WORKING WITH PROSE

Otto Reinert

UNIVERSITY OF WASHINGTON

working with

Prose

HARCOURT, BRACE AND COMPANY, NEW YORK

Preface

Working with Prose is a collection of contemporary readings, accompanied by comments and exercises, that invites close study of the ways of good prose. From experiencing the interdependence of form and content as a fact of language, the student will gain respect for the right word in the right place, for structure in sentence, paragraph, and complete work. The readings have been chosen for interest and significance, but interest and significance are here less ends in themselves than means to an end. The exciting sense of having something to say does not automatically bestow the ability to say it. What the student in class discussion and themes says about what he reads can only be as valuable as his skill with language allows it to be. Interest itself ultimately depends on such skill.

The readings are divided into two parts. Part I contains brief examples of the traditional four main types of prose: narrative, description, exposition, and argument, in about as high a degree of purity as one is likely to meet in ordinary reading. Each section begins with a definition of rhetorical type. Each selection is followed by a critical commentary and four kinds of exercises: (1) true-false questions on content, to insure comprehension; (2) questions on form and style, to relate structure and rhetoric to meaning; (3) a multiple-choice vocabulary quiz; and (4) a list of suggestions for theme writing.

Part II provides examples of prose as one more commonly meets it: the types blending and interacting and cooperating in any number of more or less "impure" ways. Here a subject-matter division seemed natural, though the four sections do not pretend to any systematic treatment of their respective subjects. The selections in *Vocation and Recreation* are more concerned with attitudes than with specifics about jobs and relaxations; those in *Nature and Science* deal with a few aspects of man's relationship with the physical world; those in *Self and Society* with his relationship with himself and others; those in *Language and Learning* with his relationship with words in his search for truth. Each section is introduced by a brief précis of the selections. Part II has no commentary or analysis of the individual selections but includes the same four kinds of exercises as Part I.

For help in choosing selections, for criticism of commentary and exercises, and for agreements and disagreements in discussing with me the theory of composition teaching on which this anthology is based, I am grateful to Professors Glenn Leggett, Robert Stanton, Paul Dietrichson, and Peter Lisca.

O. R.

Seattle
August 1958

Contents

1. Types of Prose   1

NARRATIVE   3

1. Thor Heyerdahl   *Man Overboard!*   4
2. Charles A. Lindbergh   *Emergency Jump–I*   10
                            Emergency Jump–II   11
3. *Time*   *The Well-Digger's Ordeal*   16
4. John Steinbeck   *How Mr. Hogan Robbed a Bank*   20

DESCRIPTION   31

5. Frieda Landfried Taylor   *This Is Home*   32
6. Rebecca West   *Miss Furness*   36
7. Loren Eiseley   *The Slit*   41
8. Ivan T. Sanderson   *Moles*   45
9. Wolfgang Langewiesche   *The U.S.A. from the Air*   49

EXPOSITION   56

10. U.N. Recipes   *Sweet Roll—Brioche*   57
11. *World Book Encyclopedia*   *The Hydraulic Press*   59
12. Ernest Havemann   *The Psychologist, the Psychiatrist, and
    the Psychoanalyst*   63
13. Waldemar Kaempffert   *Weather Fronts*   66
14. *Consumer Reports*   *Motaloy: Claims vs. Tests*   71
15. Mortimer J. Adler   *Baseball and Reading*   77
16. Arthur C. Clarke   *The Earth and Its Neighbors*   81

ARGUMENT   92

17. Robert Hatch   *Music Spoils the Picture*   94
18. Philip Wylie   *Safe and Insane*   99
19. Sloan Wilson   *The Case Against Fraternities*   110
20. Herbert L. Brown   *The Case For Fraternities*   119

2. The Types in Action   129

VOCATION AND RECREATION   130

21. Carl Sandburg   *First Paydays*   131
22. Hanson W. Baldwin   *Number Six*   135

23. Roger Angell   *Two Women*   144
24. E. B. White   *The Decline of Sport*   149
25. Alec Waugh   *What Rugby Means to England*   154
26. Frederick Lewis Allen   *King of Swing*   161
27. Bernard De Voto   *Heavy, Heavy, What Hangs Over?*   165

NATURE AND SCIENCE   172

28. Leonard Hall   *The Pond*   173
29. Alexander Petrunkevitch   *The Spider and the Wasp*   179
30. Beirne Lay, Jr.   *The Jet That Crashed Before Take-Off*   186
31. Berton Roueché   *Eleven Blue Men*   192
32. I. M. Levitt   *Schedule for the Space Age*   202

SELF AND SOCIETY   209

33. Charles W. Cole   *American Youth Goes Monogamous*   210
34. Mark Van Doren   *Know What You Want*   219
35. Edmund G. Love   *Subways Are for Sleeping*   225
36. Mark Ethridge, Jr.   *Turmoil in the South*   237
37. Ruth Suckow   *Four Generations*   242
38. Edith Hamilton   *The Greek Way*   253
39. Patricia Alvis Kosobud   *Interim*   262

LANGUAGE AND LEARNING   268

40. Robert U. Jameson   *How to Stay in College*   269
41. Rixford Knight   *Street Elbow*   275
42. S. I. Hayakawa   *Classification*   279
43. Darrell Huff   *The Semi-Attached Figure*   284
44. Joseph J. Seldin   *Selling the Kiddies*   289
45. Peg Bracken   *The New Mallarkey*   292
46. Marchette Chute   *Getting at the Truth*   297
47. James Thurber   *The Moth and the Star*   305
48. Joseph Wood Krutch   *The Golden Mean*   307

WORKING WITH PROSE

1. Types of Prose

Narrative

Description

Exposition

Argument

The selections in Part One are divided according to the four traditional types of prose: Narrative, Description, Exposition, and Argument. Whether a given piece of prose is classified as one or the other is, of course, important only insofar as such classification leads to a greater understanding of how prose works. Is the story told for its own sake or because it clarifies an idea? Does the description help to prove a point, throw light on a character, add color to the action—or is it an end in itself? What is the *main* impression received from this passage? What seems to have been the author's *main* purpose in writing this? Answers to such questions as these are important in helping the reader realize the function of the rhetorical elements in what he reads.

The ideal reader does not tuck bits of prose away in labeled boxes. He uses his awareness of the different natures and purposes of the different types of prose to further his understanding and enjoyment of what he reads. He experiences good writing as a single, meaningful whole, a blend of elements which he no longer needs to distinguish and analyze because he sees with the author's eyes, shares his feelings, thinks his thoughts. But such reading skill can be the product only of long practice in reading good prose and of an awareness, born of conscious study, of why the prose *is* good.

Narrative

HEYERDAHL • LINDBERGH • TIME • STEINBECK

Narrative is writing that answers the question, "What happened?" "The dog barked. The child cried. The dog jumped. The child screamed and ran"—that is narrative. Though each of the four sentences states a different action, we feel there is connection between them. We assume that the dog that barked in sentence 1 is the dog that jumped in sentence 3 and that the child that cried in sentence 2 screamed and ran in sentence 4. The four sentences tell a single story.

But if we read, "The dog barked. The man read. The sun shone. The child ate and slept," it is difficult to feel any connection. Most of us are so used to finding that narrative sentences like these *do* hang together that we are likely to assume or invent a connection: "The dog barked, but the man read on. Though the sun was shining, he had to stay in to feed the child and put him to bed." Nevertheless, in the absence of a context common sense forces us to conclude either that the sentences really deal with four separate actions and four separate characters, or that they are a very badly told narrative. The first set of sentences told about a dog frightening a child. It would be difficult to sum up the second set in a similar statement. As the sentences are given here they do not seem to make up a single, unified story.

Narrative sentences may be connected in several ways. Most narratives are arranged in time sequence: first one thing happened, then the next, and so on. But chronology alone may not be enough to create unity. Often, as in both examples above, the reader, consciously or unconsciously, will seek some closer connection between the actions than the simple fact that they followed one another in time. Such connection may be logical or causal ("the child cried because the dog barked"), but it need not be. Some narratives are held together by similarity and contrast in situation or characterization or setting or "mood," and so forth, between their separate scenes. Or narrative unity and coherence may be achieved by more than one method. It is unwise to lay down rules for *all* narratives, for in the art of writing exceptions always seem to appear to upset any general rule. Still, it is reasonably safe to say that if the reader is not aware of *some* kind of connection in what he reads, chances are that he will find the narrative to be no story at all, but separate bits of action haphazardly thrown together, meaningless, irritating, boring. Some-

3

how, he must be made to feel that what he reads "hangs together." Yet he
should be warned that the connection is not always so simple as in the
examples given here. And if he fails to discover the nature of the unity of
subtle narratives, the fault may be his own and not the author's.

1
THOR HEYERDAHL
Man Overboard!

1   . . . On July 21 the wind suddenly died away again. It was oppressive and absolutely still, and we knew from previous experience what
this might mean. And, right enough, after a few violent gusts from east
and west and south, the wind freshened up to a breeze from southward,
where black, threatening clouds had again rushed up over the horizon.
Herman was out with his anemometer all the time, measuring already
fifty feet and more per second, when suddenly Torstein's sleeping bag
went overboard. And what happened in the next few seconds took a
much shorter time than it takes to tell it.

2   Herman tried to catch the bag as it went, took a rash step, and fell
overboard. We heard a faint cry for help amid the noise of the waves, and
saw Herman's head and a waving arm as well as some vague green object
twirling about in the water near him. He was struggling for life to get
back to the raft through the high seas which had lifted him out from the
port side. Torstein, who was at the steering oar aft, and I myself, up in
the bow, were the first to perceive him, and we went cold with fear. We
bellowed "Man overboard!" at the top of our lungs as we rushed to the
nearest life-saving gear. The others had not heard Herman's cry because
of the noise of the sea, but in a trice there was life and bustle on deck.
Herman was an excellent swimmer, and, though we realized at once that
his life was at stake, we had a fair hope that he would manage to crawl
back to the edge of the raft before it was too late.

3   Torstein, who was nearest, seized the bamboo drum round which
was the line we used for the lifeboat, for this was within his reach. It was
the only time on the whole voyage that this line got caught up. Herman
was now on a level with the stern of the raft but a few yards away, and
his last hope was to crawl to the blade of the steering oar and hang on to

MAN OVERBOARD! From *Kon-Tiki: Across the Pacific by Raft* by Thor
Heyerdahl. Copyright 1950 by Thor Heyerdahl. Published in the U.S. by
Rand McNally & Company. Reprinted by permission of Rand McNally & Com-
pany and George Allen & Unwin Ltd., London.

it. As he missed the end of the logs, he reached out for the oar blade, but it slipped away from him. And there he lay, just where experience had shown we could get nothing back. While Bengt and I launched the dinghy, Knut and Erik threw out the life belt. Carrying a long line, it hung ready for use on the corner of the cabin roof, but today the wind was so strong that when it was thrown it was simply blown back to the raft. After a few unsuccessful throws Herman was already far astern of the steering oar, swimming desperately to keep up with the raft, while the distance increased with each gust of wind. He realized that henceforth the gap would simply go on increasing, but he set a faint hope on the dinghy which we had now got into the water. Without the line, which acted as a brake, it would perhaps be possible to drive the rubber raft to meet the swimming man, but whether the rubber raft would ever get back to the *Kon-Tiki* was another matter. Nevertheless, three men in a rubber dinghy had some chance; one man in the sea had none.

4   Then we suddenly saw Knut take off and plunge headfirst into the sea. He had the life belt in one hand and was heaving himself along. Every time Herman's head appeared on a wave back Knut was gone, and every time Knut came up Herman was not there. But then we saw both heads at once; they had swum to meet each other and both were hanging on to the life belt. Knut waved his arm, and, as the rubber raft had meanwhile been hauled on board, all four of us took hold of the line of the life belt and hauled for dear life, with our eyes fixed on the great dark object which was visible just behind the two men. This same mysterious beast in the water was pushing a big greenish-black triangle up above the wave crests; it almost gave Knut a shock when he was on his way over to Herman. Only Herman knew then that the triangle did not belong to a shark or any other sea monster. It was an inflated corner of Torstein's watertight sleeping bag. But the sleeping bag did not remain floating for long after we had hauled the two men safe and sound on board. Whatever dragged the sleeping bag down into the depths had just missed a better prey.

5   "Glad I wasn't in it," said Torstein and took hold of the steering oar where he had let it go.

6   But otherwise there were not many wisecracks that evening. We all felt a chill running through nerve and bone for a long time afterward. But the cold shivers were mingled with a warm thankfulness that there were still six of us on board.

Comment

Thor Heyerdahl's narrative is part of a book about six men on a raft in the Pacific. But the episode forms one complete story: a man falls overboard and is rescued. Everything that happens is the direct result of the action told in the first sentence of the second paragraph: "Herman tried to catch the bag as it went, took a rash step, and fell overboard." And this happened because the

sleeping bag blew overboard. As far as we and the men on the raft are concerned, the sequence of causally connected events begins with the strong wind.

But Heyerdahl does not begin with the "few violent gusts from east and
west" that preceded the wind. Instead he begins his story with wind*lessness*.
This may seem illogical, but actually it makes as much sense as the broad-
jumper's walking away from the take-off line in order to get momentum for his
jump. Heyerdahl succeeds in creating an ominous quiet before the storm with
his first few sentences. We know that something dramatic and dangerous is
about to happen. The opening builds up suspense.

What is told here actually happened. It is "truth," not "fiction." Obviously,
the event was packed with fear, excitement, relief, for the men involved. Does
this mean that the story could be left to tell itself—that all Heyerdahl needed
to do was to set down what actually happened to make an exciting, suspenseful
piece of narrative? In other words, does the fact that the incident actually took
place in real life make the narrator's task simple and easy? Before you say "yes"
to these questions, ask yourself if you have never failed to find words to
express to others the quality of an experience you had—and failed all the worse
the more exciting, significant, and unique the experience? *You* knew the "truth"
—not just the facts but the whole set of feelings that went with the facts—of
what had happened to you, but you also found that you could not communicate
that truth to others. If you have ever had this feeling of being isolated by your
lack of expressive words, this frustrating sense of "if only I could say what I
mean!"—then you will know that the expression of truth can be a difficult thing.

Heyerdahl's task here was not simple and easy. He did not have to invent
characters and situations for them to get involved in, but, for the very reason
that he was dealing with truth and not fiction, he was tied down to the facts.
He could not freely use his imagination and tell what did not happen. At the
same time, he obviously could not tell *everything* that happened. Out of the
hundreds of little actions that went into the making of the incident of Herman's falling overboard and being rescued by Knut, Heyerdahl could select
only a few. He tells us what Herman was doing when the sleeping bag went
overboard, both because Herman is the chief character, whose circumstances
at the beginning of the action are part of the information we reasonably expect
to get from a story like this, and because wind-measuring is a relevant detail
in a story where wind is so important. But we do not learn what happened to
the anemometer when Herman fell. We do not learn what Torstein did after
he failed to throw the line for the lifeboat to Herman. We do not hear of all
the separate little manual operations that must have been performed "while
Bengt and I launched the dinghy," or while the men on the raft hauled Herman and Knut aboard. Such unreported happenings were just as true and real
as those we do hear about. Heyerdahl does not mention them, because they are
unimportant to the story of the rescue—or, rather, because he chooses to make
them unimportant. Heyerdahl has exercised the right every narrator necessarily
must exercise: the right to be selective about the details that go into his story.
When we report a real life event to which we have been eyewitness, we all tell
different stories. Some of the accounts will not differ widely, and some will
differ only in a few trivial details, but no two will be identical. This is not because we are all liars. Our stories will differ because all of us report the event as

it appeared to our senses and our interests, and two persons' sense impressions and interests (or preoccupations or attitudes or moods) are never exactly alike.

This selection—which sometimes is deliberate and sometimes not, but which always is inevitable—is what distinguishes the good storyteller from the bad one. The art consists in telling neither too much nor too little, but just enough to do justice to both facts and feelings and thus to the meaning, the truth—the whole truth—of what happened. We don't mind not being told what each of the others was doing at the moment Herman went overboard; in fact, we might have minded if we had been told. Such detailed accounts would slow up an action which was, above all, fast and thus actually falsify it, though the details themselves would, of course, be true. On the other hand, we would not have been greatly excited by such a flat (though, again, factually true) version of the story as this: "One day Herman fell overboard in a windstorm, but fortunately he was rescued by Knut, who swam after him with a lifebelt attached to a line." And we might well have been irritated if the narrator had ended his story this way: "Oh yes, I should have told you before that it was blowing terribly hard and that there was no way in which the raft could be turned back so we could pick up Herman." Such versions of the story would be bad narratives, not just because they are unskillful, but because they leave us bored or irritated, and boredom and irritation, in this case, are feelings that are untrue to the actual experience.

Heyerdahl's version of what happened is not the only one possible. Other details might have been added and some of those that are included might have been omitted, without damage to the story, though not without changing it, however little. But this account is held together by a single line of action, and every detail in it contributes to the effect of the whole. For example, consider how some of the drama of the narrative disappears if the detail about the steering oar is omitted, or the mysterious green monster that turned out to be a sleeping bag, or the even more mysterious, and frightfully more real, monster that dragged it down. Such details are not essential to the main line of the story, but each of them adds to its concreteness and vividness and hence to its interest and effectiveness. Or take Torstein's remark near the end: "Glad I wasn't in it." It is certainly safe to assume that other things were said and shouted during and after the rescue. Why does Heyerdahl choose to record just this one speech? The story would have made sense without it, the action would have been complete, but we would have lost something—some sense of how close events came to make even such a mild wisecrack impossible and of the state of mind, relieved but spent, feeble as the joke itself, of the men after it was all over.

The most casual look at Heyerdahl's story will show that it did not just tell itself. Even a reporter of factual truth must be something of a literary craftsman: selecting, arranging, distributing emphasis, finding the words that do justice not only to the bare facts of the event but to its "feeling" as well. Certainly, in one sense the narrator of a narrative like this sets down "what actually happened." But as far as the reader is concerned, what actually happened is what the narrator says happened. The truth of the story must be found in the story itself, for we were not there, we cannot check the author's truthfulness. His job is to get the truth, as he saw it, into his story and so over to us.

Exercises

CONTENT

True or false? If you think the statement represents what the selection says or implies, mark it "True"; if you do not think so, mark it "False." The true-or-false exercises that follow each selection in this book test your understanding of it by asking you whether or not the author makes or implies the statements listed. You are *not* being asked for your opinion of the selection—you will have a chance to express this in class discussion or in themes. Here you are simply being asked what the author says and does not say. Without such knowledge opinion is meaningless.

1. The wind was blowing almost a hundred feet per second when the sleeping bag blew overboard.
2. Herman fell in on the port side.
3. What made the situation especially dangerous was the fact that Herman was not a good swimmer.
4. Herman's last hope of getting back on the raft by his own efforts was to catch hold of the stern of the raft.
5. The wind made it impossible to throw out a life belt.
6. One of the men was called Erik.
7. The men on the raft mistook a corner of the sleeping bag for the triangular fin of a shark.
8. The raft was navigable in any direction.
9. The name of the raft, Kon-Tiki, is the name of an old Norse god of sailing.
10. Because it was his sleeping bag that caused the accident, Torstein apologized to Herman.

FORM AND STYLE

1. Point out exactly where the "introduction" ends and the action begins.
2. Discuss why or why not "Then everything began to happen fast" would have been preferable to "And what happened in the next few seconds took a much shorter time than it takes to tell it" (Paragraph 1, last sentence).
3. Show in detail the parallelism of grammatical structure in "Nevertheless, three men in a rubber dinghy had some chance; one man in the sea had none" (Paragraph 3). Can you explain what is meant by saying that the sentence "pivots on the semicolon"?
4. What is the function of "Nevertheless" in that sentence?
5. What effect on the story would the omission of "And there he lay,

just where experience had shown we could get nothing back" have (Paragraph 3)?

6. Try to find a phrase or sentence that sums up each of the six paragraphs. These "titles" for the different parts of the narrative should suggest the relationship between them.

7. Why do you think Heyerdahl put Torstein's remark (Paragraph 5) in a separate paragraph?

VOCABULARY

Which of the four words or phrases to the right seems to you to be *closest* in meaning to the word in heavy type to the left? Put a check mark after your choice. The words will *not* be identical; two words are almost never identical in meaning. If you feel that the word to the left could have more than one possible meaning, match it with that word to the right that comes closest to the meaning the word has *in this particular context.* [For example: Which of the following four words comes closest in meaning to the word FENCE in the sentence, "The thieves sold the silver to a fence": (a) a barrier, (b) to fight with swords, (c) to enclose, (d) a receiver of stolen goods? Obviously, though FENCE can have all four meanings, *in this sentence* only meaning (d) is possible.] The number in parentheses after the word refers to the paragraph in which the word occurs in context.

oppressive *(1)*   depressing . . . heavy . . . hot . . . burdensome . . .

anemometer *(1)*   camera . . . instrument for measuring humidity . . . instrument for measuring speed of wind . . . instrument for measuring speed of waves . . .

twirling *(2)*   spinning . . . moving up and down . . . floating . . . turning over . . .

aft *(2)*   again . . . in the stern . . . forwards . . . afterwards . . .

perceive *(2)*   see . . . miss . . . hear . . . discover . . .

in a trice *(2)*   in three seconds . . . suddenly . . . quickly . . . soon . . .

inflated *(4)*   water-sogged . . . prominent . . . triangular . . . blown up . . .

prey *(4)*   bite . . . prize . . . victim . . . meal . . .

THEME SUGGESTIONS

A close call

Three reasons for learning how to swim

The Kon-Tiki expedition

Relate this incident first from Herman's, then from Knut's point of view, with "I" as narrator in both cases.

2

CHARLES A. LINDBERGH
Emergency Jump—I

1 . . . At 5,000 feet the engine sputtered and died. I stepped up on the cowling and out over the right side of the cockpit, pulling the rip cord after about a 100-foot fall. The parachute, an Irving seat service type, functioned perfectly; I was falling head downward when the risers jerked me into an upright position and the chute opened. This time I saved the rip cord. I pulled the flashlight from my belt and was playing it down towards the top of the fog when I heard the plane's engine pick up. When I jumped it had practically stopped dead and I had neglected to cut the switches. Apparently when the ship nosed down an additional supply of gasoline drained to the carburetor. Soon she came into sight, about a quarter mile away and headed in the general direction of my parachute. I put the flashlight in a pocket of my flying suit preparatory to slipping the parachute out of the way if necessary. The plane was making a left spiral of about a mile diameter, and passed approximately 300 yards away from my chute, leaving me on the outside of the circle. I was undecided as to whether the plane or I was descending the more rapidly and guided my chute away from the spiral path of the ship as rapidly as I could. The ship passed completely out of sight, but reappeared in a few seconds, its rate of descent being about the same as that of the parachute. I counted the five spirals, each one a little further away than the last, before reaching the top of the fog bank.

2 When I settled into the fog I knew that the ground was within 1,000 feet and reached for the flashlight, but found it to be missing. I could see neither earth nor stars and had no idea what kind of territory was below. I crossed my legs to keep from straddling a branch or wire, guarded my face with my hands and waited. Presently I saw the outline of the ground and a moment later was down in a cornfield. The corn was over my head and the chute was lying on top of the corn stalks. I hurriedly packed it and started down a corn row. The ground visibility was about 100 yards. In a few minutes I came to a stubble field and some wagon tracks which I followed to a farmyard a quarter mile away. After reaching the farmyard I noticed auto headlights playing over the roadside. Thinking that someone might have located the wreck of the plane I walked over to the car. The occupants asked whether I had heard an airplane crash and it required some time to explain to them that I had been piloting the plane, and yet was searching for it myself. I had to display the parachute as evidence before they were thoroughly convinced. The farmer was sure, as were most others in a 3-mile radius, that the ship had just missed his house and crashed nearby. In fact, he could locate within a few rods the spot where he heard it hit the ground, and we spent an unsuccessful quarter hour hunting for the wreck in that vicinity before going to the farmhouse to arrange for a searching party and telephone St. Louis and Chicago.

3　I had just put in the long distance calls when the phone rang and we were notified that the plane had been found in a cornfield over two miles away. It took several minutes to reach the site of the crash, due to the necessity of slow driving through the fog, and a small crowd had already assembled when we arrived. The plane was wound up in a ball-shaped mass. It had narrowly missed one farmhouse and had hooked its left wing in a grain shock a quarter mile beyond. The ship had landed on the left wing and wheel and skidded along the ground for 80 yards, going through one fence before coming to rest in the edge of a cornfield about 100 yards short of a barn. The mail pit was laid open and one sack of mail was on the ground. The mail, however, was uninjured.

4　The sheriff from Ottawa arrived, and we took the mail to the Ottawa Post Office to be entrained at 3:30 A.M. for Chicago.

Emergency Jump—II

1　I was 5000 feet high when my engine cut the second time. I unbuckled my safety belt, dove over the right side of the fuselage, and after two or three seconds of fall pulled the rip cord. The parachute opened right away. I was playing my flashlight down toward the top of the fog bank when I was startled to hear the sound of an airplane in the distance. It was coming toward me. In a few seconds I saw my DH, dimly, less than a quarter mile away and about on a level with me. It was circling in my direction, left wing down. Since I thought it was completely out of gasoline, I had neglected to cut the switches before I jumped. When the nose dropped, due to the loss of the weight of my body in the tail, some additional fuel apparently drained forward into the carburetor, sending the plane off on a solo flight of its own.

2　My concern was out of proportion to the danger. In spite of the sky's tremendous space, it seemed crowded with traffic. I shoved my flashlight into my pocket and caught hold of the parachute risers so I could slip the canopy one way or the other in case the plane kept pointing toward me. But it was fully a hundred yards away when it passed, leaving

EMERGENCY JUMP—II. Reprinted from *The Spirit of St. Louis* by Charles A. Lindbergh (copyright 1953 Charles Scribner's Sons) with permission of the publisher.

me on the outside of its circle. The engine noise receded, and then increased until the DH appeared again, still at my elevation. The rate of descent of plane and parachute were approximately equal. I counted five spirals, each a little farther away than the last. Then I sank into the fog bank.

3   Knowing the ground to be less than a thousand feet below, I reached for the flashlight. It was gone. In my excitement when I saw the plane coming toward me, I hadn't pushed it far enough into my pocket. I held my feet together, guarded my face with my hands, and waited. I heard the DH pass once again. Then I saw the outline of the ground, braced myself for impact, and hit—in a cornfield. By the time I got back on my feet, the chute had collapsed and was lying on top of the corn tassels. I rolled it up, tucked it under my arm, and started walking between two rows of corn. The stalks were higher than my head. The leaves crinkled as I brushed past them. I climbed over a fence, into a stubble field. There I found wagon tracks and followed them. Ground visibility was about a hundred yards.

4   The wagon tracks took me to a farmyard. First, the big barn loomed up in haze. Then a lighted window beyond it showed that someone was still up. I was heading for the house when I saw an automobile move slowly along the road and stop, playing its spotlight from one side to the other. I walked over to the car. Several people were in it.

5   "Did you hear that airplane?" one of them called out as I approached.

6   "I'm the pilot," I said.

7   "An airplane just dove into the ground," the man went on, paying no attention to my answer. "Must be right near here. God, it made a racket!" He kept searching with his spotlight, but the beam didn't show much in the haze.

8   "I'm the pilot," I said again. "I was flying it." My words got through that time. The spotlight stopped moving.

9   "*You're the pilot?* Good God, how . . ."

10   "I jumped with a parachute," I said, showing him the white bundle.

11   "You aren't hurt?"

12   "Not a bit. But I've got to find the wreck and get the mail sacks."

13   "It must be right near by. Get in and we'll drive along the road a piece. Good God, what went wrong? You must have had *some* experience! You're sure you aren't hurt?"

14   We spent a quarter hour searching, unsuccessfully. Then I accompanied the farmer to his house. My plane, he said, had flown over his roof only a few seconds before it struck the ground. I asked to use his telephone. The party line was jammed with voices, all talking about the airplane that had crashed. I broke in with the statement that I was the pilot, and asked the telephone operator to put in emergency calls for St. Louis and Chicago. Then I asked her if anyone had reported the exact

location of the wreck. A number of people had heard the plane pass overhead just before it hit, she replied, but nothing more definite had come in.

15 I'd hardly hung up and turned away when the bell rang—three longs and a short.

16 "That's our signal," the farmer said.

17 My plane had been located, the operator told me, about two miles from the house I was in. We drove to the site of crash. The DH was wound up in a ball-shaped mass. It had narrowly missed a farmhouse, hooked one wing on a grain shock a quarter mile beyond, skidded along the ground for eighty yards, ripped through a fence, and come to rest on the edge of a cornfield. Splinters of wood and bits of torn fabric were strewn all around. The mail compartment was broken open and one sack had been thrown out; but the mail was undamaged—I took it to the nearest post office to be entrained.

Comment

Two stories of the same parachute jump are told by the same author at two different times. The first version appeared in *We,* the book Colonel Lindbergh published a few months after his sensational solo flight from New York to Paris in 1927. The second is part of a much longer autobiography, *The Spirit of St. Louis,* he published in 1953.

The later account is about three hundred words longer than the earlier one. More important than mere length, however, is the difference in the quality of the feeling they create in the reader. The 1927 version is taken word for word from the official report mail pilot Lindbergh submitted after the crash, whereas in the later version he tries to re-create as vividly as possible the circumstances and the emotions of the dramatic moments years earlier. The passage from *We* is simple, clear, direct, factual, fast moving, but rather impersonal, without many descriptive details. Its temperature of feeling is lower than that of the account in *The Spirit of St. Louis,* and it creates a less sharp and less full picture in our minds. In 1927 Lindbergh "stepped up on the cowling and out over the right side of the cockpit." In 1953 this has become: "I dove over the right side of the fuselage." In 1927 he "put the flashlight in a pocket." In 1953 he "shoved the flashlight into my pocket." "Dove" and "shoved" are clearly more dynamic, dramatic, specific words than "stepped" and "put." Similarly, in the 1927 account we find this bit of factual and emotionally neutral narrative:

> Presently I saw the outline of the ground and a moment later was down in a cornfield. The corn was over my head and the chute was lying on top of the corn stalks. I hurriedly packed it and started down a corn row. . . .

In the later version, the narrative has been slowed up and made more specifically descriptive. The result is both a clearer picture and a sense of heightened drama. To the latter even such a minor device as the dash after "hit" contributes. For a brief moment it holds up the meaning and thus creates suspense.

Then I saw the outline of the ground, braced myself for impact, and hit—
in a cornfield. By the time I got back on my feet, the chute had collapsed
and was lying on top of the corn tassels. I rolled it up, tucked it under my
arm, and started walking between two rows of corn. The stalks were higher
than my head. The leaves crinkled as I brushed past them. . . .

But where the two accounts differ most is in telling about the meeting
with the farmers. The report has two brief sentences; in *The Spirit of St. Louis*
we find a little play staged for us, with sharply visualized physical setting and
lifelike dialogue. To generalize: the greater number of concrete details makes
the later version the livelier, the more vivid, the more dramatic, the more
literary of the two.

Is this the same as saying that it is better? Not necessarily. First, we will
have to answer another question: "Better for what purpose?" For a book entitled *Exciting Tales from Life*, undoubtedly yes. But imagine how Lindbergh's
superiors in the mail service would have reacted to the corn leaves "that
crinkled as I brushed past them" or to the conversation with the unbelieving
farmers! Chances are they would have found these details irrelevant and inappropriate and concluded that Lindbergh did not know how to make out an
official report. And they would have been right.

Exercises

CONTENT

True or False? If you think the statement represents what the selection says or implies, mark it "True"; if you do not think so, mark it
"False."

1. Lindbergh had to jump because his plane caught fire.

2. It took some agonizing seconds before the parachute began to
open.

3. The night was clear and moonlit.

4. For a moment it looked as if the pilotless plane was going to hit
Lindbergh.

5. The fact that the plane continued flying on its own proves that
the jump really was not necessary.

6. We never learn exactly where the jump occurred.

7. Lindbergh's shoulder was badly bruised by the impact of the
landing.

8. Each of the farmers thought the plane had "just missed" his house.

9. The crashed plane was easily located.

10. Most of the mail was undamaged.

FORM AND STYLE

1. If you were to divide the former of the two accounts into three
parts, exactly where would you make the divisions? Do they coincide
with breaks between paragraphs? If not, why not?

2. Explain how descriptions of physical movement help organize the narratives. Find the point in each narrative where the direction of the movement changes.

3. Which part of the story has been given proportionately larger emphasis in the later than in the earlier account? Assuming that Lindbergh's purpose in writing was not the same in both cases, how do you account for the shift in emphasis?

4. Write a brief comparative analysis of the two versions of the scene where Lindbergh fears that the pilotless plane is going to hit him. Compare amount of detail given and kind of words used.

5. Is there any evidence that Lindbergh had the earlier account in front of him when he wrote the passage from *Spirit of St. Louis?* If so, what is the evidence?

VOCABULARY

Which of the four words or phrases to the right seems to you to be *closest* in meaning to the word in heavy type to the left? Put a check mark after your choice.

preparatory (*I, 1*)   happening before something else . . . for the purpose of . . . after . . . making ready . . .

descent (*I, 1*)   circular movement . . . downward movement . . . speed . . . decency . . .

straddling (*I, 2*)   hitting . . . with a leg on each side of . . . being hurt by . . . ruining . . .

display (*I, 2*)   stop playing . . . hand over . . . show . . . spread . . .

locate (*I, 2*)   find . . . estimate . . . point to . . . make local . . .

vicinity (*I, 2*)   spot . . . district . . . conviction . . . neighborhood

radius (*I, 2*)   area . . . distance . . . distance from center of circle to circumference . . . diameter . . .

fuselage (*II, 1*)   a padded metal strip rimming the cockpit . . . gas tank on an airplane . . . body of an airplane . . . place for cargo . . .

canopy (*II, 2*)   dome-shaped top . . . drawstring . . . parachute . . . any means of rescue . . .

braced (*II, 3*)   prepared . . . relaxed . . . tensed . . . pulled oneself into a ball . . .

impact (*II, 3*)   hurt . . . possible danger . . . readiness . . . collision . . .

THEME SUGGESTION

Write two brief versions of the same event. The event may be something that really happened to you—at home, in class, on a date, in camp,

on a trip, during a sport—or you may invent it. One version should be as
neutral and impersonal as possible; in the other, you should try to suggest what the events felt like to you. You may find it helpful to imagine
that one account is being written as an objective report (for a superior
or employer or some official institution like the police), the other as a
letter to a close friend with whom you want to share an exciting experience. But keep in mind that the main facts of the event itself should be
the same in both accounts.

3

TIME

The Well-Digger's Ordeal

1 When he began digging the well under Brooklyn's Sixteenth Avenue Garage, brawny, heavy-shouldered Dominick Atteo took all the
short cuts he could. He had done hundreds of such sweaty, commonplace
jobs, and all the garage owner wanted was a hole to supply water for
car washing during the New York water shortage. At 50 Dominick had six
children and a pretty auburn-haired wife, and had to stretch dollars as
far as they would go.

2 He didn't bother to take out a city permit (which would have
called for inspection of the job) or to bring timber to shore up his
shaft. He just ripped up a patch of concrete flooring near the garage's
main support pillar and began to dig. At 18 feet, as he was trying to dislodge a big rock, a cave-in buried him up to the waist in loose sand and
gravel. When he tried to wriggle out he discovered that he was trapped;
his right leg was doubled beneath him and pinned immovably by the
boulder.

3 *Help.* Overalled cops from the police emergency squad were
finally called in. They cut the ends of an oil drum, lowered it around
him as protection against further caving and then began to shore the well
with lumber and rig supports under the roof in case digging weakened
the pillar. A crowd gathered. Photographers fired flashbulbs down the
hole; Dominick grinned up sheepishly.

4 But as evening came it was evident that he would be down in the
well a long time. Encased in his oil drum, he filled the bottom of the

THE WELL-DIGGER'S ORDEAL. From TIME, May, 22, 1950. Courtesy
TIME, The Weekly Newsmagazine; copyright Time Inc., 1950.

hole; it was virtually impossible to dig beneath him. For a while he tried to dig himself out. But finally, dirty and aching with fatigue, he gave up.

5 *Fire.* His wife arrived and peered down the hole in fright. He reassured her. But the police sent for a doctor and a priest. Oxygen was piped down the hole. Big floodlights were brought in; they threw a harsh, garish light over the scene and heated the air until the toiling cops were wet with sweat. At 8:30 there was a terrible interruption. A lighted cigarette was lowered down the well in a tin can; a few minutes after it reached the bottom there was an explosion—apparently caused by oxygen and seeping gasoline fumes. Fire filled the well.

6 A workman threw a bucketful of water down on Dominick. Another squirted a fire extinguisher at him. The fire puffed out. Dominick had made no sound, but he had endured fearful burns. His shirt was all but gone, he had breathed flame, and his throat and lungs were scorched. The rescue work stopped and Dr. Harold Berson, a young intern from Coney Island Hospital, was lowered to him. He greased the burns and gave Dominick morphine; a priest was lowered, performed the last rites of the Catholic Church.

7 As the night wore on, rescue workers—now numbering 150—tried a new scheme: men with pneumatic jack hammers began the ear-splitting job of tearing up the garage floor. A huge bucket crane rumbled ponderously into the garage. The rescuers began digging a deep slanting ditch to connect with the well. All night, all through the early morning, as the frantic work went on, people took turns kneeling at the mouth of the well to encourage Dominick.

8 *Death.* The doctor made five trips into the hole to give the trapped man stimulants, and a transfusion of plasma. Warm milk was lowered to him. He sipped at it listlessly. After daylight, his wife knelt at the mouth of the well and dropped religious medals into the excavation; she rose with her face white, her hands fumbling with her rosary. A policeman called, "How are you feeling, Dom?" The well-digger replied quietly, "I am going to die."

9 His eldest son, John, a black-haired husky of 27, called in a quavering voice: "Pa . . . Pa, don't get excited." Dominick moaned, and his blackened head dropped. But at 2:40 in the afternoon, as the excavators reached him and began digging the dirt away from his legs he was still conscious and still uncomplaining. He asked for a bottle of Coca-Cola and drank it.

10 Lifting tackle was rigged under his arms, hauled tight. He groaned with pain. Fifteen minutes, a half hour, three quarters of an hour passed before his rescuers freed his leg. Then, after 27½ hours, he sagged limply. "Pa!" his son called. "Pop!" There was no answer. The mud-stained, exhausted doctor climbed down into the pit, came up slowly with his face lined and sad. Dominick was dead.

Comment

The Well-Digger's Ordeal tells of one of those desperate rescue attempts that from time to time keep the whole nation glued to radio and TV sets, for the latest report from mine shafts, abandoned wells, cave-ins, and holes in the ground. It is a story packed with what newspapermen call "human interest," and *Time*'s account skillfully squeezes the story for all the drama and pathos it carries. The skill consists in the seemingly straightforward simplicity of the telling. There is no direct appeal to our emotions; we are not being tricked into feelings of pity by some sob sister's fake sentimentality shamelessly pulling our heartstrings. If we are moved by Dominick's fate, it will not be because we are victims of a shrill appeal for sympathy, but because we respond spontaneously to human suffering. Our feelings will almost seem part of the stark facts of the tragedy.

The effect is the result of several devices. The story begins by plunging us into a situation that promises to be dramatic ("When he began digging. . . ."). The hero's plight is seen to be the result of his own negligence (no city permit, no timber for shoring), but a negligence which we probably understand only too well and are willing to sympathize with. Don't we all try to stretch our dollars? Then there is the careful selection of concrete details that serve to make Dominick real to us: the sheepish grin, the desire to smoke, the religious medals, the Coke. The exactness of facts and figures—"at 18 feet," "at 8:30," "after 27½ hours"—gives the air of a technical report which is all the more terrifying because of the unstated pathos. The story is full of adjectives— "brawny, heavy-shouldered," "pretty auburn-haired," "dirty and aching," "harsh, garish"—but because of the general compactness and brevity of style they appear to be factually descriptive and necessary to the narrative rather than superfluously sentimental. The effect of emotionalism underplayed and controlled is aided also by the many short, clipped sentences (for instance, in Paragraphs 5 and 6) and by the almost self-conscious absence of expressed emotion in the two climactic ones: "Fire filled the well" (Paragraph 5) and "Dominick was dead" (Paragraph 10). The position of "Fire filled the well" in the paragraph contributes to its force. We get a kind of "cliff-hanger" effect, a sudden break-off in the exciting narrative at the very point where it is most exciting. We expect and demand that the paragraph continue, but it doesn't, and so we are teased into reading on by our own impatient sense of intolerable suspense: we, not the writer, hasten the story forward.

This analysis is not meant to suggest that *Time* has taken advantage of the reader by unfair means. It *is* a successful narrative of a moving event; Dominick's death has been treated with honesty, dignity, and sympathy. But for a fuller understanding of the ways and means of prose we must realize that the narrative, though apparently straightforward news reporting, ungarnished by literary devices, is not quite so simple, direct, and artless as it may seem. Considerable art has gone into its fast-moving simplicity. To seem natural in writing often calls for conscious skill.

Exercises

CONTENT

True or False? If you think the statement represents what the selection says or implies, mark it "True"; if you do not think so, mark it "False."

F 1. This was Dominick's first well-digging job.

F 2. The boulder broke his leg.

T 3. It took hours before anybody realized that Dominick was trapped in the well.

T 4. Dominick died from burns.

F 5. Dominick was a Baptist.

F 6. All Dominick's children were present when he died.

F 7. Dominick died just before noon.

T 8. If Dominick had been given medical aid sooner, he might have survived.

F 9. The moon threw a garish light over the rescue attempts.

T 10. It is against the law in New York City to dig wells without a city permit.

FORM AND STYLE

1. At the time of the accident the French film comedy *The Well-Digger's Daughter* (with Raimu and Fernandel) was playing successfully in New York. Assuming that *Time* expects the reader to catch the reference to the movie, do you find the title of *Time*'s story about Dominick Atteo in good taste? Explain your answer.

2. How relevant are the adjectives "brawny, heavy-shouldered" in the first sentence in Paragraph 1? The chief subject of the sentence is clearly not Dominick's appearance; hence, do the adjectives belong? Do they perhaps have a purpose beyond that of simply telling what Dominick looked like?

3. What is the connection between the first sentence in Paragraph 1 and the first two sentences in Paragraph 2?

4. Where does the reader get the first hint that Dominick will not survive? When fire started

5. What is implied by "Dominick had made no sound, but he had endured fearful burns"?

6. Why is John in the story? Is it simply because he happened to be present at the scene, or because he also serves the reporter's ends in the telling of a newsworthy story? If so, how?

VOCABULARY

Which of the four words or phrases to the right seems to you to be *closest* in meaning to the word in heavy type to the left? Put a check mark after your choice.

brawny (1)   strong . . . stocky . . . quarrelsome . . . big . . .
evident (4)   possible . . . accidental . . . clear . . . believed . . .
encased (4)   shut in . . . in a case . . . surrounded . . . protected . . .
fatigue (4)   pain . . . tiredness . . . strain . . . wear . . .
endured (6)   suffered . . . survived . . . withstood . . . lasted . . .
ponderously (7)   heavily . . . with difficulty . . . noisily . . . finally
frantic (7)   with wild motions . . . fast . . . expert . . . with intensity . . .
stimulants (8)   pain-killers . . . injections . . . drugs . . . things that influence . . .

THEME SUGGESTIONS

Trapped

A stylistic analysis of *Time* magazine's news reporting. Pick an item in any issue of the magazine that seems to you to be typical of *Time*'s style, and try to define the qualities of that style. Slow? Fast? Vivid? Colorless? Do certain grammatical constructions predominate? What parts of speech are most heavily employed?

The psychology of the mass interest in accidents like the one reported in *The Well-Digger's Ordeal*. (Why, for example, do mine disasters that involve the loss of many human lives often, or even usually, receive less publicity and seem less tragically fascinating to the public than an individual accident like Dominick Atteo's?)

4

JOHN STEINBECK

How Mr. Hogan Robbed a Bank

1   On the Saturday before Labor Day, 1955, at 9:04½ A.M., Mr. Hogan robbed a bank. He was forty-two years old, married, and the father of a boy and a girl, named John and Joan, twelve and thirteen respectively. Mrs. Hogan's name was Joan and Mr. Hogan's was John, but since they

called themselves Papa and Mama that left their names free for the children, who were considered very smart for their ages, each having jumped a grade in school. The Hogans lived at 215 East Maple Street, in a brown-shingle house with white trim—there are two. 215 is the one across from the street light and it is the one with the big tree in the yard, either oak or elm—the biggest tree in the whole street, maybe in the whole town.

2 John and Joan were in bed at the time of the robbery, for it was Saturday. At 9:10 A.M., Mrs. Hogan was making the cup of tea she always had. Mr. Hogan went to work early. Mrs. Hogan drank her tea slowly, scalding hot, and read her fortune in the tea leaves. There was a cloud and a five-pointed star with two short points in the bottom of the cup, but that was at 9:12 and the robbery was all over by then.

3 The way Mr. Hogan went about robbing the bank was very interesting. He gave it a great deal of thought and had for a long time, but he did not discuss it with anyone. He just read his newspaper and kept his own counsel. But he worked it out to his own satisfaction that people went to too much trouble robbing banks and that got them in a mess. The simpler the better, he always thought. People went in for too much hullabaloo and hanky-panky. If you didn't do that, if you left hanky-panky out, robbing a bank would be a relatively sound venture—barring accidents, of course, of an improbable kind, but then they could happen to a man crossing the street or anything. Since Mr. Hogan's method worked fine, it proved that his thinking was sound. He often considered writing a little booklet on his technique when the how-to rage was running so high. He figured out the first sentence, which went: "To successfully rob a bank, forget all about hanky-panky."

4 Mr. Hogan was not just a clerk at Fettucci's grocery store. He was more like the manager. Mr. Hogan was in charge, even hired and fired the boy who delivered groceries after school. He even put in orders with the salesmen, sometimes when Mr. Fettucci was right in the store too, maybe talking to a customer. "You do it, John," he would say and he would nod at the customer, "John knows the ropes. Been with me—how long you been with me, John?"

5 "Sixteen years."

6 "Sixteen years. Knows the business as good as me. John, why he even banks the money."

7 And so he did. Whenever he had a moment, Mr. Hogan went into the storeroom on the alley, took off his apron, put on his necktie and coat, and went back through the store to the cash register. The checks and bills would be ready for him inside the bankbook with a rubber band around it. Then he went next door and stood at the teller's window and handed the checks and bankbook through to Mr. Cup and passed the time of day

How Mr. Hogan Robbed a Bank. From *The Atlantic Monthly*, March, 1956. Copyright © 1956 by John Steinbeck. Reprinted by permission of McIntosh and Otis, Inc.

with him too. Then, when the bankbook was handed back, he checked
the entry, put the rubber band around it, and walked next door to Fettucci's grocery and put the bankbook in the cash register, continued on
to the storeroom, removed his coat and tie, put on his apron, and went
back into the store ready for business. If there was no line at the teller's
window, the whole thing didn't take more than five minutes, even passing the time of day.

8   Mr. Hogan was a man who noticed things, and when it came to
robbing the bank, this trait stood him in good stead. He had noticed, for
instance, where the big bills were kept right in the drawer under the
counter and he had noticed also what days there were likely to be more
than other days. Thursday was payday at the American Can Company's
local plant, for instance, so there would be more then. Some Fridays
people drew more money to tide them over the weekend. But it was even
Steven, maybe not a thousand dollars difference, between Thursdays and
Fridays and Saturday mornings. Saturdays were not terribly good because
people didn't come to get money that early in the morning, and the bank
closed at noon. But he thought it over and came to the conclusion that
the Saturday before a long weekend in the summer would be the best of
all. People going on trips, vacations, people with relatives visiting, and
the bank closed Monday. He thought it out and looked, and sure enough
the Saturday morning before Labor Day the cash drawer had twice as
much money in it—he saw it when Mr. Cup pulled out the drawer.

9   Mr. Hogan thought about it during all that year, not all the time,
of course, but when he had some moments. It was a busy year too. That
was the year John and Joan had the mumps and Mrs. Hogan got her
teeth pulled and was fitted for a denture. That was the year when Mr.
Hogan was Master of the Lodge, with all the time that takes. Larry
Shield died that year—he was Mrs. Hogan's brother and was buried from
the Hogan house at 215 East Maple. Larry was a bachelor and had a
room in the Pine Tree House and he played pool nearly every night. He
worked at the Silver Diner but that closed at nine and so Larry would go
to Louie's and play pool for an hour. Therefore, it was a surprise when he
left enough so that after funeral expenses there were twelve hundred
dollars left. And even more surprising that he left a will in Mrs. Hogan's
favor, but his double-barreled twelve-gauge shotgun he left to John
Hogan, Jr. Mr. Hogan was pleased, although he never hunted. He put
the shotgun away in the back of the closet in the bathroom, where he
kept his things, to keep it for young John. He didn't want children handling guns and he never bought any shells. It was some of that twelve
hundred that got Mrs. Hogan her dentures. Also, she bought a bicycle
for John and a doll buggy and walking-talking doll for Joan—a doll with
three changes of dresses and a little suitcase, complete with play make-
up. Mr. Hogan thought it might spoil the children, but it didn't seem to.
They made just as good marks in school and John even got a job deliver-

ing papers. It was a very busy year. Both John and Joan wanted to enter the W. R. Hearst National "I Love America" Contest and Mr. Hogan thought it was almost too much, but they promised to do the work during their summer vacation, so he finally agreed.

2

10 During that year, no one noticed any difference in Mr. Hogan. It was true, he was thinking about robbing the bank, but he only thought about it in the evening when there was neither a Lodge meeting nor a movie they wanted to go to, so it did not become an obsession and people noticed no change in him.

11 He had studied everything so carefully that the approach of Labor Day did not catch him unprepared or nervous. It was hot that summer and the hot spells were longer than usual. Saturday was the end of two weeks heat without a break and people were irritated with it and anxious to get out of town, although the country was just as hot. They didn't think of that. The children were excited because the "I Love America" Essay Contest was due to be concluded and the winners announced, and the first prize was an all-expense-paid two days trip to Washington, D.C., with every fixing—hotel room, three meals a day, and side trips in a limousine—not only for the winner, but for an accompanying chaperone; visit to the White House—shake hands with the President—everything. Mr. Hogan thought they were getting their hopes too high and he said so.

12 "You've got to be prepared to lose," he told his children. "There're probably thousands and thousands entered. You get your hopes up and it might spoil the whole autumn. Now I don't want any long faces in this house after the contest is over."

13 "I was against it from the start," he told Mrs. Hogan. That was the morning she saw the Washington Monument in her teacup, but she didn't tell anybody about that except Ruth Tyler, Bob Tyler's wife. Ruthie brought over her cards and read them in the Hogan kitchen, but she didn't find a journey. She did tell Mrs. Hogan that the cards were often wrong. The cards had said Mrs. Winkle was going on a trip to Europe and the next week Mrs. Winkle got a fishbone in her throat and choked to death. Ruthie, just thinking out loud, wondered if there was any connection between the fishbone and the ocean voyage to Europe. "You've got to interpret them right." Ruthie did say she saw money coming to the Hogans.

14 "Oh, I got that already from poor Larry," Mrs. Hogan explained.

15 "I must have got the past and future cards mixed," said Ruthie. "You've got to interpret them right."

16 Saturday dawned a blaster. The early morning weather report on the radio said "Continued hot and humid, light scattered rain Sunday night and Monday." Mrs. Hogan said, "Wouldn't you know? Labor Day."

And Mr. Hogan said, "I'm sure glad we didn't plan anything." He finished his egg and mopped the plate with his toast. Mrs. Hogan said, "Did I put coffee on the list?" He took the paper from his handkerchief pocket and consulted it. "Yes, coffee, it's here."

17   "I had a crazy idea I forgot to write it down," said Mrs. Hogan. "Ruth and I are going to Altar Guild this afternoon. It's at Mrs. Alfred Drake's. You know, they just came to town. I can't wait to see their furniture."

18   "They trade with us," said Mr. Hogan. "Opened an account last week. Are the milk bottles ready?"

19   "On the porch."

20   Mr. Hogan looked at his watch just before he picked up the bottles and it was five minutes to eight. He was about to go down the stairs, when he turned and looked back through the opened door at Mrs. Hogan. She said, "Want something, Papa?"

21   "No," he said. "No," and he walked down the steps.

22   He went down to the corner and turned right on Spooner, and Spooner runs into Main Street in two blocks, and right across from where it runs in, there is Fettucci's and the bank around the corner and the alley beside the bank. Mr. Hogan picked up a handbill in front of Fettucci's and unlocked the door. He went through to the storeroom, opened the door to the alley, and looked out. A cat tried to force its way in, but Mr. Hogan blocked it with his foot and leg and closed the door. He took off his coat and put on his long apron, tied the strings in a bowknot behind his back. Then he got the broom from behind the counter and swept out behind the counters and scooped the sweepings into a dustpan; and, going through the storeroom, he opened the door to the alley. The cat had gone away. He emptied the dustpan into the garbage can and tapped it smartly to dislodge a piece of lettuce leaf. Then he went back to the store and worked for a while on the order sheet. Mrs. Clooney came in for a half a pound of bacon. She said it was hot and Mr. Hogan agreed. "Summers are getting hotter," he said.

23   "I think so myself," said Mrs. Clooney. "How's Mrs. standing up?"

24   "Just fine," said Mr. Hogan. "She's going to Altar Guild."

25   "So am I. I just can't wait to see their furniture," said Mrs. Clooney, and she went out.

3

26   Mr. Hogan put a five-pound hunk of bacon on the slicer and stripped off the pieces and laid them on wax paper and then he put the wax-paper-covered squares in the cooler cabinet. At ten minutes to nine, Mr. Hogan went to a shelf. He pushed a spaghetti box aside and took down a cereal box, which he emptied in the little closet toilet. Then, with a banana knife, he cut out the Mickey Mouse mask that was on the back. The rest of the box he took to the toilet and tore up the cardboard and

flushed it down. He went into the store then and yanked a piece of string loose and tied the ends through the side holes of the mask and then he looked at his watch—a large silver Hamilton with black hands. It was two minutes to nine.

27 Perhaps the next four minutes were his only time of nervousness at all. At one minute to nine, he took the broom and went out to sweep the sidewalk and he swept it very rapidly—was sweeping it, in fact, when Mr. Warner unlocked the bank door. He said good morning to Mr. Warner and a few seconds later the bank staff of four emerged from the coffee shop. Mr. Hogan saw them across the street and he waved at them and they waved back. He finished the sidewalk and went back in the store. He laid his watch on the little step of the cash register. He sighed very deeply, more like a deep breath than a sigh. He knew that Mr. Warner would have the safe open now and he would be carrying the cash trays to the teller's window. Mr. Hogan looked at the watch on the cash register step. Mr. Kenworthy paused in the store entrance, then shook his head vaguely and walked on and Mr. Hogan let out his breath gradually. His left hand went behind his back and pulled the bowknot on his apron, and then the black hand on his watch crept up on the four-minute mark and covered it.

28 Mr. Hogan opened the charge account drawer and took out the store pistol, a silver-colored Iver Johnson .38. He moved quickly to the storeroom, slipped off his apron, put on his coat, and stuck the revolver in his side pocket. The Mickey Mouse mask he shoved up under his coat where it didn't show. He opened the alley door and looked up and down and stepped quickly out, leaving the door slightly ajar. It is sixty feet to where the alley enters Main Street, and there he paused and looked up and down and then he turned his head toward the center of the street as he passed the bank window. At the bank's swinging door, he took out the mask from under his coat and put it on. Mr. Warner was just entering his office and his back was to the door. The top of Will Cup's head was visible through the teller's grill.

29 Mr. Hogan moved quickly and quietly around the end of the counter and into the teller's cage. He had the revolver in his right hand now. When Will Cup turned his head and saw the revolver, he froze. Mr. Hogan slipped his toe under the trigger of the floor alarm and he motioned Will Cup to the floor with the revolver and Will went down quick. Then Mr. Hogan opened the cash drawer and with two quick movements he piled the large bills from the tray together. He made a whipping motion to Will on the floor, to indicate that he should turn over and face the wall, and Will did. Then Mr. Hogan stepped back around the counter. At the door of the bank, he took off the mask, and as he passed the window he turned his head toward the middle of the street. He moved into the alley, walked quickly to the storeroom, and entered. The cat had got in. It watched him from a pile of canned goods cartons. Mr. Hogan went to the toilet closet and tore up the mask and flushed it. He took off his coat and put on his apron. He looked out into the store and then moved to the cash register. The revolver went back into the charge account drawer. He punched No Sale and, lifting the top drawer, distributed the stolen money underneath the top tray and then pulled the tray forward and closed the register, and only then did he look at his watch and it was 9:07½.

30 He was trying to get the cat out of the storeroom when the commotion boiled out of the bank. He took his broom and went out on the sidewalk. He heard all about it and offered his opinion when it was asked for. He said he didn't think the fellow could get away—where could he get to? Still, with the holiday coming up—

31 It was an exciting day. Mr. Fettucci was as proud as though it were his bank. The sirens sounded around town for hours. Hundreds of holiday travelers had to stop at the roadblocks set up all around the edge of town and several sneaky-looking men had their cars searched.

32 Mrs. Hogan heard about it over the phone and she dressed earlier than she would have ordinarily and came to the store on her way to Altar Guild. She hoped Mr. Hogan would have seen or heard something new, but he hadn't. "I don't see how the fellow can get away," he said.

33 Mrs. Hogan was so excited, she forgot her own news. She only remembered when she got to Mrs. Drake's house, but she asked permission and phoned the store the first moment she could. "I forgot to tell you. John's won honorable mention."

34 "What?"

35 "In the 'I Love America' Contest."

36 "What did he win?"

37 "Honorable mention."

38 "Fine. Fine—Anything come with it?"

39 "Why, he'll get his picture and his name all over the country. Radio too. Maybe even television. They've already asked for a photograph of him."

40 "Fine," said Mr. Hogan. "I hope it don't spoil him." He put up the receiver and said to Mr. Fettucci, "I guess we've got a celebrity in the family."

41 Fettucci stayed open until nine on Saturdays. Mr. Hogan ate a few snacks from cold cuts, but not much, because Mrs. Hogan always kept his supper warming.

42 It was 9:05, or :06, or :07, when he got back to the brown-shingle house at 215 East Maple. He went in through the front door and out to the kitchen where the family was waiting for him.

43 "Got to wash up," he said, and went up to the bathroom. He turned the key in the bathroom door and then he flushed the toilet and turned on the water in the basin and tub while he counted the money. Eight thousand three hundred and twenty dollars. From the top shelf of the storage closet in the bathroom, he took down the big leather case that held his Knight Templar's uniform. The plumed hat lay there on its form. The white ostrich feather was a little yellow and needed changing. Mr. Hogan lifted out the hat and pried the form up from the bottom of the case. He put the money in the form and then he thought again and removed two bills and shoved them in his side pocket. Then he put the form back over the money and laid the hat on top and closed the case and shoved it back on the top shelf. Finally he washed his hands and turned off the water in the tub and the basin.

44 In the kitchen, Mrs. Hogan and the children faced him, beaming. "Guess what some young man's going on?"

45 "What?" asked Mr. Hogan.

46 "Radio," said John. "Monday night. Eight o'clock."

47 "I guess we got a celebrity in the family," said Mr. Hogan.

48 Mrs. Hogan said, "I just hope some young lady hasn't got her nose out of joint."

49 Mr. Hogan pulled up to the table and stretched his legs. "Mama, I guess I got a fine family," he said. He reached in his pocket and took out two five-dollar bills. He handed one to John. "That's for winning," he said. He poked the other bill at Joan. "And that's for being a good sport. One celebrity and one good sport. What a fine family!" He rubbed his hands together and lifted the lid of the covered dish. "Kidneys," he said. "Fine."

50 And that's how Mr. Hogan did it.

Comment

Here is a crime story with a difference. First of all, the criminal gets away with it—crime *does* pay. Second, he is clearly not the "criminal type." He seems to be the average American breadwinner, good husband and father, living an ordinary kind of life in an ordinary-looking house at an ordinary-sounding address, working at an ordinary, respectable, unglamorous job in a grocery store. And his family, too, is nice in the same ordinary, average way. Perhaps his children seem a bit brighter and better behaved than most children their age, but this just adds to our general favorable impression of Mr. Hogan.

And this takes us to the third and most startling point about the manner in which the story differs from most crime stories: not only does Steinbeck let Hogan get away with an eight-thousand-dollar bank robbery, he does not even condemn him. Not a word is said about Mr. Hogan being a bad man who does a bad thing. We found Heyerdahl, Lindbergh, and the *Time* reporter using what we ordinarily think of as "literary" devices in reporting real and truthful events. Here Steinbeck does the reverse: he uses the manner of a reporter in writing fiction, i.e., a form of literature. Throughout, he is objective, factual, composed, a little distant—like a reporter calmly observing the ordinary behavior of rather likable strangers. Steinbeck writes as if he thought robbing a bank no more unusual or wicked than polishing your car or making a coffee table. The very title of the story suggests that we have to do with a "how-to" piece for the do-it-yourself-er. The procedure outlined evidently works; Mr. Hogan's way seems indeed to be the way to rob a bank successfully. We leave him pleasantly seated at his dinner table in front of his favorite dish, chatting amiably with his wife, proud of his hopeful son. And there is no evidence that his happiness is about to be interrupted by the arrival of cops with difficult questions.

The story is almost upsetting in its calm acceptance of crime. What are we to make of it? Has Steinbeck simply written a crime story with a new twist? If so, can he not be accused of recklessly teaching his readers how to break the law? Even worse, isn't the story frankly immoral? May it not contribute to juvenile delinquency? Is it proper reading for college students?

Maybe Steinbeck is not quite so irresponsible as such questions suggest. His purpose may be less sinister than to instruct us in crime. It may be that the story is a satire.

Satire is writing that criticizes a person, a belief, or a thing by ridiculing it. The making fun may be more or less open and direct. Here it is indirect. Isn't the clue to Steinbeck's real purpose found in the Hogan family's very ordinariness and niceness? And doesn't the story get its "point" from the clash between what Mr. Hogan *is* and what he *does* and from his own apparent unawareness of that clash? Naturally, he is rather nervous about being caught, but that seems to be as far as his emotions are involved. There is not the slightest indication that he is aware of doing anything morally wrong or even unusual for a man in his position or that he suffers from guilty conscience either during or after his crime. And yet, he is clearly, in all other respects, a normal, pleasant, nice, *ordinary* American, a regular guy who loves his family, is trusted by his employer, believes in the right things, wants to lead a good life. Put the two facts together. A decent, average kind of man commits a serious crime for no urgent motive and gets away with it. Neither the law nor his own conscience punishes him.

Could it not be that Steinbeck is writing with his tongue in his cheek? Perhaps he wants us to identify ourselves with Mr. Hogan and all he stands for —solid middle-class virtues. Before we indignantly accuse Steinbeck of confusing right and wrong, maybe we should ask ourselves if it is not the Mr. Hogans of our society who have developed a rather odd sense of values. Hogan's complete indifference to the *sinfulness* of the robbery suggests that he has accepted a belief that quite a few of us have accepted or are on our way to accepting, whether we realize it or not: that anything that works, that is profitable, that is successful, is really quite all right. Why does Mr. Hogan rob the bank? Not, obviously, because he likes to run risks; the care with which he plans the crime proves that. He robs because he is a good provider. What motive could be more admirable?

If Steinbeck had written an essay telling us that behind our surface niceness and decency we really are thoroughgoing materialists, we might either have felt insulted or yawned and muttered "Oh, I suppose so," and gone on to something else. But by dramatizing his point in the story of Mr. Hogan and by attacking our values indirectly, from behind, he both catches our attention and disturbs us. Whether we fully understand the satire or not, Steinbeck will have made us feel that something, somewhere, somehow, is wrong. It could be that that vague sense of things somehow being wrong is exactly what Steinbeck wanted to create in us.

Exercises

CONTENT

True or False? If you think the statement represents what the selection says or implies, mark it "True"; if you do not think so, mark it "False."

T 1. Mr. Hogan's first name was John.

F 2. The robbery took place the day after Labor Day.

T 3. Mrs. Hogan had just inherited some money.

T 4. Mrs. Hogan was superstitious.

F 5. The beauty of his plan, Mr. Hogan told himself, was that it did not require carrying a gun.

F 6. The cat in the storeroom may turn out to be proof of Mr. Hogan's guilt.

F 7. Mr. Hogan intended to use the money for a trip to Europe with his family.

F 8. Joan Hogan won second prize in the "I Love America" contest.

F 9. The Hogans were not popular people.

F 10. The story proves that the police are often stupid in investigating crime.

Question for Discussion.

Even assuming that Steinbeck's purpose with the story was what the comment above suggests, couldn't it still be said that this story should not be read by susceptible people, perhaps particularly young people, because it may give them wrong ideas? Explain your answer.

FORM AND STYLE

1. Does the nature of the contest which the Hogan children enter have any significance? Would it have made a difference if they had been competing in some sort of box-top contest? Explain your answer.

2. Why do you think Mrs. Hogan's church activity has been emphasized?

3. Considering the "character" of Mickey Mouse and the qualities he is usually associated with (for example, in TV's "Mickey Mouse Club"), can you think of any reason why Steinbeck had Mr. Hogan commit the robbery in a Mickey Mouse mask? Why not just any kind of mask?

4. In Paragraph 43 Mr. Hogan's Knight Templar's uniform is de-

scribed as well as the amount of loot. The uniform box is then used as a hiding place for the money. Why do you think Steinbeck wanted the Lodge uniform and the loot brought together in this way?

5. Do you see any connection among your four previous answers?

6. Define "hanky-panky" (Paragraph 3).

7. Aside from the robbery itself, what evidence, if any, can you find that the Hogans are materialists?

8. What do you think goes on in Mr. Hogan's mind as indicated in this sentence (Paragraph 20): "He was about to go down the stairs, when he turned and looked back through the open door at Mrs. Hogan"?

9. Discuss briefly the means by which Steinbeck has given the story an air of reality, like that of a factual report or a detailed newspaper account. (You may find it helpful to study style and content of Paragraph 22.)

10. Why has so much space been given to the preparation for the robbery?

VOCABULARY

Which of the four words or phrases to the right seems to you to be *closest* in meaning to the word in heavy type to the left? Put a check mark after your choice.

respectively (*1*) full of respect . . . in the order mentioned . . . in a respectable manner . . . looking backward . . .

venture (*3*) business . . . enterprise . . . adventure . . . investment

obsession (*10*) possession . . . obstacle . . . something that shows clearly . . . fixed idea . . .

chaperone (*11*) companion for the sake of propriety . . . temporary maid . . . friend . . . guide . . .

indicate (*29*) show . . . make certain . . . force . . . suggest . . .

celebrity (*40*) someone who is stuck up . . . a fortunate person . . . one who celebrates . . . someone famous . . .

plumed (*43*) fanciful . . . with a big brim . . . provided with feathers . . . crumpled . . .

THEME SUGGESTIONS

A character sketch of either Mr. Hogan or Mrs. Hogan
An unsolved crime
Why foreigners call Americans materialists
Crime comics—how they affect(ed) me

Description

TAYLOR · WEST · EISELEY · SANDERSON
LANGEWIESCHE

The writer of description tries to create in our minds impressions of the physical world we experience with our senses. These imaginary equivalents of real-life sense impressions—the sights, sounds, smells, tastes, and feel of things that the reading of description calls up in our minds—are known as *images*. Writing that does not cause images to form in the reader's mind is not descriptive, whatever else it may be. You *describe* your room or your room-mate or a new dress or a sunset or the smell and taste and feel of fresh corn, or you *describe* your feelings on your first date or when you flunked math or when your grandmother died. It is a simplification, but not an altogether misleading one, to say that in narrative writing the verbs are emphasized, in description the adjectives and the adverbs are emphasized. This is not to say that nouns ever are or ever should be unimportant. It *is* to say that in narrative the writer tells what the nouns do or have done to them, while in description he tells what the nouns look like, feel like, and so on.

Of course, in practice we do not often make distinctions like this, and even if we should want to, we are rarely able to do so. For we almost never meet the different types of prose in their pure form. It is hardly possible to *narrate* an action without *describing* it at the same time. Only a dull reader would fail to receive images of shapes, colors, movements, of shouts and spray and angry winds from Heyerdahl's account of the raft incident. Insofar as *Man Overboard!* called up such mental pictures, it may be called descriptive. "It was oppressive and absolutely still" can hardly be called a narrative statement; nor are "black, threatening clouds," "measuring already fifty feet and more per second," and "some vague green object twirling about in the water near him" narrative phrases. The point is not that *Man Overboard!* is not an example of narrative; it is. The point is that narratives almost invariably include descriptive elements and that the narrative elements themselves are image-forming. We visualize a dog and a child (however vaguely) and hear the dog's bark and the child's cry in the sample sentences in the discussion of Narrative on page 3, above. The reverse is also true: few descriptions are without narrative elements. In her description of her home in Germany, *This Is Home*, which follows, Frieda Landfried Taylor refers to several actions: cats claw at the willow tree, a child is slapped, old men are marched off to prison or concentration camp. In his zoologist's description of moles (page 46), Ivan Sanderson turns out as pure a piece of narrative as this: "Whereupon he promptly takes her captive and if any other male appears he seals her up in a side-hole, then quickly hollows out an arena and goes to work on the interloper."

What is true of narration and description is true of all types of prose. The types are not mutually exclusive. Much more often than not, they are found in one combination or another, cooperating for a common end.

5

FRIEDA LANDFRIED TAYLOR
This Is Home

1   To many people it is only a place on a map and to most people it's not even that. But to me it's the center of the universe.

2   The land is flat and the soil is rather sandy. It is miserly and gives of itself only grudgingly—and then only upon payment of much backbreaking and time-consuming work.

3   The summers are hot and dry; the winters bitterly cold. Autumn brings the icy west wind from the North Sea and freezes the still unharvested crops. All seasons bring with them sudden floods and unexpected thunderstorms and hunger and danger and fear. Only spring is good to us. With it come soft gentle breezes that stir the dead leaves and hopes into life again. Everyone and everything seems to thrive in the new warmth of the sun, and everyone knows that it will be a better year than ever before. We tell each other that never before has the air felt so much like spring, and never have the first blades of grass come up in just such a way. We know that the wheat crop will be good and that we will be able to harvest it, because last year, when our fields were flooded, there was a different wind, and the clouds weren't as fluffy.

4   Following spring is the same hot, dry summer of the years before; but we tell ourselves to be patient: next year will be different. For years we've gone on—looking forward to a new spring and to larger and better crops. Yet each year comes as the one before, and with it come floods, droughts, and thunderstorms; but we don't mind, because we love this place: it is Home.

5   It is the place that gave me my first experiences with death and love and happiness. This is the place where I tasted my first banana and took my first train ride. I remember the ferry boats, with the sea gulls

THIS IS HOME. Student theme. Reprinted by permission of the author.

circling around the stern. I remember the willow tree by the kitchen window—the one with the sparrow nest in the lowest crotch. I can still see the cats clawing in anger and frustration at the foot of the tree because they were unable to get past the barbed wire that Grandfather had put up to protect the birds!

6 It is here that I witnessed the transformation of human beings into savage animals whose only emotions were hate, fear, and self-preservation. I knew of a mother who slapped down her crying child and left him in the street while she shoved her way past a group of injured to take up someone else's place in the bombshelter. I've seen elderly men being marched off because their sons had turned them in to gain favor for themselves.

7 But it is here also I saw the human people: those who believed in the worth of others, those who loved and who sacrificed for what they loved. They gave up shelter and food when they had little to give. They passed out clothing when their own was threadbare. They sacrificed honesty and lied and stole to protect and feed the refugees. They gave of themselves to perfect strangers, with whom their only kinship was fear of obliteration and fear of being afraid.

8 I also remember the whine of the siren: three short blasts for a warning, and a constant high-pitched scream—like the Wednesday noon practice alert, only much more high-strung—for complete evacuation. Even now, the smell of sulphur and burning wool brings back the stench of the war with double force. Every day in the chemistry lab I again see the rubble and the smoke screens, the bathtub and radiator hanging by only a thread of a pipe from what is left of an apartment house. I see the crock of preserved eggs standing perfectly intact in front of what is left of the house in which my parents and nineteen others died. Now it seems merely ironic, but then it was painful mockery. At these times I taste again the bitter gall of terror and then feel the fear subside to leave a hollow, empty numbness.

9 Yet after all this, when I now think of this place, the small black, unnamed dot on the map of Germany, I feel myself drawn toward it with longing. I see it as I want to see it, and the emotions aroused by the Wednesday noon whistle and the odor of the chem lab are completely obliterated by the memory of the trees and the North Sea breeze and the train ride and the banana.

Comment

An American college freshman, faced with a blank sheet of paper and the ordeal of recording on it his impressions of "My Home Town," may read *This Is Home* and feel envious of the author because of the unusualness of her home environment: "With a background like that I, too, could write an interesting descriptive theme!"

But *This Is Home* is superior descriptive writing not because it describes something interesting (though it does that), but because of the *manner* of the description. Its distinction lies in the author's selection of many different, sometimes contrasting, details of landscape and soil and climate, of seasonal change, of animals and people, war and peace, kindness and cruelty, then and now, of the trivial and the solemnly significant. The marvel is that in a description as short as this there has been room for so many separate details which all combine to make a single sharp and vivid picture of what a wartime childhood in a little German town was like. And it is because the many concrete details have been chosen with such sure sense of rightness of what belongs in the complex but unified image the author wants to evoke in us, that they are able to communicate not just sights and sounds and smells and tastes, but also moods and feelings: pleasure, nostalgia, pity, horror, understanding.

If you felt when you read "This Is Home" that you responded not so much to *what* happened as to *how* it happened and how it felt to the author when it happened and what the memory feels like to her now, then you have understood something of the importance of the descriptive ingredient in language.

This Is Home was written in a class in regular freshman composition. And English is not the writer's native language.

Exercises

CONTENT

True or False? If you think the statement represents what the selection says or implies, mark it "True"; if you do not think so, mark it "False."

1. The author's home was in south Germany.
2. Agriculture was the main occupation in the district.
3. The worst threat to the crops came from almost yearly droughts.
4. The author had never eaten a banana till she came to America.
5. Her parents died in a fire.
6. Her parents died in an Allied bombing raid.
7. Because of her horrible war memories, the author's feelings about her home are wholly painful.
8. Her memories tend to prove that war always brings out the worst in people.
9. Twenty-three persons died in the apartment house where she lived.
10. Her account of how she miraculously escaped death is the most dramatic part of the whole theme.

Question for Discussion.

In Paragraph 7 occurs this sentence: "They sacrificed honesty and lied and stole to protect and feed the refugees." First define and then try to explain and justify your feelings about "They." Is knowledge of Germany in World War II relevant in this connection?

FORM AND STYLE

1. Comment on the change in the "feeling" of the sentence if "my home town" were substituted for "it" in the first sentence of Paragraph 1.

2. How would you justify the ungrammatical lack of specific reference for the pronoun "it" throughout the paragraph?

3. The second sentence in Paragraph 1 is in figurative language. More specifically, it is a metaphor. A metaphor is a compressed comparison, with the words "like" or "as" left out. For example, "he eats like a pig" is a nonmetaphorical comparison; "he is a pig" is a metaphor. What is being compared to what in the metaphor in this selection? What does the metaphor say? Does it say it better than a nonmetaphorical statement would have?

4. Explain this comment: "The connecting link between Paragraphs 3 and 4 is that between expectation and disappointment."

5. Why do you think "death" is mentioned before "love and happiness" in Paragraph 5? Does simple chronology seem to be the reason?

6. If the theme were to be divided into two main parts, the division could be made after either Paragraph 4 or Paragraph 5. Explain and justify both divisions by defining the subject matter of each of the two parts in both cases. Try to find a single phrase for each definition. Which of the two ways of dividing the essay do you prefer? Explain your answer.

7. Paragraphs 5 and 6 are placed next to one another for the sake of contrast. State the nature of the contrast and point out a concrete detail in each paragraph that strengthens the contrast.

8. Why are the eggs in the theme (Paragraph 8)? Why the chemistry lab (Paragraph 9)?

9. Discuss the manner in which repetition gives coherence to Paragraph 7.

10. Discuss whether or not the theme would have been improved if the author had concluded not with the train ride and the banana but with a sentence like this: "I love this place: it's Home." Explain your answer.

VOCABULARY

Which of the four words or phrases to the right seems to you to be *closest* in meaning to the word in heavy type to the left? Put a check mark after your choice.

miserly (2)   ugly . . . sparingly . . . poor . . . unwilling to give . . .

thrive (3)   be happy . . . wake up . . . be thrifty . . . do well . . .

refugees (7)   unfortunates . . . members of the underground . . . the rescued . . . people who flee . . .

kinship (7)   family relation . . . similarity . . . kindness . . . bond
obliteration (7)   extinction . . . death . . . punishment . . . intoler-
       able pain . . .
ironic (8)   amusing . . . strange . . . meaningful in an unexpected
       way . . . curious, for no reason . . .
evacuation (8)   emptiness . . . protection . . . moving out . . .
       danger . . .
crotch (5)   branch . . . angle between branches . . . hollow . . .
       nesting place . . .
transformation (6)   deformation . . . degradation . . . passage . . .
       change . . .
crock (8)   shelf . . . box . . . earthenware container . . . wooden
       container . . .

THEME SUGGESTIONS

Where I grew up
The day people changed
My earliest memory
A childhood incident, perhaps one you feel changed your life

6

REBECCA WEST

Miss Furness

¹   There was a geography mistress whom we rather liked, Miss Furness, one of the few teachers we could imagine ourselves choosing to go
on knowing when we had grown up. She had a timid, wavering voice,
and green eyes, with flecks of dark green on a light green iris, like goose-
berries, and sandy hair which curved across the front of her head in a
high hollow crescent, the shape of a boat turned upside down. We used
to imagine her walking across England and coming to the Severn or the
Wye or the Ouse, and taking off this crescent and launching it the right
way up and floating in it to the opposite shore, shading her green eyes
and calling apologetically, "Ahoy, there." She obviously wanted to be
nice, she flushed and had to force her voice when it came to saying, "And
now for those girls who failed," and she taught her subject in a quite in-

MISS FURNESS. From *The Fountain Overflows* by Rebecca West. Copyright ©, 1956, by Rebecca West. Reprinted by permission of The Viking Press,
Inc. and Macmillan & Co. Limited, London.

teresting, gasping way. Even physical geography, which tells so many things one does not want to know, such as why there is night and day, was interesting because she spoke of the stars with such wistful respect. So we were very pleased when she asked us to tea, particularly as she lived in a part of Lovegrove we liked very much, where a dozen early-Victorian villas stood white and betowered and battlemented round a three-corned scrap of village green, shaded by a row of tall old limes.

2   The house was as nice as we had expected. Miss Furness's grandfather had bought it from the builder and her father and mother had moved there when he had given up teaching epigraphy at Oxford. There was a feeling that the same people had always lived there, and that there had always been enough money, which we liked very much. Nothing was shabby. She showed us everything, moving and speaking as hesitantly as if she were not hostess but guest. She put a timid forefinger to the curtains, to the wallpapers, which alike were a rich-coloured paste of little flowers, and told us that they were the work of William Morris; and she took us to the fireplaces, where huge fires glowed orange, and pointed down at the tiles, which showed windmills and castles and men in armour, and said they were made by the clever Mr. William de Morgan, who made tiles better than anybody had made them for hundreds of years. There was much furniture, so highly polished that its very solidity made it the more airy, there were such broad surfaces reflecting the warmed and ruddy light. The winter day, which was blanched and cold, was annulled; and we were happy, particularly when Miss Furness took us to see her mother, who now never left her room. She wore a huge silver chignon, through which ran some streaks as sandy as her daughter's hair. We had always known that the other girls were talking nonsense when they said that the curious hollow crescent across Miss Furness's head was a transformation. Mrs. Furness had had a relative who was one of the first English amateur photographers, and she showed us some portraits, very sharp and linear and refined, almost like drawings, except for the pale, milky blacks, of Lewis Carroll and some little girls at a tea-party he gave to celebrate the publication of *Alice in Wonderland*. What amused us so much that we could hardly keep our minds on the photographs was that Mrs. Furness had an asthmatic pug lying beside her which was exactly like the pug we had made up when we were younger and had first come to Lovegrove Place. Finally we had to tell her, in case she thought we were rude, and she and her daughter quite understood.

3   Then we went down to tea in the dining room. It was a very good tea, with cherry cake that had cherries all the way through, and not just at the bottom. It was a pity that Mrs. Furness could not come down, we had liked her so much. There was a big clock on the chimney-piece, with a beautiful tick, almost like a purr, but this room was not as nice as the others, for it was hung with large photographs, framed in reddish oak, of stones bearing inscriptions in ancient languages, with notices in black

letters underneath saying where they had been found. They introduced a look of schoolroom squalor. When we had finished, Miss Furness did not rise, we just went on sitting at the table. We listened to the agreeable tick of the clock, and we looked round the room. Mary asked Miss Furness if the inscriptions had ever turned out to be interesting when they had been translated. Miss Furness looked embarrassed, and then smiled, and said with an air of daring, "Do you know, never. Never to me. The most interesting are laws. But such dull laws." Then she relapsed into silence again. We did not mind, this was such a very safe, well-cared-for house, we liked being there.

Comment

A little girl describes her and her sisters' visit to one of their teachers. The description is only a small fragment of a novel, and though its effect in the context of the whole novel necessarily is different from what it is here since the characters have a life in the novel beyond the few brief episodes of the fragment, we can still feel that it has reality. We can visualize Miss Furness, her gooseberry eyes and timid voice, her house, the polished furniture, her mother, the wheezy dog, the photographs, the cake.

More important, we can form an attitude toward her. And our attitude is not quite that of the girl who is supposed to be describing her. The girl is perhaps ten or twelve years old, certainly not much older. The author's prob-lem has been to make us believe in the reality of the girl-as-author. Rebecca West has succeeded in doing this. The sentences have a childlike ring (though undoubtedly of a rather precocious child), the viewpoint throughout is that of a young girl. Read over again the scene where the sisters are so amused by the resemblance between Mrs. Furness's dog and their own imaginary one that they pay no attention to the photographs they are shown, are embarrassed by their own childishness, and apologize to the two grown-ups. Ask yourself if this scene does not carry with it the feel of childhood and childhood visits to kindly aunts who tried in vain to enter into your child's world of precious silli-ness and covered up their helplessness by "understanding."

And it is exactly because we are so fully aware of the describer as a child that we can see more in what she describes than she does herself. Quite a complex attitude toward Miss Furness is set up in us. We see her with the child's eyes: kindhearted, interesting, a little funny looking, a little odd and comical altogether. But we also sense something which the child, being a child, does not sense, or, if she does, does not have the words for (her description begins and ends with the general, vague word "like": "we rather liked [Miss Furness] . . . we liked being there"). Gradually we become aware of good-ness and sensitivity and intelligence and learning, of a prim, neat, peaceful existence at school and in the old, still house, of quiet interests, of secret dreams not quite dead but never to be fulfilled, of spinsterishness, but also of humor and gentle sadness. Quite possibly, words like these are too definite for the subtle delicacy of the portrait of Miss Furness. If you feel something like this, you are proving that the implied, the unsaid, contributes at least as much to the portrait as the direct description, although it does so only *through* the direct description. We have been allowed to see both with the child's eyes and with the wiser eyes of the mature and deliberate novelist. In this doubleness of vision lies the excellence of the description.

Finally, a note on a point of organization. The first paragraph deals mainly with Miss Furness herself. Its last sentence, however, introduces the description of the house which is continued in the first sentences of the second paragraph. The description of the house serves, in other words, as *transition* between the two paragraphs. It could not have done so if it had been complete in either one or the other of the two paragraphs. And yet it has not been split arbitrarily. The last sentence of Paragraph 1 describes the exterior of the house, the first sentences of Paragraph 2 describes its interior—a perfectly natural division, since Paragraph 1 deals with a time before the visit and Paragraph 2 with the visit itself.

Exercises

CONTENT

True or False? If you think the statement represents what the selection says or implies, mark it "True"; if you do not think so, mark it "False."

1. The scene of the story is England.
2. Miss Furness taught geography.
3. She had red hair.
4. The area she lived in was called Lovewood.
5. She invited the girls to tea because she wanted to show them the ancient stones.
6. Miss Furness and her mother were evidently not well off.
7. Mrs. Furness was silver-haired.
8. Miss Furness did not share her father's interests.
9. The girls thought there was something supernatural about Miss Furness.
10. Miss Furness had been the little girl who was Lewis Carroll's model for Alice of *Alice in Wonderland*.

Question for Discussion.

Characterize Miss Furness so as to suggest the reason(s) why the girls liked her.

FORM AND STYLE

1. Although there is no one "right" answer to this, what meaning do you find in this sentence from Paragraph 1: "We used to imagine her walking across England and coming to the Severn or the Wye or the

Ouse, and taking off this crescent and launching it the right way up and floating in it to the opposite shore, shading her green eyes and calling apologetically, 'Ahoy, there.' "

2. How can a forefinger be "timid" (Paragraph 2)?

3. Disregarding your own personal interests for the moment, can you think of any reason why anybody should *not* want to know "why there is night and day" (Paragraph 1)? Do you find any connection between or consistency in this and the girl's general attitude to Miss Furness and the visit?

4. Do you agree or do you not that the style and the whole manner of telling about the visit is like a child's? Support your opinion by pointing out specific passages in the selection that strike you as being childlike (or not) in form or attitude or both.

VOCABULARY

Which of the four words or phrases to the right seems to you to be *closest* in meaning to the word in heavy type to the left? Put a check mark after your choice.

timid (*1*)   rasping . . . frightened . . . low . . . soft . . .

flecks (*1*)   areas . . . streaks . . . spots . . . circles . . .

crescent (*1*)   top . . . sweep . . . line . . . curve . . .

apologetically (*1*)   musically . . . like a sailor . . . shyly . . . as if apologizing . . .

wistful (*1*)   wishing . . . longing . . . unknowing . . . knowing . . .

epigraphy (*2*)   study of epics . . . study of inscriptions . . . study of stones . . . study of writing . . .

ruddy (*2*)   reddish . . . pleasant . . . cozy . . . friendly . . .

blanched (*2*)   white . . . bleak . . . dreary . . . blank . . .

annulled (*2*)   forgotten . . . changed . . . made unimportant . . . made void . . .

chignon (*2*)   comb . . . net . . . knot . . . wig . . .

linear (*2*)   full of lines . . . close . . . clear . . . angular . . .

squalor (*3*)   miserableness . . . terror . . . squareness . . . boredom

relapsed (*3*)   collapsed . . . slipped . . . fell back . . . muttered . . .

THEME SUGGESTIONS

The high school teacher I liked best/least

An embarrassing visit

The day I changed my opinion of —— (fill in a person's name)

Tell about an episode from your childhood that seems more significant to you now than it did then.

7

LOREN EISELEY

The Slit

1   Some lands are flat and grass-covered, and smile so evenly up at the sun that they seem forever youthful, untouched by man or time. Some are torn, ravaged and convulsed like the features of profane old age. Rocks are wrenched up and exposed to view; black pits receive the sun but give back no light.

2   It was to such a land I rode, but I rode to it across a sunlit, timeless prairie over which nothing passed but antelope or a wandering bird. On the verge where that prairie halted before a great wall of naked sandstone and clay, I came upon the Slit. A narrow crack worn by some descending torrent had begun secretly, far back in the prairie grass, and worked itself deeper and deeper into the fine sandstone that led by devious channels into the broken waste beyond. I rode back along the crack to a spot where I could descend into it, dismounted, and left my horse to graze.

3   The crack was only about body-width and, as I worked my way downward, the light turned dark and green from the overhanging grass. Above me the sky became a narrow slit of distant blue, and the sandstone was cool to my hands on either side. The Slit was a little sinister—like an open grave, assuming the dead were enabled to take one last look—for over me the sky seemed already as far off as some future century I would never see.

4   I ignored the sky, then, and began to concentrate on the sandstone walls that led me into this place. It was tight and tricky work, but that cut was a perfect cross section through perhaps ten million years of time. I hoped to find at least a bone, but I was not quite prepared for the sight I finally came upon. Staring straight out at me, as I slid farther and deeper into the green twilight, was a skull embedded in the solid sandstone. I had come at just the proper moment when it was fully to be seen, the white bone gleaming there in a kind of ashen splendor, water worn, and about to be ground away in the next long torrent.

5   It was not, of course, human. I was deep, deep below the time of man in a remote age near the beginning of the reign of mammals. I squatted on my heels in the narrow ravine, and we stared a little blankly at each other, the skull and I. There were marks of generalized primitiveness in that low, pinched brain case and grinning jaw that marked it as

lying far back along those converging roads where . . . cat and man and weasel must leap into a single shape.

6   It was the face of a creature who had spent his days following his nose, who was led by instinct rather than memory, and whose power of choice was very ,small. Though he was not a man, nor a direct human ancestor, there was yet about him, even in the bone, some trace of that low, snuffling world out of which our forebears had so recently emerged. The skull lay tilted in such a manner that it stared, sightless, up at me as though I, too, were already caught a few feet above him in the strata and, in my turn, were staring upward at that strip of sky which the ages were carrying farther away from me beneath the tumbling debris of falling mountains. The creature had never lived to see a man, and I, what was it I was never going to see?

Comment

A distinction is often made between *objective* and *subjective* writing. Lindbergh's two accounts of his parachute jump on pages 10-13 are examples: the earlier version is objective, the later version subjective. As we should expect, much writing is neither all objective nor all subjective but first one, then the other, or somewhere in between the two extremes. These extremes may—roughly—be defined as follows.

In objective writing, the writer tries to keep his own personal feelings, interests, and prejudices from interfering with his expression of factual, scientific truth as that truth would appear to a neutral and accurate observer or to a recording instrument. Subjective writing, on the other hand, does not try to express universal, absolute, scientific truth; instead it deals with how things seem or feel to the individual. Its subject matter is precisely what cannot be expressed in the objective terms of science: feelings and attitudes, beliefs and hunches, dreams and visions, hopes, longings, prejudices—everything that has to do with the uniqueness of the individual personality. "Four-door Cadillac sedan, green, license plate AAB 6794" is an objective description of what the adman subjectively has in mind when he tells you "you'll feel like a million dollars when you take off for the stars in your new Cadillac." And "the cute little co-ed with eyes like a clear sky in April and hair like ripe wheat" may turn up as "height 5'4", eyes blue, hair light brown" in the Registrar's files. The Cadillac and the girl are the same; only the viewpoint has changed.

Loren Eiseley, the author of *The Slit*, is a scientist whose field—anthropology—combines physical and social science. Here he writes about finding a prehistoric animal skull embedded in sandstone inside a deep, narrow gorge somewhere on the prairie lands of the American Midwest. But even a casual reading will show that this is not an objective, scientific report. The land, the slit, and the skull are not described as a scientist would describe them. To a scientist lands don't "smile," and it is irrelevant that the slit reminds him of "an open grave." And though Eiseley may feel that the skull "stared" at him he could not, *as a scientist*, say that it did. Rather, these things are described subjectively, as they appear to a sharp-eyed observer gifted with vivid imagination, a sense of beauty, a philosophic cast of mind, and a sufficient command of words to express these values. In one sense, therefore, the description is as much of the observer himself as of the objects he describes. It would be possible to argue that *The Slit* really is closer to being a kind of poetry in prose than it is to being science. It is not so much about topography and bone collecting as it is about man's mysterious sense of his own position somewhere in the vast stretches of Nature's measureless time.

Exercises

CONTENT

True or False? If you think the statement represents what the selection says or implies, mark it "True"; if you do not think so, mark it "False."

1. We never learn why the author went down into the slit.
2. The author drove a car across the prairie.
3. The slit is located in North Dakota.
4. The slit was actually an old Indian grave.
5. A geologist would find the slit interesting.
6. Its sides revealed earth formations almost one million years old.
7. The skull's snout pointed downward.
8. The skull was of an animal that must have been one of man's ancestors.
9. The skull was removed only with great difficulty.
10. At the end, the author thinks he is trapped in the slit.

FORM AND STYLE

1. Synonyms are words of the same or very similar meaning (though they may differ in "emotional quality," or *connotation,* as "drunk" and "intoxicated" differ). "Car" and "automobile" are synonyms. In *The Slit,* Eiseley uses three synonyms for the slit. What are they?
2. What gives unity to Paragraphs 2 and 3 is the sense the reader gets of physical movement. Compare the physical movement of the two paragraphs.
3. Does "the broken waste beyond" (Paragraph 2) refer to something mentioned earlier?
4. Point out the words in Paragraph 2 that link it with Paragraph 1.
5. What justification is there for calling the twilight "green" in Paragraph 3?
6. When he writes, "we stared a little blankly at each other, the skull and I," Eiseley suggests that the skull and he somehow are equal—both alive, both wondering. Of course, Eiseley knows as well as you do that a million year old bone is not alive; scientifically speaking, the sentence

is nonsense. Why, then, did he write it? In other words, can you think of a sense in which the sentence is *not* nonsense? The similarity between man and skull suggested in the final paragraph is relevant to this question.

7. What is the meaning of "cat and man and weasel must leap into a single shape"? Do you see any significance in the fact that "man" is mentioned in the middle?

8. How can Eiseley be sure that the skull belonged to a male animal? If he cannot be sure, why does he refer to the animal (or rather, to the skull) as "he"? Why not "it" (Paragraph 6)?

9. Explain the verb form in "*were* staring upward . . ." (Paragraph 6).

10. In what sense is the slit "an open grave" (Paragraph 3)?

VOCABULARY

Which of the four words or phrases to the right seems to you to be *closest* in meaning to the word in heavy type to the left? Put a check mark after your choice.

ravaged (*1*)   ragged . . . violated . . . wrinkled . . . mad with old age . . .

convulsed (1)   ragged . . . rolling . . . shaken . . . haggard . . .

profane (*1*)   pitiful . . . blasphemous . . . unholy . . . wicked . . .

verge (2)   spot . . . slope . . . edge . . . side . . .

devious (2)   winding . . . long . . . angular . . . secret . . .

descend (2)   enter . . . crawl . . . explore . . . go down . . .

sinister (3)   crooked . . . dangerous . . . scary . . . evil . . .

ashen (4)   spooky . . . lonely . . . like ash . . . strange . . .

splendor (4)   whiteness . . . horror . . . glory . . . beauty . . .

torrent (4)   rainfall . . . flood . . . slide . . . hailstorm . . .

remote (5)   removed . . . distant . . . mysterious . . . early . . .

converging (5)   long . . . separate . . . moving apart . . . moving together . . .

forebears (6)   ancestors . . . early bears . . . primitive mammals . . . parents . . .

emerged (6)   appeared . . . combined . . . came out . . . developed

tilted (6)   turned . . . inclined . . . buried . . . in view . . .

strata (6)   earth . . . developments . . . slits . . . layers . . .

debris (6)   weight . . . ruins . . . fragments . . . small stones . . .

THEME SUGGESTIONS

When I met the past

Amateur naturalist

Christianity and the theory of evolution

Report on American excavations, A.D. 196,000

8

IVAN T. SANDERSON

Moles

1   The true moles are divided into two great clans, one composed of
the original European mole and three allied genera in Asia, one of which
spreads to the Pacific. The other, which we shall meet next, comprises
eight genera spread around the Northern Pacific, with an outlier of two
types in eastern North America. Moles have since time immemorial intrigued human beings. There is something quite unexpected about a
mammal living underground; and the appearance of the animal and its
extraordinary strength have given rise to all sorts of weird beliefs about
its habits and potentialities. Moles naturally prefer areas where the soil is
loose and by long association with man they tend to infest his gardens
and farmlands. There they burrow along about two inches below the
surface in search of food. This consists mostly of earthworms but they
will eat any small animals, including mice, shrews or even their own kind.
The latter happens when they bumble into another mole's run and one is
defeated in the battle that inevitably takes place. They also maintain
large dwelling-burrows placed at a lower level and usually under the
roots of a tree. This is lined with leaves, moss and other soft material and
has an escape exit.

2   Moles go out to eat morning, noon, and night, literally, for when
they are full they fall asleep but invariably wake up in about six hours
and unless they start eating at once soon collapse of starvation. They put
away about twice their own weight per day. Their bodies are bun-shaped,
the head pointed, the eyes minute and either covered by skin or buried in
the fur, and there are no visible ears though they have very acute hearing, especially for earth-borne sounds. The tail is short and naked but
carries a few sensitive bristles. The hind legs are very short but the feet
fairly normal and made for shoving the animal forward; the front feet
stick out sidewise, are very short but sturdy, and end in huge handlike
paddles with their palms pointing backwards. The nails are tremendous
and there is a "sixth finger" made of an extension of one of the wrist
bones. When digging, the spade-hands are shoved forward in front of the
nose alternately and the earth is then scooped backwards past the head
and under the body. The hind feet then take over and shoot it on backwards into the tunnel. Every now and then the animal makes a vent and
erupts the excess out on to the surface, thus making a molehill. Some

MOLES. From "Eurasian Moles," in *Living Mammals of the World* by
Ivan T. Sanderson (Hanover House, 1955). Reprinted by permission of the
publishers, Doubleday & Company, Inc. (Hanover House). Fully protected by
copyright.

species, however, manage to get along without these periodical eruptions and all moles hardpack the walls of their tunnels.

3   The fur of moles is very soft and silky and it grows straight up so that its lay will not hinder the animals in going either backwards or forwards. Moles, like many Shrews and other Insectivores, swim very well and, in fact, delight in entering water either in search of food or when moving from one locality to another. At this time, those moles whose eyes are not covered by skin make good use of what sight they have. The speed with which moles can get about even on the surface of the earth is almost unbelievable, but underground they can move faster than a man normally walks above! The love-life of the common mole is remarkable. Normally, he lives alone but at the appropriate season he either burrows into the tunnel system of a female or one breaks into his. Whereupon he promptly takes her captive and if any other male appears he seals her up in a side-hole, then quickly hollows out an arena and goes to work on the interloper. He fights until death and the winner takes the female. Meantime, she is busily engaged trying to dig her way to freedom. In time the pair settle down together and work alongside each other in the endless pursuit of food. When the young are due, the female hollows out a nest at a crossroads in the tunnel system where there are plenty of escape routes, and lines the hole with soft material. Three to seven young are born at a time; their eyes are closed and their ears are covered with skin and they are naked. Moles make rather solicitous parents and take a long time to wean the babies. There is always a great dearth of females! The true moles are distributed all over Europe and Asia and one species is found on the southern slopes of the Himalayas and in Assam, but none occurs down on the plains of India or in the Indonesian region.

Comment

Moles is taken from a work of popular science—science written for the layman rather than for the specialist. Some people look disdainfully at popular science, calling it "inexact" and "oversimplified." No doubt such scorn is sometimes justified, but not always and not in Sanderson's description of moles. Surely, there is room for—and need for—scientifically valid writing that addresses itself to the interested and educated nonexpert, presenting the facts and phenomena of nature and science in plain, nontechnical prose.

The classification of moles in the beginning of Paragraph 1 establishes the author as a man who knows his subject; it is the most obviously "scientific" part of the essay. But once the author's authority has been established, the description stresses reader interest by piling up vivid and concrete details, rather than rigorous scientific classification according to an elaborate system of zoological description. Strictly speaking, the account goes beyond mere description, inasmuch as only Paragraph 2 and the first sentence of Paragraph 3 deal specifically with the appearance of the mole. The other parts of the essay deal with such matters as his habitat, food, feeding habits, and love life. The organization is fairly loose, in keeping with the author's evident intention of being casually informative, almost entertaining, about his subject. Though the article is full of accurate detail—for example, the anatomy of the "sixth finger" in Paragraph 2—the style is also casual: "all sorts of weird beliefs," "they bumble into another mole's run," "put away about twice their own weight," "manage to get along."

From the point of view of the student of composition, perhaps the most important thing about *Moles* is that it proves the possibility of combining scientific accuracy and a wealth of factual information with descriptive liveliness and a style that does not frighten the layman.

Exercises

CONTENT

True or False? If you think the statement represents what the selection says or implies, mark it "True"; if you do not think so, mark it "False."

1. There are no moles on the Pacific islands.
2. Earthworms are the main food of moles.
3. Moles live in colonies.
4. Their hearing is very good.
5. They eat about one-half their weight every day.
6. Moles are sometimes cannibalistic.
7. Underground a mole can move faster than a man can walk above ground.
8. All moles are blind.
9. Moles are among the few mammals that lay eggs.
10. Though male moles often fight for females, they never kill each other.

FORM AND STYLE

1. Two of the sentences in Paragraph 1 begin with the word "moles," one with "the true moles." What else do the sentences have in common? (The correct answer explains the sameness of beginning.)

2. What does "The latter" in "The latter happens when . . ." (Paragraph 1) refer to? Has the word been properly used?

3. What is the meaning of "literally" in the first sentence in Paragraph 2?

4. The bulk of Paragraph 2 is a physical description of the mole. The first sentence of Paragraph 3 also deals with physical appearance, while the following sentences deal with other matters. Can you think of any

reason why the division between paragraphs was not made *after* rather than *before* sentence 1 in Paragraph 3?

5. A case could be made for dividing Paragraph 3 into two paragraphs. Where would the division be made and what would be the topic sentence for the second of the two paragraphs?

6. The organization of the essay breaks down at the end. Explain.

VOCABULARY

Which of the four words or phrases to the right seems to you to be *closest* in meaning to the word in heavy type to the left? Put a check mark after your choice.

genera *(1)*   small animals . . . mammals that live underground . . . kinds . . . branches . . .

comprises *(1)*   refers to . . . compromises . . . consists of . . . generalizes about . . .

outlier *(1)*   class . . . farther out . . . one that lies out . . . colony

immemorial *(1)*   well remembered . . . without memory . . . unrecorded . . . lost . . .

intrigued *(1)*   pestered . . . tricked . . . fascinated . . . confused . . .

weird *(1)*   odd . . . horrible . . . superstitious . . . frightening . . .

potentialities *(1)*   ways of living . . . abilities . . . powers . . . possibilities . . .

collapse *(2)*   die . . . become unconscious . . . break down . . . become paralyzed . . .

minute *(2)*   sixty seconds . . . sharp . . . blind . . . tiny . . .

extension *(2)*   appendix . . . growth . . . stretching out . . deformity . . .

erupts *(2)*   throws up . . . gets rid of . . . breaks . . . shoves . . .

insectivores *(3)*   a class of small insects . . . rodents . . . animals living in the ground, like some insects . . . insect-eaters . . .

appropriate *(3)*   predetermined . . . instinctive . . . fitting . . . mating . . .

arena *(3)*   tunnel . . . place for fighting . . . grave . . . circular hole

solicitous *(3)*   lonesome . . . scrupulous . . . careless . . . bothersome

dearth *(3)*   demand . . . death . . . loss . . . lack . . .

THEME SUGGESTIONS

"Mountains out of Molehills"
Superstitions about moles
A description of an animal
"From the Diary of a Mole"

9

WOLFGANG LANGEWIESCHE

The U. S. A. from the Air

1   Now, flying has changed. You have more speed, more radio, perhaps two engines. Even with only one, the forced landing obsession has
faded out. You try again to treat the country with contempt. You try to
think of it as pure expanse—graph paper, yours to make lines on. But it
still doesn't work out that way. The country still makes itself felt. In fact,
speed sometimes makes you feel it more. It's like a phonograph record:
the needle has to slide to bring out the tune.

2   I like to see East change to West. I like that moment, on the New
York-Pittsburgh-St. Louis route, when you get to the last ridge, called
Laurel Ridge. There, at the end, the dislikable Alleghenies are almost
real mountains. On the brow of the ridge, facing west, there is a bald,
stony strip, scoured clean by the west winds and the sleet and the rain.
An airway beacon stands up there, alone. Then the stuff falls steeply away
under you. You slide out across there, and you enter the Middle West. It
feels different. It feels easy-like. Not that the country turns nice right
away. Right around Pittsburgh, it is a tortuous jumble—small, steep hills,
slag fields, deep-cut railroad tracks, lots of smoke. But you know it will
calm down. A pilot gets the habit of "thinking ahead of the airplane."
The Now and Here is no longer so important in the faster airplane: now
and here, the engine percolates, the weather is okay, the gadgets work,
you have lots of gas. What's ahead is what matters. And so you study
cloud shapes, listen to weather reports, and feel out the situation ahead.
And there, you know, comes flat country, come open fields, come comfortable cities, big airports, runways with clear approaches. The squeeze,
that makes the Easterner elbowy and unfriendly, squeezes also in flying.
In the East, airports are small, obstructed by power lines, hills, gas works,
squeezed in between the cemeteries and the insane asylums. West of the
Alleghenies, they give you room.

3   So now, if the ceiling is low, you can stay under it and push on;
you know the terrain gets better all the time. Or you can go on top of
the overcast; you know that when you want to get down, no hills will
stick up into a low ceiling. And so you feel, ahead of time, way up in the
air, that certain ease and plenty of the Middle West.

4   Presently, you pick up the section lines. Now *that* is something.
It is really one of the odd sights of the world, and it is strictly an air-

THE U.S.A. FROM THE AIR. Part II of "The U.S.A. from the Air" by Wolfgang Langewiesche. From *Harper's Magazine*, October, 1950. Copyright, 1950,
by Wolfgang Langewiesche. Reprinted by permission of *Harper's Magazine*
and the author.

sight: a whole country laid out in a mathematical gridwork, in sections one mile square each; exact, straight-sided, lined up in endless lanes that run precisely—and I mean precisely—north-south and east-west. It makes the country look like a giant real estate development: which it is. One section has 640 acres. A quarter section, 160 acres, is the historical homestead. You sold your goods, you crossed the sea somehow, and they *gave* you *that!* "Land-office business" used to be done in this matter, and no wonder.

5   Get this right. These section lines are not something that an attentive eye can distinguish in the landscape. They *are* the landscape. Compared to this gridwork, the natural landscape—flat here, a little rolling there, a river valley, a pond—just can't quite catch your attention. In fact, the natural landscape has long fitted itself to this scheme. A man has a wood lot, his neighbor a cornfield; the boundary between woods and field is of course the fence line; but the fence line is part of the grid. More than people know, all their coming and going is channeled by that grid. Their roads—except for the biggest highways—run and jog along the grid. In fact, from the air, the lines are mostly marked by roads.

6   For flying, the section lines are wonderful. They make this country in reality just what a pilot wants country to be—graph paper. You can time your shadow with a stop watch across two lines, and get your exact speed. You can head the airplane down a section line and check your compass. But you hardly need a compass. You simply draw your course on the map and see what angle it makes. Then you cross the sections at the same angle. You can't miss. If you want to go exactly west, you get on a fence and follow it. The fence presently leaves off; the line becomes a highway. The highway curves off, but the line goes on as a fence again, as a lane between fields, as a farm road, then perhaps as the main street of a town, a highway again. It is easy on the brain.

7   It's true what the foreigners say—it all looks pretty much alike. A town comes out of the haze, moves through below you, falls back—only (you sometimes think) to run through some secret passageway and plant itself again in front of you!

8   Flying, you tell these towns apart as you tell stars—by constellation. This one, of about the fourth magnitude, with a smaller one to the north of it—that must be this one on the map. Those three-in-line, that's those.

9   What is it like, this American town? Well it isn't crowned by a castle, that's for sure; nor by a cathedral either. By an insurance skyscraper, more likely; or by a hotel, perhaps; but most likely by nothing. It is not fortified, and never was: no crowded Old Town, no ring-shaped boulevard where the walls used to be. Neither is it like a town I once saw in the South—a company town with a street-plan like this

>>>>>>>□

with the mill at the head. And it is not a village.

10 It is always a small city. It is laid out with streets at right angles, and has at its center a little Downtown, perhaps only two streets crossing each other, perhaps a few blocks. In there, it's naked and stony; it achieves a certain businesslike ugliness. There is a well-developed parking problem. And at night, that downtown core glows with bright lights and red neon signs, where the seller entertains the buyer and the boy the girl.

11 The rest is quiet streets with little houses and lots of trees. It fades out into the farmland in an indifferent way—streets and avenues already marked out on the ground, but still empty. You can tell—it expects to grow. Add a few blocks on the outskirts, and the downtown gets a bit more stony. Keep adding, and Farmerville becomes Bloomington, Bloomington becomes Springfield, Springfield becomes, say, Indianapolis.

12 There is always a Wrong Side of the Tracks to the town. In the thirties, when the price of paint made a bigger difference, this used to show up plainly. There is always a giant high school, and certain other standard furniture—a gasoline bulk plant, race track, "institution" (may be a veterans' hospital, may be a teachers' college, may be a county poorhouse). These things are marked on the flying maps, not because it is remarkable that a town should have them, but because it helps you tell the towns apart. This town has its high school at the east end. If this is the town I think it is, there should be an institution on the north edge. Sure, there it is. You make a pencil mark on the map and fly on.

13 Somewhere now, about a third of the way across the country, you notice something has changed. The fields are bigger; the air is clearer. Things have opened up. There is less junk around the landscape—I mean by junk, I guess, things of which a pilot cannot immediately see the sense and purpose: a clump of trees here, a different-colored patch of field there, an old abandoned factory building—that sort of thing. The landscape is tidier. Each farmhouse sits on its land as if it had just been set there; each fence shows straight and strong, as if it had just been strung. Each town seems to say: "Look, I am a town." Things have a sharper edge to them.

14 What's happened is that you have crossed the line between the forest and the prairie—the line that was there in Indian days. The white man has cleared the forest and plowed the prairie, and has made them both superficially alike—both farmland. But still the difference shows. Maybe it's the different color of the soil. Maybe it's that up to here, the country has been darkened by the last poor remnants of the old dark forests—a clump of trees, a wood lot—and here the trees leave off. Maybe it is simply the drier, clearer air. At any rate, you have moved one more notch west.

15 Here, in the less cluttered country, your map reading must change. A town may be so small that it would rate only a circle, o, further east: here, it gets the full treatment. The map shows it as a yellow area, shaped like the town's built-up area. A town may be so small that further east it wouldn't be on the map at all: here it gets at least an o, and a name. This, I like. It reminds you of the way each person counts for more out west. Go West, young man, and put yourself on the map.

16   And I like the names of those towns. It used to be that a prince would graciously call a town after himself—Williamstown or Fredericksburg or Charles' Rest, or what not. Out here, the ordinary man sat himself down, founded himself a town, and named it, by gosh, after himself. I like to check them as I fly: here comes Charlie. Howdy, Riley. *Wie geht's*, Hoehne. Hello, Kline. Landusky, Henderson, Milliken, Goessel, Weir, Swink, McPhee: how are you doing?

17   Or the man would name the town after a woman of his: Beulah, Maybell, Dolores. I had often flown over a town named Beatrice, Nebraska, and I had thought: "Poor Beatrice, whoever you were (farmer's wife? railroad president's daughter?)—that really wasn't much of a present to give a woman." It is a nice town and all that, but it isn't exactly—you know—it hasn't got *glamour*, out here in the sun-blasted country between Omaha and Wichita. (It hasn't got glamour if you were over Manhattan yesterday and will be over the Hollywood hills tomorrow.) Well, I came over Beatrice again one night. Now people don't know this, but a town at night is the most beautiful thing made by man in the past hundred years—especially an American town, where they don't spare the current. A brave sight, too, out there, where towns are far apart, with a lot of darkness in between. People went out into this vastness, built a home town here, and lit all those lights. A proud sight, just by being there. And I thought: "Beatrice, wherever you are now, you ought to be proud. It looks real nice."

18   Now, halfway across the country, come the Great Plains. It happens fast, in a matter of minutes. A grassy butte sticks up right through the fields. A bit of badlands shows up. The pattern of the farms opens up to detour around it and comes together again. A gully shows up—Grand Canyon in miniature. You know the signs. You are getting west another notch. You hitch yourself up in your seat and take new notice.

19   Ahead, the country rises a step, and the step is a bluff: its face is eroded; it grins at you like the teeth of a skull. As you pass over, the farms fall back. The last you see of them is a mile-square wheat field draped over some hump, abandoned. It reminds you of a wrecked ship on a beach—tried to go where it should not be, and got in trouble. Ahead are the vast khaki plains, rising toward the West. There's nothing to see but vastness, clarity of air, distance. The sun glistens on a window of some ranch house, fifty miles away. A train, very far away, is a small black thing under a smoke plume, like a ship at sea.

20   You head straight out there, and the world fades out: badlands; the dry, bare hills. That fellow yammering about the "Lone Prairie"— he's been there. You suddenly remember you have no water aboard, no strong shoes, no big hat. You are lucky if you see a ranch, hidden deep down in some secret canyon, in a patch of green. More likely, you see next to nothing: a barbed wire fence; some cattle; a windmill pumping beside a water hole.

21 You fall in line and follow the railroad. Everybody and everything else does, in that country; even the Civil Airways. Now the U.S.A. slenders down to a mere strip—river-plus-railroad-plus-highway. Along this strip are the irrigated fields, the towns, the airports. And the railroad is the great sight—doubly great by default of everything else. Its long straightaways and mathematical curves, the way it goes on and on through empty country up toward the West.

22 Finally these bright yellow-green plains rise under you like a wave about to break; over the crest comes a white spot that turns out to be snow. There, between two high mountains, is a gateway, where the river comes out. Toward this gate you have been steering all along; so was the railroad; so was the highway; so were the radio beams along the airway. You go in through that gate, and East has changed to West.

Comment

In *How Mr. Hogan Robbed a Bank* and again in *Miss Furness* we sensed a difference between the real and the pretended author—between Steinbeck, the satirist, and the objective reporter who fails to condemn Mr. Hogan, and between Rebecca West, the novelist, and the little girl who describes her visit at her teacher's. In both instances the real authors have assumed a distinct personality whose particular point of view contributes to the meaning of the story.

In *The U.S.A. from the Air* Langewiesche also uses the device of viewpoint, though in a somewhat different way from Steinbeck's and Miss West's. He does not create for himself a mask or dummy through whose eyes the scenes and action are viewed. Rather, he casts himself in the role of a man casually and informally describing a plane trip across the country to an intimate friend. And the friend is "you." Only the literal-minded reader would object that "I have never piloted a plane and I resent being talked to as if I had." The rest of us realize that the "you" both is and is not to be taken seriously. The author, we assume, describes his own experience (the occasional use of "I" serves as reminder of that), not "yours" or "ours." The use of "you" *is* a device, a literary trick. But it is more than that. It serves at least two important purposes. First, it universalizes the description. What the author saw and felt and thought while flying over the Midwest "you"—that is, anybody—sees and feels and thinks. Second, the direct address to the reader makes the description more intimate and immediate: *you* are in the cockpit, it is *your* impressions you are reading. And your awareness of the device *as* device no more ruins its effect than your awareness of being at the movies ruins the movie.

If such uses of viewpoint in writing are effective, it is not because we are really being taken in by them, but because we enjoy pretending that we are,

And the fact that the device is deliberate does not make the writing insincere. The skilled craftsman who consciously employs his skills is not necessarily less sincere than the enthusiastic amateur who blunders ahead. To understand technique is not to lose respect for what the technique produces. Watching a skilled writer manipulate the tools of his trade is an exciting, not a disillusioning, experience.

Exercises

CONTENT

True or False? If you think the statement represents what the selection says or implies, mark it "True"; if you do not think so, mark it "False."

1. The Alleghenies are not real mountains.
2. The section lines are roads, highways, railroads, and other distinguishable lines in the landscape.
3. The section lines confuse the navigator.
4. The typical American small town is laid out with streets at right angles, except in the outlying districts.
5. The individual—town or man—counts for more in the West than in the East.
6. Paint cost more in the 1930's than today.
7. The emptiness of the prairie gives the pilot a feeling of loneliness.
8. At the end of the essay the pilot sees the Pacific ocean in the distance.
9. Before the white man came most of the prairie was forested.
10. Place names tell something about the way in which the Midwest was settled.

Question for Discussion

Which of these two statements do you consider the more accurate?

(a) The purpose of this essay is to describe the gradual change in the physical appearance of the United States as one flies in an airplane from the East to the beginning of the Rocky Mountains.

(b) The purpose of this essay is two-fold: first, to prove that the United States is an interesting but not a beautiful country when seen from the air, and, second, to give the reader a feeling that he is flying a plane across the United States.

FORM AND STYLE

1. This essay is the second part of a longer essay originally written in three parts. Can you tell from the first sentence what the first part of the original essay probably was about?

2. What is the topic sentence of Paragraph 2?

3. What is the meaning of "the stuff" and "elbowy" in Paragraph 2? Why do you think Langewiesche uses such words? Consider also "easy-like" (rather than the more conventional "easy") in the same paragraph.

4. What evaluation of eastern towns—or life in eastern towns—is implied in "squeezed in between the cemeteries and insane asylums" (Paragraph 2)? Explain your answer.

5. What determines the organization of the essay?

6. How would you describe the relationship, the tone or "atmosphere," Langewiesche tries to establish between his reader and himself? Support your answer by reference to specific words and phrases that seem to you to contribute to the relationship. Your answer to question (3) above ought to be relevant in answering this larger question.

VOCABULARY

Which of the four words or phrases to the right seems to you to be *closest* in meaning to the word in heavy type to the left? Put a check mark after your choice.

expanse (*1*) abstraction . . . routine . . . big area . . . distance . . .

tortuous (2) tortured . . . twisted . . . painful . . . gruesome . . .

precisely (4) straight . . . always . . . exactly . . . as if cut with a sharp instrument . . .

scheme (5) plan . . . method . . . appearance . . . something artificial . . .

constellation (8) group of stars . . . brightness . . . position . . . astronomical measurement . . .

magnitude (8) brightness . . . power . . . size . . . importance . . .

achieves (10) places to keep old documents . . . has . . . suggests . . . attains . . .

tidier (13) duller . . . neater . . . smaller . . . prettier . . .

remnants (14) what is left . . . survivors . . . examples . . . speci-mens . . .

eroded (19) wrinkled . . . uneven . . . folded . . . worn away . . .

irrigated (21) cultivated . . . plowed . . . dried up . . . watered . . .

default (21) absence . . . defect . . . mistake . . . defeat . . .

THEME SUGGESTIONS

My first airplane trip
Small town vs. big city
The Midwest vs. the East
Walking down Main Street

Exposition

U. N. RECIPES · WORLD BOOK ENCYCLOPEDIA

HAVEMANN · KAEMPFFERT · CONSUMER REPORTS

ADLER · CLARKE

Exposition is writing chiefly addressed to the remembering and reasoning mind, rather than to the senses or the feelings. To generalize, it deals with ideas rather than with actions and images. But here again we must qualify our definition, for, like narrative and description, exposition is almost never "pure" but usually includes elements of the other types of prose.

Exposition informs, explains, analyzes, reasons. Its typical raw materials are facts, ideas, logical relationships. Most of the selections in this book are expository. Essays and articles in magazines, most newspaper items, lectures, and college textbooks (except literature anthologies) are expository. "Two and two makes four" is an expository statement (at least, in most circumstances); so is "Napoleon lost the battle of Waterloo," and "To every force there is an equal and opposite reaction force." "The chief purpose of a liberal arts education is to educate the student to educate himself" is also expository. It is an opinion and you are free to disagree with it, but that does not make it any less expository.

The purpose of exposition is to communicate what to the writer seems to be *true*—true about ancient Greek drama, forestry, radioactivity, elementary education, U.S. foreign policy, cancer of the lungs, hippopotami, mountain climbing, vitamins, advanced calculus, Bulgarian agriculture, French grammar, or whatever the writer writes about. Exposition makes statements, and the writer of exposition is willing (or should be willing) to have the truth of his statements tested by facts or by reason or by both. The judge of the truth of expository statements is not the writer himself or his emotions or fantasies or sense impressions (as in literature). It is the world outside him: facts, general human experience, logic, other people, physical objects, the laws of nature.

The examples in this section illustrate some, though by no means all, of the main types and devices of exposition. Such types and devices can, of course, combine in innumerable ways. As we have observed before, which type of prose a given piece of writing belongs to does not often matter very much, but you should remember that there are many other possible kinds of expository writing than are illustrated by these seven selections.

10

Sweet Roll—Brioche

Sweet Roll—Brioche

1

1 cup milk	¼ cup lukewarm water
½ cup butter or margarine	4 eggs beaten
1 tsp. salt	1 tsp. grated lemon peel
½ cup sugar	4½ cups sifted all-purpose flour
2 yeast cakes	melted butter

2   Scald milk in upper part of double boiler and pour into mixing bowl. Stir into it the butter, salt, and sugar. Cool until lukewarm. Dissolve yeast in lukewarm water and add eggs and lemon peel. Add to milk mixture. Add flour, beat well. Cover lightly with a cloth and let rise in a warm, not hot, place until doubled in bulk, about 3 hours.

3   Knead and cut off one quarter of the dough for "head" of the *brioches.*

4   Rub muffin pans with butter or lard. Shape remaining ¾ of dough into balls and place in muffin rings. Make an indentation in each ball and brush with melted butter. From the reserved one quarter of the dough, make small, pear-shaped balls. One small ball of dough, pointed side down, should be pressed into each of the larger balls. Brush the tops with melted butter. Let pans stand uncovered in a warm, not hot, place about 30 minutes. Bake in a hot oven (425° F.) about 20 minutes. Remove at once from the pans. Makes approximately 32 two-inch *brioches.* Delicious when split and toasted, even after one week old.

Comment

A recipe is a good example of *directions*—that is, writing that tells how to do something. Other examples of this kind of exposition can be found on cans of paint, mix-it-yourself plaster, or insect-killers or on the sheets of diagrams and instructions that accompany sets of unassembled furniture. Compared to some of these, recipes in respectable and best-selling cook books are models of orderliness and clarity. The example above is no exception.

Although simple—or *because* it is simple, its organization is excellent, at least up to the last two sentences. Ignoring them for the moment, we find that the recipe consists of two parts: the first lists the ingredients, the second lists each step in the mixing of the ingredients and the baking of the rolls. The

SWEET ROLL—BRIOCHE. From *Favorite Recipes from the U.N.* Reprinted by permission of the United States Committee for the United Nations, 816 21st St., N.W., Washington 6, D.C.

very obviousness of the organization is proof of its excellence. Part one insures against chaos and confusion during the process outlined in part two.

The last two sentences fall outside this organization, though this does not reduce the practical value of the recipe. The first tells how many rolls the recipe makes—necessary information, but not part of the directions. A more natural place for it would be immediately after the list of ingredients, although the position it occupies here seems to be standard in most recipes. The second sentence is a variety of advertisement: the reader is encouraged to try making these delicious and long-keeping rolls. It also gives relevant and useful information: the cook may well want to know how best to serve the rolls and how long they will keep. But this information might also reasonably have been given sooner. And as a "commercial" the sentence comes late. Anybody taking the trouble to read the recipe all the way through is most likely already quite willing to give it a try.

Exercises

CONTENT

True or False? If you think the statement represents what the selection says or implies, mark it "True"; if you do not think so, mark it "False."

1. The recipe includes a list of utensils needed.
2. Total time for making the rolls is just about four hours.
3. After the dough has been prepared it is divided into three parts.
4. Sugar is not an ingredient.
5. The recipe recommends serving the rolls unbuttered but with marmalade.

FORM AND STYLE

1. Explain why it is or is not a weakness in the recipe that such terms as "scald" and "sift" are left unexplained.
2. Why are the sentences generally so brief and jerky?
3. What determines the order of the sentences?
4. Why are so few articles used? For example, why "Scald milk" rather than "Scald *the* milk" and why "in upper part of double boiler" rather than "in *the* upper part of *a* double boiler?" Can you explain the presence of the articles you *do* find, or is the author just inconsistent?
5. Do you consider the bald, clipped, inelegant style a virtue or not? Keep in mind the purpose and presumed audience for which the recipe was written.
6. In what grammatical mood is the recipe (exclusive of the list of ingredients) written? Find two sentences that deviate from the general pattern.
7. In order to be stylistically consistent with its context, how should

"One small ball of dough, pointed side down, should be pressed into each of the larger balls" (Paragraph 4) be rewritten?

8. Do you agree that "Knead and cut off one quarter of the dough for 'head' of the *brioches*" ought to form a paragraph by itself? If so, why?

9. The last sentence of the recipe lacks a subject (in other words, it is a sentence fragment). Does that matter? Explain your answer.

10. The last phrase in the final sentence ("even after one week old") is a mixed construction—i.e., a confused and confusing combination of two expressions. What two expressions?

VOCABULARY

Which of the four words or phrases to the right seems to you to be *closest* in meaning to the word in heavy type to the left? Put a check mark after your choice.

indentation *(4)*   cross . . . hole . . . mark . . . dent . . .
reserved *(4)*   kept . . . put aside . . . remaining . . . last . . .
approximately *(4)*   almost . . . about . . . usually . . . easily . . .

THEME SUGGESTIONS

Write a set of detailed directions for a process you feel you know well—how to rotate tires on a car, how to bind a book, how to sew a doll's dress, how to give a baby a bath, how to prune rose bushes—anything except a recipe.

11
WORLD BOOK ENCYCLOPEDIA
The Hydraulic Press

1 *The Hydraulic Press* is a machine which uses water power to lift great weights. It consists of a small piston, a large piston, and a vessel containing fluid. It operates on a principle discovered by the great physicist, Blaise Pascal, during the 1600's. Pascal discovered that pressure exerted upon any part of a liquid enclosed in a vessel will create equal pressure per unit of area on everything which the liquid touches. Thus, a piston which has an area of one square inch is pushed at 100 pounds

pressure into one end of a vessel containing water. At the other end of the vessel is a piston which has an area of 500 square inches. Since water transmits pressure equally on every part of the vessel, each square inch of the larger piston is now under a pressure of 100 pounds. This makes the total pressure of the large piston 50,000 pounds. In other words, 100 pounds pressure on the small piston of the hydraulic press lifts 50,000 pounds on the larger piston.

2   The distance that the weight can be lifted is in proportion to the area of the pistons. If the small piston is forced into the water for a depth of six inches, it will displace six cubic inches of water. This amount spread over 500 inches of the larger piston means that the large piston is raised only 1/500 of six inches, or 0.012 inches.

Comment

The purpose of this excerpt from an encyclopedia article on hydraulic machines is to define an object. The definition involves explanation of a process, for the object to be defined is a machine and a machine is best defined by describing its manner of operation.

A definition is a statement that explains the meaning of a word or term by identifying what the word refers to. The "what" referred to may be called the *referent*. Referents can be anything—physical objects (including people), processes, institutions, abstract concepts. A definition usually begins by putting the referent into the class or category to which it belongs: "The hydraulic press is a *machine* . . . ," "democracy is a *system of government* . . . ," "an oboe is a *musical instrument* . . . ," "Football is a *game* . . . ," "A fish is a *cold-blooded animal*. . . ." But watches and lawn mowers and chewing-gum dispensers are machines too; aristocracies and dictatorships are systems of government, just as democracies are; and there are other cold-blooded animals than fish—for example, snakes and crocodiles. Clearly, something more than *classification* is needed to make the definition complete: the referent must be distinguished or *differentiated* from the other members of its class. The hydraulic press differs from other machines by using "water power to lift great weights." "Democracy" is *that particular* system of government "according to which power rests with the people." An oboe is a musical instrument (but so are violins and drums and trumpets) "of the woodwind group, having two reeds" (which cannot be said of the other instruments mentioned). Football is a game "played by two teams of eleven players each, with an ellipsoidal ball, which each team tries to carry across the other team's goal line." Fish is a cold-blooded animal "that lives in water and breathes by gills and has a backbone, fins, and—usually—scales." The words in quotation marks in each definition constitute its *differentiation*.

A good definition fulfills two requirements: (1) It must not exclude any referent referred to by the word being defined. For example, a definition of "scissors" as "a metal instrument with two opposing cutting edges, used for cutting paper" is unsatisfactory because it excludes scissors used for other purposes—nail scissors, for instance, or garden shears. The inclusion of purpose in this case carries the differentiation so far that the definition becomes *exclu-*

sive. (2) A good definition must also not include any referent not referred to by the word being defined. For example, a definition of "scissors" as "a metal instrument used for cutting" is unsatisfactory because it includes knives. In this case the differentiation does not go far enough, and as a result the definition is *inclusive*.

The definition of hydraulic press fails to meet the first requirement: it is exclusive. It leads us to conclude that when a fluid-powered machine, having one large and one small piston, is used to compress rather than to lift, it is no longer a hydraulic press but something else. That hardly seems reasonable. We might as well say that a wagon wheel used as a gate ornament is not a wagon wheel or that a lamp is not a lamp when the light is turned off. The exclusiveness of the definition here is all the more remarkable as the word "press" is part of the term being defined.

Exercises

CONTENT

True or False? If you think the statement represents what the selection says or implies, mark it "True"; if you do not think so, mark it "False."

1. A hydraulic press will not operate with liquids other than water.

2. It was invented by a physician.

3. If the small piston is 2 square inches in area and the large piston is 10 square inches, the pressure on the large piston will be five times as great as that on the small piston.

4. The greater the relative difference in area between the two pistons, the more powerful the machine. For example, a hydraulic press in which the small piston is 1 square inch and the large piston 5 square inches (ratio 1/5) is more powerful than one in which the small piston is 5 square inches and the large piston 10 square inches (ratio 1/2), provided the pressure is the same in both machines.

5. Pressure applied to liquid in a vessel creates equal pressure per unit of area on all sides of the vessel.

Questions for Discussion

1. Give a definition of the hydraulic press that would be faulty by being inclusive—that is, by including under the definition referents not referred to by the term "hydraulic press."

2. Is this definition inclusive or exclusive: "An American is a human being who lives on the American continent"? Explain how your answer depends on whether or not you would normally refer to Canadians, Mexicans, Brazilians, etc., as "Americans."

3. Discuss the relevance of a statement like "all entomologists are zoologists, but not all zoologists are entomologists" (or "all Chevrolets

are cars, but not all cars are Chevrolets") to the question of exclusiveness
and inclusiveness of definitions.

FORM AND STYLE

1. Find a sentence in Paragraph 1 that is not necessary to the understanding of how the hydraulic press works. Can you justify its inclusion?

2. What is the logical relationship between the two parts of Paragraph 1?

3. "Thus" means "in this manner." When it begins a sentence, it usually means something like, "An example of what has just been said
is . . ." Has the word been properly used in the fifth sentence of Paragraph 1?

4. Paragraph 1 deals with the *force* of the pressure, Paragraph 2 with
the *distance* over which the pressure operates. Explain why you think this
is or is not a good organization.

5. What is the logical relationship between sentences 1 and 2 in
Paragraph 2? Is or is not this relationship the same as that asked about in
question 2?

VOCABULARY

Which of the four words or phrases to the right seems to you to be
closest in meaning to the word in heavy type to the left? Put a check
mark after your choice.

exerted (*1*)   extended . . . used . . . pressed . . . caused to act . . .
vessel (*1*)   ship . . . tube . . . tank . . . container . . .
piston (*1*)   cylinder . . . valve . . . hammer . . . pistol . . .
total (*1*)   overall . . . actual . . . approximate . . . average . . .
hydraulic (*1*)   mechanical . . . high-powered . . . water-powered
      . . . movable . . .
transmits (*1*)   causes . . . forces . . . sends . . . possesses . . .
proportion (2)   relationship . . . accordance . . . dependence . . .
      part . . .
displace (2)   take the place of . . . substitute . . . show . . . mis-
      lay . . .

THEME SUGGESTIONS

Describe the structure and operation of a machine you know well

Look up "Pascal's law" in another reference book, compare the definition of it there with the account of the hydraulic press you have read
here, and account for the difference between the two articles.

Physics and I

A report on a successful experiment in the physics laboratory

12

ERNEST HAVEMANN

The Psychologist, the Psychiatrist and the Psychoanalyst:
Three Definitions

1 . . . The psychologist, the psychiatrist and the psychoanalyst all operate within the general area delineated by the old saws about the nature of man, with these differences:

2 The *psychologist* searches for a scientific understanding of how people see and hear, his interests thereby overlapping those of the physiologist. He also tries to find out how they learn, how they feel and express their emotions and how they get along (or do not) with their fellow men, at which point he and the sociologist are on somewhat similar ground. The psychologist once was chiefly a research specialist and teacher; he began by applying scientific methods of observation and measurement to human behavior, and instructing others in what he found. Many psychologists are still interested only in "pure science"—that is, in fact and theory. A majority of them, however, have branched out into applied psychology, attempting to use their knowledge to help people live happier and more efficient lives. Some of them, for example, counsel young people on what vocations to choose or advise businessmen on how to provide better working conditions for their employees. Quite a number of them work at what is called clinical psychology, which is an attempt to help individuals who have emotional problems and personality maladjustments.

3 The *psychiatrist* is also interested in human psychology, but as a physician attempting to understand and treat the people in whom something has gone wrong. He specializes in the care of what used to be called insanity (but what he now calls psychosis, the victims being known as psychotics) and less severe mental disorders (which he calls neuroses, the victims being called neurotics). Most psychiatrists work in public and private hospitals. About two thirds of them also have private practices, in which they treat patients whose difficulties are not severe enough to require hospitalization.

4 The *psychoanalyst* is a special kind of psychiatrist. He too is a physician who treats the mentally ill. (At least he usually is a physician, though there are some excellent "lay analysts" who have never taken an M.D.) But he uses a special type of treatment originally developed by

THE PSYCHOLOGIST, THE PSYCHIATRIST, AND THE PSYCHOANALYST: THREE DEFINITIONS. From *The Age of Psychology* by Ernest Havemann (Simon and Schuster, 1957). Reprinted by permission of the publishers.

Dr. Sigmund Freud: the analyst spends hundreds of hours listening to the patient discuss his past and present life, his dreams and his daydreams—until finally the patient's pattern of hidden or "unconscious" problems emerges to the point where it can be straightened out.

Comment

Here are some more definitions—not of objects that can be experienced with the physical senses but of abstractions that cannot be seen or touched. You may object that the definitions deal with people and that people can be seen and touched. But people as individuals are not really being defined; their professions are. And you cannot lay eyes or hands on a profession as such (though, of course, many of the actions that belong to certain professions—medicine, for example—are physical and concrete).

The purpose of the four paragraphs is obvious: to define the meaning of three words that are often confused. There are two main reasons for such confusion: The words are similar in sound, for all three contain the syllable "psych–," which is derived from the Greek word for "soul." And all three refer to activities within the same general area of study: the human mind. By identifying precisely what each of these three professions is concerned with, the definitions succeed in distinguishing clearly among them—just as the encyclopedia article on the hydraulic press distinguished one kind of machine from other kinds. What the reader should learn from these definitions is that the professional activities of the psychologist, the psychiatrist, and the psychoanalyst, while related and to some extent overlapping, represent distinctly different ways of studying and healing the human mind or "psyche."

The organization of the article is equally obvious. The first paragraph introduces the three terms and defines their area of common meaning. Each of the next three paragraphs defines one of the three terms. Notice that the order of the definitions is the same as the order of the terms in the first paragraph. As a result, the reader has a sense of structure and direction. At any one point he knows exactly where he is, where he has been, and where he is going to go next.

Exercises

CONTENT

True or False? If you think the statement represents what the selection says or implies, mark it "True"; if you do not think so, mark it "False."

1. A psychiatrist is an M.D.
2. Psychoanalysts study nothing but people's sex life.
3. A big corporation with problems of employee morale is more likely to hire a psychologist than a psychiatrist.
4. The professional staff in an insane asylum is most likely to be made up of psychoanalysts.
5. All three fields have in common the study of mental disorder.

6. Two of the three professions are more closely related than either of them is to the third.

Question for Discussion

In one sentence for each profession, distinguish among psychology, psychiatry, and psychoanalysis.

FORM AND STYLE
1. Write a topic outline of this essay.
2. List the grammatical subjects of all the sentences in Paragraphs 2-4. How many different persons or things do the subjects refer to, and how are the references distributed? Do your findings help you to understand how each paragraph hangs together as a unified whole? Explain your answer.
3. Can you think of any reason why the three terms were defined in this particular order?
4. Why are "lay analysts" and "unconscious" (Paragraph 4) in quotation marks?
5. What single word in the second sentence of Paragraph 4 connects that paragraph with Paragraph 3?

VOCABULARY
Which of the four words or phrases to the right seems to you to be *closest* in meaning to the word in heavy type to the left? Put a check mark after your choice.

delineated (*1*)   made with a ruler . . . described . . . limited . . . outlined . . .
old saws (*1*)   generalities . . . tiresome truths . . . useless tools . . . proverbial sayings . . .
sociologist (2)   one who studies human society . . . socialist . . . one who lives in society . . . one who likes to be sociable . . .
efficient (2)   useful . . . workable . . . successful . . . practical . . .
psychosis (3)   lack of soul . . . neurosis . . . soulfulness . . . a form of mental illness . . .
severe (3)   difficult . . . painful . . . serious . . . dividing . . .
lay (*4*)   private . . . self-trained . . . amateur . . . without a medical degree . . .

THEME SUGGESTION
Write a definition of a profession or a field of study you are interested in and try to distinguish it clearly from related but different fields or professions (e.g., electronics from electrical engineering, archaeology from geology, physical chemistry from biochemistry).

13

WALDEMAR KAEMPFFERT

Weather Fronts

1   Whether a meteorological service is good or bad depends on the number of reporting stations and on the accuracy of the reports. Because the air is everywhere, because it is fluid, nothing short of a world-wide system of observing stations will do. What happens in the atmosphere over the poles or in the Gulf of Mexico is just as important as what happens in our own country. Weather is made not in our backyards but at the antipodes—the chief reason why we need thousands of weather stations instead of the few hundred we have, and why there must be the closest international cooperation if forecasts are to be more accurate than they are.

2   A world war inevitably disrupts any international system of weather observation and prediction, as the Norwegians discovered in 1914. Their fisheries and their shipping depended for profits on helpless weather men. Two distinguished meteorologists, Professor V. Bjerknes and his son Jakob, rose to the occasion by developing air-mass analysis. Weather prediction used to be two-dimensional, in the sense that observations were made on the ground, generally at sea level, and for practical purposes not much attention was paid to what was happening 2 or 3 miles up. The two Bjerkneses showed how much better it was to study the vertical segments of the atmosphere, and taught us to talk of various "fronts," such as a "polar front," a "warm front," a "stationary front," and an "occluded front."

3   The facts about these various fronts are gathered on the ground, at sea, and in the lower stratosphere. Airplanes in the more progressive countries rise as high as they can to measure temperatures, to study clouds, and even to ride over tornadoes. Pilot balloons are released and followed from the ground with theodolites until they are lost to view —all to see which way and how fast the wind is blowing. Radiosonde balloons rise 50,000 feet and more and their automatic transmitters radio back to the ground code messages that say to the weather man, "It's 40 degrees below zero up here, and the wind is blowing 80 miles an hour." Since the Second World War radar has been supplementing such information, for with radar a distant thunderstorm, a cloud, even birds on the wing, can be spotted.

4   The purpose of all this probing is to form a picture of the atmos-

WEATHER FRONTS. From "Doing Something About the Weather," in *Explorations in Science* by Waldemar Kaempffert. Copyright, 1947, by the New York Times, 1953 by Waldemar Kaempffert. Reprinted by permission of The Viking Press, Inc., N.Y.

phere as a whole. Piecing a weather mosaic together was nothing new, but the interpretation of the mosaic in accordance with Norwegian principles was not only new but revolutionary. To the old-fashioned weather man "highs" and "lows" were the very essence of weather; to Vilhelm and Jakob Bjerknes they were only indications of what was happening to titanic masses of air that were rushing along, side by side, in opposite directions. Of the two titanic masses, miles in depth, one is known as the "tropical" or warm front and the other as the "polar" or cold front.

5   Of these two masses or currents of air, the polar is heavy and dry, the tropical light and moist. The speeds of the two are not the same, nor are the temperatures. Because of these and other differences the two cannot long flow peacefully side by side. In fact, the military word "front" was adopted because a battle ensues. The cold polar air wedges itself under the warm tropical mass, and the warm tropical mass in turn rides up the slope of cold polar air like surf on a beach. Obviously the warm air cools as it rises, and as it cools it contracts and thus squeezes the water out of itself in the form of rain or snow. Since the air is now denser the pressure falls. As for the cold polar air, it expands as it is warmed and loses density, so that the pressure rises. We have what we would call a "draft" in a room, meaning a wind, because air rushes from a place where the pressure is high to a place where it is low, and the greater the contrast the greater is the wind.

6   This is the roughest and simplest sketch of polar and tropical fronts that can be given in words. We must think of invisible curling eddies, tongues that shoot out here and there. If there are cumulus-nimbus clouds in the sky and it looks as if there would be a thunderstorm we may be sure that cold air has been heated and that it is rising. On the other hand if it is misty or there are stratus clouds we may be equally sure that warm air is being cooled from below. North American polar air comes down from Alaska, as might be supposed. Little happens to it for hundreds of miles because in the north the ground below is not much warmer, especially in winter. When it strikes a body of water like the Great Lakes the moving mass of air soaks up moisture, with the result that in the East we may have one of the characteristic cold clammy days of an early New England winter. But if a polar front has picked up water from the Pacific it is as likely as not to deposit it on the Sierras and Rockies and arrive in Pennsylvania warm and dry.

7   It should be evident that though the Bjerknes method of air-mass analysis is simple in principle it is not easy to apply, because the earth is partly land, partly water; partly mountainous, partly flat; partly desert and partly overgrown with dense forests. Weather may be foggy and cold on one side of a mountain range and sunny and warm on the other. Equally marked differences may prevail on the seashore and only 50 miles inland. The forecaster has to decide not only how far and in what direction fronts and pressure systems will move tomorrow and the day

after, but how they will change in themselves and how the face of the country over which a front passes will affect the local weather.

Comment

Kaempffert's essay explains certain facts about the weather and certain principles and methods of weather forecasting. The explanation includes definition of two key terms that are likely to be unfamiliar to non-meteorologists: warm and cold fronts.

Let us go through the essay paragraph by paragraph to see what it says. From Paragraph 1 we learn that the quality of a meteorological service depends on the number and the accuracy of weather reports and why this is so: "Weather is made not in our backyards but at the antipodes. . . ." Paragraph 2 explains, first, how World War I made necessary a new kind of meteorological study that did not depend on international communication of weather reports (the war interrupted such communication), and, second, what the new method was. Paragraph 3 deals with the ways in which information about the weather "fronts" is gathered. Paragraphs 4-6 explain what the concept of "weather fronts" means. Specifically, Paragraph 4 states what the fronts are ("titanic masses of air . . . rushing along, side by side, in opposite directions"), Paragraph 5 explains what happens when the two fronts collide, and Paragraph 6 states the practical consequences of the collision as far as weather is concerned and gives a specific example of how the principle of fronts works over the United States. Finally, Paragraph 7 deals with some of the practical difficulties that often make the basically simple principle of weather fronts hard to apply in actual forecasting.

Obviously, weather fronts is the main subject matter of the essay; that is what it "is about." But oneness of subject matter does not automatically provide the essay with unity and coherence (i.e., the quality in it that makes the reader feel that the discussion "hangs together" and moves forward). Here we move from the Gulf of Mexico and the antipodes—via World War I, Norwegian fisheries, definition of technical terms in meteorology, and explanation of how weather reports are gathered—to the Rockies, Pennsylvania, and the local weather. And yet the essay *is* coherent. Though the immediate subject of the discussion may change (as it does between Paragraphs 1 and 2), there are no confusing and abrupt breaks in thought between the paragraphs, and within the paragraphs the sentences all connect. How is this continuity maintained?

Generalizations are dangerous, and rather than try to list all possible ways in which an essay like this could have been organized (an almost impossible task), let us look at perhaps the most important of the organizational methods actually used. This is a method of such general usefulness and so much an integral part of our language structure that it is found in practically all organized writing. It is the use of words and phrases to refer to something mentioned before. Pronouns are words whose only function is to be such references; they are, literally, "instead-of-nouns." For example, in a short story the author does not need to refer to his hero by name every time. Once he has introduced him to his readers he can refer to him simply as "he"—at least as long as there is no other male character around with whom "he" could be confused. But, although the most common, pronouns are by no means the only kind of reference words. For instance, in Kaempffert's essay the phrase "international system of weather observation and prediction," with which Paragraph 2 opens, sums up the topic of Paragraph 1; the references to the "two" in the first two sentences of Paragraph 5 make sense only when they are interpreted as references to the two kinds of weather fronts; and "the Bjerknes method" in Paragraph 7 is a kind of shorthand term for what was explained in Paragraph 2. It refers to that paragraph in much the same manner that the pronoun "their" in the second sentence of Paragraph 2 refers to "the Norwegians." It would be possible to go through the whole essay and show how sentences and paragraphs interlock by means of such reference words.

Such a system of interconnecting references avoids awkward repetition and saves words. Another example of sentence economy occurs near the end of Paragraph 3, where the words "such information" sum up the itemized list of the kinds of weather data obtainable by modern methods which is given earlier in the paragraph: temperatures, cloud conditions, speed and direction of wind, weather conditions at different altitudes, and so on. In somewhat the same manner a word like "furniture" stands for particular chairs, tables, beds, and bookshelves. When used alone, such general references (some of them— like "furniture"— are called *collectives*) tend to make the writer's meaning vague and lifeless. But once he has particularized his details, such words are handy word-savers. It is much more convenient to have available a word like "family" than to have to refer to "Mom and Dad and Grandma and Kitty and Bob and the dog and me" every time.

Exercises

CONTENT

True or False? If you think the statement represents what the selection says or implies, mark it "True"; if you do not think so, mark it "False."

1. Weather forecasting improves during wartime when nations are cut off from one another.
2. Whether a meteorological service is good or bad depends less on the number of reporting stations than on their location.
3. Air is fluid.
4. The "air-mass analysis" method is two-dimensional.
5. It was developed by the Bjerknes brothers in Denmark.
6. Warm air is lighter than cold air.
7. Cool air has less volume than warm air.
8. The absence of high mountains between the Great Lakes and New England sometimes affects the New England weather.
9. The word "front" was chosen to refer to the moving air masses because of its military connotations.
10. Flying birds can be seen on the radar screen.

FORM AND STYLE

1. What is the topic sentence of Paragraph 1? Is its position in the paragraph a common one for topic sentences?

2. Which one of the following pairs would you choose as most accurately descriptive of the relationship between the first sentence and the rest of the paragraph in Paragraph 1: comparison–contrast, cause–effect, generalization–specification, statement–explanation, rule–example?

3. What three-word phrase in Paragraph 4 serves as a collective reference for all of Paragraph 3? Its function is a clue to its position in the paragraph.

4. What is the relationship between the second half of Paragraph 6 (beginning with "North American polar air comes down from Alaska . . .") and the rest of the paragraph?

5. What is the purpose of the reference to a " 'draft' in a room" in Paragraph 5?

VOCABULARY

Which of the four words or phrases to the right seems to you to be *closest* in meaning to the word in heavy type to the left? Put a check mark after your choice.

antipodes (*1*)   poles . . . all other places . . . on the opposite side of the earth . . . areas great distances away . . .

disrupts (2)   interrupts . . . destroys . . . breaks . . . prevents . . .

inevitably (2)   unavoidably . . . always . . . unfortunately . . . generally . . .

prediction (2)   measurement . . . forecast . . . fortune-telling . . . discussion . . .

segments (2)   layers . . . columns . . . parts . . . bits . . .

vertical (2)   parallel to the horizon . . . numerous . . . upright . . . moving . . .

stratosphere (3)   empty space . . . the cloudy or cloud-forming part of the atmosphere . . . air . . . the upper part of the atmosphere . . .

progressive (3)   technological . . . forward-moving . . . socialistic . . . prosperous . . .

theodolites (3)   big balloons . . . a kind of telescope . . . instrument for measuring speed of wind . . . instrument for measuring angles . . .

supplementing (3)   adding to . . . supplying . . . contributing . . . supporting . . .

mosaic (4)   pertaining to Moses . . . a picture made up of several small pieces . . . meteorological chart . . . puzzle . . .

essence (4)   principle . . . substance . . . something one cannot do without . . . definition . . .

indications *(4)*   directions . . . symptoms . . . external characteristics
    . . . symbols . . .
titanic *(4)*   dangerous . . . fast . . . complicated . . . huge . . .
ensues *(5)*   follows . . . intervenes . . . appears . . . is fought . . .
prevail *(7)*   triumph . . . dominate . . . be the case . . . exist before-
    hand . . .

THEME SUGGESTIONS

Why the weather is such a popular topic for conversation
Helping the weather gods, or Artificial rainmaking
The picnic that was not supposed to be rained out, or My experience
as amateur weatherman
The blizzard (tornado, hurricane, flood, drought, heat wave)

14

CONSUMER REPORTS

Motaloy: Claims vs. Tests

(For $6 you can drop four pill-size metal tabs into your gas tank. The
big question is, will they do the "ring and valve job" the ads promise?)

1   "A complete . . . ring and valve job while you drive! . . . Good
for the life of your engine! Stops costly oil burning! Increases gas mileage!
Raises compression!"

2   Thus runs some of the advertising for *Motaloy*—a product which
comes in a small cardboard package in the form of four metal pills, each
a little larger than a tablet of aspirin. The price is $6.

3   As a rule, CU [Consumers Union] does not attempt to keep tabs
on the short cut items, gimmicks, additives, pepper-uppers, and whatnot
that are advertised, particularly to automobile owners, in such vast
variety. The claims of many of these products are so general as to defy
analysis. But the claims for *Motaloy* are, at least, refreshingly specific;
they can be checked. It seemed to CU's engineers that if *Motaloy* could
deliver for $6 even a reasonable facsimile of a ring-and-valve job—which
would cost at least $100 at a garage—consumers ought to welcome it with
open arms. And if not—since even $6 still has some value these days—
consumers ought to know.

4   So CU's shoppers went out and bought some. CU's engineers read

MOTALOY: CLAIMS VS. TESTS. From *Consumer Reports*, March, 1954. Reprinted by permission of Consumers Union.

with interest the techniques and the theory of the automotive wonder drug as contained in the accompanying literature. And an automotive consulting laboratory employed by CU set out to see what it could do.

5   The operational theory of *Motaloy,* it seems, is quite simple. You open the cardboard package, drop the set of four tabs into the gas tank, and drive off. Soon, according to *Motaloy's* brochure, things begin to happen to your car's worn, sluggish engine:

Motaloy will give increased compression, better pick-up, reduced oil consumption, better gas mileage, smoother performance, and will reduce hard carbon deposits. Piston slap will be deadened or eliminated. . . . Gives improved performance with regular (cheaper) gasoline.

6   The brochure illuminates these claims with the cold, hard light of science:

The tabs are activated as the vehicle is being driven. The friction of the tabs in the fuel tank and the sloshing of the fuel begins a chemical process as *Motaloy* passes through to the combustion chambers and cylinders where the flash fire and intense heat create a reaction dissolving hard carbon. Then, a metallic plating is deposited on the surfaces of the pistons, cylinder walls, rings, and valves and is gradually worked into any pores, as well as pitted or scratched spots. This is an anti-friction plating which provides a smoother, more powerful and quieter engine.

7   It all sounds perfectly reasonable to the non-technical reader. Indeed, thousands of consumers have apparently responded to the *Motaloy* advertisements, and hopefully dropped the little metal pellets into thousands of gas tanks. This new phenomenon in the additive field was also greeted with guarded enthusiasm by such publications as *Business Week* and *The Wall Street Journal.* There was a quite different reaction at the headquarters of the National Better Business Bureau, which issued a report casting serious doubt on *Motaloy's* claims. The National Better Business Bureau pointedly suggested that all media which carry advertising have a responsibility to protect the public from claims which the manufacturer cannot back up with conclusive proof. Nevertheless, advertisements for *Motaloy* have continued to appear, and the public has presumably kept on buying.

CU's tests

8   CU's interest in *Motaloy* dates back to last August, when there were indications that the product might establish a more-or-less permanent place in the American market. It was decided to test *Motaloy* by actual field tests on worn engines in order to determine what improvements, if any, would result from its use.

9   For its tests, CU picked three *Chevrolet* engines of 1952 vintage which had accumulated, respectively, 45,000, 92,000, and 110,000 miles in taxicab service. All were road tested in the same 1953 *Chevrolet* sedan,

over the same route, under similar conditions. The worn engines were operated with no special preparation or repair work except for a tune-up job on their carburetors and ignition systems. Each engine powered the test car over an 8000-mile route without the benefit of *Motaloy,* and then two of the three ran up another 8000 miles over the same route, with *Motaloy* in the gasoline tank. (The test on the engine with 110,000 miles on it had to be discontinued about half-way during the 8000-mile *Motaloy* run; the engine had deteriorated to such a degree that further testing with it was impossible.) A new set of *Motaloy #1* tabs (recommended for cars making eight miles or more per gallon of gas) was used with each engine; these tabs were weighed before and after use. Engine compression was measured and acceleration tests were performed before and after each 8000-mile run. A record of gasoline and oil consumption was kept throughout the tests, and measurements were made of gasoline consumption at constant speed over a test course.

Conclusions

10 After testing *Motaloy* over a three-month period, CU is forced to the regretful conclusion that it can't tell its readers how to save $100 or more by spending $6. In fact, if the claims made for *Motaloy* were re-cited in the true-or-false technique of the quiz shows, CU's consultants would be forced in all honesty, on the basis of the tests made, to give the following answers:

11 "*Motaloy* improves acceleration." *False.* The time required to accelerate the test car from 10 to 60 miles per hour increased as steadily during the 8000-mile run with *Motaloy,* as in the previous 8000 miles without it. On one engine, for example, acceleration time was 31.6 seconds as received, 34.6 seconds after 8000 miles without *Motaloy* and 41.4 seconds after 8000 miles with *Motaloy* in the gas tank.

12 "*Motaloy* gives you better gas mileage." *False.* Both on the basis of total mileage, and on gasoline consumption during constant-speed, measured-mile tests, gas consumption became poorer as the engines accumulated wear. During the constant-speed tests over a measured mile, gas mileage fell off on the average of 1.5 miles per gallon after 8000 miles with *Motaloy* in the tank.

13 "*Motaloy* reduces oil consumption." *False.* Throughout the tests, oil consumption increased in all three engines as they accumulated wear, with or without *Motaloy.*

14 "*Motaloy* improves engine compression." *False.* Engine compression declined constantly as the three engines accumulated mileage; the decline was least on the engine with the lowest previous mileage and greatest on the engine with the most mileage. In no case did the loss of compression seem to be slowed by the use of *Motaloy.*

15 "*Motaloy* dissolves the carbon deposits in the engine." *False, if the claim means that Motaloy dissolves all carbon deposits.* Although the performance figures indicated clearly that *Motaloy* had not performed a "ring and valve job" as claimed for it, the test engines were torn down and checked visually. The finding was that all contained heavy deposits of carbon; certainly whether or not *Motaloy* dissolved any carbon, there was still plenty left in the engines.

16 "*Motaloy* puts an anti-friction metallic plating on cylinder walls, pistons, rings, and valves." *On this point, no categorical answer can be made.* Of the three sets of *Motaloy* tabs used in the three engines, one set of four lost no weight during the 8000-mile run, one was one milligram lighter at the end of the run, and one was two milligrams lighter. There are about 28,000 milligrams in one ounce; one milligram is about .00004 ounce. Examination of the engine showed no metal plating. But whether or not any loss in weight of *Motaloy* distributed itself in a neat layer over the pistons, cylinder walls, rings and valves, is beside the point; there was no evidence in CU's tests that it did anything for the engine's performance.

17 "Good for the life of your engine." *True.* If you put a set of four *Motaloy* tabs in your gas tank, they'll probably still be there when the car reaches the scrap heap.

Comment

Motaloy: Claims vs. Tests appeared in *Consumer Reports* magazine. The report itself suggests (particularly in Paragraph 3) the purpose of the magazine: to protect the ordinary buyer from false advertising and to give him factual information about products which will help him get the best buy possible for his money. Its style seeks to combine objective technicality with clarity and lightness of tone. Since it is written for the layman, the language in *Consumer Reports* cannot be too technical; in this selection unavoidable technical terms like "combustion chamber," "pistons," "rings and valves," "acceleration," "engine compression" are clear to most readers. The purpose of the report will certainly be clear to all. Obviously, its purpose would be defeated if any reader at the end were left wondering whether he had been advised to buy or not to buy.

The report consists of four main parts—five if the introductory paragraphs are counted: (1) The general claims made for Motaloy are quoted (Paragraphs 5, 6); (2) the reactions of some publications to these claims are discussed (Paragraph 7); (3) the procedure for testing Motaloy is outlined (Paragraphs 8, 9); (4) the results of the test are given, first in a general statement (Paragraph 10) and then in a series of findings on seven specific claims (Paragraphs 11-17).

The last of these findings calls for further comment. In form it is similar to the six that have gone before, and it is this similarity that makes its difference in content so effective. For the fraction of a second we think we have finally come upon a "True" after such a long list of "False"—here is at least one claim that the test supports. And then we see the sense in which "good for the life of your engine" is true. It is not the sense the adman intended.

Exercises

CONTENT

True or False? If you think the statement represents what the selection says or implies, mark it "True"; if you do not think so, mark it "False."

1. The claims made for Motaloy by the ad are vague and unspecific.
2. Motaloy was tested by an independent car testing laboratory.
3. The ad claims improved engine performance even with regular gas.
4. Before the appearance of the *Consumer Reports,* only *The Wall Street Journal* had warned the public against Motaloy.
5. Taxicabs were chosen as test cars on the theory that cabdrivers are more careful than ordinary drivers.
6. The tests took four months.
7. All three cars completed the tests.
8. The Better Business Bureau brought suit against the manufacturers of Motaloy for false advertising.
9. The tests proved conclusively that Motaloy dissolved no carbon deposits.
10. The loss of weight in two of the Motaloy tabs was too small to be practically significant.

FORM AND STYLE

1. In view of the main purpose of the report, how effective is its opening? In writing that is against something, is it wise to start off by quoting the "enemy's" strongest, most persuasive phrases? Explain your answer.

2. What evidence is there in the report that the Consumers Union tests are reliable?

3. Point out exactly where you begin to realize that the report is going to be negative.

4. Do you feel that the light, at times even humorous (as in the last paragraph), tone of the report makes it less effective by making it seem less trustworthy, less serious? Discuss.

5. Six of the seven last paragraphs begin with the word "Motaloy" followed by a verb. It would have strengthened the parallelism if the seventh paragraph had begun the same way. The reason why it does not may be either (a) that the Motaloy brochure did not use the exact wording of the sentence, "Motaloy is good for the life of your engine," and that the author therefore did not feel free to quote as if it did, or (b) that the author wanted to mark the difference between the one positive and the six negative reports by means of a change in form. Which of the two reasons do you think is the more likely one?

VOCABULARY

Which of the four words or phrases to the right seems to you to be *closest* in meaning to the word in heavy type to the left? Put a check mark after your choice.

defy (3)   make impossible . . . avoid . . . fight . . . ruin . . .

facsimile (3)   substitute . . . resemblance . . . version . . . copy . . .

automotive (4)   self-moving . . . having to do with cars . . . mechanical . . . engineering . . .

brochure (6)   pamphlet . . . advertising . . . technical description . . . book . . .

additive (7)   mechanical . . . adding . . . added . . . to be added

responded (7)   answered . . . been taken in . . . reacted to . . . made oneself responsible . . .

media (7)   publications . . . methods . . . instruments . . . middlemen . . .

conclusive (7)   absolute . . . final . . . actual . . . convincing . . .

presumably (7)   blithely . . . innocently . . . frequently . . .supposedly . . .

accumulated (9)   traveled . . . collected . . . been driven . . . registered . . .

deteriorated (9)   worn away . . . weakened . . . grown worse . . . corroded . . .

consumption (9)   ratio . . . use . . . waste . . . loss

declined (14)   grew worse . . . increased . . . failed . . . slowed up . . .

categorical (16)   certain . . . positive . . . arrogant . . . stated . . .

THEME SUGGESTIONS

Analyze an ad in a national magazine. Obviously, you cannot be expected to run an actual performance test on the product, but you can discuss whether the ad appeals to your reason or to your emotions, whether it tells you something worth knowing about the product, and whether its claims seem meaningful, exaggerated, relevant, logical, and so forth. Your analysis need not be negative, but it should include your evaluation of the ad.

Consumer Reports has been objected to on the grounds that the American economic system is based on free enterprise and that reports of the type it publishes tend to discredit, or at least make less effective, the system of advertising on which free enterprise is based. Write a discussion of this opinion.

An example of false advertising
TV commercials

15

MORTIMER J. ADLER
Baseball and Reading

1   No one doubts that writing and speaking are active undertakings, in which the writer or speaker is clearly doing something. Many people seem to think, however, that reading and listening are entirely passive. No work need be done. They think of reading and listening as *receiving* communication from someone who is actively *giving* it. So far they are right, but then they make the error of supposing that receiving communication is like receiving a blow, or a legacy, or a judgment from the court.

2   Let me use the example of baseball. Catching the ball is just as much an activity as pitching or hitting it. The pitcher or batter is the *giver* here in the sense that his activity initiates the motion of the ball. The catcher or fielder is the *receiver* in the sense that his activity terminates it. Both are equally active, though the activities are distinctly different. If anything is passive here, it is the ball: it is pitched and caught. It is the inert thing which is put in motion or stopped, whereas the living men are active, moving to pitch, hit, or catch. The analogy with writing and reading is almost perfect. The thing which is written and read, like the ball, is the passive object in some way common to the two activities which begin and terminate the process.

3   We can go a step farther with this analogy. A good catcher is one who stops the ball which has been hit or pitched. The art of catching is the skill of knowing how to do this as well as possible in every situation. So the art of reading is the skill of catching every sort of communication as well as possible. But the reader as "catcher" is more like the fielder than the man behind the plate. The catcher signals for a particular pitch. He knows what to expect. In a sense, the pitcher and catcher are like two men with but a single thought before the ball is thrown. Not so, however, in the case of the batter and fielder. Fielders may wish that batters would obey signals from them, but that isn't the way the game is played. So readers may sometimes wish that writers would submit completely to their desires for reading matter, but the facts are usually otherwise. The reader has to go after what comes out into the field.

4   The analogy breaks down at two points, both of which are instructive. In the first place, the batter and the fielder, being on opposite sides, do not have the same end in view. Each thinks of himself as successful only if he frustrates the other. In contrast, pitcher and catcher are suc-

BASEBALL AND READING. From *How to Read a Book* by Mortimer J. Adler (Simon and Schuster, 1940). Reprinted by permission of the publishers.

cessful only to the extent that they co-operate. Here the relation of writer and reader is more like that between the men on the battery. The writer certainly isn't trying *not to be caught,* although the reader may often think so. Successful communication occurs in any case where what the writer wanted to have received finds its way into the reader's possession. The writer's and the reader's skill converge upon a common end.

5 In the second place, the ball is a simple unit. It is either *completely* caught or not. A piece of writing, however, is a complex object. It can be received more or less completely, all the way from very little of what the writer intended to the whole thing. The amount the reader gets will usually depend on the amount of activity he puts into the process, as well as upon the skill with which he executes the different mental acts that are involved.

6 Now we can define the second criterion for judging reading ability. Given the same thing to read, one man reads it better than another, first, by reading it more actively, and second, by performing each of the acts involved more successfully. These two things are related. Reading is a complex activity, just as writing is. It consists of a large number of separate acts, all of which must be performed in a good reading. Hence, the man who can perform more of these various acts is better able to read.

Comment

Baseball and Reading is an example of explanation through analogy. Analogy is a form of comparison, but what is compared are not two objects (or two persons or places or ideas) but two *relationships.* When someone says that "a rock is to a shipwreck as a nail is to a flat tire," he is using analogy. He does not mean that a rock resembles a nail, or a shipwreck a flat tire, or that it is interesting and worthwhile to see how these things are alike and how they differ. He *does* mean that the *relationship* between the rock and the shipwreck is like the *relationship* between the nail and the flat tire. Both situations involve a cause and effect relationship.

Similarly, the point of Adler's essay is not that baseball and reading are like one another. Nobody would confuse the two activities. In fact, they are so *un*like that it seems silly to point out how they differ. A zoologist may want to compare a lion and a house cat, hardly an oyster and a kangaroo. What Adler is doing is pointing out that, however different they are in almost all respects, baseball and reading have in common a relationship between their respective human elements: the pitcher or batter is to the catcher or fielder what the author is to the reader. And the ball in baseball is to the receiver (catcher or fielder) what the content of the book is to the reader. He shows that the relationship between two people (giver–receiver in baseball) is like the relationship between two other people (author–reader in reading).

Writers use analogy for different purposes. Most commonly, perhaps, they use it to clarify and make understandable something complex and abstract by means of an illustration that is simple and concrete. For example, in the essay on weather fronts, Kaempffert explained the movement of weather-making air masses by means of analogy with something as familiar as a draft in a room. What happens to atomic particles during nuclear bombardment is sometimes compared to the scattering of balls on a pool table, bouncing off one another and the sides of the table in all directions. Certain books or movies are said to affect the young and innocent mind as poison does the body. The spring of the year is to fall and winter what childhood is to old age and death. In all these examples the items compared are not alike in themselves—only in their relationship with other items.

Proverbs and political cartoons are full of analogies. The bird in the hand is what you have but may lose if you try for the uncertain more, represented by the two birds in the bush. Donkeys and elephants, a bear and Uncle Sam are drawn in situations that are meant to be analogous—i. e., similar in relationship —to those of Democrats and Republicans, Russians and Americans. Sometimes people try to use analogies to prove whatever they want to prove. If you think the President of the U.S. should be given more power, you say that the country is like a ship and the President like the captain. And just as the captain has absolute command on board the ship, so the President ought to be given absolute command in governing the country. If you feel that students don't have enough voice in college affairs, you say that a college is like society, with the student body the citizens. And just as the citizens in a democratic society have the right to vote and decide who is to govern them and how, so the student body should be given the right to appoint the faculty and decide what courses should be taught and how.

Actually, of course, these analogies do not prove anything. No analogy ever does. It would be foolish to deny that, skillfully used, analogy can score points in an argument, but such points do not amount to logical proof. The fact that two relationships are alike does not prove identity or similarity between the parts of the relationships. The relationship between cow and calf is analogous to that between mother and baby, but that does not turn a woman into a cow as soon as her baby is born. Again, though you may say that "juvenile delinquency is a cancerous growth on the social body" and make a rather meaningful analogy, you have not proved that youthful criminals should be exterminated by law the way cancer cells are exterminated by X-ray or surgery.

Adler does not use analogy here in order to prove a likeness between baseball and reading. He is trying to clear away a common misconception about the nature of reading by means of an analogy between reading and a sport he assumes is familiar to his readers. He explains the more difficult and unfamiliar in terms of the simple and familiar, for though we all read, not very many of us may have thought of exactly what goes on during the act of reading. In short, Adler uses baseball to explain reading.

Exercises

CONTENT

True or False? If you think the statement represents what the selection says or implies, mark it "True"; if you do not think so, mark it "False."

1. Passive reading is bad reading.

2. In the baseball–reading analogy, the bat is the book that propels ideas at the reader.

3. The reader is more like a fielder than a catcher because the catcher usually calls the pitch.

4. If the reader could tell the author what to write, he would be more like the catcher.

5. A pitcher is to a batter as a writer is to a reader.

6. The content of the book passes from writer to reader in the way the baseball passes from fielder to catcher.

7. Adler admits that the analogy breaks down on two points.

8. One of them has to do with the fact that it is possible to understand only part of what one reads.

9. The analogy, therefore, is really not helpful at all.

10. Good readers are born, not made.

Question for Discussion.

Is "Baseball is fun; therefore, reading is fun" a sound conclusion to be drawn from Adler's essay? Explain your answer.

FORM AND STYLE

1. Find an example in this essay of another analogy than the baseball one.

2. How many paragraphs are given over to the baseball analogy?

3. What is the connection between the first sentence in Paragraph 4 and Paragraph 5?

4. Explain the manner in which Paragraphs 4 and 5 help in understanding the nature of reading, even though they deal with points on which the analogy breaks down.

5. What kind of reader would not understand any more about the nature of reading from reading Adler's essay?

VOCABULARY

Which of the four words or phrases to the right seems to you to be *closest* in meaning to the word in heavy type to the left? Put a check mark after your choice.

communication (*1*)   messages . . . exchange of thought . . . information . . . words . . .

legacy (*1*)   bequest . . . legation . . . heredity . . . will . . .

initiates (*2*)   speeds . . . starts . . . signs . . . . causes . . .

terminates (*2*)   determines . . . influences . . . calls . . . stops . . .

inert (*2*)   dead . . . important . . . not ert . . . inactive . . .

submit (*3*)   come down . . . summon . . . yield . . . listen . . .

instructive (*4*)   like a teacher . . . important . . . destructive . . . capable of teaching . . .

converge (*4*)   run together . . . cooperate . . . conspire . . . be based . . .

executes (*5*)   kills . . . commands . . . performs . . . exercises . . .

criterion (*6*)   element . . . factor . . . standard . . . manner . . .

separate (*6*)   apart . . . different . . . many . . . divided . . .

THEME SUGGESTIONS

Choose a common proverb ("Haste makes waste," "A rolling stone gathers no moss," "When the cat's away, the mice will play," "It's too late to lock the barn when the horse has been stolen," "A stitch in time saves nine," "A burnt child shuns the fire," etc.) and use it to illustrate and illuminate or explain a situation, a process, or experience.

The fact that two things are alike in one respect does not prove them alike in others. Analyze an argument (in a newspaper editorial, in a news commentary, in an ad, in a discussion with friends) where the writer or speaker uses analogy in this fashion to "prove" his point.

Write a simple little story (fables about animals are often useful for this purpose) that can serve as an illustrative analogy of some general public issue—for example, the cold war, lowered taxes, the crisis in education, big-time college football. (Thurber's *The Moth and the Star* on page 305 is an example of an analogical animal fable.)

My leisure reading

16

ARTHUR C. CLARKE

The Earth and Its Neighbors

> Beneath the tides of day and night
> With flame and darkness ridge
> The void, as low as where this earth
> Spins like a fretful midge.
>
> D. G. ROSSETTI—*The Blessèd Damozel*

1   The first difficulty one encounters in trying to envisage interplanetary flight is that of scale. The distances involved are so enormous, so much greater than those we meet in everyday life, that at first they are

THE EARTH AND ITS NEIGHBORS. From *The Explorations of Space* by Arthur C. Clarke. Copyright, 1951, by Arthur Charles Clarke. Reprinted by permission of Harper & Brothers.

quite meaningless. However, this is something that (with practice) can be fairly easily overcome.

2   There are still primitive peoples to whom a hundred miles is an inconceivably great distance—yet there are also men who think nothing of travelling ten thousand miles in a few days. As speeds of transport have increased, so our sense of distance has altered. Australia can never be as remote to us as it was to our grandfathers. In the same way, one's mental attitude can adapt itself to deal with interplanetary distances, even if the mind can never really envisage them. (And, after all, can the mind *really* envisage a thousand miles?)

3   The first step in this "familiarization procedure" is the scale model. To begin with, let us concentrate on Earth and Moon alone, ignoring the other planets. We will take a scale on which a man would still be visible to the naked eye, our reduction factor being 1,000 to 1. The Earth is now a sphere 8 miles in diameter, and 240 miles away is another sphere, the Moon, 2 miles across. On this scale, a human being would be a little less than a twelfth of an inch high, the speed of the fastest aircraft would be under a mile an hour, and that of a V.2 rocket about three and a half miles an hour. The twelfth-of-an-inch-high man contemplating the gulf between Earth and Moon is thus in much the same position as an intelligent ant trying to picture the size of England.

4   To bring in the planets, we must alter the scale again, making the man sink far below visibility. With a reduction of a million-fold, the Earth is now 40 feet in diameter, the Moon 10 feet across and a quarter of a mile away. The Sun is 93 miles away and almost a mile across; 36 and 67 miles from it, respectively, circle Mercury and Venus. Mercury is 15 feet across, Venus 38—a little smaller than the Earth. Beyond the Earth's orbit is Mars, 20 feet in diameter and 140 miles from the Sun. It is accompanied by two tiny satellites, only about half an inch across.

5   Outwards from Mars is a great gulf, empty save for thousands of minor planets or "asteroids," few of which on this scale are much larger than grains of sand. We have to travel 483 miles from the Sun—340 beyond Mars—before we meet Jupiter, the largest of all the planets. In our model he would be over 400 feet in diameter, with eleven satellites ranging in size from 15 feet to a few inches across.

6   You may feel that our model is getting somewhat unwieldy despite our drastic reduction of a million-to-one, but we are still nowhere near the limits of the Sun's empire. There are four more planets to come—Saturn (diameter 350 feet); Uranus (150 feet); Neptune (160 feet) and Pluto (20 feet). And Pluto is 3,700 miles from the Sun. . . .

7   This model of our Solar System shows very clearly the *emptiness* of space, and the difficulty of representing on the same scale both the sizes of the planets and the distances between them. If we reduced the Earth to the size of a table-tennis ball, its orbit would still be half a mile across, and Pluto would be ten miles from the Sun.

8 A pictorial attempt to show the planets, their satellites and their orbits to the correct scale is given in Figure 1. Even in the most "magnified" of the diagrams, however, it is not possible to represent the smaller satellites accurately.

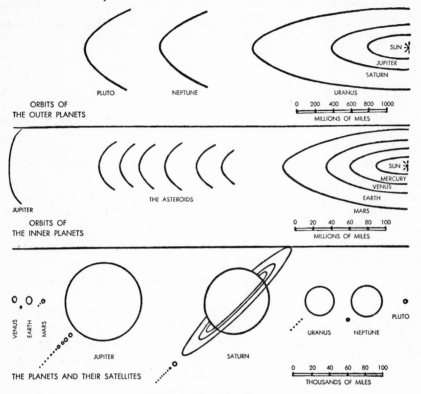

Figure 1. The Solar System

9 Three other points remain to be mentioned before our picture of the Solar System is complete. In the first place, it is not a stationary affair. All the planets are moving, and in the same direction round the Sun. The innermost planet, Mercury, takes only 88 days to complete one revolution, while Pluto takes 248 years—so that astronomers will have to wait until A.D. 2178 before it returns to the part of the sky where it was discovered in 1930. This increase in period from Mercury to Pluto is not merely due to the greater distances which the outer planets have to travel. They also move more slowly, for reasons which we will discuss in Chapter 4. Mercury is moving in its orbit at 107,000 m.p.h., the Earth at a more modest 68,000 and Pluto at a mere 10,000 m.p.h.

10 The second important point is that almost all the planets lie in or very near the same plane, so that the Solar System is virtually "flat." There are exceptions to this rule, the worst being Pluto, whose orbit is inclined at an angle of 17 degrees to that of the Earth's, but on the whole it is fairly well obeyed—and it certainly simplifies the problem of inter-planetary navigation.

11 Finally, the shapes of the orbits. They are very nearly circular, with the Sun at the centre. Only Mercury, Mars and—once again—Pluto depart seriously from this rule, their orbits being appreciably elliptical. That of Pluto, in fact, is so eccentric that it can sometimes come closer to the Sun than does Neptune.

12 This, then, is the family of planets of which our world is a rather junior member. Despite its size, it forms a virtually isolated system in space, owing to the remoteness of even the nearest stars. (We shall discuss the scale of the stellar universe in Chapter 16.) With perfect precision, age after age, the planets swing in their orbits round the Sun—for they are moving in an almost total vacuum, beyond the reach of friction or any force which might check their speed.

13 The airlessness of space must have seemed an insuperable barrier to interplanetary voyages in the days when it was first realized that the atmosphere extends only a little way from the Earth. Today we know better—for if there was any appreciable amount of matter in space, it would not be possible to reach the speeds which are required for journeys to other worlds. However, this would be rather a theoretical considera-tion, since those worlds themselves would long ago have ceased to exist: the resistance to their motion would have made them spiral inwards until they dropped into the Sun.

14 There will be opportunity later to look more closely at the other planets, and to see what is known about their physical conditions. We must now return to Earth, which for a long time to come will be the start-ing point for all our voyages, and consider what obstacles we will have to overcome if we wish to leave it.

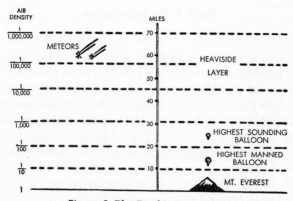

Figure 2. The Earth's Atmosphere

15 As we have already mentioned, the atmosphere is both a help and a hindrance. We cannot live if the pressure of the surrounding air falls below about one-half of its sea-level value, and most men would be practically incapacitated well before this figure was reached. As we ascend from the Earth's surface, the pressure and density of the air fall steadily, and in Figure 2 an attempt has been made to show this on the correct scale. The greatest height at which men can live permanently is three and a half miles, and this requires a long period of adaptation.

16 The absence of atmosphere does not, of course, merely affect men, but also machines. Aeroplanes—whether propelled by airscrews or jets —are air-burning devices just as much as men are, the difference being that in the human engine the combustion is gentler and the conversion of energy to power rather more subtle. In addition, aircraft require the atmosphere for support: wings and airscrews would both be useless in a vacuum. These factors set a limit to the height at which conventional aircraft can ever operate. That limit is between 10 and 15 miles—or, roughly speaking, where the air pressure is more than one-twentieth of its sea-level value.

17 Balloons can function at considerably greater altitudes—up to 25 miles if only carrying very light instruments—but presently they too reach a level where the surrounding air is little denser than the hydrogen in the envelope, and so can give them no more buoyancy. Until the advent of the giant rocket, no object made by man had ever risen above this level —with the single exception of the shells from the Paris gun (usually mis-named "Big Bertha") in the 1914 War. These had a peak altitude of 30 miles, and, if the gun could have been fired vertically, would have reached a height of over 40 miles.

18 The atmosphere, however, does not come to an end at the level where balloons will rise no further: indeed, it never comes to an end at all, but dwindles with distance as a musical note dies away with time, until at last there is no means of detecting its presence. Fifty miles up there is still enough to play a very important rôle in our modern lives, for here the tenuous gases are ionized to form the reflecting layer (the ionosphere or Heaviside layer) which makes long-distance radio com-munication possible and provides many of the strange noises which oc-casionally intrude upon our listening. Around this level most of the mete-ors which come racing into the atmosphere at speeds of 100,000 m.p.h. or more meet their doom, for at these velocities even the ionosphere can produce tremendous frictional resistance.

19 The last indication we have of the atmosphere's presence is given by the aurora, whose ghostly beams and curtains of light we seldom see in southern latitudes, but which are common enough near the magnetic poles. The aurora is produced by electrical discharges very similar to those in neon signs, and its outermost streamers extend to heights of six hundred miles. Well below this altitude, however, we are in a vacuum better than any that can be produced in the laboratory.

20 It might be thought that, because the atmosphere is so relatively shallow, it could be ignored as far as interplanetary flight is concerned.

This is not the case: as we shall see later, it sets a limit to the speed we can develop near the Earth's surface on the way into space and—much more important—it offers a means of making a safe landing on the return.

21 This thin blanket of air, without which life as we know it would be impossible, is held tightly to the Earth by the force of gravity. If gravity were weaker by a factor of four or five, the atmosphere would have escaped into space—as has happened in the case of the Moon. So we can be thankful for gravity in this respect, even though when we contemplate the task of leaving the Earth we may wish it had a much smaller value.

22 Of all natural forces, gravity is the most universal and it dominates any discussion of space-flight. Here on the Earth's surface we can never escape from its influence, and its value is practically constant over the whole of the planet. With increasing altitude it slowly diminishes, though so slowly that even at the greatest height yet reached by rocket (250 miles) it still has 90 per cent of its value at sea level. As the distance from the Earth lengthens into the thousands of miles, the reduction becomes substantial: twelve thousand miles up, a one-pound weight would weigh only an ounce. It follows, therefore, that the further away one goes from the Earth the easier it is to go onwards. (A practical example of the saying that nothing succeeds like success.) As far as gravity is concerned, leaving the Earth is rather like climbing a hill which at first is very steep but later becomes more and more gentle until finally it is almost perfectly flat. Yet it is never quite flat: the Earth's gravitational pull extends throughout the universe, even if for almost all purposes it can be ignored after a distance of a million miles or so.

23 This picture of gravity as producing a hill, up which we have to climb to get away from the Earth, is a very useful one, and we will employ it again later. In the meantime, Figure 3 will give some visual idea of the way in which gravity falls off with distance—and should help to dispel the surprisingly common impression that it simply finishes when one is still quite close to the Earth.

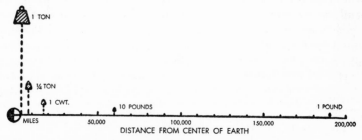

Figure 3. The Reduction of Gravity with Distance

24 If we ever hope to build spaceships, therefore, we must bear in mind two fundamental points. In the first place, any method of propulsion which depends on the atmosphere will be useless. And secondly, even if we have a device which can produce thrust in an airless vacuum, our ship must be provided with enough energy to fight its way outwards for thousands of miles against the pull of Earth's gravity.

25 The first condition, as we shall see in the next chapter, is easily fulfilled. It is the second—the energy problem—which is by far the more serious: yet even that can be solved without invoking any new and fundamental discoveries. We do not have to wait until someone produces "anti-gravity" before we can travel to the planets: the means is already at hand. It is the rocket.

Comment

The Earth and Its Neighbors is interesting not only for its subject matter but also as an illustration of how different expository purposes and techniques can combine in a unified and effective piece of writing. The main purpose of the essay is to give information about (1) the solar system, and (2) the earth's atmosphere. But in the process of being informative it also *explains* (for instance, the movements of the planets, the causes of the northern lights [or aurora borealis], the nature of gravity) and *defines* (asteroids, ionosphere). In giving information about the solar system the essay also *describes* it and *analyzes* its structure. And in so doing it makes use of two *analogies:* it "translates" astronomical distances into earthly ones which are easier for our minds to grasp— man is to the distance between earth and moon as an ant is to the size of England—and, second, it explains the difficulty of leaving earth's gravitational pull by the analogy between gravity and climbing—space flight is to gravity what climbing is to a hill. One might perhaps even say that the essay suggests the giving of directions in a "how-to" piece, since it mentions the chief requirements for successful space travel.

At this point it may be useful to introduce two terms that are frequently found in discussions about writing: *subject matter* and *theme*. The terms are often used interchangeably, but they are of more service if a distinction is made between them. Subject matter is what the essay (or weekly theme or term paper or article or story or book) is about—Charlemagne, termites, labor unions, modern art, President Roosevelt. Theme is what the writer says about the subject matter: "Termite societies are highly organized," "This is how to get rid of termites," "Roosevelt was the greatest of American presidents," "Roosevelt was responsible for today's 'creeping socialism' in America," and so on. The subject matter of Adler's *Baseball and Reading* is the nature of reading. The theme is that reading is an active process, not a passive one, just as catching and fielding in baseball are *activities* although both involve receiving rather than giving. *Motaloy: Claims* vs. *Tests* provides an even more obvious illustration of the contrast between subject matter and theme: the subject matter is Motaloy, the claims made for it, and the tests of the claims; the theme is that Motaloy is not worth buying.

Students often mistake subject matter for theme. When the instructor asks the student for a statement of topic for his term paper, the student may answer "New Orleans jazz" or "synthetic fabrics" or "the United Nations" and be surprised when the instructor tells him he still does not know what is going to be in the paper. "What *about* the United Nations? Are you going to praise New Orleans jazz, condemn it, analyze it formally like a music critic, trace its origins, discuss its influence? What is your theme?"

In *The Earth and Its Neighbors,* the subject matter is the solar system and the atmosphere (both of which are the "Neighbors" of the title). The theme is facts about the earth's neighbors pertaining to the conditions for space flight, although such flight is mentioned only in the very beginning and again at the very end of the essay. A theme (as defined here) *need* therefore not be a state-ment of proof, or of opinion, or of argument, though of course it very often is, as both *Motaloy* and *Baseball and Reading* had opinions as themes.

Since exposition is the kind of writing most commonly called for in colleges, and since organization often proves the student's biggest obstacle in successful writing, it seems useful to examine the organization of *The Earth and Its Neigh-bors,* a selection less limited in its expository aim than the others in this section. Though variations in detail are possible, no outline of *The Earth and Its Neigh-bors* would depart very radically from the following one. (See also pages 116-18, 126-27, for a further discussion of outlines.)

Paragraph(s)

I. Introduction: reduction of distances in space to earthly   1,2
   scale necessary before space flight can be conceived of

II. The solar system   3-12
   A. Scale models of planets   3-8
     1. Earth and its satellite, the moon   3
     2. Other planets   4-7
       a. Inner planets   4,5
       b. Outer planets   6
   B. Three other points about the solar system   9-11
     1. It is not stationary   9
     2. It is almost flat   10
     3. Most orbits are nearly circular   11
   C. The stellar isolation and frictionless vacuum of our   12
     system

III. Earth's atmosphere   13-23
   A. Shallowness of atmosphere and airlessness of space   13
     not obstacles but necessities for space travel
   B. Obstacles in the way of leaving earth: atmosphere,   14-23
     gravity
     1. Atmosphere   15-20
       a. Necessity   15-17
         (1) For humans   15
         (2) For aircraft   16
         (3) For other airborne objects   17
       b. The outer reaches of the atmosphere   18,19
         (1) The ionosphere   18
         (2) The aurora   19
       c. As both a hindrance and a help to space travel   20

Paragraph(s)
2. Gravity   21-23
    a. Holds atmosphere to earth   21
    b. Diminishes with distance from earth   22,23
IV. Conclusion   24,25
    A. Independence of atmosphere for propulsion and   24
    energy sufficient to escape earth's gravity are both
    necessary conditions for space travel
    B. Both conditions fulfillable   25

Exercises

CONTENT

True or False? If you think the statement represents what the selection says or implies, mark it "True"; if you do not think so, mark it "False."

1. In a sense the earth has become smaller in this century.
2. The earth is a planet.
3. Our moon is the only one in our solar system. (Artificial moons don't count.)
4. The sun is a star.
5. The closer a planet is to the sun, the shorter its solar year.
6. Jupiter is the planet farthest from the sun.
7. There are all together three scale models referred to in Paragraphs 3-7.
8. Space is cluttered with tiny planets called asteroids.
9. The regularity of the planetary orbits is due to the size of the planets.
10. The airlessness of space is a help to space travel because of the lack of friction in a vacuum.
11. Without gravity, earth would lose its atmosphere.
12. The ionosphere prevents the earth from being pelted with meteors.

Questions for Discussion

1. Point out the statements in the essay that are relevant to determine whether or not artificial earth satellites orbit beyond the force of gravity.
2. Aside from the fact that without the force of gravity life on our earth, as we know it, would be impossible, does Clarke say that gravity is both a help and a hindrance to space travel, or does he say it is just a hindrance?
3. On the basis only of information given in this essay explain why

"any method of propulsion which depends on the atmosphere will be useless" in space travel.

FORM AND STYLE

1. Explain how the word "again" in the first sentence of Paragraph 4 can be said to be incorrectly used.

2. What determines the order of Paragraphs 3-7?

3. Complete these analogies from Paragraph 7:

The earth is to the diameter of its orbit as a table-tennis ball is to _____?

The earth is to a table-tennis ball as _____ is to ten miles.

4. Explain exactly how Paragraph 12 functions as the transitional paragraph between the two main parts of the essay.

5. The second sentence in Paragraph 14 begins "We must now return to Earth. . . ." Where have we been? Comment upon the appropriateness of the phrase in this essay. Can you think of a kind of astronomical writing in which the phrase would be inappropriate?

6. Pick out phrases and references that show this essay to be part of a book.

7. On the basis of this essay only, make an intelligent guess as to what the next chapter in the book is about. (Your guess can be intelligent without necessarily being right.) Explain your answer.

VOCABULARY

Which of the four words or phrases to the right seems to you to be *closest* in meaning to the word in heavy type to the left? Put a check mark after your choice.

envisage (*1*)   imagine . . .analyze . . . see . . . understand . . .

inconceivably (*2*)   incapable of being measured . . . enormously . . . incapable of being thought of . . . uncomfortably . . .

remote (*2*)   unknown . . . mysterious . . . interesting . . . distant

adapt (*2*)   change . . . adopt . . . accustom . . . force . . .

contemplating (*3*)   imagining . . . measuring . . .thinking about . . . visualizing . . .

satellites (*4*)   objects in the sky . . . moons . . .objects that circle . . . planets . . .

drastic (*6*)   vigorous . . . very great . . . extreme . . . sudden . . .

stationary (*9*)   simple . . . revolving . . . standing still . . . stagnant . . .

virtually (*10*)   practically . . . full of virtue . . . actually . . . nearly

appreciably *(11)*   highly . . . pleasantly . . . measurably . . . approximately . . .

eccentric *(11)*   strange . . . off center . . . not moving in a regular circle . . . wild . . .

insuperable *(13)*   difficult . . . superior . . . incapable of being overcome . . . impenetrable . . .

density *(15)*   weight . . . consistency . . . thickness . . . speed . . .

buoyancy *(17)*   lightness . . . floatability . . . bounciness . . . altitude . . .

advent *(17)*   coming . . . invention . . . addition . . . development

tenuous *(18)*   rare . . . thin . . . high . . . positively charged . . .

intrude upon *(18)*   bother . . . ruin . . . interfere with . . . enter into . . .

velocities *(18)*   heights . . . speeds . . . circumstances . . . distances

substantial *(22)*   important . . . unimportant . . . considerable . . . substandard . . .

employ *(23)*   refer to . . . work . . . use . . . need . . .

dispel *(23)*   disprove . . . clear away . . . break . . . kill . . .

THEME SUGGESTIONS

Flying to the moon
Jules Verne
The day gravity stopped
Write a brief explanatory introduction to your chief interest or hobby
—scientific or not—in the manner in which Clarke here introduces the
general reader to the astronomy of our solar system.

Argument

HATCH • WYLIE • WILSON • BROWN

Contrary to widespread belief, argument is not simply a fight in words ("I had an argument with my roommate last night, and today we aren't talking"). It is the use of language for the purpose of persuading the reader or listener to accept a certain opinion or belief as true or good, to feel in a certain way about something, to act in a certain way. An argument may seek to prove that cigarettes cause lung cancer, that Nixon will make a better president than Kennedy, that movie censorship threatens democracy, that Ted Williams is a greater baseball player than Mickey Mantle, that Sparkol gives whiter teeth. Argument is sometimes hard to distinguish from exposition. If the arguer is honest—the world, unfortunately, is full of dishonest arguments—the argument communicates something which he thinks is true in some objective, absolute sense. The analysis of the advertising claims made for Motaloy was an argument insofar as it tried to convince the reader of Motaloy's worthlessness. And it was a successful argument to the extent the reader could feel its factual evidence (the purely expository element) to be reliable. In science, too, the proof of a hypothesis is often expository. That is, it may be the result of a laboratory test, a meter reading, a set of statistics, that clinches the scientist's argument for his theory. Still, argument can be distinguished from exposition. It does not only inform, explain, analyze, and reason, though it may do all of these. Its distinctive characteristic is that it seeks to *influence* its audience (reader or listener) in one way or another.

Arguments appeal to our reason or to our feelings or to both. The subject of the argument, the circumstances under which it is presented, and the nature of the audience determine which kind of appeal is possible and justified and most effective. The appeal to pure reason that often makes a scientific argument convincing would very likely cause a different kind of argument to fail—for instance, a marriage proposal. Cold, clear logic or systematic reference to facts and figures would be as absurdly out of place in a romantic young man proposing marriage to a starry-eyed girl in a moonlit garden, as sighs and sweetly whispered nothings would be in a scientist arguing for the validity of his hypothesis.

But, life and human nature being what they are, none of us are neither all intellect nor all emotion. This is probably why most arguments in everyday life address themselves to both reason and feeling—sometimes more to one than the other but rarely to one alone. Besides, what may be simply facts and clear thinking to one person may be a highly emotional issue to another. A psychologist can discuss sex in a state of mind quite different from that of a troubled adolescent.

Whatever the nature of your argument, however, both you and your audience will probably be better off if you realize what the argument involves, what kind of appeal it makes, whether it rests on facts or on feelings. To say that "Jones never goes to church; last Tuesday I saw him having lunch downtown with a young girl" is to state facts. But to preface the facts with a statement such as "Jones leads an immoral life" or "Jones is a disgrace to the neighborhood" is to draw conclusions from the facts, to make judgments, to express feelings. Jones may indeed be a monster of sin, but that has not been proved by the facts mentioned. And anyone who thinks that "Jones never goes to church" is the same kind of state-ment as "Jones leads an immoral life" is confusing facts and judgments and lays himself wide open for justifiable criticism. Facts can usually be checked; judgments can not. "Water boils at 212° F.," "The invasion of Normandy took place on June 6, 1944," "Mice are rodents," "Wichita, Kansas, had a population of more than 166,000 in 1950" are all factual statements and can be checked. The statement, "On the morning of Au-gust 29, 1958, 9,259,807 glasses of orange juice were drunk in New York City," is a factual statement, even though it most probably is false, and it most certainly cannot be checked. That we cannot determine its va-lidity does not affect its factuality. But statements like "Mozart is a greater composer than Beethoven" or "Love is a many-splendored thing" or "C— is not a fair grade for this paper" do not state facts but judg-ments. They refer to personal feelings and evaluations. Such feelings and judgments are neither "true" nor "false"; they simply *are*. You may share them, approve of them, disagree with them, resent them, argue against them, think they are ruining the country, consider them ridiculous or wicked—but you cannot prove them either true or false the way you can prove Mount Whitney to be 14,495 feet high. (Even if you don't trust the recorded measurement, you could—theoretically—climb the mountain and measure for yourself.)

Judgments and feelings are legitimate parts of many arguments, and the world would be a sorrier place if we could not use them to influence one another. We do not want to do without them; obviously, we couldn't even if we wanted to. But we *do* want to distinguish them from facts. For to confuse feelings with facts is to risk believing that the nonexistent exists and to surrender to our prejudices the sovereignty of our minds.

17

R O B E R T   H A T C H

Music Spoils the Picture

1   In a picture soon to be released there is said to be a moment of drama so exquisitely intense that for the duration of the episode—some four or five minutes—musical accompaniment is to be suspended. The studio making this announcement apparently feels that the innovation is daring and so *outré* that an unprepared public might fail to grasp the artistic intention and complain of faulty engineering. I wish that some producer would now have the boldness to drop the symphonic background entirely, even if a stand-by orchestra had to be paid to keep Mr. Petrillo tranquil.

2   Modern pictures carry music on the sound track because their forerunners had no sound track. It was thought that the atmosphere of a dead silent theater was not festive, so a piano or other more elaborate music was provided to give the ears something to do while the eyes scanned the subtitles, and incidentally to cover the whir of the projector and the rustle of candy wrappers. It may have been a proper solution to the screen's vexing dumbness. I recall silent movies at camp that were accompanied by no sound except the laughs, cheers, and strangled cries of the campers, and they were vivid beyond anything I saw in those years at conventional theaters with conventional mood music. But these treats were festive by long anticipation and the audience boiled as soon as the light went out. In any case, music on the sound track is as clearly an anachronism as the buggy-whip sockets that were installed in the earliest automobiles.

3   It is more than an anachronism, though; it is a real disfigurement of the movies as a form of art or a means of entertainment. The screen is cousin to the stage. It has its own genius (actually, it has a more particular genius than Hollywood, devoting its major energy to "adapting" from Broadway, is willing to recognize); nevertheless it too is engaged in arresting our attention with selected and selective fragments of experience. Music in its own right is an expression of experience, but it is not used in its own right when it drones along behind some picture that was conceived and executed entirely in nonlyric terms. No sane theater producer would suggest that "Death of a Salesman" or "The Shrike" or "Julius Caesar" should be performed before such a background, but when these plays are moved to the screen—meticulously decked out with the bits of

Music Spoils the Picture. From "Films," in *The Nation,* September 24, 1955. Reprinted by permission of *The Nation.*

verisimilitude that the camera makes possible—a score is provided and everyone loves and suffers, triumphs and dies to music.

4   In one way—a bad way—the orchestration makes the job easier for directors and actors. If the heroine has no passion in her heart or in her voice, violins filling in behind her can raise the pitch as she plods through her lines. If a moment of suspense has failed to reach its calculated tension, oboes and a staccato beat in the bass will do much to make the audience crane forward. But this is encouraging actors to be incompetent and debases the movies even as an industry.

5   Movie music is rarely music in any real sense, but has a quality of its own. The men who write it try to fit their notes and phrases to the galloping of hoofs, the lingering kiss, the death, and the lifted mortgage. But above all they struggle with the problem of keeping an orchestra at work on some kind of intelligible sound for a stretch of two hours or more without giving them anything to play that would really catch the hearer's attention. So the score for one picture is about as appetizing and arresting as that for another—it is the cream sauce that does as well for chicken or lamb croquettes or cauliflower or the hanging of wallpaper.

6   Pictures, I think, have more individuality today than they once had. You cannot type them as easily as Westerns, domestic comedies, gang thrillers, or whatever. This does not mean, unfortunately, that there is more inventiveness in the studios; rather that pictures are being borrowed from somewhat more inventive sources. But the music which is poured over them indiscriminately and which encourages the actors to lean back and ride on the tremolo does a good deal to blur the originality that the movie scouts so industriously smell out.

7   I do not advise a return to the silent screen. Voices should be heard, obviously, and so should music, when it can be used as music and not as an absence of silence. More than that, the movies can use sound with a virtuosity impossible in the theater. All the noises of life—large crashes and the faint clink of glass, city chatter and the chatter of the fields—are available to them. What you hear can be edited as shrewdly as what you see, and for the same narrative and emotional purposes. Of course such sound is used now, but it cannot be used very well when it is carried along in a wash of ambitionless instrumentation.

Comment

The quality of an argument does not depend on the value of the opinion argued. Bad arguments are arguments that ignore or twist relevant evidence, sidestep the issue, cloud it over by gushing jargon, jump to conclusions or draw false ones or otherwise violate logic, and assert (sometimes shout) rather than prove. The list could be longer, for there are almost as many kinds of bad arguments as there are arguers. Bad arguments can be (and have been) given in defense of such things as equal justice for all, better schools, and the preservation of individual freedom. If someone says he is against the narcotics trade, you will (I hope) agree with him. But if he adds, "Because the stuff costs too much," you will hardly feel that the opinion has been well defended. It is also quite possible to give a good argument in favor of something "bad." People who succeed in convincing other people that war or the torture of human beings is a fine thing can be both eloquent and ingenious. Nor do facts and reason invariably support the good against the evil. On most issues something can usually be said for and against both sides.

There is more to judging an argument, then, than simple agreement or disagreement. That you, too, think that movie makers should drop background music does not prove Hatch's argument sound. Nor does your delight in such music prove it *unsound*. Its soundness has not been proved even if Hatch has succeeded in changing your mind.

But whether you find Hatch's opinion acceptable or unacceptable is less important than your awareness of his method of argument. Notice, for example, his frequent use of concrete detail in examples and analogies. Such use of detail is quite common in argument designed for general, nonprofessional consumption. It serves both to substantiate the writer's thesis and to enliven and brighten the style. It can also—as here—serve the subtler purpose of "selling" the arguer's personality to his audience. A man who can compare a musical score to cream sauce "that does as well for chicken or lamb croquettes or cauliflower or the hanging of wallpaper" is not a stuffy bore. Our interest in him as a person makes us more willing to listen sympathetically to his argument.

Exercises

CONTENT

True or False? If you think the statement represents what the selection says or implies, mark it "True"; if you do not think so, mark it "False."

1. Hatch wants to return to the silent movies.

2. The reason movies have background music is that the public demands it.

3. The reason movies have background music is that the musicians' union demands it.

4. There was never any musical accompaniment to silent movies.

5. The silent movies Hatch saw in camp were accompanied by music from a phonograph.

6. Horsewhip holders were installed in early automobiles.

7. Titles of three Broadway plays are mentioned in Paragraph 3.

8. A bad actor or actress benefits from movie music.

9. Most movie music does not even catch the attention of the audience and fits one movie just as well as it does another.

10. Hatch is unmusical.

Questions for Discussion

1. Which of the following statements is true? (give reasons for your choice): Hatch is opposed to background music in movies because (a) he wants better movies, (b) he likes music and dislikes movies, (c) he wants to raise musical tastes in America.

2. Discuss Hatch's argument. Do you agree or disagree with him? How fair is he? How convincing are his reasons?

FORM AND STYLE

1. Using the formal topic outline of *The Earth and Its Neighbors* on pp. 88-89 as model, arrange the following scrambled items from Hatch's essay in a meaningful outline:
   (a) It encourages bad acting.
   (b) Background music should be dropped altogether.
   (c) Movies can use sound better than can the theater.
   (d) Reasons for dropping background music
   (e) It blurs the originality of movies.
   (f) Introduction
   (g) It is old-fashioned.
   (h) Movies should use sound.
   (i) It is unusual for a movie to have even a single scene without background music.
   (j) It is bad for the movies.
   (k) Conclusion
   (l) It is bad as music.

2. Mr. Petrillo, who is mentioned at the end of Paragraph 1, was president of the American Federation of Musicians, the musicians' union. Is this information (a) essential for an understanding of the essay; (b) essential for an understanding of the paragraph; (c) helpful, but not essential; (d) unimportant; (e) irrelevant; (f) insulting to the reader, since everyone knows who Mr. Petrillo is?

3. Why are the candy wrappers mentioned (Paragraph 2)?

4. What is meant by, "The screen is cousin to the stage (Paragraph 3)? When you have decided what it means, can you think of a reason why Hatch put it the way he did rather than using more direct language?

5. What is the name of the form of figurative language represented by "The screen is cousin to the stage"?

6. What do the items in this list have in common: "the galloping of hoofs, the lingering kiss, the death, and the lifted mortgage" (Paragraph 5)?

7. What kind of person is likely to suffer "the death" in the list above?

8. Paragraphs 2 and 5 each end with a comparison. The comparisons deal with quite different objects—buggy-whips and cream sauce—but can they not be said to be of the same nature, to have the same purpose? Explain your answer.

9. What is the importance to the continuity of the essay of the word "though" in the first sentence of Paragraph 3?

10. "A wash of ambitionless instrumentation" (Paragraph 7) refers to the same thing as a phrase in Paragraph 1. Which phrase? Is the difference in "feeling" between the two expressions justified? If so, how so?

VOCABULARY

Which of the four words or phrases to the right seems to you to be *closest* in meaning to the word in heavy type to the left? Put a check mark after your choice.

exquisitely (*1*) forcefully . . . excellently . . . unusually . . . beautifully . . .

suspended (*1*) eliminated . . . muted . . . made full of suspense . . . held up . . .

modern (*2*) fashionable . . . technologically advanced . . . characteristic of the 20th century . . . present day . . .

festive (*2*) interesting . . . like a feast . . . joyous . . . attractive . . .

vexing (*2*) questionable . . . fetching . . . growing . . . irritating

anachronism (*2*) old-fashioned . . . something out of its proper time . . . ridiculous practice . . . anarchy . . .

drones (*3*) hums . . . male bees . . . jars . . . plods . . .

meticulously (*3*) soberly . . . carefully . . . incongruously . . . always . . .

verisimilitude (*3*) likeness to truth . . . something very similar . . . multitudes . . . detail . . .

plods (*4*) stumbles . . . speaks without conviction . . . works heavily . . . falls . . .

debases (*4*) disgraces . . . brings down . . . makes evil . . . makes doubtful . . .

intelligible (*5*) nice . . . understandable . . . intelligent . . . informative . . .

inventiveness (*6*) ability to invent . . . genius . . . quality . . . intensity . . .

virtuosity (*7*) virtue . . . fascination . . . technical skill . . . realism

edited (*7*) produced . . . arranged as by an editor . . . collected . . . represented . . .

THEME SUGGESTIONS

The case for / against background music in the movies

The danger of generalization, or What Hatch overlooks

The movies—entertainment for 12-year-olds

A comparison of musicals from the 1930's and musicals from the 1950's (for students who watch old movies on TV)

18

PHILIP WYLIE

Safe and Insane

1

1   The past fifty years of what we call civilization have utterly ruined childhood. The automobile, by restricting children to the yard or the block, by conditioning their very impulse to chase a ball, and by hooting at them like a beast whenever they appear on the margins of its sacred raceways, has taken away their last rights. The city itself is, of course, no place for children. Today the millionaire's son is as much immured as the child in Victorian slums; perhaps the chauffeur drives him to and from school, but he is walled in by the hooting iron and is altogether cut off from Nature.

2   The needs of children are perfectly described by those recent psychological discoveries which show that the development of each person follows the evolution of the entire species. The infant is the instinctual animal; the tot, a savage with the savage's fears, curiosities, unwitting cruelties, and naïveté; the grade pupil is the advancing barbarian, full of lawless enterprises, excitements, rituals, outdoor achievement, and tribal activity; the adolescent is the medieval mystic; after him comes the adult —*if* all the other stages have been thoroughly experienced and assimilated. But in the modern city, suburb, town, and even to a great extent in the village, the child has been deprived of any normal opportunity to engage in these cultural phases.

3   There is no adequate way for children to wage war against this fierce and universal imprisonment. Their parents try increasingly to barricade them from perils, to fence up their schoolyards, and to hire more supervisors for them, more life guards, more cops at corners, more counselors at camp. Their own so-called adult properties and interests constantly militate against childhood necessities. Their very working hours and pastimes make children a handicap rather than an interest. Indeed, the American child is impounded as soon as it can crawl in what is wretchedly called a play pen—a convenience to every mother which keeps the tot from chewing through electric wires and the like, but which frustrates its every vital instinct.

4   The expression of natural instincts in towns and cities, limited to the unnatural material at hand, is necessarily of an "illegal" nature. In

open country—woods, fields, farms, lakesides—the world is every child's oyster. In towns and cities, everything is "owned" save that which lies in the gutter. This presents the child with total dilemma, total frustration. His environment ought to belong to him and he ought to be a free agent in it. But if he even takes the bark off a tree to make a miniature boat to float in a pool, the urban child destroys somebody's birch, his dad has to pay, and the old lady who owns the goldfish pond has him chased by policemen.

5   The rebellion of city children naturally takes the form of property destruction, for property has become their enemy instead of their friend. They steal from stores; they steal cars; they smash windows; they set fires; they interfere with traffic; they damage trees and public benches; they paint brick walls and iron deer. Most of these are enterprises in which I, myself, have engaged. Generally, I was not caught; when I was caught, my family could pay. But the children of families who cannot pay, when caught in such activities and others analogous, are known as juvenile delinquents, taken before judges, sent to reform schools, and cemented into criminal habits.

6   Such rebellion, however, is merely a negative act which expresses resentment over the fact that the child has been deprived of all suitable opportunity to practice his impulses. The child of modern civilization takes his real revenge—or makes his compensation—when he has shaken off the trap of youth and has become, legally at any rate, an adult. The great majority of Americans alive today are preoccupied with such acts of revenge and compensation. They are performed in three principal categories, besides outright criminality.

7   The overweening passion of grown Americans for games, play, pleasures, and vicarious sports via stadiums, ball parks, radio, movies, and newspapers is the first great evidence of misspent—or, rather, unspent—childhoods. The second is the aggressive, hostile, irresponsible exploitation seen so commonly in businessmen—the littlest along with the greatest. Disguised as "go-getters," "individualists," "builders," and "progressives," they usurp as much power as they can, with total disregard for human welfare—as a revenge for and a protection against the damage society did them in childhood. They feel that by becoming owners they can make up for having lived for many years amidst universal deprivation. The third category results from a complete ruin of the adult by the distortions of childhood environment, and in it are some 20 per cent of the population: the hopeless neurotics and the insane. These people are popularly supposed to be unable to face the grown-up world; actually, they are unable to face the terrible destitutions of their childhood.

8   Children have been sacrificed to "civilization" as much as if they had been poured by millions into the belly of a red-hot idol. The cost, as any good psychologist would expect, is to be found in the national pall of adult infantilism and regression. Most adults remain children all

their lives, often even those who are known as statesmen, senators, generals, admirals, and industrial tycoons.

9   The life of a child ought to be a process of adventure, experience, and exploit, graduated upward to suit his rising consciousness—which, as I have said, follows the unfolding pattern of all instinct. In this process, if he is to become truly adult and thus mentally and emotionally secure, he must make contact with the evolutionary experiences of his forebears, for only thus can his emotions mature and only thus can he get a biological sense of those fundamentals of human life and society which sustain civilization even at its most citified summits. But instead of aiding and abetting this procedure, we have done everything we can think of to shield and protect our children from the facts of life.

2

10   All my adult life I have been appalled at the absence of basic experience in my associates. They think they know what they are doing, but they live in a world of dreams; and the very fact of their ignorances inevitably fills them with enormous hostilities and with immense insecurities.

11   I have met countless people who are active in various health, hospital, welfare, and hygiene societies, but who have never seen a chicken killed or a kitten born. They cross the Atlantic, but they cannot swim. They have slept in hotels in Cairo and Bombay but never in the woods. They drive to the top of Pikes Peak, but they have never shinnied a tree or climbed a cliff. They install automatic heating plants in their homes and air-conditioning in their offices, but they could not be trusted to burn trash in a back yard. They make ice in their kitchens, but they have never skated or skied or snowshoed. They eat all their lives, and wear carnations and orchids, but they have never planted a seed or raised a crop.

12   Now, these people, for all their wonderful accomplishments, such as the atom bomb, are not really conscious, because they have had no true primary experiences in life. They do not know what it is like to feel alive or to be alive. All of them are terribly frightened of their civilization. Their fears run from an entirely rational anxiety about crossing their own streets to the equally rational panic over the possibility that they may get into another war. Such fears, of course, make them aggressive—which greatly increases the chances of wars. They vacillate between worry and escapist work and play. They are, that is, supremely childish.

13   Communism and fascism, from this point of view, merely represent attempts to manage the increasingly infantile behavior of all people in our increasingly industrial societies. They are systems of treating adults as permanent children—of making the state into a universal father and mother; systems of ruling populations by absolute authority (by cajolery on the one hand and physical punishment on the other) not only over the activities of every individual but over his mind and his emotions as well.

And the more childish we Americans become in compensation for our destruction of American childhood, the more vulnerable we become to some form of state absolutism.

14 Most of this change took place in my own lifetime, and today most parents are themselves the products of the sort of background I have described. The fears they feel concerning the world they do know are projected ignorantly, hence doubly, upon that normal, real, and natural childhood environment of which they lack the knowledge. Thus they keep eliminating, forbidding, and discouraging the very sorts of activity which are essential for youngsters. This is done in the name of safety and sanity. Its purpose is to protect the young from danger and from shock—such shock, that is, as would upset these very unstable and subnormal adults. Actually, of course, the adult world is more terribly dangerous than it ever was in history. Actually, ignorance itself is dangerous, and the only hope of security lies always in understanding. And actually, of course, it is dangerous every minute to be alive anywhere at any time.

15 A normal childhood is normally dangerous. It is only through an experience of dangers, graduated to his age, that any child can grow up emotionally. Excessive protection is, for him, famine. A real adult will have real self-reliance and true independence, and will be deeply trustworthy, only if he has successfully passed through a great many experiences in which his own mistake could have caused his serious injury or even his death. A human being who has never had such experiences is likely, for instance, to be unqualified even to drive an automobile, since it represents the constant equation of "error equals injury and death." However, for the sake of adult convenience, of adult "freedom from worry"—and because of the projection of adult neurosis on childhood—safety and protection have been legislated into childhood to a degree that is murderous of adult personality. Not only are the unnatural restrictions of the city and town placed upon the youngster, but to them are added all the sickly prejudices, squeamishnesses, and ignorant dreads of the average urban parent.

16 Our "safe and sane" Fourth of July is an example. It is true that fireworks used to maim and kill children. Not many—as child-killing goes in this nation—but a few. There are, however, no statistics to show how many children who would have been maimed and killed because of their ignorance, poor instruction, untrained recklessness, and general incompetence in using fireworks were saved by the ban. Quite likely, the majority of all such still do get maimed and killed from other causes: falling off the backs of hopped trucks, setting fire to themselves, drowning, and other little dooms that are reserved for the ignorant, stupid, overreckless, and incompetent among youngsters as amongst us all.

17 The institution of the "quiet Fourth" destroyed the greatest and most emotionally potent national fiesta America ever had. Its ceremony

was handed down through generations. My father saluted sunrise on Independence Day with a brass cannon charged and fired by himself. He worked and saved to set rockets spattering the high dark of every July Fourth night. Bands, parades, and oratory were part of the celebration and they tied his emotions, by music, sights, and words, to the stirring deeds of his Revolutionary forebears. But the seal on that relationship was made by Father's own loud, glamorous, explosive *participation* in the proudest and most important memory we Americans possess.

18 I was taught, at a very early age, to shoot off fireworks. Little fireworks at first, big ones in later years, and rockets and Roman candles when I was ten. The Fourth of July was the day of my greatest boyhood independence. I was allowed by public sanction to help wake up the whole town at the crack of dawn. I was permitted all day to make as much noise as I pleased. At night, it was my privilege to play gorgeously with fire. Instinct, tribal custom, fundamental human culture, here bound me gloriously to a supreme tradition of the fight of a bold people for liberty. In the whole adventure of being a boy there is no event so altogether satisfactory as a proper Fourth of July; the ritual is primitive and valuable beyond price.

19 When I was twelve, we moved to another State and the Fourth of July became a Boy Scout parade in hot uniforms, a lot of speeches, formal wreathlaying—in, of all places for such a day, the cemetery!—a long walk home, a late dinner, and fireworks distantly viewed that evening in a park.

20 In my thirteenth year, I accidentally discovered at a public library in this benighted State a book which told how to make black powder. I was not permitted by the librarian to take out this book on my card; so, naturally, I took it out under my coat—for good. In three different drugstores I purchased sulphur "for the roses," potassium nitrate "for the plants," and powdered charcoal "for dad's indigestion." These, when mixed according to directions, gave off a fine flash. I then made a cannon by boring an oak block in the manual training shop, loaded it with my powder, packed it with toilet paper and blue stone from the driveway, and touched it off by lighting a newspaper.

21 The first explosion was slow but fiery. After further reading, however, I caught on to such ingredients as potassium chlorate—then in use as a gargle—tannic acid, and other substances. And my extreme delight can be imagined when, one day, the charge in my gun gave a mighty bang and the chipped stones smashed several cellar windows in the house next door. Father paid for the windows.

22 Chapters from the story of my childhood usually cause my present friends and acquaintances to gasp with anxiety or even to snort with unbelief. Of what they consider perils and hardships, onerous duties and inordinate responsibilities, I had a far greater share than most of my friends. My busy parents let me go my way—even urged me to take chances when I was reluctant; but they saw to it, first, that I had the knowledge and the disciplines necessary for the undertakings. That is the point. I lived a great deal in the out-of-doors when I was young— and that is where all mankind lived for a million years and until the few last unsatisfactory thousands of years.

23 I should like to point out to every protective mother and father that, while I got hurt many times—cut, skinned, bruised, sprained, and so on—through independent acts, the most careful supervision failed to spare me from harm. My worst burn was sustained when, a baby in my mother's arms, I reached out as she stirred jam stewing on a wood stove and pressed my hand into its white-hot surface. My worst hurt occurred when I was about four and my grandmother was bathing me, standing, in a washbowl; somehow she let me fall. And the closest I ever came to death—during any protracted period—resulted from a bellyache for which my parents innocently called an old-fashioned osteopath. On three successive days he treated, by kneading, what had been from the start a ruptured appendix. I sustained my only severe fracture during a school gym period.

3

24 A great deal of attention has been paid by psychologists to the early sex training of children. Freud's discoveries have shown how crazily we behave in this dominant aspect of life. But it is only part of the background of childhood, one facet in the direct contact with Nature which the child requires. Sex difficulties, of a certainty, are the commonest expression of our modern human incompetence. But beneath them lies the fact that the form and purpose of the last few millenniums of man's development have been increasingly hostile to every opportunity for natural childhood.

25 Modern educators have followed the lead of modern psychologists and have attempted to set up systems which would give room for the development of the child's ego in relation to its playmates and to mother-child-father situations. In some schools, all formal discipline has been abandoned to "liberate" young personalities. This is futile. The one discipline which the child is emotionally equipped to learn, and indeed must know to live successfully as an adult, is the natural discipline of cause and effect—the perfect honesty of Nature and the absolute inviolability of its laws. For in natural law is the basis of all human morality; but because it can be assimilated only through experience, we regularly observe—with absurd regret—that there seems to be no other way by which each generation can learn anything. The regret is absurd simply because it arises from our fallacious notion that somehow civilization could or should reach the child vicariously, without risk to it or worry or bother to its parents.

26 The fact is that nearly all the properties, buildings, streets, ma-

chines, gadgets, higher courses of learning, governments, armies, navies, weapons, monetary systems, and other "advanced" aspects of civilization are superficial to *life*. Indeed, people who lack them all seem to be both wiser and more contented than the average American. To a child, these things are *totally* superficial—wretched excrescences that filch his necessary environs and replace them with deadly walls. To think, as parents do, that children can be morally educated and emotionally prepared for maturity in such a setting, and by means which substitute, at best, supervised samplings of natural life for the child-long experience of it, is like thinking that a man could be prepared to live on Mars by occasional squints at the stars.

27 Essays such as this are, by "civilized" custom, supposed to conclude with neat plans to solve any difficulties or problems which they present. Obviously, the cardinal idea here implied is that the entire way of life of Western man is wrong and has been wrong since before Greece and Rome. The reader, granting my premises, will hardly feel equipped to set out to arrest and redirect a process in being for thousands of years. Yet the reader, if a parent, can do precisely that within the limits of one family and perhaps with good effect on several families.

28 He can do it by understanding the true needs of childhood, by realizing that the needs are "rights," and by serving those rights above and beyond all other rights. Parents have no right, for example, to live in cities if they can possibly live outside them. Children have the right to observe and experience every fact of Nature—animal, mineral, and vegetable. They have a right to learn to be, step by step, independently able to live in natural environments. They have a right to take on such responsibilities as their age makes possible. They have a right to learn such truths and consequences as their emotional development permits, in environs that are not property—environs where they can dig, pluck, hoard, build, saw, cut, walk, swim, chop, paint, paddle, and pole without let or hindrance; environs where their normal impulse is neither inhibited by blue-jacketed guardians of every object nor confined by the artificial hazard of rushing, iron monstrosities. Children have the right to take, every day, such natural risks as their teaching in Nature gives them the competence to face.

29 Only that adult who is able to live successfully in a primitive world can bring enough knowledge and experience to civilized living to make it worth while. Without a realistic childhood background, he (or she) is a mere gadget himself. And a human being is not designed to be a by-product of a pile of buildings and a slew of machines or a parasite upon them.

30 I know that some readers, anxious mothers, will think this is a ghastly theory, and that I have never had charge of a child. The fact is, my brother and sister and I did most of the "bringing up" of our much younger half-brother and half-sister. The fact is that, as I write, my own daughter, who is fourteen, has just recovered from a badly broken arm which she sustained while riding a rough horse—I spent part of last summer encouraging her to ride by riding with her. I swam with her in "shark-infested waters," too, last summer. And when I found that she had gone swimming alone over the Bahaman coral reefs, it gave me quite a turn. "I came in," she said, "when I looked down and saw an enormous purple sting ray right underneath me."

31   The reader will see that I have taught her to be prudent. And a few readers, perhaps, may see that my daughter has a good opportunity of growing up into a person with some experience of Nature—and a fair quantity of self-reliance. Such, anyhow, is my hope for her.

Comment

Philip Wylie does not approve of the way most children grow up these days, and he is quite emphatic and explicit in stating his disapproval. Whether one agrees with him or not, it is difficult to deny that much of the interest of his essay lies in the force with which he expresses himself. The energy and logic of his argument are impressive, and so are his keenness of observation and his way with words.

But, by being so insistently full of fight, perhaps Wylie hurts his own cause. It would not be difficult to accuse him of exaggerating or at least of being one-sided. It is a fair guess that among Americans who cross the Atlantic, more know how to swim than do not know, and there are certainly "countless people" who own refrigerators *and* ski or skate. Nor is it very obviously true that the majority of our cultural and community leaders "are terribly frightened of their civilization." We may ask what is particularly childish about vacillating "between worry and escapist work and play," what was so satisfactory about prehistoric human life (unless savagery itself be considered satisfactory), and how accurate the use of adjectives is in such a statement as this: "the very fact of their [his associates] ignorances inevitably fills them with enormous hostilities and with immense insecurities." Wylie throughout contrasts the enterprising freedom and happy "naturalness" of his own boyhood with the confined and frustrating and overcivilized experience of contemporary children. But the vehemence of his protest may suggest that he himself is not the product of an ideal childhood. In view of what he says about adult hostility and insecurity, we may well ask whether his argument gains or loses from the anger in his tone.

Exercises

CONTENT

True or False? If you think the statement represents what the selection says or implies, mark it "True"; if you do not think so, mark it "False."

1. Today only the rich city child is able to have a natural childhood.
2. A preschool child is like a savage.

3. Juvenile delinquency is a form of rebellion against restrictions.

4. Children hate adults.

5. Because of their frustrating childhoods, most adult Americans belong to one of the following four classes: the criminals, the neurotics and the insane, the unsuccessful drifters, the childish sports fans.

6. There is a kind of "evolutionary process," similar to that which the whole human race has gone through, in the development of every child.

7. Physical danger is good for a child.

8. The author explains his own neurosis as the result of an overprotected childhood.

9. Authoritarian forms of government, like fascism and communism, are childish.

10. The way of life of Western man took a wrong turn about one hundred years ago.

11. Sex education should be made compulsory in school.

12. Children should be allowed to grow up without discipline.

Questions for Discussion

1. Interpret the following statements and phrases which occur in the paragraphs indicated by the numbers in parentheses:
    (a) "the margins of its sacred raceways" (*1*)
    (b) "the adolescent is the medieval mystic" (*2*)
    (c) "the terrible destitutions of their childhood" (*7*)
    (d) "They cross the Atlantic, but they cannot swim." (*11*)
    (e) "it is dangerous every minute to be alive anywhere at any time" (*14*)
    (f) "the constant equation of 'error equals injury and death'" (*15*)
    (g) "Not many—as child-killing goes in this nation—but a few." (*16*)
    (h) "the perfect honesty of Nature and the absolute inviolability of its laws" (*25*)

2. Does the fact that Wylie himself on occasion was a "bad" boy— he committed vandalism, damaged other people's property, and once stole a book from a public library—help or weaken his argument? Explain your answer.

3. What purpose in the essay as a whole is served by the recollections of Wylie's childhood Fourth of July's? (Paragraphs 16-21).

4. Which of the following statements do you feel best expresses Wylie's thesis? (A *thesis* is the theme of an argument.)
    (a) Much of the unhappiness and nervous tension of our times is caused by the complexities and restrictions of city life.
    (b) Since it is impossible to turn the clock back and "return to nature," each individual parent has a duty to see to it that his children experience nature first hand.
    (c) By overprotecting and overrestricting our children, we make them unfit for normal, happy adulthood.

(d) Down with civilization!

(e) Safety restrictions on the free celebration of the Fourth of July should be lifted.

(f) People who are secure tend to go insane.

FORM AND STYLE

1. A paradox is a statement or phrase that seems at first glance to be contradictory, or nonsensical and hence untrue but which turns out, on inspection, to make sense. Find and discuss an important paradox in Wylie's essay.

2. With respect to argumentative strategy, what does the "old lady who owns the goldfish pond" (Paragraph 4) have in common with the "countless people" (Paragraph 11)?

3. Comment upon the author's attitude in the sentence beginning (Paragraph 12): "Now, these people, for all their wonderful accomplishments, such as the atom bomb. . . ."

4. Paragraph 12 connects with Paragraph 11, Paragraph 13 with Paragraph 12, and Paragraph 14 with Paragraph 13, all in the same way. Identify the connection.

5. Explain the division of the essay into three sections by defining the subject matter of each section.

VOCABULARY

Which of the four words or phrases to the right seems to you to be *closest* in meaning to the word in heavy type to the left? Put a check mark after your choice.

conditioning (*1*)   ruining . . . blocking . . . controlling . . . changing . . .

immured (*1*)   frustrated . . . walled in . . . made immune . . . paralyzed . . .

unwitting (2)   stupid . . . unintentional . . . unknown . . . cruel . . .

naïveté (2)   ignorance . . . quality of being new-born . . . childishness . . . credulity . . .

rituals (2)   secrets . . . rules . . . ceremonies . . . rights . . .

tribal (2)   belonging to a tribe . . . trial . . . three-fold . . . common . . .

assimilated (2)   absorbed . . . killed . . . conquered . . . left behind . . .

militate (3)   fight . . . work against . . . withhold . . . destroy . . .

impounded (3)   enslaved . . . frustrated . . . taken into custody . . . pounced upon . . .

dilemma (*4*)   difficulty . . . boredom . . . choice between two unattractive alternatives . . . pain caused by restriction . . .

cemented (*5*)   glued . . . walled . . . built . . . stuck fast . . .

resentment (*6*)   anger . . . injustice . . . frustration . . . callousness . . .

deprived (*6*)   separated from . . . stripped . . . forbidden . . . forced to give up . . .

compensation (*6*)   putting instead of . . . regret . . . frustration . . . payment . . .

hostile (*7*)   like a host . . . friendly . . . unfriendly . . . fiendish . . .

exploitation (*7*)   ruthlessness . . . exploration . . . making unfair use of . . . taking advantage of . . .

destitutions (*7*)   destructions . . . losses . . . conditions of poverty . . . desperations . . .

pall (*8*)   cloth . . . gloom . . . grief . . . disaster . . .

sustain (*9*)   hold up . . . contribute to . . . are necessary to . . . strengthen . . .

citified (*9*)   made certain . . . made citylike . . . elevated . . . heavenly . . .

abetting (*9*)   helping . . . encouraging . . . improving . . . betting on . . .

appalled (*10*)   shocked . . . made gloomy . . . surprised . . . frightened . . .

vacillate (*12*)   tremble . . . run back and forth . . . waver . . . unable to make up one's mind . . .

cajolery (*13*)   threats . . . pleasantry . . . coaxing . . . flattery . . .

vulnerable (*13*)   attractive . . . attracted . . . close . . . capable of being wounded . . .

eliminating (*14*)   putting limits to . . . outlawing . . . removing . . . lacking . . .

graduated (*15*)   given a degree . . . gradually adapted . . . graded . . . proper . . .

excessive (*15*)   too much . . . parental . . . constant . . . strong . . .

famine (*15*)   fame . . . starvation . . . death . . . something that cripples . . .

squeamishness (*15*)   fear . . . peculiarity . . . intolerance . . . excessive daintiness . . .

incompetent (*16*)   clumsy . . . incapable . . . disobedient . . . unable to compete . . .

potent (*17*)   powerful . . . important . . . sacred . . . possible . . .

fiesta (*17*)   institution . . . party . . . holiday . . . feast . . .

sanction (*18*)   decree . . . tradition . . . approval . . . permission

benighted (*20*)   aristocratic . . . covered by night and darkness . . . benevolent . . . respectable . . .

onerous (*22*)   awful . . . hateful . . . heavy . . . difficult . . .

inordinate (*22*)   extraordinary . . . not in order . . . unasked for . . .
    immoderate . . .
protracted (*23*)   remembered . . . extended . . . specific . . . pro-
    tected . . .
dominant (*24*)   complex . . . ruling . . . controversial . . . not to be
    ignored . . .
facet (*24*)   part . . . aspect . . . face . . . faucet . . .
futile (*25*)   in vain . . . idiotic . . . evading the issue . . . unneces-
    sary . . .
inviolability (*25*)   peacefulness . . . quality of not being capable of
    being violated . . . inevitability . . . mastery . . .
fallacious (*25*)   foolish . . . capable of falling . . . false . . . stupid
vicariously (*25*)   indirectly . . . by substitute . . . victoriously . . .
    without human effort . . .
excrescences (*26*)   superfluous objects . . . excesses . . . trouble-
    makers . . . abnormal growths . . .
filch (*26*)   steal . . . ruin . . . make ugly . . . make filthy . . .
environs (*26*)   desirable places . . . environments . . . playgrounds
    . . . outlets . . .
cardinal (*27*)   important . . . like a cardinal of the Roman Catholic
    Church . . . main . . . sovereign . . .
confined (*28*)   limited . . . condemned . . . threatened . . . shut up
prudent (*31*)   prudish . . . proud . . . cautious . . . brave . . .

THEME SUGGESTIONS

How to have fun growing up in a city
A mother's reply to Wylie, or Unsafe children, insane parents
Sex education—in life and school
Wylie's theory of the causes of juvenile delinquency

19

SLOAN WILSON

The Case Against Fraternities

1   Last winter a student at the Massachusetts Institute of Technology
was killed while being initiated into a fraternity. He had been left out
in the woods alone on a cold night by his "brothers" and was trying to
find his way back to his campus. While crossing a frozen pond, which

THE CASE *Against* FRATERNITIES. From *The American Weekly*, October
14, 1956. Reprinted by permission of *The American Weekly* and the author.

he may have mistaken for a snow-covered meadow in the darkness, he fell through the ice and was drowned.

2   Fraternities are allowed a good deal of latitude in the name of good clean horseplay, but they aren't supposed to kill people. All sorts of reforms were undertaken on the M.I.T. campus, and the paid executive secretaries of fraternities all around the country were kept busy writing statements about the good deeds their members have substituted for old-fashioned hazing.

3   In spite of this, the incident of the boy falling through the ice in the darkness dealt a hard blow to fraternities. A lot of people began to wonder what all these Greek letters really mean and whether fraternities aren't fundamentally vicious.

4   I think this is too bad because there is nothing vicious about fraternities. They can be called stupid, witless, juvenile and purposeless associations much like the "clubs" small boys organize in back-yard shacks, but they can't be called vicious. Most of them have a kind of Boy Scout code of honor which makes their members burst with pride.

5   It bothers me to see fraternities criticized for the wrong reasons. Fraternities can easily prove they're not vicious, and they can easily change their initiation procedures to avoid unfortunate fatal accidents. In doing this, they may seem to have undertaken important reforms, and to have justified their existence. That, of course, would be nonsense. The existence of fraternities can't be justified any more than can many other manifestations of adolescence.

6   Very few people seem to understand what fraternities (and sororities and other secret clubs) are. They are organizations of students which ask some people to be members and exclude others. The standards of acceptance are vague and are established by the fraternity members themselves.

7   The goal of each fraternity usually is to get as its members the "best" students enrolled in an institution of learning. By "best" I don't mean the most brilliant or the most moral; I mean "best" as construed by the adolescents themselves.

8   To some this means rich, handsome and white Protestants, a definition which in its guileless witlessness almost achieves innocence. To others, "best" means those possessed of the prevailing code of social behavior, or the best available after "better" fraternities have taken their pick.

9   Fraternities like to boast about getting "a good cross-section" of students as members, but on almost any campus an old hand will be able to tell which fraternities specialize in attracting the local version of socialites, which ones pride themselves on varsity athletes, and which ones are havens for the boy intellectuals. There are fraternities especially known for heavy drinking, for wild parties and luxurious living.

10   On almost any campus it is easy to find which fraternities are for

white Protestants only, which ones are largely Catholic and which ones are largely Jewish. In the past, many fraternities oafishly placed written articles of racial or religious restriction in their constitutions. Recently there have been many hasty and red-faced attempts to bring the constitutions of fraternities into line with the constitution of the United States, but no one can seriously doubt that intolerance and bigotry are still practiced by many fraternities.

11   From campus to campus and from year to year the chapters of fraternities change, but each tends to seek students of like nature. On each campus there will be the "best" fraternity—the one which has attracted the most prosperous Protestant students of athletic, academic or social distinction.

12   The "best" fraternity sometimes can make the superficially believable claim that it gets a cross-section of the "best" students. But there can be only one "best" fraternity. Many others are established to assuage the feelings of those who fail to get in the "best" fraternity. If the "ins" organize, so do the "outs." If students, for one of many reasons, are excluded from one fraternity, the thin-skinned ones frequently organize a fraternity of their own.

13   Thus every student is neatly compartmented on many an American campus, and the main purpose of a college education is, in a sense, defeated. That is the irony of fraternities: they do the most harm to their own members.

14   In the past, many tears have been shed over the plight of students who aren't asked to join a fraternity. In my opinion these students are lucky. They may have momentarily hurt feelings, and they may even spend most of their college days feeling themselves to be outcasts, but they do not suffer the invisible injuries inflicted upon those who do become fraternity members. They do not have the stultifying experience of associating only with people of their own kind for their entire college career.

15   They are not blinded by false pride in having "made" an institution which was not worth making in the first place. They can, once their wounded pride is healed, become one with those very best college students of all: those who wouldn't think of joining a fraternity.

16   Today more and more students feel that their intelligence is insulted when they are invited to participate in the trick handclasps, juvenile insignia, the paddling of posteriors, the abandonment of young boys in the woods at night, and all the rest of it.

17   For decades many American college students were notorious for their immaturity, but since the war they have shown signs of growing up. The really brilliant students nowadays are taking a hard look at the "advantages" fraternities pretend to offer and are recognizing them as childish frauds.

18   One of these "advantages" is "brotherhood," which is achieved by

denying the fundamental brotherhood of all men, by excluding people of different mien or manner.

19 Mature students are realizing that they do not need Greek letters to have friendship. The veterans of World War II who returned to college found that they could drink beer without being "initiated," and they weren't enthusiastic about being paddled or taken on "scary" expeditions by beardless youths. Most of these ex-servicemen ignored fraternities. They have set a sensible example for their younger brothers and their sons.

20 Another so-called advantage of fraternities is the development of social ease, or "savoir faire." Apparently a lot of clods who blushed at the thought of asking a woman to dance and who didn't know a salad fork from a pitch fork have, over the years, joined fraternities and found enlightenment in the field of modes and manners. Special classes for such poor souls could be provided—if fraternities should die of their own clownishness.

21 What other advantages do fraternities pretend to offer? A "sense of belonging" is one. Undoubtedly there are a few students on every campus who are afraid to stand up as individuals. For such people it is not enough to be a member of a family, a church, a college, a nation, and the human race. They like to believe they're something special, because they have achieved membership in an organization which keeps others out. Fortunately, most colleges now have psychiatric clinics for such students.

22 There is one other "advantage" which fraternities dangle before the eyes of prospective members, but even the fraternity members themselves are sometimes ashamed to boast of it. That is the "advantage" of "contacts" made at college who will later be useful in helping a fraternity member to get a job. It would seem that many of the "brothers" lack confidence in themselves and are afraid they will be unable to get a job as good as they deserve without outside aid.

23 Whatever the reason, fraternity members often show pathetic hope in, and dependence on, one another for help in earning a living. On what frail straws these poor souls lean!

24 I have been in the hiring business on several occasions, and I have been amazed at the eagerness of many fraternity "brothers" to blackball one another. On many occasions people have said to me something like this: "Jim Jones? He was a member of my fraternity in college, and I knew him well. He's a bum—a real bum!"

25 In the business world, the accuracy of the recommendations a man gives others greatly affects his own reputation, and no old-school-tie sentiment affects the judgment given by capable and ambitious men. I suppose some jobs are reserved for down-and-outers by their fraternity brothers but, fortunately, government relief programs are relieving fraternities of these responsibilities.

26 In any case, really capable students don't spend their days on the campus worrying about "contacts" for jobs after graduation.

27 No really brilliant student who is mature and psychologically whole could possibly become a member of a fraternity nowadays, any more than he could join the Ku Klux Klan, or one of those clubs whose only requirement for membership is the mailing of a cereal box top. It probably would be wise for teachers and parents to point this out to boys and girls of college age who are not bright enough to perceive it for themselves.

28 But let's not exaggerate the evils of fraternities. There is nothing vicious about the boys and girls who join such organizations. Even those initiation stunts which result in fatal accidents, like the one last winter at M.I.T., are not the product of evil thinking. They are the result of not thinking at all.

Comment

Sloan Wilson here tells us why he is against fraternities. But his purpose is not just to let us know his opinion (if it were, he would be writing pure exposition); it is to make us share it. The essay invites us to come over to his side in the debate and see, as he does, that fraternities are "a bad thing."

Wilson's argument involves both facts and feelings. For example, the first paragraph is an almost completely objective statement of an actual accident; the second paragraph proceeds to pass judgment on the social institution responsible for the accident. The judgment goes beyond merely stating facts. It interprets the facts, evaluates them, that is, expresses feelings and attitudes toward them. Attitude is implied also in Wilson's main method of attack; in fact, one might say that attitude *is* his main method of attack: the attitude that refuses to take fraternities seriously and keeps repeating that they are childish and silly "but not vicious." Since fraternity life—like most subjects of common discussion—involves more than one side of the student's existence, his emotions as well as his mind, it is quite proper that Wilson should try to appeal to both reason and emotion.

But we, his readers, should be aware of when he is doing one and when the other. In reading controversial essays on topics which are likely to engage our opinions and feelings, nothing is easier than to find a writer we disagree with prejudiced when he states a fact and a writer we agree with factual when he states a prejudice. Ideally, perhaps, we should strip ourselves of all opinion, make our minds a blank, try to read as objectively as an electronic brain. But the "ideal" is not humanly possible. To be human is to have opinions, desires, affections, grudges, prejudices. The best we can do if we are intellectually responsible and interested in truth is to try to be as open-minded as possible, to try to be aware of the slant of our own minds and of the author's, and to listen to him as calmly as we can even though we may disagree with him. You are entitled to your opinion as he is to his, but you should both know why you hold it. And you should remember that not everyone who disagrees with you is necessarily either an idiot or a scoundrel.

Exercises

CONTENT

True or False? If you think the statement represents what the selection says or implies, mark it "True"; if you do not think so, mark it "False."

1. The M.I.T. freshman's death made no impression on fraternity officials.

2. Fraternities are both stupid and vicious.

3. Only the white, Protestant, wealthy, athletic, and scholarly boys belong to fraternities.

4. Fraternities would be all right if they gave up practices that lead to fatal accidents.

5. World War II veterans were not much interested in joining fraternities.

6. Fraternity men drink too much.

7. Fraternities hurt their own members most.

8. It is bad to associate with only one kind of people.

9. Fraternity brothers are usually loyal to one another after college.

10. Though there are many serious objections to fraternities, they *do* teach their members good manners, and they *do* give them a valuable sense of belonging.

Questions for Discussion

1. What, in Wilson's opinion, is "the main purpose of a college education" (Paragraph 13)?

2. Do you agree that "the 'clubs' small boys organize in back-yard shacks" are "purposeless" (Paragraph 4)? If you do not agree, what do you think their purpose is?

3. The most serious objection usually made against fraternities is that they are discriminatory in their selection of members. When Wilson in Paragraph 14 considers the students who are not asked to join "lucky," is he weakening his own case? Obviously, if the nonfraternity men are better off for being excluded from fraternities, it no longer makes much sense to blame the fraternities for keeping them out. Or does it? Explain.

FORM AND STYLE

1. Throughout, Wilson tries to "destroy the enemy" by refusing to take him (i.e., fraternities) seriously. Point out specific words and phrases where this attempt is apparent.

2. There are few arguments on controversial topics like this that do not gain by giving the other side credit for *some* virtue and good sense.

To do so proves objectivity and fair-mindedness in the arguer. In Paragraph 10 Wilson tries to give fraternities their due. Is his admission that fraternities recently have tried to liberalize their constitutions objectively stated? How does your answer affect your attitude toward Wilson and his case?

3. "Name-calling" is a device in propaganda by which you try to discredit your opponent by saying bad things about him, without any attempt to support your attack by factual evidence or by logic. Is "no one can seriously doubt that intolerance and bigotry are still practiced by many fraternities" (end of Paragraph 10) a valid argument or is it just name-calling?

4. Why are there quotation marks around "brothers" in Paragraph 1?

5. Why does Wilson twice repeat the statement that "fraternities are not vicious"? Isn't this a rather strange admission for an antifraternity man to make?

6. Wilson's attack on fraternities consists of four main parts. Part I— the introduction—includes Paragraphs 1-5 and deals with the M.I.T. freshman's accidental death. First (I, A, Para. 1), the death is reported. Second (I, B, Para. 2, 3), Wilson mentions two consequences of the accident: one (I, B, 1, Para. 2), that fraternities were shocked into publishing defensive statements; two (I, B, 2, Para. 3), that people began to wonder whether fraternities were not really vicious. Third (I, C, Para. 4, 5), Wilson gives his reasons for thinking that fraternities should not be considered vicious: they can easily prove they are not, thus seeming to justify their existence. But, even so, they cannot be justified.

The body of the essay (II, III, Para. 6-26) supports this opinion by two reasons. One (II, Para. 6-15) is that fraternities are discriminatory, and because discrimination does more harm to him who discriminates than to him who is being discriminated against, fraternities are stupid rather than vicious. The second (III, Para. 16-26) is that the advantages claimed for fraternities are not real.

Part II, in turn, consists of two parts. The first (II, A, Para. 6-13) defines fraternities as discriminatory organizations (II, A, 1, Para. 6), the goal of which is to attract the "best" students, whatever each fraternity makes "best" mean (II, A, 2, Para. 7-12), and the result of which is to defeat "the main purpose of a college education" (II, A, 3, Para. 13). The second part (II, B, Para. 14, 15) gives Wilson's two reasons for considering the student who either is not allowed to join or does not want to join luckier than the student who joins. One reason is that the nonmember has a richer social experience than the member (II, B, 1, Para. 14), another that he does not become a discriminatory snob "blinded by false pride" (II, B, 2, Para. 15).

Part III, Para. 16-26, argues that the advantages of belonging to a fraternity really are not advantages at all. It is linked to Part II by the idea that the nonmember, in addition to being better off than the fraternity man, is also more intelligent and mature (III, A, Para. 16, 17). He shows his superiority in two ways: by refusing to take part in the childish nonsense that goes with fraternity life (III, A, 1, Para. 16) and by realizing that there are no advantages in belonging (III, A, 2, Para. 17).

The rest of Part III (III, B, Para. 18-26) lists some of these so-called advantages: the sense of brotherhood (III, B, 1, Para. 18, 19), which is both morally unsound (III, B, 1, a, Para. 18) and juvenile (III, B, 1, b, Para. 19); the acquisition of the social graces (III, B, 2, Para. 20); the sense of belonging (III, B, 3, Para. 21); and the contacts that are supposed to help the student in his later career (III, B, 4, Para. 22-26). A belief in the value of such contacts shows lack of self-confidence (III, B, 4, a, Para. 22) and has no foundation in the business world: successful businessmen don't risk their reputation for good judgment by recommending failures (III, B, 4, b, Para. 23-25). And good students don't expect their fraternity brothers to make their careers for them (III, B, 4, c, Para. 26).

The Conclusion (IV, Para. 27-28) restates two points already made. The first is the main idea of Part III, namely, that the nonfraternity man is more intelligent, more mature, and better adjusted than the fraternity man (IV, A, Para. 27). The second is the chief point of the whole essay, the idea stated already at the end of the Introduction: fraternities are "stupid, witless, juvenile, and purposeless"—but they are not "vicious" (IV, B, Para. 28).

Here is this outline in the form of a chart. With the help of the analysis above, try to find appropriate topics or "titles"—not sentences—for each of the items in the chart.

Outline	Paragraph(s)	Topic
I.	1-5	
A.	1	
B.	2, 3	
1.	2	
2.	3	
C.	4, 5	
II.	6-15	
A.	6-13	
1.	6	
2.	7-12	
3.	13	
B.	14, 15	
1.	14	
2.	15	
III.	16-26	
A.	16, 17	

Outline	Paragraph(s)	Topic
1.	16	
2.	17	
B.	18-26	
1.	18, 19	
a.	18	
b.	19	
2.	20	
3.	21	
4.	22-26	
a.	22	
b.	23-25	
c.	26	
IV.	27, 28	
A.	27	
B.	28	

VOCABULARY

Which of the four words or phrases to the right seems to you to be *closest* in meaning to the word in heavy type to the left? Put a check mark after your choice.

latitude (2)   width . . . fun . . . roughness . . . freedom . . .

hazing (2)   brutality . . . loafing . . . playing tricks . . . making hazy . . .

incident (3)   accident . . . tragedy . . . happening . . . story . . .

vicious (3)   harmful . . . wicked . . . untrustworthy . . . silly . . .

manifestation (5)   result . . . symptom . . . stupidity . . . evidence

construed (7)   built . . . interpreted . . . defined . . . qualified . . .

havens (9)   refuges . . . ports . . . heaven . . . things worth having . . .

bigotry (10)   stupidity . . . discrimination . . . narrow-mindedness . . . hatred . . .

prosperous (11)   numerous . . . popular . . . admirable . . . wealthy

compartmented (13)   separated . . . individualized . . . placed in compartments . . . satisfied . . .

plight (14)   difficulty . . . flight . . . sadness . . . pledge . . .

stultifying (14)   horrible . . . irritating . . . limiting . . . making stupid . . .

insignia (16)   marks . . . activities . . . signs . . . insignificant things . . .

mien (18)   background . . . behavior . . . appearance . . . means

accuracy (25)   value . . . meaning . . . importance . . . exactness

THEME SUGGESTIONS

Initiation night

An answer to Wilson that Brown does not make (see following selection)

A day at our fraternity/sorority house

Why I joined/didn't join Alpha Beta Gamma

20

HERBERT L. BROWN

The Case For Fraternities

1 To prove how vicious college fraternities are, Mr. Sloan Wilson last week used as his prime example a fraternity initiation at Massachusetts Institute of Technology in which a pledge fell through the ice and was drowned in a pond.

2 I am sure that on sober second thought Mr. Wilson will agree that he has not proved fraternities "stupid," "witless," "juvenile," and "purposeless" (or any of the other angry adjectives he hurled at them), by his single example of tragedy. He should be well aware that several hundred thousand college students are prevented from falling into holes by fraternities—from falling into social awkwardness, failing grades, athletic inertia, and ignorance of group living.

3 I refuse to reply to Mr. Wilson in the style of his attack; rather I will answer his "arguments" with a defense of fraternities, which I will attempt to make more well-proportioned and level-headed than his broadside.

4 What would Mr. Wilson find if he would look for the truth about college fraternities? He would find, first of all, that there are 12,000 chapters of Greek-letter societies in the United States with a total membership of four million. If fraternities are "purposeless," why have 225,000 new members joined them in the past three years? If fraternities are "unnecessary," why have 381 new chapters been established in the same period? Would so many young Americans in so many places go into organizations that are "stupid, witless, and juvenile"?

5 If Mr. Wilson believes so, then his faith in the wisdom of the American people is pretty weak. Fraternity life is continuing to flourish

THE CASE *For* FRATERNITIES. From *The American Weekly*, October 21, 1956. Reprinted by permission of *The American Weekly* and of Herbert L. Brown (past National President of Phi Sigma Kappa, past Chairman of the National Interfraternity Conference).

because fraternities exist to answer genuine student and college needs, because fraternities help in attainment of worthy educational, social, and personal goals.

6 "On our campus," says Chancellor Ethan A. H. Shepley of Washington University (St. Louis), "fraternities are a very real asset. I frankly don't know what we would do without their influence and support. We are proud of them and the record they have made." The testimony of dozens of other college presidents—men like George Bowman of Kent State (Ohio), Harlan Hatcher of Michigan, and Milton Eisenhower of Johns Hopkins University—tells the same story: fraternities are needed.

7 The reason that the great good in fraternities is so clouded is that, unfortunately, only the freak prank makes the headline; only the tragic slip arouses righteous indignation. The many valuable things that American fraternities do for their members, their colleges and their communities—their many fine purposes and achievements—go unheralded because activities like working in a community chest drive, or teaching a student how to conduct himself socially, are hardly the stuff of news.

8 When a student is accidentally hurt in what is usually harmless fun, people are quick to cry out that fraternities should be driven from the land like the plague. But when a student's marks are raised by the help he receives from his fraternity brothers, when a community Red Cross receives blood from a chapter, when a college is saved from a housing problem by a group with Greek letters, too few people know about it.

9 Exactly what are the values of American fraternities—to the student, to the school, and to the college community—values that are so often lost behind scare headlines and distorted by attacks like Mr. Wilson's?

10 Fraternities make important contributions to the minds, characters and personalities of their members.

11 First, each fraternity has a tutoring system in which members proficient in certain studies help members who are less proficient. It is often the coaching of a fraternity brother that prevents a fraternity man from failing a course.

12 Mr. Wilson mocks a fraternity's "Boy Scout code of honor which makes their members fairly burst with pride," but one great source of fraternity pride is the achievement of high scholastic marks by its members. Fraternity brothers do not tutor one another simply to prevent failure in subjects. They exchange knowledge so that the students in their chapter can make the best marks on the campus.

13 Ask any fraternity man and he will tell you how often a "seminar" with his brothers the night before an exam raised his marks. If this is a "Boy Scout" code, then to be out of the "Boy Scouts" is to enjoy being a moron.

14 It is an undisputed fact that the social programs of fraternities give members poise and polish which would develop more slowly—and per-

haps not at all—if the students were to live alone. Fraternity parties, out-
ings, dances, and sports enable a student to shed his adolescent awkwardness and learn to move with confidence among members of his own and
the opposite sex. In addition to helping a man's grades, fraternities help
him feel at ease on a dance floor, on the baseball diamond, on a committee—or in any facet of group living.

15 Fraternities develop qualities of leadership in their members. They
inculcate in them standards of good conduct, good manners, good taste,
and good sportsmanship. Most important, fraternities teach members to
live together in harmony and understanding.

16 Mr. Wilson rejoices over the advantage a college student receives
when he does *not* join a fraternity.

17 Shortly after graduation, most of these students will be asked—with
no refusal permitted—to join a larger and less friendly fraternity called
the United States Army.

18 Who does Mr. Wilson think will be better prepared to cope with
the trials of group living found in military service—the "lone wolf" or
the fraternity man? The essence of America, as President Eisenhower has
so often said, is the team—both in peace and war.

19 And does Mr. Wilson believe that the "lone wolf" can learn the
principles of self-government in his single room? He can read about them
in history textbooks; but the fraternity man works with and studies these
principles as they are alive in the political organization of his chapter.

20 Critics like Mr. Wilson are silent about the financial aid that Greek-
letter societies constantly provide for students. Through the years, many
fraternities have built up foundations to enable needier members to
continue higher education. Without grants from these foundations many
boys would never get a college education.

21 How do fraternities help the colleges? First, and most important,
they do so by housing many students. Fraternities furnish high-quality
housing facilities which many colleges could never offer. If Mr. Wilson
considers this "juvenile" then we must assume he considers it "adult" for
college students to live in tents.

22 Lest Mr. Wilson think that the only activity of college fraternities
is sending students out to fall through icy ponds, here are others that
might interest him:

23 Fraternities throughout America donate blood, work with community chest drives, give children's Christmas parties, entertain orphans
and underprivileged children. They operate foreign student exchange
programs, sell Easter and Christmas seals, collect clothing for refugees.
They raise funds for the fight against polio, cerebral palsy, heart disease,
and cancer; assist in the CARE program; and in many other ways help
local, American, and world society.

24 Such activities are typical of fraternities, which Mr. Wilson considers "stupid and purposeless." He and other critics continue to shout, "Yes, but what about 'hell week' and discrimination?"

25 All right, what about them? The people making the most noise about an occasional "hell week" abuse do not seem to hear—or care—that fraternities themselves are eliminating archaic hazing practices. And no segment of American society has been more shocked or distressed over "hell week" tragedies than the college men and women of Greek-letter societies.

26 Fraternity members are the first to admit that outmoded hazing practices are a shortcoming in the fraternity system. In the past 10 years, "hell week" has become "help week" on most campuses. Instead of getting lost in the woods, students now spend this initiation period working on chores which improve their fraternity houses, their school, and their community.

27 Fraternities have been further condemned for being selective in choosing their members, but can you, Mr. Wilson, name a single social organization in this country that does not practice some type of selectivity in the choice of its members? But just to set the record straight, a few decades ago 44 of the 58 social fraternities in the National Interfraternity Conference at that time had restrictive membership clauses based on race, color, or national origin in their constitutions. Today, no more than a dozen of the 61 groups in the Conference have such clauses.

28 People are innate joiners, Mr. Wilson. If there were no fraternities at colleges, cliques of people with similar interests would, naturally, get together anyway.

29 In fact, consider what colleges would be *without* fraternities.

30 There would be fewer students (for there would be fewer scholarships), lower marks, overcrowded dormitories, and less effective social, athletic, and self-government programs for great numbers of students.

31 Fraternities—or groups like them (whether they are called "eating clubs" or "houses" or "societies")—will always exist at colleges because they answer a definite need. Dr. Milton Eisenhower—who has been president of three colleges and who was recently appointed by his brother Dwight to help make North, Central, and South America into one big fraternity—summed it up this way: "Fraternities and sororities are workshops in understanding and cooperation. They are anvils upon which the character of individuals may be fashioned for service beyond self."

Comment

The second speaker in a debate is largely limited in what he can say by what his opponent has already said. His success depends to a considerable extent on how well he answers his opponent's arguments. If he does not at least *try* to answer them he cannot develop his own argument without being legitimately accused of "changing the subject," "evading the issue," or "arguing beside the point." If this seems like an unfair handicap, as in a duel where one man makes choice of weapons, we may keep in mind that the second speaker has an advantage the first speaker does not have: the chance to say the last word.

It is clear from Brown's many references to Wilson that he regards his own article as a defense of fraternities against Wilson's attack, although Brown chooses to concentrate on the good things that can be said about fraternities, rather than to show that the bad things Wilson says are untrue or unfair. But *as* an answer, Brown's essay is in trouble with its very first sentence. For is it true that Wilson tries to prove college fraternities are vicious? Is it not rather true that Wilson's main point is the sarcastic one that fraternities, in spite of appearances, are *not* vicious? That they are not wolves in sheep's clothing, but sheep in wolves' clothing? Brown might have said (with considerable justice) that Wilson, whatever he pretends, *really* thinks fraternities vicious, and that he is only trying to be clever and cute in saying they are not. Brown might have made it clear to us that he, too, knows how to be sarcastic by using his opening sentence as straight-faced proof that he has not been taken in by Wilson's sarcastic pretenses. But this is not the way Brown's style and method of attack work. As a result, he gives the impression of beginning his counterattack by misunderstanding his opponent's main point. We are not just quibbling over words, for though we may be willing to understand Brown's position, it is still difficult not to feel that he has been awkward in making his position clear. We can also ask if it is true, as Brown says, that Wilson uses the M.I.T. student's death as his "prime example" in proving whatever he tries to prove about fraternities.

It is unfortunate that Brown distorts Wilson's main point in this way, for by so doing he shakes our confidence in him at the very beginning. The bad opening does not mean that everything Brown goes on to say in defense of fraternities is false or worthless; as a matter of fact, he succeeds in presenting the case *for* fraternities in full and in poking holes in several of Wilson's flippancies. But the fairness of his case is clouded by the *un*fairness of his first sentence. A player who fumbles in the first quarter might still go on to score the winning touchdown, but it is likely that the coach will bench him for the rest of the game. We are the coach here. We are unjust to Brown if we do not stay to listen to his side, but we cannot be altogether blamed if we do not.

Exercises

CONTENT

True or False? If you think the statement represents what the selection says or implies, mark it "True"; if you do not think so, mark it "False."

1. The fact that more than 200,000 young Americans have joined fraternities during the last three years proves that these organizations cannot be "purposeless" and "unnecessary," as Wilson calls them.

2. Fortunately for fraternities, their good deeds receive as much publicity as their occasional accidents.

3. According to the fraternity code of honor, no member is allowed to help a brother in his academic work.

4. Fraternity life prepares a young man for life in the Army.

5. A nonfraternity student who does not raise his exam grade is a moron.

6. The most important way in which fraternities help colleges is by providing scholarships for needy students.

7. Fraternities are justified in being discriminatory in their choice of new members, for all social organizations in this country practice such discrimination.

8. Fraternities satisfy a basic human urge for being part of a group.

9. Without fraternities students would get lower grades and have less satisfactory social and athletic programs.

10. President Dwight D. Eisenhower is in favor of fraternities because they further international friendship.

Questions for Discussion

1. Apply Brown's argument in Paragraph 4 to a defense of other institutions or activities in which a great number of people participate. How sound is the argument?

2. Paragraph 13 implies a *syllogism,* a set of three logically related statements. Two of them are called *premises,* from which the third, the *conclusion,* necessarily follows. For example, from the two statements "Oklahoma is in the United States" and "Oklahoma City is in Oklahoma," the conclusion "therefore Oklahoma City is in the United States" must logically follow. And not only is this the logical and necessary conclusion; it is the *only* logical and necessary conclusion. No other statement about Oklahoma City, however true it may be, follows from these two premises.

Brown's syllogism in Paragraph 13 has not been expressed in such clear-cut terms, but it can be stated in such terms. It goes like this:

Premise 1: "Boy Scouts" [that is, in this context, fraternity men who participate in fraternity seminars] often raise their exam marks.

Premise 2: Students who often raise their exam marks are not morons.

Conclusion: Therefore, students who are not Boy Scouts enjoy being morons.

If you are all for fraternities (and perhaps even if you are not) this may at first glance look like a clincher of an argument. But it is not. The conclusion does not follow from the premises. The conclusion that *does* follow is that Boy Scouts are not morons. No other conclusion is logically possible. If it were, one could prove all sorts of interesting things:

> Girls are human beings.
> Human beings are not animals.
> Therefore, boys are animals.

Or:

> I am a man.
> A man is not a lobster.
> Therefore, everybody is a lobster except me.

In other words, from the facts that x is y and y is not z it does not follow that all that is *not* x *is* z. My family lives in Goodtown, and nobody who lives in Goodtown has ever committed a crime. I could say that this proves that nobody in my family has ever committed a crime, and I would be right in saying that. But according to Brown, I ought to say that everybody outside my family *has* committed a crime, including the other people in Goodtown!

The faulty reasoning here, by the way, proves nothing one way or the other about the usefulness of fraternity seminars or the level of intelligence among nonfraternity men. They may indeed all be morons. But Brown's argument here has not proved that they are.

With reference to Wilson's essay, set up and discuss the implied syllogism in Paragraph 21 in Brown's essay: "If Mr. Wilson considers this [high quality housing facilities] 'juvenile' then we must assume he considers it 'adult' for college students to live in tents."

3. Quite aside from the soundness or unsoundness of the logic in the syllogism discussed above, is it true that "students who often raise their exam marks are not morons," as Brown implies in Paragraph 13? A psychologist's definition of "moron" is a feeble-minded person whose I.Q. lies somewhere between 50 and 70. Is that what "moron" means here? If not, what does it mean? Does the new definition make Brown's second premise above any more necessarily true? Explain.

4. Do you find any inconsistency in the fact that in Paragraph 27 Brown first excuses discrimination on the grounds that all social organizations discriminate, and then goes on to say that discriminatory clauses in fraternity constitutions are on their way out? Explain.

FORM AND STYLE

1. In Paragraph 3 Brown says he will "refuse to reply to Mr. Wilson in the style of his attack. . . ." Comment on the difference between the two articles in style of attack. Can you think of any way in which Brown's statement of intention could be used against him?

2. The "testimonial" is a device in propaganda by which you try to support your opinion by quoting prominent and popular people who agree with you. A common form of the testimonial is the ad or commercial where a movie or baseball star is seen enthusiastically using the product advertised. Point out examples of the testimonial in Brown's essay. Do these examples differ from those in advertising? If so, how?

3. Between Paragraphs 9 and 10 there occurs a major division in the organization of the essay. Explain.

4. In an argument to prove that the fraternity tutoring system makes "important contributions" to the student's mind, how valuable do you consider this statement (Paragraph 12): "They [the fraternity brothers] exchange knowledge so that the students in their chapter can make the best marks on the campus"? Would you say that Brown here seems to be putting secondary matters before primary ones? Explain your answer.

5. Look up the meanings of the adjective "prime" in your dictionary and determine which meanings apply and which do not apply to Brown's use of the word in Paragraph 1.

6. In Paragraphs 27 and 28 the writer's point of view has shifted from what it was in the earlier parts of the essay. Identify the shift. Can you explain it? Justify it?

7. In the second sentence in Paragraph 2, the word "holes" does not refer to actual holes; it is used in a figurative, not in a literal, sense. Why do you think Brown used the word in this way? Do you feel that a pun (a play on more than one meaning of a word) is appropriate in the context? Explain your answer.

8. Brown's essay also falls into four parts. The Introduction (I, Para. 1-8) makes three points. First (I, A, Para. 1-3), it criticizes Wilson for using a single unfortunate accident as grounds for condemning fraternities in general. Second (I, B, Para. 4-6), it asserts the purpose of and need for fraternities against Wilson's charge that they are "stupid, witless, juvenile, and purposeless." These assertions are supported by two facts: young Americans keep joining fraternities by the thousands every year (I, B, 1, Para. 4, 5), and college administrators approve of them (I, B, 2, Para. 6). Third (I, C, Para. 7, 8), the Introduction explains how Wilson came to exaggerate the significance of the M.I.T. student's death: we always hear more about the "tragic slips" in fraternity life than about its good sides, because fatal accidents make for better news copy than constructive but unsensational events.

Part II, Para. 9-24, is the main body of the essay. It deals with the value of fraternities to students (II, A, Para. 9, 10-20), to colleges (II, B, Para. 9, 21), and to college communities (II, C, Para. 9, 22-24). Their value to students comes under three categories: value to the mind (II, A, 1, Para. 11-13); value to character and personality (II, A, 2, Para. 14-19) by teaching the student manners (II, A, 2, a, Para. 14), leadership (II, A, 2, b, Para. 15-18), and self-government (II, A, 2, c, Para. 19); and value in providing financial aid to needy students (II, A, 3, Para. 20).

Part III, Para. 24-28, deals with two common targets for criticism of fraternities: "Hell week" (III, A, Para. 24-26) and discrimination (III, B, Para. 27, 28). Three points are made by way of defending fraternities against the accusation that they are discriminatory in choosing members. The first (III, B, 1, Para. 27) is that every other social organization practices discrimination of some kind, so why not fraternities? The second

(III, B, 2, Para. 27), that discriminatory practices are on their way out. The third (III, B, 3, Para. 28), that fraternities satisfy a basic human urge for congenial people to group together socially.

The Conclusion (IV, Para. 29-31) consists of two parts. One (IV, A, Para. 29, 30) asks the reader to consider what college life would be without fraternities and to realize that it would be less valuable in several respects. The other (IV, B, Para. 31) quotes a strong endorsement of fraternities by a prominent educator.

Below is Brown's essay in chart form. Try to find appropriate topics, as you did for Wilson's essay outline, above.

Outline	*Paragraph(s)*	*Topic*
I.	1-8	
A.	1-3	
B.	4-6	
1.	4-5	
2.	6	
C.	7-8	
II.	9-24	
A.	9-20	
1.	11-13	
2.	14-19	
a.	14	
b.	15-18	
c.	19	
3.	20	
B.	9, 21	
C.	9, 22-24	
III.	24-28	
A.	24-26	
B.	27-28	
1.	27	
2.	27	
3.	28	
IV.	29-31	
A.	29-30	
B.	31	

VOCABULARY

Which of the four words or phrases to the right seems to you to be *closest* in meaning to the word in heavy type to the left? Put a check mark after your choice.

hurled (2)   sneered . . . threw . . . used . . . shot . . .

inertia (2)   lack of skill . . . failure . . . laziness . . . inferiority complex . . .

attainment (5)   establishment . . . ambition . . . achievement . . . satisfaction . . .

prank (7)   accident . . . death . . . event . . . trick . . .

righteous (7)   correct . . . virtuous . . . unfair . . . moral . . .

unheralded (7)   ignored . . . unpublicized . . . without a herald . . . forgotten . . .

proficient (11)   skillful . . . professional . . . talented . . . experienced . . .

inculcate (15)   exemplify . . . inoculate . . . encourage . . . teach

donate (23)   give . . . collect . . . help with . . . send . . .

archaic (25)   vicious . . . dangerous . . . crazy . . . outmoded . . .

segment (25)   part . . . organization . . . element . . . class . . .

selective (27)   prejudiced . . . snobbish . . . discriminating . . . difficult . . .

clauses (27)   reasons . . . sentences . . . regulations . . . practices

innate (28)   born . . . original . . . definite . . . veteran . . .

anvils (31)   trials . . . evils . . . models . . . blocks . . .

THEME SUGGESTIONS

From hell week to help week
To cheat or to be unbrotherly, that was the question
A fraternity/sorority seminar
The judge's verdict in the debating contest between Wilson and Brown

2. The Types in Action

Vocation and Recreation

Nature and Science

Self and Society

Language and Learning

Vocation and Recreation

SANDBURG • BALDWIN • ANGELL • WHITE • WAUGH

ALLEN • DE VOTO

This section might, more simply, have been entitled "Man at Work and Play," but only at the loss of some relevant connotations. For these selections deal less with occupations than with *vocation,* a sense of calling, and less with leisure activities than with *recreation,* man's making himself over—or failing to make himself over—physically, mentally, spiritually, after the rigors of work.

Sandburg tells about an eleven-year-old boy's first job in a small-town real estate office before the turn of the century, and of his pride in being a wage earner. Baldwin shifts the scene—in space, though not so much in time—in his story of dedication and heroism in a sunken Japanese submarine before the First World War. Angell takes us into our contemporary world in contrasting two hardworking women: one a glamorous movie star, the other an obscure Indian social worker. White combines the fantastic and the familiar in a futuristic satire on the consequences of too much and too many spectator sports in the life of a pathetic little ordinary man. Waugh's description of his life as an amateur Rugby player implies, perhaps, a solution to the problem of preventing White's prophecy from coming true. Allen deals with a musical craze from the 1930's and proves incidentally that there is nothing new about such teen-age fads. And De Voto heaps scorn on the frantic intensity with which certain American travelers relax, suggesting—like Angell and White—some serious questioning of our system of values.

21

CARL SANDBURG

First Paydays

1   I was eleven when I had the first regular job that paid me cash. There had been odd jobs for earning money and there were Saturdays and after school hours when we took gunny sacks and went around streets, alleys, barns, and houses hunting in ditches and rubbish piles for rags, bones, scrap iron, and bottles, for which cash was paid us, my gunny sack one week bringing me eighteen cents. Now I was wearing long pants and every Friday was payday.

2   My employer was the real estate firm of Callender & Rodine, their office on the second floor of a building on Main midway between Kellogg and Prairie. Mr. Callender was a heavy man with a large blond mustache. His head was wide between the ears and in front of him, at his middle, he had a smooth, round "bay window," easy to carry. Mr. Rodine was the lean member and had a pink face with blue eyes. If a customer spoke Swedish and was a temperance man, it seemed Mr. Rodine handled him. If he was Irish and liked his whisky or a German who liked beer, it seemed Mr. Callender took care of him. They had their signals and worked together something like that when a man wanted to buy or sell a house, a lot, or a farm.

3   Their office was large and I would guess it was ten paces from the west wall where Mr. Callender had his desk to the east wall where Mr. Rodine had his big roll-top desk with pigeonholes to stick papers in and try afterward to remember into which pigeonhole this or that paper had been stuck. It was Mr. Callender who told me about pigeonholes in a desk and what they are for. It came into my head, but I didn't mention it to Mr. Callender, that some of the pigeonholes were so thin you couldn't find a pigeon so thin that it could fly into one of those holes. Nor did I mention to Mr. Callender that it would be fun to bring in five or six pigeons and put them in the pigeonholes of the two desks so that when Mr. Callender and Mr. Rodine rolled back the tops of their desks the first thing in the morning, the office would be full of pigeons and wings flapping and fluttering. This idea, this scheme, I liked to roll around in my head and I told other boys about it, but no grownups. One of the boys said, "If you did that, they would prosecute you." So we made the boy tell us what it is to be prosecuted and for several weeks we saluted him, "Hello, Prosecutor" and "Here's Little Prosecutor again."

4   Mr. Callender and Mr. Rodine treated me nice and fair. The longest talk I had with either of them was when Mr. Callender told me what was expected of me, what my work was to be and how I should do it. After that, for month after month, about the only talk between us was on Friday morning when Mr. Callender handed me my pay, saying, "Here you are," and I said, "Thanks," and skipped.

5   They gave me a key to the office and I unlocked the door about a quarter to eight each morning, Monday through Friday. I took a broom made of broomcorn grown near Galesburg and manufactured at Mr. Boyer's broom factory at the northwest corner of Kellogg and Berrien. I swept out the office. I came to know every floorboard of that office, the cracks and corners where I had to dig in and push to bring out the dust. I swept the office dust out into the hall. I swept it along the hall six or eight feet to the top of the wide stairway leading down to the street. Reaching the bottom of the stairs I swept the accumulations of my earnest and busy broom out onto the sidewalk of Main Street and across the sidewalk. With two or three grand final strokes of my broom I threw a half-bushel of dust and paper and string and cigar butts and chewing-tobacco cuds out on the cobblestones to join other sweepings and layers of horse droppings. If a strong east wind was blowing, it would be no time until my sweepings had been scattered all along Main Street.

6   I would go up the stairs to the office, stand the broom in a corner, and then pick up the wide, round, flat brass spittoon that stood at Mr. Callender's roll-top desk. If the day before had been a busy day with plenty of callers, the spittoon might be filled to capacity with fluid content in which floated cigar butts and tobacco cuds. I carried this container out in the hall to a cubbyhole with a faucet and running cold water. I dumped, washed, rinsed, and rinsed again and took the honorable and serviceable spittoon back to its place at Mr. Callender's desk. Then I did the same cleaning on Mr. Rodine's spittoon. About once in six or eight weeks I polished the spittoons till they were bright and shining.

7   This morning service of mine for Callender & Rodine took less than a half-hour. Sometimes I could whisk through all the motions in fifteen or twenty minutes. If at the time a man had come to me and said he was organizing a Spittoon Cleaners' Union, I would probably have joined, if only to meet with other spittoon cleaners to see what they looked like and to talk with them about our work and our wages, fellow craftsmen enjoying fellowship. At no time did I make a complaint to Mr. Callender or Mr. Rodine. I was pleased and thankful when on Friday morning Mr. Callender would bring his right hand out of a pocket and with a look on his face as though he had almost forgotten it, he would hand me a coin with those three words, "Here you are." And I would take the coin in my hand, say, "Thanks," skip down the stairway holding the money, and on the Main Street sidewalk open my hand to see what it held and there it was, twenty-five cents of United States money, a silver quarter of a dollar.

Exercises

CONTENT

True or False? If you think the statement represents what the selection says or implies, mark it "True"; if you do not think so, mark it "False."

1. The boy's family was poor.
2. None of the other boys worked.
3. The work disgusted him.
4. Callender and Rodine were lawyers.
5. Rodine spoke Swedish.
6. Callender was often drunk.
7. The boy worked from 8 till 12 noon every weekday.
8. He did not sweep very carefully.
9. He refused to help organize a Spittoon Cleaners' Union.
10. A silver quarter in those days was the equivalent of almost five dollars today.

Questions for Discussion

1. What is the boy's attitude to his job with Callender & Rodine? Do you feel that the nature of the work and the pay he received for it justify the attitude?

2. Most of us would feel that young Sandburg was badly underpaid for the work he did for Callender & Rodine. Which paragraph specifically contributes to this impression?

3. Which of these phrases do you think comes closest to describing Sandburg's intentions with the essay: (a) to encourage young boys to get paying work; (b) to describe his feelings about his first job; (c) to shock the reader into realizing the awful conditions of child labor in the 19th century; (d) to illustrate how the value of money has gone down since those days.

FORM AND STYLE

1. Paragraphs 2 and 3 are descriptive paragraphs. What is the subject of description in each?

2. In Paragraph 4 Sandburg says that Callender and Rodine "treated me nice and fair." In Paragraph 7 he once again expresses his appreciation and gratitude. This attitude seems more significant, makes more of an impact upon the reader, in the latter than in the former paragraph. Why?

3. A "dead" metaphor is a word or expression originally used to point to a similarity between two otherwise dissimilar objects but now, through long and frequent usage, no longer suggestive of such comparison. For example, we no longer think of an actual cap, something to cover our head with, when we speak of the "cap" for a tube of toothpaste, and we don't visualize two men walking when we hear that somebody is "following in his father's footsteps." Sometimes, however, in certain contexts or when we are not familiar with the purely metaphorical meaning of the word or expression, we interpret the metaphor literally, bring it back to life. This may be confusing, as when an electrician's mention of "juice" is taken to refer to a breakfast fruit drink. Explain how a "dead" metaphor amusingly and confusingly comes "alive" in Paragraph 3.

4. What purpose is served by all the proper names in "I took a broom made of broomcorn grown near Galesburg and manufactured at Mr. Boyer's broom factory at the northwest corner of Kellogg and Berrien" (Paragraph 5)?

5. What contribution to the theme of the essay is made by the heavy emphasis on the weekly pay at the end?

VOCABULARY

Which of the four words or phrases to the right seems to you to be *closest* in meaning to the word in heavy type to the left? Put a check mark after your choice.

lean (2)   junior . . . sullen . . . thin . . . small . . .

temperance (2)   mild-tempered . . . irritable . . . moderate in the use of alcohol . . . teetotaler . . .

paces (3)   yards . . . old-fashioned units of measuring distance . . . steps . . . meters . . .

scheme (3)   crime . . . plan . . . vision . . . thought . . .

prosecute (3)   bring suit against . . . punish . . . fire . . . get mad at . . .

saluted (3)   kidded . . . greeted . . . yelled at . . . tormented . . .

capacity (6)   overflow . . . brim . . . repulsiveness . . . extent of space . . .

fluid (6)   dirty . . . liquid . . . smelly . . . horrid . . .

THEME SUGGESTIONS

My first job
My first boss
Should school children take paying jobs?
It's all in the way you feel about it

22

HANSON W. BALDWIN

Number Six

1   It was the year 1910 when Tatsuta Sakuma died with his men in the foul air of the sunken submarine *Number 6.* Sakuma was already, at thirty-one, a veteran of danger. He had participated in the Russo-Japanese War five years before; as a pioneer in the development of submarines he had often been close to death.

2   His command, the *Number 6,* had been in service four years. Launched September 28, 1905, at Kawasaki Shipyards, Kobe, and completed at the submarine base at Kure six months later, she was one of the first, the most awkward, and the strangest of Japanese submarines; but she had never been in serious trouble, and her crew—struggling against difficulty, discouragement, and constant mechanical defects—had kept her running. She was the smallest of Japan's nine submarines: seventy-three feet long, beam seven feet, fifty-seven tons displacement, a great, ungainly bathtub of a "boat," a she-devil for crankiness. She was always having propeller trouble; she had only two feet freeboard and was no good in the open sea: even when running on the surface the smallest wave washed clean over her so her crew must always be imprisoned in the steel shell. During maneuvers she was usually left behind; she was too fickle and untrustworthy for offshore work except in a smooth and glassy summer ocean.

3   *Number 6,* like other contemporary Japanese submarines, was gasoline-powered for surface running, with some rather primitive electric motors for submerged propulsion. But the electric motors were slow and unsatisfactory; they could be used only a short time before the batteries were discharged, and so, sticking above the surface like a sore thumb, just aft of the crude conning tower and the periscope, was a great intake or ventilating pipe, to provide air for the gasoline engines both when the boat was running partially submerged, and during rough weather on the surface. The pipe could be closed by a sluice valve when its intake was completely below the surface, and the electric motors were being used.

4   The valve was open that spring day in 1910, when the cherry trees blossomed on the Japanese islands and Lieutenant Sakuma took his ship to her fate. *Number 6* had been ordered to join in the maneuvers on April 11, and under tow of the *Rekizan Maru,* her mother ship, she left port for the maneuver area in Hiroshima Bay. The exercises—as far as little *Number 6* was concerned—were to determine how long the sub-

NUMBER SIX. From *Sea Fights and Shipwrecks* by Hanson W. Baldwin. Copyright, 1938, by Hanson W. Baldwin. Copyright ©, 1955, by Hanson W. Baldwin. Used by permission of the publishers, Hanover House (Doubleday).

marine could remain completely submerged. On April 12 and 13 she operated successfully, though never much more than a hundred feet away from the *Rekizan Maru*. On the fourteenth she stayed under water for two and a half hours, a feat for those days; and on the fifteenth she began her fatal voyage.

5 She cast off her lines to the mother ship and got under way—slowly and awkwardly—at about nine-thirty in the morning. The sun was shining on the sea. Sakuma was in the conning tower; Engineer Lieutenant Harayama was in the engine room; Sublieutenant Hasegawa bent above gauges; the eleven members of the crew were at their posts by valve wheels or engines. Shortly before ten Sakuma gave the order to submerge. Slowly the conning tower, air-intake pipe, the periscope disappeared beneath the surface. . . .

6 Aboard the *Rekizan Maru* it was logged as another routine test.

7 *Number 6* started down, as she had submerged so often before, with the water gurgling into the ballast tank and the green sea swirling and frothing up above the thick glass of the conning tower ports. She was cranky, but with a stern master she would obey. Then suddenly there came a lurch—unexplainable, unexplained, a last awkwardness of the "boat"—and the thing was done. She had gone too deep.

8 Water poured in through the air intake. Sakuma's crisp voice calmly uttered orders. A sailor tried to close the air-intake sluice valve, but the chain slipped off the sprocket wheel; the water gushed in. Frantically he shut the valve with his bare hands, but it was too late. Old *Number 6* was heavy with the water of the sea.

9 She had always had a tendency to nose down on submerging, so her bow had been kept up, her stern down. The flooding water, rushing in through the intake aft, added to their stern inclination; and she started down for the bottom like a rotted log, at an angle of twenty-five degrees.

10 The electric switchboard was close to the opening of the ventilating tube; and the salt water gushed over the copper contacts. There were flaring blue sparks and hissing arcs of flame, the stench of a short-circuited burning cable, and then the lights went out. To die in darkness. . . .

11 Sakuma's voice still gave sharp, precise commands; each of the fourteen stood to his post.

12 The power was gone, the water was reaching toward the batteries —the scourge of the submarine: chlorine!

13 Sakuma's quiet, calm voice continued.

14 The hand pump! The hand pump was their chance for life. Blow out the main ballast tank, pump out the sea, lighten ship to compensate for that flood water in the hull; shoot her to the surface! The pump began to wheeze and suck and sigh in the darkness as sailors found its handle and fumbled with the valve wheels of its manifold in that black hulk beneath the sea.

15 But down she went—down. Water ruffled past the thick glass peep-holes in the conning tower; the needle of the depth gauge quivered slowly around the dial—20 feet—30—40—50. . . .

16 She struck stern first in the mud of Hiroshima Bay, and the needle of the gauge settled at 52. She was planted solidly at a thirteen-degree tilt: lifeless, inert, solid. Already there was that fearful, faint tickling in the throat; already the men's nostrils seemed to flare wider to suck for air. The pump still heaved and sighed.

17 There was no need now for further orders. The men took their appointed turns at the hand pump, bending and straightening there in the dark, with the insulation of the burning cable fusing noxiously in the blackness, and the sweet stench of the chlorine tickling their tiny nostril hairs.

18 They worked, each in his own appointed turn, and then they felt their way back to their posts, forward by the torpedo, aft by the engines, amidships by the controls. Sakuma had come down out of the conning tower to see what could be done. There was not much, and they were doing it there in the dark; but still—with the slow pump wheezing and the tide of their lives ebbing on swift minutes—the needle of the depth gauge did not flicker. It pointed motionless to the measure of their fate, the boundaries of their grave—fifty-two feet. Sakuma left Sublieutenant Hasegawa in charge at the pump and returned, stumbling in the black-ness, to the conning tower. Here the dim gray-green light, filtered through the water, filtered through the glass, shed a kind of sepulchral twilight over gauges and valve wheels and the cold, painted steel. Tatsuta Sa-kuma, conscious of his duty, sat down to report to his Emperor and to Japan.

19 He started to write—vertical columns from right to left, the well-remembered characters he had learned so long ago:

20 "I am sorry—" (first an apology from one so humble, one who had failed). "I am sorry that my carelessness sank the Emperor's submarine and killed the Emperor's sailors."

21 (He knew then that there was no hope. The unmoving needle pointed with awful finality to 52.)

22 "But every man of the crew has bravely done his duty until death."

23 (They still were doing it, and death not far, still holding death and fear at arm's length from their inner consciousness. The pump still sucked and wheezed, and the gasping lungs of fourteen men heaved now like bellows in the dark.)

24 "We are willing to die for our country, but I regret one point, that our deaths might discourage the people of the nation."

25 (He could not know it, but their names were to live far more in death than they would have done in life.)

26 "My sincere hope, gentlemen, is that this accident will give you material to study diligently the problems of submarine design and construction, and thus insure future submarine development. If this be done, we die without regret."

27 Sakuma paused—still the slow sucking of the pump, and in his throat the thinning air. Hurry; his pencil now must race to scribble out this last message, to tell the world how they had died, so that others might live.

28 "When we started on the gasoline-submarine exercise the ship went too deep, so we tried to close the sluice pipe valve. But the chain gave way, and before we could close the valve by hand, water flooded in, the stern filled; we tilted to 25 degrees and sank."

29 Recapitulation of disaster; these things he wrote seemed centuries past, yet they had happened so brief a time ago. Each breath now was a heavy period in time; each character he formed, each phrase he wrote, an eternity of effort. But quickly: the world must know.

30 "Stern inclination is 13 degrees. Switchboard wet, lights gone. Telegraph cable burned. Bad fumes came out, began to be hard to breathe. Sank on April 14, about 10 A.M.

31 He was fumbling now; the date was wrong. His mind was hazy, confused with images of the past, filled too with the insistence of little details that must be set down while he still could write.

32 "Breathing bad fumes we tried to drain the water with hand pumps. When the sinking began we immediately commenced to drain the main ballast tank. The lights are out; I cannot see the gauge, but I think we have blown the main ballast tank empty."

33 But still the needle stood inflexible at 52; still *Number 6* stuck in the mud of Hiroshima Bay, inert and unmoving, like the skeleton of a ship long sunk. The ballast tank was empty—empty, what could yet be done? The pump wheezed futilely. . . . Sakuma laid down his pencil, picked it up again.

34 "Cannot use current at all. Battery fluid is slightly flooded. No more sea water is coming in. No more chlorine gas is being produced. About 500 pounds of air left. Only thing we depend on is hand pumps. (The above note I wrote in the control room 11:45.)"

35 Five hundred pounds of air in the air tanks, but it was hissing swiftly out in the dark to keep fourteen pairs of lungs moving and fourteen hearts throbbing. The main ballast tank was clear; what else could be done to lighten her? The gasoline! Sakuma gave orders to pump out the gasoline. Valves were opened and closed in the darkness; the pump soughed to a stop briefly, and then sucked again, this time at the gasoline. Sakuma once more began to write.

36 "The flooding water wet our clothes and we are cold. . . . I think that a submarine's crew should always be calm and pay strict attention, and at the same time they must be brave. Otherwise we cannot hope for progress."

37 Progress, progress . . . they must not die in vain.

38 "Overstrict attention sometimes causes fear."

39 No fear was in Sakuma's soul, and those others in the dark below gave no sign.

40 "But I told them not to be afraid."

41 The code of the Samurai was triumphant still.

42 "People may laugh at this philosophy after this failure, but I am confident that my words are right."

43 In the darkness the pump still sucked at the gasoline.

44 "The depth gauge in the control room shows 52 feet. Efforts to drain continued until twelve o'clock, but no movement was made. Depth of the location around here is 58, so I think 52 is the right figure."

45 It was twelve o'clock now; and what would they be thinking on the surface, on the *Rekizan Maru,* and on the shore where the spring blossoms had come? Twelve o'clock; the air was fouler; hurry, hurry.

46 "The crew of a submarine should be a carefully selected crew, for you may have difficulties such as this. Fortunately my crew have done their duty to the best of their ability, and I am fully satisfied."

47 Obituary enough for Hasegawa and Harayama, for Chief Petty Officer Kadota, for Seaman Endo and those gasping in the black, dead hull. They would want no higher praise than this.

48 "I always expected death whenever I left home."

49 It was close upon him now—his lungs were like leather, his mouth open wide.

50 "Therefore my will is already at Karasaki. (This, of course, refers only to my private affairs, and it is not necessary to mention it. Messrs. Taguchi and Asami, please hand my will to my humble father.)"

51 In the blackness there is a sudden sharp crack aft of the main ballast tank and forward of the engines, and *Number 6* fills with the fumes of gasoline. They could not read the gauges in the darkness; they could not tell the pressure on the line; it had broken, and now more deadly fumes fill the fetid air. The pump stops wheezing; its work is done. Hasegawa and Kadota feel their way to the break in the pipe line, fumble futilely about the burst metal. The others stand stolid at their posts, Petty Officer Yokoyama in the bow by his torpedo; Harayama and Endo near him, not far from the pump; Warrant Mechanician Suzuki far aft, in the stern near the electric motor. This was the end; they all knew it. Sakuma picked up his pencil again, and traced wavering characters in the growing dark.

52 "Reverently I write to the Emperor; please do not let the bereaved families of my crew suffer. . . ."

53 It was hard to write; somehow his hand was heavy; the pencil dragged across the paper; his eyes blurred, his throat burned; he could feel the bulging veins in his neck and temples.

54 "Do not let them suffer. This is the only thought in my mind now.

My regards to the following: Minister Saito—Vice-Admiral Shimamura—
Vice-Admiral Fujii—Rear Admiral Nawa—Rear Admiral Yamashita—Rear
Admiral Narita (air pressure so high that my ear drums feel they are
breaking).”

55 Blood beating in his ears, congested in his brain, white specks
leaping in the air before his eyes; hold on—hold . . . The pencil has-
tened, scribbling the names.

56 “Capt. Oguri—Captain Ide—Commander Junichi Matsumura—Lieu-
tenant-Commander (Kike) Matsumura (my brother)—Captain Funakoshi
—Professor Kotaro Narita—Professor Koinji Ikuta.”

57 The list was almost done. “12:30 very hard to breathe, gasping—”

58 This then was death, this wracking gasp and flailing heart, this
skin so cold and clammy, smeared with sweat; this body crying for
air . . .

59 “I thought to blow out the gasoline, but I am befuddled by the
fumes. Capt. Nakano . . .”

60 The characters grew broad and sprawling; the pencil faltered.
Below was silence; long since the pump had stopped. The men stood by
their posts in the loneliness of death. In the conning tower the green filtered light shone faintly upon Sakuma’s barely moving hand. There was
no sound from the world above down here, no temple bells, no sound at
all save the gentle play of the water against the peep-hole glass—and the
roaring in his ears.

61 “It is now 12:40. . . .”

62 Within, the needle pointing to 52; without, the fluted ripples weaving patterns on the dead steel hulk of *Number 6*, mud-bound, water-
logged, drowned, at the bottom of Hiroshima Bay.

63 The *Rekizan Maru* was not concerned until eleven o’clock, an hour
after *Number 6* had disappeared beneath the surface of the bay. Then
the search began—the search that did not end until the sunken submarine
was found next day, April 16, at 3:38 P.M. She was raised less than five
hours later, but they could not open the conning-tower hatch; she was
half towed, half carried, to a shallow inlet not far away. At 10 A.M. on
the seventeenth, two days to the hour after her fatal plunge, she was
opened; the water was pumped out of her; scavenging air was pumped
in. It rushed in freshly, the pure spring air; but long too late to help those
gasping lungs.

64 Commander Yoshikawa and First Lieutenant Nakajo went in together. All others were kept out; these first must ascertain how Sakuma
and his men had died; at all costs the honor of the Empire must be saved.
But there was no need to fear; they found the bodies calm and peaceful
in their death—no signs of panic or disorder, each at his post save Lieutenant Hasegawa and Kadota, who had died by the break in the gasoline
pipe they had tried to mend.

65 The honor of the Japanese Navy was proved.

66 They found the notes Sakuma had written; they have become part of the heritage of the old Japan. They brought the bodies to Kure aboard the *Toyohashi,* and there at the torpedo station the families wept proudly for their dead. The Grand Chamberlain of the Emperor Matsuhito came to Kure to pay his tribute; and at Kure on the twentieth, twenty thousand people, breathing the fragrance of spring flowers, hearing the tolling of the bells, mourned at the funeral.

67 It was the end—and a beginning. The nation gave 57,000 yen: 35,000 for the families of the victims, 22,000 for a memorial at the Kure naval station. And years later *Number 6* was lifted out of water and placed on land at the submarine school, in commemoration of one of the proud episodes of Japan's navy.

Exercises

CONTENT

True or False? If you think the statement represents what the selection says or implies, mark it "True"; if you do not think so, mark it "False."

1. The Russo-Japanese War took place in 1895.
2. In 1910 Japan had already more than a hundred submarines.
3. The ventilating pipe was needed for the crew's air supply.
4. If the pump had worked, *Number 6* would not have sunk.
5. The men died of chlorine gas poisoning.
6. The men died from drowning.
7. Sakuma early realized there was no hope, but his crew didn't.
8. Sakuma wrote his report mainly to explain the cause of the disaster to his superiors in the navy.
9. *Number 6* was raised just barely too late to save the men.
10. As far as the Japanese navy was concerned, Sakuma and his men had not died in vain.

Questions for Discussion

1. What does Paragraph 3 contribute to the story, beyond continuing the description of the submarine?

2. A pacifist is a person who is against war for any purpose. If you were a pacifist, which of the following reactions to *Number Six* do you think you would most likely have? If you *are* a pacifist, which reaction *do* you have? Explain your answer.

    (a) A silly and pointless story. The deaths serve no purpose.

    (b) A harmful story, since it glorifies the kind of bravery and loy-alty that often are responsible for war.

(c) He who lives by the sword shall die by the sword.

(d) The disaster was, of course, indirectly caused by war and war preparations. But Baldwin's story is not about war but about the death of brave men. I don't see anything objectionable in it.

(e) Sakuma and his men died for a bad purpose, but I respect their manner of dying. The story is a useful illustration of the sad truth that men can act admirably for wrong causes.

FORM AND STYLE

1. In which paragraphs does the main action begin and end? How would you describe the function of the parts of the story that precede and follow the main action?

2. Why are there so many references to the blossoming cherry trees, to sunshine, and to fresh spring air?

3. Why are there so many short paragraphs?

4. Explain the use of parentheses in Paragraphs 20-25.

5. There were no survivors. How can Baldwin know Sakuma's thoughts and feelings?

6. Find passages where Baldwin can have had no factual evidence for what he writes—where, in other words, he leaves off reporting and begins to write fiction? Can such passages be justified? If so, how?

VOCABULARY

Which of the four words or phrases to the right seems to you to be *closest* in meaning to the word in heavy type to the left? Put a check mark after your choice.

crankiness (2)   difficulty . . . orneriness . . . ugliness . . . mechanical defects . . .

fickle (2)   unreliable . . . weak . . . dangerous . . . tricky . . .

propulsion (3)   operation . . . forward movement . . . power . . . action of propeller . . .

inclination (9)   slantedness . . . tendency . . . quality of being down . . . angle . . .

arcs (10)   sparks . . . spots . . . bursts . . . curves . . .

scourge (12)   doom . . . any cause of serious trouble . . . heart . . . whip . . .

compensate (14)   get rid of . . . outweigh . . . make up for . . . substitute . . .

fusing (17)   melting . . . burning like a fuse . . . mixing . . . consuming . . .

noxiously (17)   poisonously . . . noisily . . . steadily . . . hurtfully

sepulchral *(18)*   greenish . . . as in a grave . . . eerie . . . dim . . .

apology *(20)*   confession . . . politeness . . . excuse . . . justification . . .

diligently *(26)*   eagerly . . . carefully . . . expertly . . . directly . . .

recapitulation *(29)*   review . . . repetition . . . surrender . . . new emphasis . . .

inflexible *(33)*   still . . . unbendable . . . stuck . . . without wavering . . .

code *(41)*   secret language . . . honor . . . system of moral rules . . . strength . . .

samurai *(41)*   Japanese naval academy . . . Sakuma's family name . . . military class of old Japan . . . Japanese sailors . . .

obituary *(47)*   gravestone . . . praise . . . epitaph . . . notice of death . . .

reverently *(52)*   humbly . . . full of veneration . . . finally . . . pleadingly . . .

ascertain *(64)*   make certain . . . make an official report . . . see . . . state . . .

fragrance *(66)*   loveliness . . . perfume . . . pollen . . . blossoms . . .

episodes *(67)*   heroic achievements . . . tragedies . . . stories . . . incidents . . .

THEME SUGGESTIONS

From the first sentence, we know the outcome of the story. Write a brief critical discussion of whether the story would have been better, worse, or simply different, if the reader were kept in suspense as to the fate of Sakuma and his men.

Suppose *Number Six* had appeared in print in the U.S. on December 8, 1941? Describe, analyze, and evaluate possible reactions.

The death of a hero

Confessions of a claustrophobic

Sakuma—hero or "hero"?

23

ROGER ANGELL

Two Women

1

1 The greatest Italian discovery since spaghetti is a 26-year-old, fawn-eyed, heavy-chested movie actress named Gina Lollobrigida. Although a good three quarters of the many millions of Europeans and Americans who have seen this extraordinarily beautiful girl in films cannot spell or even pronounce her name, this has proved no handicap: in any language, Gina Lollobrigida is currently pronounced "Wow!" Today, after a mere five years and 21 movies, Gina Lollobrigida is the undisputed queen of the booming Italian film industry, receives $100,000 per picture, and is the hottest item in show business east and west of Marilyn Monroe. Nor is this all. Most experts now believe that her supersonic-speed rise to the ionosphere of feminine stardom is sure to continue until Gina takes her place at a level previously occupied only by a few celestial bodies like Theda Bara and Jean Harlow. Who is this phenomenon, this new goddess?

2 Gina's rise to fame has all the flat, familiar overtones of a B picture: the daughter of a poor manufacturer, she was "discovered" on the street by a director, and was an extra and a stand-in and a beauty contestant before instantly making good in her first big part. Today, although Gina is probably more fascinated with her own success than anyone else, she is not naïve about it. She knows she was lucky: her truly incredible physical attributes came before the cameras at the very instant when the new Italian film industry badly needed new stars. She considers these attributes and their effect on men rather as a huge joke she plays on the world. She tries to rise above them by her truly devoted hard work. As a result, she is now known in the business as a real pro, a smart girl who is trying, with some success, to become an actress as well as just a statue, however breathtaking, of the Female Incarnate.

3 But goddesses have a hard time on earth—and little time for private, human affairs. Gina's husband, Dr. Mirko Skofic, has given up his physician's practice to help her with contracts, publicity, scripts, fan mail, the color of her hair for a new film. They have no children (the studios won't hear of it); little leisure (Gina works a 14-hour day, reads scripts and her clippings in the evening); few friends (Gina is surrounded always

Two Women. From "World of Women" by Roger Angell, from *Holiday Magazine* (The Curtis Publishing Company), February, 1955. Reprinted by permission of the author.

by cameramen, make-up men, directors, publicity men, dress designers and fans); no privacy (Gina owns a flame-red Lancia, as a star should); few pastimes (Gina recently spent all of three rare free days making a catalogue of her huge wardrobe); no time, until their recent trip to the U.S.A. and England, even to enjoy their money (they live in a small Rome apartment, have seen little of their big new country house).

4 To an outsider, it appears that somewhere along the line Gina and Mirko have lost themselves, have become mere slaves and acolytes to Gina the Goddess. Gina's beauty and work have made her independent and famous, but she cannot for a moment be independent of that fame. Here is a lovely woman who works terribly hard at an odd, curiously sad way of living—if living is the right word.

2

5 The temptation to turn one's back on ugliness is very great. For the well-to-do, particularly the well-to-do woman, it is more than a temptation: it is the custom. And in most countries where ugliness—poverty, ignorance, superstition, ignominy—is at its worst, the custom is strongest. It takes courage and intelligence and firm conviction for one of these rich women to involve herself with the realities of her time and place. In no country has the division between the many poor and the few rich been greater than in India; in no other country have poor women been more overworked and rich women more protected and isolated. And yet in India today an astonishing thing is happening: well-born, well-educated women in considerable numbers have suddenly broken away from their ancient position of luxurious serfdom. They are figuring prominently in economic and political life. They are bringing ideas of education and even of individualism to their poorer countrywomen. Qamar Khalil Ahmed, a 27-year-old Moslem social worker, is one of these.

6 Qamar is Labor Welfare Officer for the big India United Mills, Ltd., in Bombay. Here, doing a tough job never before held by a woman, she has already made herself both respected and beloved. Serious and serene in a white sari, she walks through the fetid, heavy air of a great room which roars with the clatter of looms and machines. As she passes, dark faces look up and smile, women wave to her from their spindles, men stop her to tell her some problem. In four years at her 9-hour-a-day, 7-day-a-week job, Qamar has made herself personally known to all 7000 mill workers. The range of her activities is phenomenal. She runs literacy classes (hugely attended) for the workers, and nursery classes for their children. She investigates and improves (if possible) both their working conditions and their living conditions. She has introduced a cheap canteen, in order to add to their wretched diets. She lectures and pleads with workers on everything from hygiene and safety to family planning to the need for insurance. She hears and acts on complaints, wage disputes, personnel problems. She takes a sick worker or his child to an over-crowded hospital and even gives bribes to get him admitted.

7   At the end of this terrible day, Qamar drives home to the austere, 3-room Bombay flat she shares with her younger sister, Akhter, who is a social worker in a hospital. These girls are daughters of one of the best families of Central Asia. Their father was a high government minister, their mother a rich Persian of high birth. It was their mother, oddly enough, who urged the girls to break away, to find jobs for themselves. Although she had never worked, she saw the changing of her world and told the girls, after the death of their father, to find careers. Qamar became a Red Cross officer and later, during the bloody Partition fighting, ran a refugee camp for Hindus, where she was often in great danger because of her Moslem faith.

8   Although they are very close, Qamar and Akhter are very different in personality. Akhter is moody, restless, stricken with moments of violent energy. Sometimes, tired out from her work, she bursts out at Qamar and at their work. "We are overplaying our parts, I tell you!" she shouts. But Qamar is always calm, serious, sure of herself—as only a young girl with a mission can be sure. To an outsider, she explains: "Our social revolution is now and I must feel a part of it. I don't find my work easy. There have been many disappointments and hardships. Fighting tradition, the tradition against women, has been the hardest. But this work I must do."

9   Qamar is clearly idealistic. She is intelligent and well-read, and has opinions on every subject. Her interests range unchecked: from movies to dancing to collecting saris to studying comparative religion. Her great ambition is to open an orphanage in Bombay. And Qamar is also young and has a very normal, young interest in marriage and in men. Probably she could have been married long ago, but there is a problem—the old (new in India) problem of career and husband. "My brothers disapprove of my work," she says, "but they cannot touch me. But if I marry some day, my husband would probably disapprove, too, and want me to give up my beloved career."

10   Visiting this intense, eager, dedicated girl; watching her climb to the top floor of a filthy tenement to see a sick child; listening to her patiently negotiating with a shouting mill foreman; seeing her throw herself down at home, utterly exhausted after her soul-wringing day, you are apt to feel suddenly sorry for her and for her admirable, youthful devotion and her hard, self-chosen path. But Qamar is perceptive and she sees this look in your face. "Listen," she says, laughing and patting her dog, "I am really so fortunate. On my job I can help my countrymen where they most need help. For myself, it is only today that women of India can hold responsible positions. Five years ago, my job would have been considered unlikely; ten years ago, impossible; fifty years ago, a dream. Truly, I am lucky. Think of me that way."

Exercises

CONTENT

True or False? If you think the statement represents what the selection says or implies, mark it "True"; if you do not think so, mark it "False."

1. Gina Lollobrigida in 1955 was even better known in America than Marilyn Monroe.
2. Theda Bara and Jean Harlow were famous film stars of the past.
3. Gina was discovered on the street by a director.
4. Gina has twin girls from her first marriage.
5. Gina is not satisfied with just being a goddess of sex.
6. Only a very few well-born Indian women are active in their country's political and economic life.
7. Qamar Khalil Ahmed's work involves both teaching and nursing.
8. Although devoted to her career as social worker, Qamar thinks she may some day get married.
9. Qamar's high-born Persian mother urged her to find a career.
10. Qamar considers herself a fighter for progress in India's social revolution.

Questions for Discussion

1. In Paragraph 4 Angell calls Gina a slave of her career. Qamar apparently works just as hard at her crueler job and for far fewer material rewards. Can you explain why Angell does not call *her* a slave?
2. Angell clearly implies that he finds Qamar's life the more successful of the two. On what system of values does he seem to base his judgment? What evidence is there that he tries to be fair to Gina? Do you agree with him? Give reasons why or why not. Be sure to think through your answer. Do not just give the stock response you think you are "supposed to" give: that hard work is better than glamorous luxury, unselfishness than selfishness, things of the spirit than material things, personal satisfaction and idealism than fame and money.

FORM AND STYLE

1. What attitude to Gina is suggested by the phrase, "the greatest Italian discovery since spaghetti"? Is there any phrase similar in tone used about Qamar?
2. Explain the double meaning in "Gina takes her place at a level previously occupied only by a few *celestial bodies* . . ." (Paragraph 1).
3. What is the connection between the last sentence in Paragraph 1 and Paragraphs 2 and 3?

4. Explain the function of the parenthetical clauses in Paragraph 3. Would the style be improved if "she" were substituted for "Gina" in at least some of them? Explain your answer.

5. What does "these," the last word in Paragraph 5, refer to? Use your answer to define the logical relationship between Paragraph 5 (minus the last sentence) and the rest of the description of Qamar.

6. The first two sentences of Paragraph 5, where Qamar has not yet been introduced, are connected with the description of Gina by means of contrast. What is being contrasted with what?

7. The last six sentences in Paragraph 6 all begin with the word "She." Is the repetition successful or just simply awkward and monotonous? Explain.

VOCABULARY

Which of the four words or phrases to the right seems to you to be *closest* in meaning to the word in heavy type to the left? Put a check mark after your choice.

celestial (*1*)   exalted . . . celebrated . . . heavenly . . . beautiful . . .

naïve (*2*)   cynical . . . surprised . . . simple-minded . . . curious . . .

incredible (*2*)   not to be believed . . . lovely . . . credulous . . . fantastic . . .

devoted (*2*)   intense . . . given wholly . . . admirable . . . genuine

incarnate (*2*)   beauty . . . embodied . . . sexual . . . goddess . . .

pastimes (*3*)   friendships . . . things that are fun . . . recreations . . . hobbies . . .

catalogue (*3*)   estimate . . . list . . . description . . . fashion show

acolytes (*4*)   religious attendants . . . worshipers . . . converts . . . appendices . . .

ignominy (*5*)   anonymity . . . disease . . . disgrace . . . humiliation . . .

ancient (*5*)   protected . . . old . . . honored . . . favored . . .

prominently (*5*)   constantly . . . popularly . . . well . . . outstandingly . . .

serene (*6*)   noble . . . beautiful . . . kind . . . calm . . .

fetid (*6*)   hot . . . humid . . . sickening . . . stinking . . .

sari (*6*)   nurse's gown . . . face mask . . . overalls . . . garment worn by Indian women . . .

phenomenal (*6*)   extraordinary . . . large . . . wonderful . . . beyond belief . . .

austere (*7*)   small . . . cramped . . . charming . . . severely simple

dedicated (*10*)   hard-working . . . splendid . . . devoted . . . good-natured . . .

negotiating (*10*)   arguing . . . conferring . . . planning . . . dealing
perceptive (*10*)   keen . . . thoughtful . . . responsive . . . understanding . . .

THEME SUGGESTIONS

The failure of success   Why I want to become a social worker
What is success?   Hollywood's ideal woman

24

E. B. WHITE

The Decline of Sport
(*A Preposterous Parable*)

1   In the third decade of the supersonic age, sport gripped the nation
in an ever-tightening grip. The horse tracks, the ballparks, the fight rings,
the gridirons, all drew crowds in steadily increasing numbers. Every time
a game was played, an attendance record was broken. Usually some other
sort of record was broken, too—such as the record for the number of consecutive doubles hit by left-handed batters in a Series game, or some such
thing as that. Records fell like ripe apples on a windy day. Customs and
manners changed, and the five-day business week was reduced to four
days, then to three, to give everyone a better chance to memorize the
scores.
2   Not only did sport proliferate but the demands it made on the
spectator became greater. Nobody was content to take in one event at a
time, and thanks to the magic of radio and television nobody had to. A
Yale alumnus, class of 1962, returning to the Bowl with 197,000 others to
see the Yale-Cornell football game would take along his pocket radio and
pick up the Yankee Stadium, so that while his eye might be following a
fumble on the Cornell twenty-two-yard line, his ear would be following
a man going down to second in the top of the fifth, seventy miles away.
High in the blue sky above the Bowl, skywriters would be at work writing
the scores of other major and minor sporting contests, weaving an interminable record of victory and defeat, and using the new high-visibility pink
news-smoke perfected by Pepsi-Cola engineers. And in the frames of the
giant video sets, just behind the goalposts, this same alumnus could watch
Dejected win the Futurity before a record-breaking crowd of 349,872 at

Belmont, each of whom was tuned to the Yale Bowl and following the World Series game in the video and searching the sky for further news of events either under way or just completed. The effect of this vast cyclorama of sport was to divide the spectator's attention, over-subtilize his appreciation, and deaden his passion. As the fourth supersonic decade was ushered in, the picture changed and sport began to wane.

3   A good many factors contributed to the decline of sport. Substitutions in football had increased to such an extent that there were very few fans in the United States capable of holding the players in mind during play. Each play that was called saw two entirely new elevens lined up, and the players whose names and faces you had familiarized yourself with in the first period were seldom seen or heard of again. The spectacle became as diffuse as the main concourse in Grand Central at the commuting hour.

4   Express motor highways leading to the parks and stadia had become so wide, so unobstructed, so devoid of all life except automobiles and trees that sport fans had got into the habit of travelling enormous distances to attend events. The normal driving speed had been stepped up to ninety-five miles an hour, and the distance between cars had been decreased to fifteen feet. This put an extraordinary strain on the sport lover's nervous system, and he arrived home from a Saturday game, after a road trip of three hundred and fifty miles, glassy-eyed, dazed, and spent. He hadn't really had any relaxation and he had failed to see Czlika (who had gone in for Trusky) take the pass from Bkeeo (who had gone in for Bjallo) in the third period, because at that moment a youngster named Lavagetto had been put in to pinch-hit for Art Gurlack in the bottom of the ninth with the tying run on second, and the skywriter who was attempting to write "Princeton 0—Lafayette 43" had banked the wrong way, muffed the "3," and distracted everyone's attention from the fact that Lavagetto had been whiffed.

5   Cheering, of course, lost its stimulating effect on players, because cheers were no longer associated necessarily with the immediate scene but might as easily apply to something that was happening somewhere else. This was enough to infuriate even the steadiest performer. A football star, hearing the stands break into a roar before the ball was snapped, would realize that their minds were not on him, and would become dispirited and grumpy. Two or three of the big coaches worried so about this that they considered equipping all players with tiny ear sets, so that they, too, could keep abreast of other sporting events while playing, but the idea was abandoned as impractical, and the coaches put it aside in tickler files, to bring up again later.

6   I think the event that marked the turning point in sport and started it downhill was the Midwest's classic Dust Bowl game of 1975, when Eastern Reserve's great right end, Ed Pistachio, was shot by a spectator. This man, the one who did the shooting, was seated well down in the

stands near the forty-yard line on a bleak October afternoon and was so saturated with sport and with the disappointments of sport that he had clearly become deranged. With a minute and fifteen seconds to play and the score tied, the Eastern Reserve quarterback had whipped a long pass over Army's heads into Pistachio's waiting arms. There was no other player anywhere near him, and all Pistachio had to do was catch the ball and run it across the line. He dropped it. At exactly this moment, the spectator— a man named Homer T. Parkinson, of 35 Edgemere Drive, Toledo, O.— suffered at least three other major disappointments in the realm of sport. His horse, Hiccough, on which he had a five-hundred-dollar bet, fell while getting away from the starting gate at Pimlico and broke its leg (clearly visible in the video); his favorite shortstop, Lucky Frimstitch, struck out and let three men die on base in the final game of the Series (to which Parkinson was tuned); and the Governor Dummer soccer team, on which Parkinson's youngest son played goalie, lost to Kent, 4-3, as recorded in the sky overhead. Before anyone could stop him, he drew a gun and drilled Pistachio, before 954,000 persons, the largest crowd that had ever attended a football game and the *second*-largest crowd that had ever assembled for any sporting event in any month except July.

7   This tragedy, by itself, wouldn't have caused sport to decline, I suppose, but it set in motion a chain of other tragedies, the cumulative effect of which was terrific. Almost as soon as the shot was fired, the news flash was picked up by one of the skywriters directly above the field. He glanced down to see whether he could spot the trouble below, and in doing so failed to see another skywriter approaching. The two planes collided and fell, wings locked, leaving a confusing trail of smoke, which some observers tried to interpret as a late sports score. The planes struck in the middle of the nearby eastbound coast-to-coast Sunlight Parkway, and a motorist driving a convertible coupé stopped so short, to avoid hitting them, that he was bumped from behind. The pileup of cars that ensued involved 1,482 vehicles, a record for eastbound parkways. A total of more than three thousand persons lost their lives in the highway accident, including the two pilots, and when panic broke out in the stadium, it cost another 872 in dead and injured. News of the disaster spread quickly to other sports arenas, and started other panics among the crowds trying to get to the exits, where they could buy a paper and study a list of the dead. All in all, the afternoon of sport cost 20,003 lives, a record. And nobody had much to show for it except one small Midwestern boy who hung around the smoking wrecks of the planes, captured some aero news-smoke in a milk bottle, and took it home as a souvenir.

8   From that day on, sport waned. Through long, noncompetitive Saturday afternoons, the stadia slumbered. Even the parkways fell into disuse as motorists rediscovered the charms of old, twisty roads that led through main streets and past barnyards, with their mild congestions and pleasant smells.

Exercises

CONTENT

True or False? If you think the statement represents what the selec⸗ tion says or implies, mark it "True"; if you do not think so, mark it "False."

1. Television contributed to the sports mania.
2. Only artists and people in the academic profession protested against the rage for sports.
3. Pepsi-Cola engineers invented a new kind of smoke for skywriting.
4. Interest in sport began to decline after an event in the Rose Bowl game.
5. The fourth supersonic decade began before 1975.
6. Parkinson's son played soccer.
7. Cheering lost its stimulating effect on the players because they could no longer be sure why the crowd cheered.
8. Some coaches equipped their teams with tiny earphones.
9. The public still found spectator sports relaxing.
10. A two-day work week was instituted during the late 1960's.

Questions for Discussion

1. Using *The Decline of Sport* as evidence, what do you think is White's attitude to sport?
2. Mention as many as you can of the factors contributing to the decline of sport.
3. There is a "straw-that-broke-the-camel's-back" situation implied in the climax of the story. Exactly what is the straw?
4. Name, in the right order, each of the "falling dominoes" in the chain reaction disaster told about in Paragraph 6.
5. What characteristic is common to the records "usually broken" at the sport events of the supersonic age?
6. What does the last paragraph add to the meaning of the story?

FORM AND STYLE

1. What does White gain by telling the story from a point of view in time at which the future has already become the past?
2. Explain the symbolic significance of the names in "watch Dejected win the Futurity . . ." (Paragraph 2). Can you find other names in the story that seem to suggest more than a single meaning?
3. What purpose in the organization of the story is served by the last sentence in Paragraph 2?

4. What is the logical relationship between Paragraph 6 and Paragraphs 4 and 5?

5. Normally, of course, Princeton beats Lafayette, and a score of 0-43 in the latter's favor is certainly highly unusual. Why did White introduce this bit of near absurdity?

6. Why is the "small Midwestern boy" (end of Paragraph 7) in the story?

7. Write a topic outline of the story.

VOCABULARY

Which of the four words or phrases to the right seems to you to be *closest* in meaning to the word in heavy type to the left? Put a check mark after your choice.

supersonic (*1*)   jet powered . . . fast . . . beyond the speed of sound . . . colossal . . .

consecutive (*1*)   conservative . . . successive . . . following . . . consistent . . .

proliferate (*2*)   become more popular . . . become widespread . . . succeed . . . multiply . . .

interminable (*2*)   endless . . . undetermined . . . not permanent . . . unstoppable . . .

cyclorama (*2*)   dramatic cycle . . . spectacle . . . CinemaScope . . . picture in the round . . .

diffuse (*3*)   complicated . . . difficult . . . without a spark . . . spread out . . .

infuriate (*5*)   confuse . . . disappoint . . . upset . . . enrage . . .

dispirited (*5*)   sober . . . downcast . . . materialistic . . . angry . . .

saturated (*6*)   tired . . . angry . . . frustrated . . . fed up . . .

deranged (*6*)   confused . . . insane . . . dangerous . . . abnormal . . .

cumulative (*7*)   overwhelming . . . unforeseen . . . added up . . . causing disaster . . .

ensued (*7*)   followed . . . pursued . . . sued . . . crashed . . .

congestions (*8*)   views . . . pleasures . . . surprises . . . traffic jams

THEME SUGGESTIONS

Active vs. passive sports
Leisure—for what?
My experience with sports mania
A football/baseball game of the future
Why spectator sports will *not* decline, or A fan answers White

25

ALEC WAUGH

*What Rugby Means
to England*

1   I am now in my middle 50s. A short while ago I was playing golf with a near contemporary who had gone to Princeton. After the game we fell to talking about the '20s, which he had spent mainly in New York while I had been in London. We compared our separate experiences during that hectic period. Suddenly an idea struck me. "I believe," I said, "that this is the chief minor difference between us—I as a Londoner every Saturday afternoon between mid-September and mid-April was playing Rugby football while you as a New Yorker were shooting squash in the Racquet Club."

2   He looked surprised and his eyes ran me over. I am short and stocky, 5 foot 6, and my weight since my late teens has vacillated between 150 and 160. "You played Rugby till you were nearly 30?" He is quite a bit bigger than I, but he had played no football after he had left high school. He hadn't been heavy enough to make the team, he felt, and there were other games. "Weren't you exceptional?" he asked.

3   I shook my head. "I was a very average player. One of many thousands. Rugby is played in the majority of our public schools. Most of us who are any good go on playing afterwards."

4   "Rugby every Saturday between mid-September and mid-April. That's quite a thing!" he ruminated. "It must fill a very special place in English life."

5   Now, in retrospect, I can see it does. But at the time, to play Rugby every Saturday through the winter was the most natural thing for me to do, for the very simple reason that it was the thing I wanted to do most.

6   I have joined in many arguments as to which is the best game to watch. Much is to be said for many. But I have little doubt that the best winter game for a young man to play is Rugby football. It has everything to recommend it. It is fast and hard; it is rough but it is not dangerous. You get bruised and shaken but bones are rarely broken; no special padding is prescribed; you wear shorts and a jersey. Dexterity and speed are as important as weight and strength. It is essentially a team game, but it is highly individualistic. The majority of points are scored not as the out-

WHAT RUGBY MEANS TO ENGLAND. First published in *Sports Illustrated,* February 4, 1957. Copyright ©, 1957, by Alec Waugh. Reprinted by permission of Brandt & Brandt.

come of a concerted movement but through an opportunist taking advantage of an opponent's slip. Each player develops his own style.

7 It is, moreover, a very simple game. You learn it by playing it. No long apprenticeship is served. My own experience is that of many thousand others. At my preparatory school, from 9 years to 13, I played soccer. On my first afternoon at Sherborne, my public school, I was instructed with 20 other new boys in the rudiments of Rugby. It bears resemblance to American football. It would be surprising if it didn't; after all, both games stem from the same source. *Tom Brown's Schooldays,* in its account of a school-house match at Rugby School in the 1830s, describes that source. Both fields look alike, with a similar type of goal post, and the object of each game is the same, to get the ball over the opponent's line, after which you are allowed a free kick at the goal. But whereas the game that was introduced into America via Canada in the 1870s developed rapidly into its present form, Rugby stayed the way it was. My younger son is playing today at Sherborne virtually the same game that his grandfather played there 75 years ago.

8 In Rugby there are few complications. The ball cannot be passed forward; it is fatter and less pointed than the American ball, and you cannot fling long one-handed passes with it. There is as much dribbling with the feet and the gaining of ground by long kicks into touch as there is running with the ball under the arm. Body blocking is not allowed. There are no substitutes, no huddles, no interruptions except for serious injuries. The rules consist of a few straightforward DON'TS.

9 There are 15 players on each side, and I was told on that first afternoon how they are disposed—eight forwards, six backs and as a last line of defense a single fullback. I was then shown how the eight forwards form themselves into a three-row phalanx—it is called a scrum—and, with bent backs and arms around each other, join issue with the opposing pack. The ball is then slid by one of the backs under their feet, and the two packs shove and struggle in an attempt to heel it to the backs, who are spread out behind them in the open, waiting to initiate an attack.

10 My first lesson lasted for half an hour. I was then ordered to watch a practice game on the upper ground. It was the first Rugby match that I had watched. I was fascinated by its speed and its variety. In all athletics I doubt if there is a finer sight than a fast backfield movement, the ball heeled quickly from the scrum, each back running straight, making all the ground he can, drawing his opponent before he passes laterally till finally the ball reaches the wing man, who makes for the corner flag in a desperate attempt to outswerve and outpace the fullback. I longed for the day when I should be big enough to play in such a game.

11 That half hour of explanation and the watching of that "upper" was all the preliminary instruction I received. The next day I was posted to a house game. I cannot say that I enjoyed it. I was playing with boys bigger than myself. I felt very lost. I was terrified of making myself con-

spicuous by doing the wrong thing. I was equally terrified of doing nothing. The game was watched by a prefect who urged us to keener efforts. Abuse was mingled with his exhortations. "Go low. Drop on the ball, run straight, don't funk," he shouted. I was afraid that my ignorance would be mistaken for cowardice, and at half time I surreptitiously rubbed mud into my knees to give the impression that I had plunged adventurously under the feet of the attacking forwards. I was infinitely relieved when the final whistle went. But within a week I had found my feet.

12 The simplicity of Rugby is one of its great merits. It is easy for a novice to pick it up, and it is possible for the ex-public school boy to continue playing it after he has come down when he is working in an office, with no time available for midweek practice, which is impossible, I fancy, in American football, with its profusion of "plays," its elaborate deception schemes, its mathematical positionings.

13 The proof of Rugby's excellence lies in the fact that so many men play it after they leave college. Games are compulsory at English schools, and it is natural for a schoolboy to be anxious to succeed at them. Prestige and popularity depend upon his prowess on the field. The reputation and standing of a school is in large part determined by the skill of its footballers and cricketers, and it stands a man in good stead in later life to be able to say he was in his school XV. "A ribboned coat" is the opening to many appointments. But it is quite another matter to go on playing Rugby after you have left school, when you are under no compunction, with no rewards attached, obscurely before an uncrowded touch line, simply out of a love of the game. And that is what thousands of men do.

14 My own case is typical. When I was posted to the army reserve after World War I at the age of 21, I joined Rosslyn Park, a London Club. For seven years I turned out every Saturday between mid-September and mid-April. I had been in the first XV at Sherborne, but as a forward weighing 150 pounds. I was too small to earn a regular place in the first Rosslyn Park side. For the most part I played for the second or "A" XV against public schools, second-class clubs, and the "A" XVs of other first-class clubs. That Saturday match determined the pattern of my week.

15 Each Monday evening the selection committee met and on the Tuesday morning I would receive a card. "You are selected to play vs. Bishop's Stortford. Train 1:15 Liverpool Street. Meet at barrier. Tickets taken." I observed no training rules, but I kept fit. I confined wild parties to the first half of the week. On Friday I dined at my parents' house and was in bed by 10.

16 Sometimes when I woke on the Saturday, I would wonder why I still went on playing football. It was cold and wet. Liverpool Street station at 12:30 on a Saturday is a shambles. I should lunch in a crowded

buffet off a soggy sandwich. The train would be packed and I should have
to stand. The ground would be a quarter of an hour's walk from the station. The pavilion would be a drafty converted army hut. There would
be small wash tubs, tepid water, and no electric light. Why on earth was
I still playing Rugby?

17 Now and again I felt like that on a wet Saturday morning, but the
moment I reached the barrier and saw the familiar faces that mood left
me. From week to week the side changed little, and the nucleus was
carried on from one year to the next. We had a fund of jokes to share.
Though I had to stand in the train, the journey passed so quickly that I
was surprised to find we had arrived. It was still spattering with rain, but
that made it, I reminded myself, perfect football weather for a forward.
The pavilion was indeed drafty, but I did not notice it. I was impatient,
like a horse at the starting point. I was young, fit, tingling with a sense
of battle. It would be a game in which nothing was at stake, no caps or
cups were to be won: afterwards there would be no elation in victory, no
deep despondency in defeat. I can remember in detail every house and
school match in which I played at Sherborne, but of my seven years with
Rosslyn Park I can only recall occasional incidents and the look of certain grounds. Yet, though there was no drama in that later football, I enjoyed the actual playing of it more than I had at school.

18 And after the game, despite the tepid water in the shallow tub, I
was suffused with the agreeable languor that follows violent exercise.
Next day I should be stiff and slow in movement, but at the moment my
bruises were still soft. I felt pleasantly exhausted, no more than that.
After the game there would be a heavy tea with fruitcake and thick fish-
paste sandwiches. We would be too tired for much talking, that could
wait till afterwards. For always after the game seven or eight of us, on
our return to London, would raid Dehem's oyster bar off Shaftesbury
Avenue and drink many pints of lukewarm beer, eat a steak and kidney
pudding and argue about this and that till closing time. So it went on
every Saturday from mid-September to mid-April for seven years.

19 Rugby football made the pattern of winter life for me, as it does
in Britain year after year for many thousands of ex-public school boys. I
was lucky to have that pattern. The seven years between 21 and 28 are
crucial in a young man's life. He is establishing himself in his career, he
is falling in and out of love, he is discovering himself. Myself, I had at
that time a half-time job as an editor in a publishing house. On the other
days I was writing articles, short stories, novels. I had many problems,
emotional and professional. It was an immense relief to me to be taken
every week out of the circle of those problems into the wholesome atmosphere of football. It was a relief to all of us.

20 It is a curious two-dimensional friendship that links the members
of a Rugby side. In one sense we all knew each other very well. We knew

who was reckless and who was cautious, who was a fair-weather player and who was at his best in an uphill fight. We all liked each other, for that is the great merit of team games, that you only play with congenial people; however brilliant as an individualist a player may be, if he is boastful and a bully, he soon ceases to receive that Tuesday morning postcard. In one sense I knew inside out the men with whom I played regularly with Rosslyn Park. In another sense I scarcely knew them. I knew little of their backgrounds. I knew to which school each had been, and the kind of job he worked at. But I had no idea who his parents were or from what kind of home he came. For the most part we were bachelors, but more than once I was surprised to find that someone I had known for three seasons was married and a father. When we parted outside Dehem's at closing time we passed out of each other's lives until we met at the station barrier on the following Saturday.

21   There is a quality of anonymity about football friendships, and sometimes on Saturday evenings when I caught the tube back to my flat in Kensington I found myself thinking ruefully of the inevitable day when I should give up Rugby. Very few men play it after 30: you lose your speed, your wind gets short and your bones brittle, you are shaken badly when you are brought down heavily. I had seen many friends drop out of the game, usually in the same way. They caught a chill, or a minor injury prevented their playing for three weeks. When they played again they were out of training; they excused themselves on the following Saturday; they vowed to get back into training and never did. If the rhythm is once broken, it is not resumed when you are nearing 30.

22   One day that would happen to me, and as my tube rattled westward I vowed to myself that when my turn came to stop playing, I would not drop out of the game altogether; I would become a referee or a touch judge so that a winter Saturday would still mean football for me. It didn't though. When my time came, I was like all the others. I let golf and matrimony impose their own new pattern.

23   That is the one sad thing about Rugby football. When you give up playing it, you drop out of the game altogether. I am a life member of Rosslyn Park but I never go to the old Deer Park to see them play. I have lost touch with every former member of the side. As a retired cricketer I go to Lord's on a summer evening, certain of meeting half a dozen old friends in the pavilion, but a Rugby international in the vast arena at Twickenham provides no common meeting ground.

24   When you walk off a Rugby field for the last time, you walk out of the world of Rugby. Maybe that foreknowledge adds a keener savor to one's enjoyment of the game during the years when one can play it. Certainly the savor I got from it lingers still upon the palate. For me, in retrospect, the early 1920s do not mean wild parties and the fast dollar half as much as they mean Rugby football.

Exercises

CONTENT

True or False? If you think the statement represents what the selection says or implies, mark it "True"; if you do not think so, mark it "False."

1. Waugh was a professional Rugby player.
2. American football and Rugby developed from the same source.
3. Rugby was invented in the 1830's by an Englishman named Tom Brown.
4. Forward passes are not allowed in Rugby.
5. Rugby would be a much safer game if the players would wear helmets and padding.
6. The "scrum" is an important backfield formation used in defensive play.
7. Waugh played Rugby in his twenties mainly for the exercise.
8. The Rugby ball is less pointed than an American football.
9. Many Englishmen continue playing Rugby well into their forties.
10. Substitutes are allowed in Rugby only under exceptional circumstances.

Questions for Discussion

1. Exactly what does Waugh say Rugby *does* mean to England? In other words, what does he say he got out of the game? Be specific.
2. What are some of the differences between Rugby and American football? What seem to you to be advantages and disadvantages to player and spectator of each game? Be as objective as you can.

FORM AND STYLE

1. Why is the American friend in the essay?
2. *What Rugby Means to England* falls into three main divisions: introduction, description of the game and how an English boy learns it, description of Waugh's post-graduation Rugby career. Where do the divisions occur? Comment on the transitions—what are they? Are they well worked out, or too slow, too obvious, not clear enough?
3. What is the connection between Paragraphs 16 and 17?
4. Does the first sentence in Paragraph 21 have unity? Explain.
5. Find words or expressions that show that the writer is not an American.

VOCABULARY

Which of the four words or phrases to the right seems to you to be *closest* in meaning to the word in heavy type to the left? Put a check mark after your choice.

hectic (*1*)   far-off . . . restless . . . fabulous . . . exciting . . .

ruminated (*4*)   wondered . . . pondered . . . repeated . . . exclaimed

dexterity (*6*)   speed . . . strength . . . skill . . . courage . . .

concerted (*6*)   collective . . . planned ahead . . . individual . . . direct . . .

opportunist (*6*)   a player on your team . . . one who is appropriate . . . an expert player . . . one who makes use of the opportunity . . .

rudiments (*7*)   rules . . . aspects . . . first principles . . . pleasures

phalanx (*9*)   arrow . . . attacking group . . . army . . . line-up . . .

laterally (*10*)   literally . . . sideways . . . often . . . beautifully . . .

preliminary (*11*)   basic . . . real . . . introductory . . . not limited by time . . .

conspicuous (*11*)   despised . . . looking silly . . . neglected . . . noticeable . . .

exhortations (*11*)   encouragements . . . compliments . . . pieces of advice . . . warnings . . .

funk (*11*)   waver . . . hesitate . . . fumble . . . be a coward . . .

surreptitiously (*11*)   hurriedly . . . on the sly . . . fearfully . . . falsely . . .

novice (*12*)   young person . . . one who is lightweight . . . one who knows . . . beginner . . .

profusion (*12*)   complexity . . . multitude . . . confusion . . . long list . . .

prowess (*13*)   fame . . . skill . . . success . . . superiority . . .

compunction (*13*)   sense of guilt or duty . . . force . . . order . . . urgency . . .

tepid (*16*)   too little . . . cold . . . lukewarm . . . scalding . . .

nucleus (*17*)   majority . . . core . . . stem . . . elite . . .

elation (*17*)   triumph . . . celebration . . . joy . . . pride . . .

despondency (*17*)   hopelessness . . . regret . . . envy . . . dejection

suffused (*18*)   overspread . . . filled . . . suffering pleasantly . . . lazy . . .

languor (*18*)   lassitude . . . stupor . . . sleepiness . . . stiffness . . .

congenial (*20*)   nice . . . generous . . . jovial . . . likeminded . . .

ruefully (*21*)   sadly . . . regretfully . . . frequently . . . wistfully

savor (*24*)   touch . . . quality . . . flavor . . . knowledge . . .

THEME SUGGESTIONS

My favorite sport
E. B. White reads Alec Waugh

Team sports vs. individual sports

Write about an experience you have had similar to the one Waugh describes in Paragraph 11: you are self-conscious, you want to make good, you are scared you'll make a fool of yourself or ruin things for the others.

26

FREDERICK LEWIS ALLEN

King of Swing

1   One morning in the winter of 1937-38 a crowd began to gather outside the Paramount Theatre in Times Square, New York, as soon as it was light. By 6 A.M. there were three thousand people assembled in the otherwise empty streets—mostly high-school boys and girls in windbreakers and leather jackets. By 7:30 the crowd had so swelled that ten mounted policemen were sent from the West 47th Street station to keep it under control. At 8 o'clock the doors of the theatre were carefully opened to admit 3,634 boys and girls; then the fire department ordered the doors closed, leaving two or three thousand youngsters out in the cold.

2   Benny Goodman and his orchestra were opening an engagement at the Paramount. Benny Goodman was the King of Swing, and these boys and girls were devotees of swing, ready to dance in the aisles of the theatre amid shouts of "Get off, Benny! Swing it!" and "Feed it to me, Gene! Send me down!" They were jitterbugs, otherwise "alligators," equipped with the new vocabulary of swing ("in the groove," "spank the skin," "schmaltz," "boogie-woogie," "jam session," "killer-diller," and so on endlessly); members of that army of young swing enthusiasts all over the country who during the next year or two knew the names and reputations of the chief band leaders and instrumentalists of swingdom—Goodman, Tommy Dorsey, Artie Shaw, Gene Krupa, "Count" Basie, Teddy Wilson, Louis Armstrong, Jack Teagarden, Larry Clinton, and others without number—as a seasoned baseball fan knows his professional ball players.

3   To trace fully the origins of this craze one would have to go back very far. Suffice it to say here that during the nineteen-twenties, the jazz craze—which had begun long before in the honky-tonks of New Orleans and had burst into general popularity with the success of "Alexander's Ragtime Band" and the rising vogue of the one-step and fox-trot as dances between 1911 and 1916—had become tamed into decorum and

formality; but that even during this time there were obscure jazz bands, mostly of Negro players, which indulged in a mad improvisation, super-imposing upon the main theme of the dance music they were playing their own instrumental patterns made up on the spur of the moment (and sometimes later committed to writing). During the early years of the Depression there was little popular interest in this "hot jazz" in the United States; what a worried public wanted was "sweet" music, slow in rhythm and soothingly melodious, like "Some Day I'll Find You" (1931) and "Star Dust" (very popular in 1932), or poignantly haunting, like "Night and Day" (1932) and "Stormy Weather" (1933). But Europe had acquired a belated enthusiasm for jazz rhythms and in France there grew up something of a cult of "le jazz hot." Phonograph records of the playing of such experts as Louis Armstrong and his band sold well abroad. In the fall of 1933—at about the time of the NRA parades and the coming of Repeal—an English company arranged with a young New Yorker who was crazy about hot jazz to try to get some good records made by a band of American whites; and young John Henry Hammond, Jr., persuaded the scholarly-looking clarinetist, Benny Good-man, who was playing in a radio orchestra, to gather a group of players for this purpose.

4   The resulting records not only sold well in England but made an unexpected hit in the United States; and thus began a public enthusi-asm for "swing"—as the hot jazz full of improvisation came to be called —which welled to its climax in the winter of 1937-38, when the bespec-tacled Mr. Goodman, playing at the Paramount and later in Boston and elsewhere, found that the boys and girls so yelled and screamed and cavorted when his band began to "send" that a concert became a bedlam. When in the spring of 1938 a Carnival of Swing was held at Randall's Island in New York, with twenty-five bands present, over 23,000 jitterbugs listened for five hours and forty-five minutes with such uncontrollable enthusiasm that, as a reporter put it in the next morning's *Times,* the police and park officers had all they could do to protect the players from "destruction by admiration."

5   Among many of the jitterbugs—particularly among many of the boys and girls—the appreciation of the new music was largely vertebral. A good swing band smashing away at full speed, with the trumpeters and clarinetists rising in turn under the spotlight to embroider the theme with their several furious improvisations and the drummers going into long-drawnout rhythmical frenzies, could reduce its less inhibited audi-tors to sheer emotional vibration, punctuated by howls of rapture. Yet to dismiss the swing craze as a pure orgy of sensation would be to miss more than half of its significance. For what the good bands produced —though it might sound to the unpracticed ear like a mere blare of dis-cordant noise—was an extremely complex and subtle pattern, a full ap-

preciation of which demanded far more musical sophistication than the simpler popular airs of a preceding period. The true swing enthusiasts, who collected records to the limit of their means and not only liked Artie Shaw's rendering of "Begin the Beguine" but knew precisely why they liked it, were receiving no mean musical education; and if Benny Goodman could turn readily from the playing of "Don't Be That Way" to the playing of Mozart, so could many of his hearers turn to the hearing of Mozart. It may not have been quite accidental that the craze for swing accompanied the sharpest gain in musical knowledge and musical taste that the American people had ever achieved.

Exercises

CONTENT

True or False? If you think the statement represents what the selection says or implies, mark it "True"; if you do not think so, mark it "False."

1. The essay begins with an incident in the Roxy Theater in New York.
2. Teen-age slang has no meaning.
3. Allen's list of bandleaders includes Duke Ellington.
4. Allen's references to hit songs from the 'thirties do *not* include "Begin the Beguine."
5. Swing was not popular during the early years of the Depression.
6. Benny Goodman wears glasses.
7. "Hot jazz" became popular in Europe before it became popular in the United States.
8. "Swing" is the same as "hot jazz."
9. There is not much difference in behavior between the teen-age swing enthusiasts of the 1930's and the rock-'n'-rollers of today.
10. Swing spoils one's appreciation of classical music.

Question for Discussion

What is Allen's point in Paragraph 5? Do you agree with him?

FORM AND STYLE

1. Which of the following terms best describes the function of Paragraph 1 in relation to the rest of the essay? (a) analogy, (b) illustrative anecdote, (c) contrast, (d) generalization, (e) cause.
2. Which of the following terms best describes the method of development within Paragraph 1? (a) spatial movement, (b) example-

general rule, (c) comparison-contrast, (d) movement in time, (e) cause-effect.

3. Outline the essay by assigning a topic phrase to each of the five paragraphs.

4. Point out as many examples as you can of the use of specifics (dates, names, titles, etc.) in the essay. What do your findings teach you concerning ways of getting interest, substance, and authority into your own writing?

VOCABULARY

Which of the four words or phrases to the right seems to you to be *closest* in meaning to the word in heavy type to the left? Put a check mark after your choice.

devotees (2)   crazy persons . . . followers . . . "cats" . . . fanatics
suffice (3)   allow . . . be enough . . . suffer . . . be important . . .
decorum (3)   boredom . . . niceness . . . decency . . . propriety . . .
obscure (3)   excellent . . . unknown . . . radical . . . original . . .
indulged (3)   practiced . . . improvised . . . took pleasure in . . . gave themselves up to . . .
superimposing (3)   putting on top of . . . supervising . . . substituting . . . making more impressive . . .
poignantly (3)   exquisitely . . . painfully . . . touchingly . . . pointedly . . .
haunting (3)   beautiful . . . like a ghost . . . recurring . . . suggestive . . .
belated (3)   postponed . . . late . . . joyful . . . strange . . .
cavorted (4)   yelled . . . kicked . . . pranced . . . wriggled . . .
bedlam (4)   dance hall . . . madhouse . . . chaos . . . jam session
vertebral (5)   muscular . . . sensual . . . pertaining to the vertebrae . . . emotional . . .
punctuated (5)   separated . . . marked . . . exploded . . . intensified . . .
rapture (5)   excitement . . . delight . . . ecstasy . . . approval . . .
orgy (5)   wildness . . . ceremony . . . excess . . . organization . . .
mean (5)   usual . . . contemptible . . . evil . . . average . . .

THEME SUGGESTIONS

A brief history of swing
The development of my musical tastes
Teen-age fashions in music from Goodman to Presley
The psychology of rock-'n'-roll

27

BERNARD DE VOTO

Heavy, Heavy, What Hangs Over?

1   Europeans have made a cliché of saying that nothing is so sad as the sight of Americans having a good time. They see us in special but revealing circumstances, making a job of what is supposed to be a pleasure trip, exercising our native resolution, doggedness, and grit. The qualities were indispensable to creating the standard of living that enables the American to make his tour, but they are a formidable handicap while he is making it. They professionalize his pleasure, put it on a sound business basis, make an investment of it. It has got to show a profit—pay off in self-improvement, culture, *savoir-faire*, small talk about restaurants and exchange rates. There must be no red ink representing lost time or wasted effort. Are we investing for safety of principal, for income, or long-term appreciation? Program this trip accordingly—budget it, it's costing plenty, isn't it?

2   One infers a kind of point system in which the Tower of London, say, counts fifteen, the changing of the Guard ten, and Stonehenge five. The tourist is playing against bogey. Or he is making a judicious determination of par. Given total length of tour, how many days shall the work-sheet allot to Paris? How many hours to Montmartre, the Invalides, Sainte-Chapelle, Fontainebleau? What are permissible alternatives? Should he play it with a number-four iron or should he sell out at the market and get into something else? And don't think the metaphor is mixed, for the tourist is likely to play golf so that it will show a return, too, he hopes.

3   There may be a vagrant thought that, given an afternoon in Paris, he would have a fine time simply sitting at a sidewalk table and watching the girls' skirts blow, or drifting down the Seine while getting mildly buzzed on bad beer and watching the light change. But if he is on a conducted tour he won't get a chance for there are stern obligations to be met. If he is on his own he won't dare to, for he hasn't seen the Mona Lisa yet and so is still in the red. Besides, the idea of a free afternoon is a dangerous thought.

4   We begin to sniff certain anxieties. They affect the most popular of American vacations, the automobile tour. I eagerly admit that it is my most dependable source of pleasure and I indulge my liking for it whenever I can afford, and all too often when I can't. I am therefore often in contact with fellow Americans who are making desperately hard labor of what they undertook for fun. They exhibit the indomitability I have described and they tend to be strained, harried, and tired out. So they are fretful, querulous, bad-mannered, childish, and in a hell of a hurry. Having succeeded in getting a headlock on pleasure, they have gone on to choke it to death.

5   Watch the arrivals at any famous scenic point, say one of the overlooks on the edge of the Canyon of the Yellowstone River in Yellowstone Park. A car pulls into the parking space, a family piles out of it at the double, and everyone lines up along the edge. They perform the ceremonial rite of littering the place with Kleenex (known as the national park flower) and chewing-gum wrappers. Pop takes a color shot that with luck will have both Mom and the Lower Falls in it, or runs off some footage of Junior leaning over the railing to see if he can spit into the river. Having thus made sure that he will have something to prove they have seen the Canyon, he puts the camera back in the case and looks at his watch. Got it in eight minutes, by God!—and they are off with a squeal of tires to Old Faithful. If they get there five minutes after an eruption they will be miserable, for here is an enforced wait of fifty-five minutes with absolutely nothing to do.

6   If they can cut it a little finer, understand, then maybe they can get away from Yellowstone a day sooner than the schedule calls for. If so, then maybe they will be able to restore the Columbia Gorge to their itinerary.

7   One has a vision of the family sedan streaking into Montana at seventy-five miles an hour, diving through the Bitterroots, hurtling past Flathead Lake, skidding into the distant prospect of Mount Hood. Oh, fleet chariot, conquering distance, annihilating space, by the miracle of technology laying a whole continent at the feet of a fortunate people, so that one more notch can be carved in the traveler's gunstock. Or with the favor of providence two notches, for if we get through the Gorge betimes and crowd ourselves, maybe we can go home by way of the Redwood Highway.

8   What has been accomplished at the Canyon of the Yellowstone, the Columbia Gorge, or the Redwood Highway? Even the tourist's claim that he has seen them is fraudulent, for he has only glanced at them. He is barely telling the truth when he claims that he has been there, for he was in process of getting somewhere else. He may have strung another celebrated name on his rosary but he has had no experience of the place. He has not even acquired a visual image of it except what will show behind Mom's blowing hair in the Kodachrome. (How often, looking at your friends' slides, have you found them unable to identify the subject?) Nothing has given significance to the countryside his winged chariot has

taken him across. He has some statistics: miles, gallons, daily average, national parks, historic sites, and a table that analyzes costs per day. He will soon get over his physical fatigue, his spiritual fatigue may last longer; but don't the Americans play just as hard as they work?

9   This compulsion to keep on the move may provide welcome protections against the anxieties I have diagnosed. What would happen to this obsessed man if he were to linger on somewhere long enough to open the possibility of perceiving and understanding? Evidently something that scares him. As at Old Faithful there might be nothing to do, as in Paris a free afternoon might be dangerous. . . . We may recall the gentleman who consulted a psychiatrist because he couldn't break the habit of talking to himself. After subjecting him to a careful study, the psychiatrist reported that he was normal enough and bade him go home and forget it—talking to himself was an innocent eccentricity that harmed no one. "But, Doctor," the appalled patient said, "I'm such a bore." What . . . keeps the tourist trying to get a varsity letter for total mileage is emptiness and incapacity, inability to fill a pause in the day's occupations with anything worth doing, justified fear of leisure time. The radio and television industries are grounded on the assumption that the American people are so poor in personal resources that they must have entertainment available at the turn of a switch twenty-four hours a day.

10   Our history has a hold on us that we have found hard to break. For one thing we got rid of aristocracies, didn't we?—of the contemptible parasites known as the Leisure Class who devoted themselves to pleasurable and unprofitable occupations? For another, subduing the continent was touch and go; our ancestors had to work from dawn to dusk and the real reason for keeping the Sabbath holy was to get back enough strength to make an early start on Monday. It followed that work was virtue and idleness was sin. It followed further that profits and sound business procedure were an outward and visible sign of an inner and spiritual grace. Conversely, anyone not practicing virtue diligently, and visibly, was a set-up for Satan.

11   When a neighbor elects to go fishing on a fine summer day and you shoulder a scythe and trudge off to cut the grass in the high mowing, it is comforting to know that he is headed straight to hell and the town poor farm. He has a jug of corn along and you reflect that if any of it is left when he gets back he will spend the evening sharing it with other sinners singing bawdy songs, and chasing off with them to find some loose women. Taxing you to support him on the poor farm is unjust but your tax bill is a certificate of righteousness for all other righteous men to see.

12   The trouble with this puritanism of labor is not only how it stigmatizes the inoffensive grasshopper but how it affects the ant. When the hay is in there comes another fine morning and you go fishing. But this is yielding to sin, and a sense of guilt keeps you from enjoying the trout stream. Like the motorist you feel uneasy. . . . How to handle this nagging self-accusation? That's easy: professionalize fishing. Methodize and systematize it and provide yourself with an efficient production line, including wind-gauge and stream-thermometer. Then fish the daylights out of the Miramichi, the Batten Kill, and any other you can add to your rosary—drive across the continent, so to speak, in four and a half days—and strive to show a credit balance in cups and record catches. Nobody can say that you have been unbusinesslike about it or accuse you of light-mindedness.

13   Like all suspicions, this one widens out to create guilt by association. It has taken the righteous a long time to lose the conviction that listening to a fiddle was flirting with temptation and playing one positively disreputable. To the upright man, the proprietor of a filling station or a vice-president in charge of sales, the intellectual has seemed a weakling and the artist a sissy if not indeed a pansy. Singers, painters, and sculptors, actors, dancers, writers—clearly they were not participating in the world's work. Worse, others took time off to derive pleasure from their activities. Worse still, these derelict ants actually paid the grasshoppers money that could otherwise have been banked, and thus in a highly illegitimate way seemed to be legitimatizing them. The solution of this dilemma was to consign the frivolities to the womenfolk, to one's wife and daughters—if there's going to be any subversion around this house, the whole world can see that I'm clean. . . . It may well be that President Eisenhower and Sir Winston Churchill, who like to paint pictures, have done more to liberate the hard-working American male to the satisfactions of the arts than all the museums in our history.

14   Ascribe some more of our incapacity for leisure to the educational system. It has increased our will to professionalize, to specialize, even our sports and games, leaving us incurious about any intellectual or sensuous experience that a specialist cannot put to use. . . .

15   They [the compulsive tourist and his like] have cultivated no appetites except for food and drink, and probably have not cultivated them very much. Apart from making a living, they have found no zest. Except in relation to their jobs, their minds are color-blind, tone-deaf, and mute. Inborn faculties whose use would create gusto and delight have fossilized. They are unskilled, they are incurious, they have no passion for learning or understanding. No wonder they are bored—and bores. No wonder that leisure scares them.

16   They are going to be scared worse. Their industriousness—plus the richest natural resources in the world—have provided Americans with steadily increasing leisure. The seventy-two-hour work week has become the forty-hour week; the grasshopper who sings the summer away is now assured a two-week vacation as his natural right. Presently it will be a month, or two months, and the forty-hour week will shrink to some now unpredictable fraction. Having endowed everyone with leisure by sub-

stituting machines for muscles, we are now fashioning machines to operate the machines, which is what automation means. Tough luck if they
intensify our neuroses and increase our unhappiness. . . .

Exercises

CONTENT

True or False? If you think the statement represents what the selection says or implies, mark it "True"; if you do not think so, mark it
"False."

1. It is silly to visit scenic places and cultural and historical land-
marks when you are traveling.

2. Europeans dislike American tourists.

3. Europeans think American tourists don't know how to enjoy themselves.

4. The typical American tourist uses material standards in evaluat-
ing his travel experience.

5. The more you see within a given amount of time, the less you
have really seen.

6. According to American values, laziness is sinful, hard work virtuous. Since Europeans make fun of Americans for these beliefs, it follows that Europeans are lazy.

7. Strangely enough, the artist has always been respected in America.

8. Sir Winston Churchill is an amateur painter.

9. De Voto is not an American.

10. The more elaborate the equipment, the more easily the hobby is
justified.

Questions for Discussion

1. Explain the relevance of the fable of the ant and the grasshopper
to De Voto's thesis.

2. Which of the following statements does, in your opinion, most accurately represent De Voto's main idea: (a) Americans work too hard; (b)
there is no value in seeing foreign places unless you live there for some
time; (c) Americans don't know how to make use of the leisure their hard
work has provided them with; (d) Americans are materialists; (e) to an
American, what is not useful is wicked.

3. How fair do you think De Voto's attack on American attitudes to
leisure is? Granting that he exaggerates (he knows as well as you do that
not *all* vacationing Americans behave like the tourists he describes), do
you think he has got hold of something fundamentally true about American values, or do you feel he is just being irresponsibly cynical, trying
to shock for the sake of shocking? Or do you feel he does not expect to

be taken seriously at all? Or that he is serious beneath all the humorous exaggeration? Or simply wrong?

4. What is the meaning of the title?

FORM AND STYLE

1. The first eight paragraphs deal mainly with examples of the American way of sightseeing. This part of the essay is divided into two sections. Where does the division come and what are the two sections?

2. The style of Paragraphs 1-8 is characterized by frequent use of a satiric device known as *parody*. When he parodies, the satirist imitates or copies the attitudes and manners of the object of his satire, in order to show the reader how ridiculous the satirized object is. A good example of parody in De Voto's essay comes at the end of Paragraph 1: "Program this trip accordingly—budget it, it's costing plenty, isn't it?" Here De Voto speaks as if he were the kind of money-minded tourist he is making fun of. Find other examples in the essay of parody.

3. Explain the meaning of ". . . so that one more notch can be carved in the traveler's gunstock." Does the metaphor serve only to give color and concreteness to the statement, or does it add to its meaning? Explain.

4. If you had time for only a single day in Paris, would you spend your afternoon in the Louvre, the world-famous art gallery, or in the manner which De Voto describes in the first half of Paragraph 3? There is no right or wrong answer to this question; your decision is a matter of taste, temperament, interest, and other personal qualities. Your answer will, however, probably indicate whether or not you agree with De Voto. Would it have been different before you read the essay? Would it have been different if De Voto had written, ". . . he would have a fine time simply sitting at a sidewalk table or drifting down the Seine . . ."? Consider the effect upon you of the loss of detail in the version given here.

VOCABULARY

Which of the four words or phrases to the right seems to you to be *closest* in meaning to the word in heavy type to the left? Put a check mark after your choice.

cliché (*1*)   saying . . . proverb . . . trite expression . . . picture . . .
grit (*1*)   endurance . . . seriousness . . . lack of humor . . . moral strength . . .
infers (*2*)   assumes . . . invents . . . plays . . . sees . . .
judicious (*2*)   like a judge . . . wise . . . careful . . . ridiculous . . .
vagrant (*3*)   fleeting . . . quick . . . secret . . . immoral . . .
stern (*3*)   important . . . cultural . . . serious . . . forbidding . . .
obligations (*3*)   activities . . . enterprises . . . duties . . . criticisms

affect (*4*) cause . . . ruin . . . act in an affected manner . . . influence . . .

indomitability (*4*) independence . . . morality . . . quality of being ungovernable . . . intensity . . .

harried (*4*) hurried . . . afflicted . . . worn out . . . nervous . . .

querulous (*4*) full of questions . . . quarrelsome . . . tired . . . irritable . . .

rite (*5*) ceremony . . . misprint for "right" . . . custom . . . practice

itinerary (*6*) list . . . program . . . route . . . sightseeing . . .

hurtling (*7*) skipping . . . hurting oneself by hurrying . . . traveling . . . rushing . . .

fleet (*7*) powerful . . . charming . . . fast . . . fleeing . . .

annihilating (*7*) conquering . . . making trivial . . . destroying . . . challenging . . .

fraudulent (*8*) absurd . . . false . . . faked . . . criminal . . .

compulsion (*9*) fascination . . . necessity . . . quality of being forced . . . habit . . .

eccentricity (*9*) abnormality . . . oddity . . . pastime . . . habit . . .

appalled (*9*) shocked . . . sad . . . pale . . . almost insane . . .

stigmatizes (*12*) punishes . . . discriminates against . . . paralyzes . . . brands . . .

righteous (*13*) correct . . . legitimate . . . smugly virtuous . . . right . . .

derelict (*13*) irresponsible . . . delinquent . . . foolish . . . without principles . . .

consign (*13*) leave . . . limit . . . resign . . . give . . .

frivolities (*13*) trifles . . . immoral deeds . . . hobbies . . . sillinesses

subversion (*13*) crime . . . stubbornness . . . corruption . . . secret affairs . . .

sensuous (*14*) sensual . . . full of good sense . . . affecting the senses . . . artistic . . .

zest (*15*) enthusiasm . . . meaning . . . fun . . . keen enjoyment

gusto (*15*) pleasure . . . refinement . . . taste . . . appreciation . . .

incurious (*15*) common . . . without curiosity . . . bored . . . boring . . .

presently (*16*) soon . . . now . . . in the manner of a gift . . . in the manner of being present . . .

THEME SUGGESTIONS

Leisure is hard work, or Whadd'ya mean, it's supposed to be fun?
The fine art of doing nothing
My trip to _____
A defense of the American traveler

Nature and Science

HALL • PETRUNKEVITCH • LAY • ROUECHÉ • LEVITT

"Nature" refers to the natural, un-manmade objects and phenomena of our physical environment. "Science" refers to man's efforts and accomplishments in trying to understand, and control, and make use of this environment.

Hall tells how natural processes of life and growth and human knowledge and techniques can cooperate in making possible the peaceful coexistence of plant, animal, and human life: his pond may be called a joint product of Nature and Science. Petrunkevitch presents a close-up of a drama in the quiet and cruel little world of small invertebrates. Lay provides a contrast in setting, though not altogether in final effect, in his report on how human errors and the ruthless logic of nature's laws destroyed a jet plane and its pilot. Roueché follows the trail of a team of medical investigators through New York's Bowery in a report that manages to be objective and moving, humorous and scientific, factual as a newspaper item and as thrilling as a good "whodunit." With Levitt, finally, we move into orbit and anticipate the development of space travel through the next fifty or sixty years. The visions he holds up for us may seem far removed from the peaceful idyll of Hall's Big Pond, but both essays deal with man's never-ending efforts to come closer to the mysteries of the universe.

28

LEONARD HALL

The Pond

1   The late Robert Coffin, who wrote of the salt-water farms of Maine, has a poem I've always liked. He tells of the farmer who rocked his troubles away in a favorite rocking chair. This chair crept across the floor as he rocked, from wall to fireplace, and by the time the old fellow had made the journey twice he was at peace with the world; ready for bed and whatever fortune tomorrow might bring.

2   Here at Possum Trot Farm we have a somewhat similar technique for ironing out our troubles, though in a little different way. When the bottom drops out of the cattle market while tractor prices go higher or aphids take the alfalfa or bugs strip the vegetable garden in spite of dusting, we find that our remedy is almost sure fire. I just tell Ginnie to pack her picnic basket and the old camp coffee pot. Then we hurry through the evening chores, load the red setters into the car along with the creel and fly rod, and head down the county road and across the fields to the Big Pond.

3   This Big Pond of ours could hardly be called an impressive body of water. It covers, in fact, just about an acre and a half. Yet it is one of the most peaceful places I know, especially in early morning or in the evening along about sunset. It is far from the house and the highway—set at the edge of a broad and sloping meadow where fat Herefords graze contentedly. And we feel about these Herefords as does our friend the sheriff of a neighboring county who came to visit one day.

4   "I'll tell you, Len," he said, as we looked over the herd and he approved the good points of each animal. "Those cattle are mighty fine property for a feller to own—even if they weren't worth a dime."

5   So, no matter what their market price, white-faced cows and calves on a green pasture make a picture we always enjoy contemplating.

6   Over to the west of the Big Pond, at a distance of perhaps three hundred yards, Saline Creek flows down its wooded course, flanked on the far side by a high limestone bluff behind which the sun sets early. But a mile to the east, where Buford Mountain raises its rounded crest, the glow lingers for moments longer while purple shadows creep up the deep hollows on its slopes. It is the hour when tree and bank swallows come to harvest insects above the water, dipping now and then to break the surface. And high above them, still in bright sunlight, the nighthawks wheel and dive in graceful, erratic flight.

THE POND. From *The Country Year* by Leonard Hall. Copyright, 1956, by Leonard Hall. Reprinted by permission of Harper & Brothers.

7   Once at the pond, we build a small Indian fire between two stones and set the coffee to boil. Then while Ginnie brings out whatever provender her basket provides, I tie on a floating lure to make a few casts for one of the big bass that live under the old snag where the water is deep. Four or five pounds, these fellows run, so that one of them is excitement enough for an evening. Then I come back to the campfire and watch the fireflies turn on their small lanterns. A barred owl calls from the woods— Old Eight-Hooter is his country name. Stars begin to wink out overhead and the day's cares are forgotten.

8   A farm pond is something you build. Its purpose, generally, is to create a supply of water for livestock in some field where you need it—or for the farm buildings, except the drinking water—or even as a reservoir for irrigation. This latter, however, takes a very deep pond with a big storage capacity. Compared with our small livestock ponds, the irrigation reservoir is expensive. We have seven ponds at Possum Trot, most of them small and serving only to water livestock, and all of them built since we came here ten years ago. The Big Pond, however, has other uses which will be explained presently.

9   It really isn't difficult to plan and build a farm pond. You decide, first of all, where you want or need a supply of water. Then it is well to have someone with experience make a few borings with a soil augur or post-hole digger to be sure the soil structure is such that it will become watertight after saturation. You would not want to dig a pond, for example, where you might hit rock close to the surface—or where there is a loose gravelly subsoil which simply won't hold water. The most successful farm ponds depend entirely on surface run-off from rainfall for their water supply, so that the next step is to be certain you have a watershed of sufficient size draining into the pond. It must be large enough, in other words, so that the normal rainfall of your region will keep the pond filled; yet should not drain so large an area that there is recurring danger of washing away the earthen fill which you make to serve as a dam. You'll have a better water supply, too, if rainfall drains in over a good grass sod, rather than over cultivated ground, since the sod acts as a filter to keep the water clear.

10   There are many reasons why surface drainage from rainfall, rather than the flow from a stream or spring, makes for an ideal farm pond. Streams have a way of flooding in times of heavy rainfall and this constitutes a danger to the dam; this same thing applying, in lesser degree, to the flow from a spring. Sometimes if a pond is built over a spring, the very weight of water above will cause its flow to stop, so that it breaks out at some other point, generally below the pond dam.

11   But the chief drawback is that a constant supply of fresh water flowing into and through the pond has a tendency to keep it sterile; that is, low in the organic matter and in all of the minute organisms which are its very life. The pond depending on rainfall for its water supply will support more aquatic life and has a greater producing capacity than one supplied by a running stream or spring.

12 There are plenty of people who can help with the details of pond planning and building: the county Extension Agent, the U.S. Soil Conservation Service engineer, a field man from the Fish and Wildlife Commission, or an experienced dirt-moving contractor who has built other ponds. Any of these can help with final selection of the location, with necessary surveying of the watershed, and with staking out the earth fill and spillway. With some knowledge of the size of dam, depth of water wanted, and rates per hour for dirt-moving equipment, they can also give a close estimate of costs.

13 The chief rules to remember, other than those already given, are to have the pond deep enough (approximately 10 feet in the deep water area), and to provide a sodded spillway big enough to handle overflow during periods of heavy rainfall. Also if you intend using the pond for livestock water, plan for a pipe through the dam with a watering tank outside. You can fence the pond against trampling by animals and thus prevent erosion, silting, and contamination.

14 When we built our Big Pond, we knew that we wanted to stock it with fish and also to create around it the best possible conditions for all forms of wildlife likely to use such an area. First step was to manure the dam heavily and seed it to pasture grasses and the big perennial legume called Sericea Lespedeza which grows six feet tall and provides dense cover, as well as some food, for songbirds, bobwhite quail, and the small furbearers. Then we built a fence around the pond, taking in an area of perhaps three acres; and here nothing was done except to spread some commercial fertilizer.

15 Once the pond had filled, the next step was to stock it with fish and this was done by our state Conservation Commission, who brought in and released about a thousand bluegill fry and two hundred fingerlings of the largemouth bass. This was done without cost, in return for our agreement to allow a reasonable amount of controlled fishing by our neighbors. Heavy fishing pressure on the farm pond—once the fish population has established itself—is altogether essential; without it, both bass and bluegill will multiply to the point of overpopulation and eventual starvation. The Commission also recommended an annual application of fertilizer to encourage miscroscopic plant growth, thus providing food and cover for the small organisms which are at the base of the pond "food chain": plankton, small crustaceans, insect larvae, nymphs, bluegills, bass.

16 The fish in a well-managed pond increase in size at an astonishing rate; and meanwhile, in the small area of wild land surrounding it, all sorts of interesting things begin to happen. A blackberry thicket spreads and grows; seedlings of multiflora rose appear along the fences where birds drop the seed; grass thrives tall and rank. A few willows take hold at the outside base of the dam and other trees show up in the enclosure: ash, winged elm, hickory, and cedar. A clump of sumac sprouts near the blackberry.

17 When spring arrives, the migrating waterfowl start dropping in. There are bands of blue and snow geese which rest on the pond and go out to graze in the fields of wheat and barley. Visiting ducks include the little teal, scaup, gadwall, ringneck, baldpate, shoveler, wood duck, and mallard. Shorebirds feed along the marshy edges of the pond; greater and lesser yellow-legs, Wilson's snipe, woodcock, sandpipers. The herons come to fish the pond and stay all summer; the great blue and little green and the American and least bitterns. The rattle of the kingfisher is a familiar summer sound. Bobwhites raise their young in the blackberry thicket and red-winged blackbirds nest in the button bushes. Kingbirds and flycatchers and phoebes frequent the pond area, as do the nighthawks and swallows.

18 All of the animal kingdom seems attracted to this small bit of wild land and water—and this with little planning or effort on our part. A pair of muskrats move in from the creek; we view these with some misgiving, since they burrow into the pond dam. Big snapping turtles take up residence, as well as harmless water snakes. Frogs come in countless numbers to lay their eggs in the shallows; little hyla crucifer—the "spring peeper," the lyrical garden toad, green and meadow and leopard frogs, and finally the big bullfrogs whose voices we can hear plainly, a half-mile away across the fields, long after we've come home to bed. Always along the water's edge we find tracks of the raccoon, an enthusiastic fisherman; and more than once, as we've sat beside our small fire, the eerie, sardonic laugh of the red fox has come floating to us across the water.

19 The farm pond, it seems to me, is one of the best examples of what can happen when man works hand in hand with nature—in this enterprise, at least up to a point, by rather intensive human management. We select the place to put the pond where it will do the most good for our own selfish purposes. Then we go in and completely upset the landscape for a time with our bulldozers and scoops; but at once start again to re-create the natural conditions. What we are doing, actually, is to build here a small new "biotic community" in which many niches are unfilled. The pond is fertilized and stocked with fish; this much is artificial, for the fish population must be kept in balance. But the rest of the things just happen. Here are good conditions of food and shelter for insects, certain reptiles, amphibians, birds, and animals; and it is not long before they take advantage of these. Here is a safe resting ground for the migrants, tired from journeying the long skyways, and down they come to visit us.

20 The fishing alone can make our Big Pond one of the most productive areas, acre for acre, on this whole farm. But there are many other values which accrue almost automatically. Besides the animals who come to stay, neighborhood youngsters come with their cane poles (and often with their parents) to catch bluegills by the dozens. To our family, the Big Pond is a sure refuge against those pressures of modern life which reach out to the farm just as surely as they do into the city apartment. It is our best proof, too, that we are still part of the community of Nature —and that she responds richly to our efforts to live in harmony with her.

Exercises

CONTENT

True or False? If you think the statement represents what the selection says or implies, mark it "True"; if you do not think so, mark it "False."

1. Possum Trot Farm is in Maine.
2. The pond covers about three and a half acres.
3. There is bass in it.
4. A farm pond is mainly used for watering the livestock.
5. The first step in building a farm pond is to sample the soil.
6. Rain is the ideal source of water for a farm pond.
7. Organic life in the pond depends on a constant supply of fresh, flowing water.
8. Permission to build a pond must be obtained from the Department of the Interior.
9. The greatest satisfaction from building a farm pond comes from the realization that you are working hand in hand with Nature.
10. The material benefits are negligible.

Question for Discussion

What is the meaning of the sheriff's remark in Paragraph 4? Name as many examples as you can of Hall's sharing the sheriff's sense of values.

FORM AND STYLE

1. A general topic outline of "The Pond" might go something like this:

    I. Introductory anecdote illustrating the need for a means of escape from worries and tensions
   II. Description of Big Pond and surroundings and of picnic
  III. How to build a pond
  IV. Nature takes over; establishment of "biotic community"
   V. Conclusion: values of the pond reasserted

   (a) Divide all twenty paragraphs among the five sections of this outline.

(b) Subdivide sections III and IV into three sections each (A, B, C) and sub-subdivide section IV B into three sections (1, 2, 3). Write topics for each subsection and sub-subsection and specify which paragraph or paragraphs each division includes.

(c) Explain the transitional function of the first sentence in Paragraph 16.

(d) What is the relationship between the first and the last paragraphs? On the basis of your answer explain the comment that the form of the whole essay is circular.

2. Find a paragraph that is almost pure narrative, one that is almost pure description, and one that is almost pure exposition.

3. Explain how the change in word order affects the quality of the statement—and hence the meaning—in the following sentences: "Four or five pounds, these fellows run . . . (sentence 3, Paragraph 7) and "These fellows run four or five pounds. . . ."

VOCABULARY

Which of the four words or phrases to the right seems to you to be *closest* in meaning to the word in heavy type to the left? Put a check mark after your choice.

aphids (2)   rabbits . . . plant lice . . . fungi . . . any kind of grass-eating worms . . .

remedy (2)   escape . . . rescue . . . cure . . . repair . . .

impressive (3)   large . . . full of impression . . . impressionable . . . causing an impression . . .

erratic (6)   without definite course . . . full of errors . . . fanciful . . . strange . . .

provender (7)   provisions . . . content . . . food . . . hay . . .

saturation (9)   excessive leakage . . . quality of being filled . . . time of rainfall . . . moisturing . . .

aquatic (11)   inorganic . . . animal (*adj.*) . . . biological . . . water (*adj.*) . . .

silting (13)   clogging . . . decomposition . . . making salty . . . sifting . . .

contamination (13)   corruption . . . making unfit for human or animal consumption . . . quality of being contagious . . . poisoning . . .

legume (14)   clover . . . water plant . . . any edible vegetable . . . bush . . .

crustaceans (15)   fish . . . snails . . . shell-covered animals . . . algae

rank (16)   straight . . . vigorous . . . offensive . . . degree . . .

misgiving (18)   fear . . . doubt . . . wrong gift . . . reluctance . . .

sardonic (18)   ugly . . . scornful . . . ghastly . . . wild . . .

biotic (*19*)   wildlife . . . natural . . . biological . . . life-giving . . .
niches (*19*)   positions . . . small recesses . . . statues . . . ranks . . .
accrue (*20*)   follow . . . develop . . . are valued . . . come by natural
        growth . . .

THEME SUGGESTIONS

Backyard biology
". . . We are still part of the community of Nature—and . . . she responds richly to our efforts to live in harmony with her." Discuss, elaborate, illustrate.
My form for escape from the world
The lake I love

29

ALEXANDER PETRUNKEVITCH
The Spider and the Wasp

1   In the feeding and safeguarding of their progeny insects and spiders exhibit some interesting analogies to reasoning and some crass examples of blind instinct. The case I propose to describe here is that of the tarantula spiders and their archenemy, the digger wasps of the genus Pepsis. It is a classic example of what looks like intelligence pitted against instinct—a strange situation in which the victim, though fully able to defend itself, submits unwittingly to its destruction.

2   Most tarantulas live in the tropics, but several species occur in the temperate zone and a few are common in the southern U.S. Some varieties are large and have powerful fangs with which they can inflict a deep wound. These formidable looking spiders do not, however, attack man; you can hold one in your hand, if you are gentle, without being bitten. Their bite is dangerous only to insects and small mammals such as mice; for a man it is no worse than a hornet's sting.

3   Tarantulas customarily live in deep cylindrical burrows, from which they emerge at dusk and into which they retire at dawn. Mature males wander about after dark in search of females and occasionally stray into houses. After mating, the male dies in a few weeks, but a female lives much longer and can mate several years in succession. In a Paris museum is a tropical specimen which is said to have been living in captivity for 25 years.

THE SPIDER AND THE WASP. From *Scientific American*, August, 1952. Reprinted by permission of *Scientific American*.

4   A fertilized female tarantula lays from 200 to 400 eggs at a time; thus it is possible for a single tarantula to produce several thousand young. She takes no care of them beyond weaving a cocoon of silk to enclose the eggs. After they hatch, the young walk away, find convenient places in which to dig their burrows and spend the rest of their lives in solitude. The eyesight of tarantulas is poor, being limited to a sensing of change in the intensity of light and to the perception of moving objects. They apparently have little or no sense of hearing, for a hungry tarantula will pay no attention to a loudly chirping cricket placed in its cage unless the insect happens to touch one of its legs.

5   But all spiders, and especially hairy ones, have an extremely delicate sense of touch. Laboratory experiments prove that tarantulas can distinguish three types of touch: pressure against the body wall, stroking of the body hair and riffling of certain very fine hairs on the legs called trichobothria. Pressure against the body, by the finger or the end of a pencil, causes the tarantula to move off slowly for a short distance. The touch excites no defensive response unless the approach is from above where the spider can see the motion, in which case it rises on its hind legs, lifts its front legs, opens its fangs and holds this threatening posture as long as the object continues to move.

6   The entire body of a tarantula, especially its legs, is thickly clothed with hair. Some of it is short and woolly, some long and stiff. Touching this body hair produces one of two distinct reactions. When the spider is hungry, it responds with an immediate and swift attack. At the touch of a cricket's antennae the tarantula seizes the insect so swiftly that a motion picture taken at the rate of 64 frames per second shows only the result and not the process of capture. But when the spider is not hungry, the stimulation of its hairs merely causes it to shake the touched limb. An insect can walk under its hairy belly unharmed.

7   The trichobothria, very fine hairs growing from disklike membranes on the legs, are sensitive only to air movement. A light breeze makes them vibrate slowly without disturbing the common hair. When one blows gently on the trichobothria, the tarantula reacts with a quick jerk of its four front legs. If the front and hind legs are stimulated at the same time, the spider makes a sudden jump. This reaction is quite independent of the state of its appetite.

8   These three tactile responses—to pressure on the body wall, to moving of the common hair and to flexing of the trichobothria—are so different from one another that there is no possibility of confusing them. They serve the tarantula adequately for most of its needs and enable it to avoid most annoyances and dangers. But they fail the spider completely when it meets its deadly enemy, the digger wasp Pepsis.

9   These solitary wasps are beautiful and formidable creatures. Most species are either a deep shiny blue all over, or deep blue with rusty wings. The largest have a wing span of about four inches. They live on

nectar. When excited, they give off a pungent odor—a warning that they are ready to attack. The sting is much worse than that of a bee or common wasp, and the pain and swelling last longer. In the adult stage the wasp lives only a few months. The female produces but a few eggs, one at a time at intervals of two or three days. For each egg the mother must provide one adult tarantula, alive but paralyzed. The mother wasp attaches the egg to the paralyzed spider's abdomen. Upon hatching from the egg, the larva is many hundreds of times smaller than its living but helpless victim. It eats no other food and drinks no water. By the time it has finished its single Gargantuan meal and become ready for wasphood, nothing remains of the tarantula but its indigestible chitinous skeleton.

10 The mother wasp goes tarantula-hunting when the egg in her ovary is almost ready to be laid. Flying low over the ground late on a sunny afternoon, the wasp looks for its victim or for the mouth of a tarantula burrow, a round hole edged by a bit of silk. The sex of the spider makes no difference, but the mother is highly discriminating as to species. Each species of Pepsis requires a certain species of tarantula, and the wasp will not attack the wrong species. In a cage with a tarantula which is not its normal prey the wasp avoids the spider and is usually killed by it in the night.

11 Yet when a wasp finds the correct species, it is the other way about. To identify the species the wasp apparently must explore the spider with her antennae. The tarantula shows an amazing tolerance to this exploration. The wasp crawls under it and walks over it without evoking any hostile response. The molestation is so great and so persistent that the tarantula often rises on all eight legs, as if it were on stilts. It may stand this way for several minutes. Meanwhile the wasp, having satisfied itself that the victim is of the right species, moves off a few inches to dig the spider's grave. Working vigorously with legs and jaws, it excavates a hole 8 to 10 inches deep with a diameter slightly larger than the spider's girth. Now and again the wasp pops out of the hole to make sure that the spider is still there.

12 When the grave is finished, the wasp returns to the tarantula to complete her ghastly enterprise. First she feels it all over once more with her antennae. Then her behavior becomes more aggressive. She bends her abdomen, protruding her sting, and searches for the soft membrane at the point where the spider's legs join its body—the only spot where she can penetrate the horny skeleton. From time to time, as the exasperated spider slowly shifts ground, the wasp turns on her back and slides along with the aid of her wings, trying to get under the tarantula for a shot at the vital spot. During all this maneuvering which can last for several minutes, the tarantula makes no move to save itself. Finally the wasp corners it against some obstruction and grasps one of its legs in her powerful jaws. Now at last the harassed spider tries a desperate but vain defense. The two contestants roll over and over on the ground. It is a terrifying sight and the outcome is always the same. The wasp finally manages to thrust her sting into the soft spot and holds it there for a few seconds while she pumps in the poison. Almost immediately the tarantula falls paralyzed on its back. Its legs stop twitching; its heart stops beating. Yet it is not dead, as is shown by the fact that if taken from the wasp it can be restored to some sensitivity by being kept in a moist chamber for several months.

13 After paralyzing the tarantula, the wasp cleans herself by dragging her body along the ground and rubbing her feet, sucks the drop of blood oozing from the wound in the spider's abdomen, then grabs a leg of the flabby, helpless animal in her jaws and drags it down to the bottom of the grave. She stays there for many minutes, sometimes for several hours, and what she does all that time in the dark we do not know. Eventually she lays her egg and attaches it to the side of the spider's abdomen with a sticky secretion. Then she emerges, fills the grave with soil carried bit by bit in her jaws, and finally tramples the ground all around to hide any trace of the grave from prowlers. Then she flies away, leaving her descendant safely started in life.

14 In all this the behavior of the wasp evidently is qualitatively different from that of the spider. The wasp acts like an intelligent animal. This is not to say that instinct plays no part or that she reasons as man does. But her actions are to the point; they are not automatic and can be modified to fit the situation. We do not know for certain how she identifies the tarantula—probably it is by some olfactory or chemo-tactile sense —but she does it purposefully and does not blindly tackle a wrong species.

15 On the other hand, the tarantula's behavior shows only confusion. Evidently the wasp's pawing gives it no pleasure, for it tries to move away. That the wasp is not simulating sexual stimulation is certain, because male and female tarantulas react in the same way to its advances. That the spider is not anesthetized by some odorless secretion is easily shown by blowing lightly at the tarantula and making it jump suddenly. What, then, makes the tarantula behave as stupidly as it does?

16 No clear, simple answer is available. Possibly the stimulation by the wasp's antennae is masked by a heavier pressure on the spider's body, so that it reacts as when prodded by a pencil. But the explanation may be much more complex. Initiative in attack is not in the nature of tarantulas; most species fight only when cornered so that escape is impossible. Their inherited patterns of behavior apparently prompt them to avoid problems rather than attack them. For example, spiders always weave their webs in three dimensions, and when a spider finds that there is insufficient space to attach certain threads in the third dimension, it leaves the place and seeks another, instead of finishing the web in a single plane. This urge to escape seems to arise under all circumstances, in all phases of life and to take the place of reasoning. For a spider to

change the pattern of its web is as impossible as for an inexperienced man to build a bridge across a chasm obstructing his way.

17 In a way the instinctive urge to escape is not only easier but often more efficient than reasoning. The tarantula does exactly what is most efficient in all cases except in an encounter with a ruthless and determined attacker dependent for the existence of her own species on killing as many tarantulas as she can lay eggs. Perhaps in this case the spider follows its usual pattern of trying to escape, instead of seizing and killing the wasp, because it is not aware of its danger. In any case, the survival of the tarantula species as a whole is protected by the fact that the spider is much more fertile than the wasp.

Exercises

CONTENT

True or False? If you think the statement represents what the selection says or implies, mark it "True"; if you do not think so, mark it "False."

1. All insect and spider behavior is blindly instinctive.
2. The female tarantula lives longer than the male.
3. One specimen is said to have lived in captivity for five years.
4. Although defective in sight and hearing, the tarantula has an excellent sense of touch.
5. The tarantula always attacks when touched.
6. The Pepsis wasp nests in huge colonies.
7. The Pepsis wasp sometimes deposits its egg on the body of the tarantula.
8. But it can do so only after it has killed the spider.
9. The reason why the tarantula does not defend itself against the wasp is that it is anesthetized by the wasp's odorless secretions.
10. The tarantula is far more fertile than the wasp.

Questions for Discussion

1. Why is the wasp throughout referred to as "she" and the spider as "it"?
2. What is the purpose of the long (Paragraphs 5-8) description of the spider's sense of touch?

FORM AND STYLE

1. Complete the following outline:

Paragraph(s)

I. Thesis statement: Pepsis wasp and tarantula exemplify   1
a case of "reasoning" vs. blind instinct in the animal
world

II.   pattern of its web is as improbable as for an inexperienced   2-8
      A.   2
      B. Dangerousness   2
      C.   3
      D. Mating   3
      E.   4
      F.   4-8
         1. Poor sight and hearing   5
         2.   5-8
            a.   5
            b. On body hair   6
            c.   7
            d.   8
            e. Generally adequate, but inadequate against   8
               Pepsis wasp
III.   9
      A.   9
      B. Method of hatching egg   9
IV. Wasp vs. spider   10-13
      A. The search   10
      B.   11
      C.   11
      D.   12
      E. Depositing the egg   13
V.   14-17
      A.   14-15
         1. Wasp's: purposeful, intelligent   14
         2.   15
      B. Interpretation of spider's behavior   15-16
         1. Not sexually stimulated   15
         2.   15
         3. Possibly fooled by body touch   16
         4. Instinctively tries to escape problem   16
VI. Conclusion: 17
      A. But not in the case of tarantula vs. Pepsis wasp   17
      B.   17

2. A scientist should, as a scientist, be as objective as possible. In view of this general rule, can you justify Petrunkevitch's use of the words "ghastly" and "terrifying" in Paragraph 12?

3. Assuming that you find the essay interesting, not only as zoological information but as a kind of "drama in nature," explain the effect of the statement in Paragraph 4 that the female tarantula "takes no care of [her young] beyond weaving a cocoon of silk to enclose the eggs."

4. Look up the technical terms that are unfamiliar to you—such

words, perhaps, as "chitinous" (last sentence, Paragraph 9), "olfactory" and "chemo-tactile" (sentence 5, Paragraph 14), and decide whether the author could have found simpler, more familiar terms to express the same meaning as accurately. What does your answer suggest about the need for and justification of technical language (special terminology, jargon) in scientific writing?

5. What is the origin and meaning of the word "Gargantuan" in the last sentence of Paragraph 9?

6. What are the transitional words and phrases in the beginning of Paragraphs 5, 8, 9, 11, 12, 13, 14, and 15?

VOCABULARY

Which of the four words or phrases to the right seems to you to be *closest* in meaning to the word in heavy type to the left? Put a check mark after your choice.

progeny (1)   eggs . . . life . . . offspring . . . larvae . . .
analogies (1)   examples . . . contrasts . . . illogicalities . . . parallels . . .
crass (1)   vulgar . . . ignorant . . . stupid . . . striking . . .
fangs (2)   teeth . . . claws . . . jaws . . . horns . . .
formidable (2)   well-formed . . . enormous . . . formless . . . terrifying . . .
response (5)   repose . . . answer . . . mechanism . . . organ . . .
vibrate (7)   shake . . . bend . . . move . . . quiver . . .
pungent (9)   powerful . . . sharp . . . unpleasant . . . paralyzing
species (10)   kind . . . specimen . . . brood . . . size . . .
evoking (11)   calling forth . . . meeting . . . making necessary . . . demonstrating . . .
molestation (11)   effort . . . injury . . . annoyance . . . exploration
persistent (11)   irritating . . . long-lasting . . . urgent . . . painful
excavates (11)   leaves a cave . . . makes . . . digs . . . causes to cave in . . .
enterprise (12)   surprise . . . undertaking . . . purpose . . . action
protruding (12)   showing . . . shielding . . . sticking out . . . using . . .
prowlers (13)   thieves . . . a kind of field mice . . . wanderers . . . burrowers . . .
simulating (15)   stimulating . . . causing to occur at the same time . . . imitating . . . applying . . .
obstructing (16)   hindering . . . destroying . . . preventing . . . making difficult . . .
encounter (17)   quarrel . . . conflict . . . occasion . . . a second fight . . .

THEME SUGGESTIONS

The value of Walt Disney's documentary nature films
Can animals think?
An object lesson in zoology
An example (or examples) of natural hostility in the animal kingdom

30

BEIRNE LAY, JR.

The Jet That Crashed Before Take-Off

1   Jet fighter Number 313 taxied onto the end of the runway, cleared for take-off. The Pilot, a young major, fastened his safety belt, set his brakes, and ran up 100 per cent rpm on his engine—a huge, long corncob that made up nearly all of his airplane. Then he released his toe brakes. The wheels rolled the first inch. And in that first inch, the Pilot of Number 313 was doomed. In effect, he was already dead.

2   A mile and a half of smooth, white concrete runway narrowed into the distance in front of the nose of the gleaming, javelin-sleek, swept-wing fighter—8,000 feet of it, more than ample for the 6,700-foot take-off distance calculated in the flight plan.

3   The weather was good, a clear bright morning with a hot sun beating down on the shimmering California desert. Surface winds were nearly dead calm. The J-79 engine was in perfect condition and turning up normal thrust. No mechanical defect lurked anywhere within the complex innards of the aircraft. The Pilot was highly experienced and could point to a spotless safety record and superior past performance. The mission, like every mission in the Air Force, had been minutely planned: gross weight at take-off figured to the pound; runway temperature, surface-wind velocity, and every other factor to insure the mathematical certainty that the wheels of Number 313 would unstick from the runway after a roll of 6,700 feet. No one connected with the planning or preparation for the mission was guilty of a fatal blunder.

4   Only one thing was wrong. A series of minor errors, already irrevocably committed, not one of which was fatal in itself, when added together spelled out a stark fact: Number 313 could not possibly get off the 8,000-foot runway safely.

5 She needed 8,100 feet, instead of 6,700 feet.

6 Why?

7 How could this happen in a precision organization like the United States Air Force, where hundreds of heavily loaded jet aircraft take off every day without incident? The Air Force emphasizes "flying safety" second only to accomplishment of its primary mission and has achieved a consistently lower accident rate each year since World War II.

8 Part of the answer is that each "routine" take-off is not really routine. Rather, it is a kind of triumph, endlessly repeated, over an unseen enemy always lying in wait to prove that an accident is "no accident." It is a triumph, illustrated in reverse, so to speak, by the case of Number 313, which highlights one of the new facts of life in the jet age: a jet take-off is more critical than the familiar take-off in a propeller-driven aircraft. Far more so.

9 Perhaps the simplest way to visualize the situation that confronted Number 313 is to think of the Pilot's safety margin—that 1,300-foot surplus between his estimated 6,700-foot take-off distance and the 8,000-foot runway—as money in the bank. As long as he had any or all of those 1,300 feet, he was in the black. But a series of petty thefts could conceivably put him in the red. Number 313 was the victim of four such thefts, plus two other contributing factors.

10 Theft number one: As the fighter was taxiing out, the control tower reported practically a dead calm, a zero wind, as forecast in the flight plan. However, by the time Number 313 actually started her take-off, she had a four-knot tailwind. This was so small a change that the tower operator either did not notice it or did not consider it important enough to relay it to the Pilot. Certainly this was no drastic windshift. But it cost the Pilot 310 feet of added take-off distance required. Unknown to him, it brought his bank balance down to 990 feet. Still plenty of margin.

11 Theft number two: Take-off had been planned for 11:15 A.M., at which time the runway temperature was forecast to be, and actually was 97 degrees. But Number 313 had taxied out half an hour late because of a valid delay while the crew chief double-checked a malfunctioning fire-warning light and replaced a bulb. During this delay and later, while the fighter was taxiing for over a mile from the parking ramp to the end of the runway, the temperature rose slightly to 101 degrees. A prolonged delay, say of an hour, would have automatically necessitated a revised flight plan, but the Pilot followed common procedure, in view of the shorter delay, when he followed his original flight plan. This unforeseen and seemingly negligible rise of four degrees of temperature robbed him of another 190 feet, since hotter air adds to the take-off roll of a jet in two ways. The engine develops less thrust, and the wings need a higher take-off speed in the thinner air. As he released his toe brakes, the Pilot did not know that his bank balance was now down to 800 feet.

12 Theft number three: The Pilot was executing his first take-off from an unfamiliar air base, having arrived the previous day as a transient. Therefore he was unaware of an optical illusion that confronted him as he stared down the runway at the desert floor, rising gradually from the far end of the runway toward a distant mountain range. To his eyes, the runway appeared to slope slightly downhill in contrast with the rising ground beyond. Actually, there was an imperceptible uphill grade, placing the far end of the runway 260 feet higher than where he sat, and requiring a take-off roll—under existing conditions of a tailwind and high temperature—of an additional 550 feet. Now, unknown to the pilot, his bank balance had shrunk to 250 feet. It was still enough, but it was getting close to bankruptcy.

13 Theft number four: Lack of sleep for the Pilot, as a result of an unexpected change in the weather during the previous night, became a pertinent factor. Confident he would be weathered in for a couple of days until a cold front passed, he had left the base on the evening before to enjoy a night on the town with a clear conscience.

14 His family and his girl lived not far from the air base, and their convivial reunion lasted into the small hours. He was awakened after three and a half hours of sleep by a call from the base notifying him of a break in the weather. Since he was under orders to return to his home base as soon as possible, there was nothing for it but to bolt a cup of black coffee, hustle on out to the base, and start wheeling and dealing.

15 You don't just leap into the cockpit of a supersonic jet fighter and take off, unless you are an interceptor pilot on twenty-four-hour alert duty. This was an extended navigational mission requiring careful planning, preflight inspections, and attention to the check lists. And there is where the lack of sufficient rest led to the final withdrawal from the already slim bank account of Number 313.

16 The Pilot arrived to find that the Assistant Operations Officer, an old pal, had lent a hand and figured the weight of fuel in the main tanks and the auxiliary wing-tip tanks, based on servicing performed the night before. It had been a cold night—an important factor. In arriving at the correct weight, it is necessary to apply a correction for temperature. This his friend had done, but inadvertently he had applied the correction the wrong way, subtracting it instead of adding it. A gallon of fuel will weigh more when it is cold and dense than when it is warm and expanded—just a fraction of a pound more, but it adds up when you're dealing with thousands of pounds of fuel.

17 The Pilot checked over his friend's figures. Partly because of confidence, based on past experience, in the other man's accuracy and conscientiousness, and partly because lack of rest had affected his alertness, the Pilot failed to spot his friend's slip-up. Thus, when the wheels of Number 313 rolled that first inch, the aircraft weighed slightly more than the Pilot thought she did. Under any other circumstances, it might not

have been a costly error, but it was enough in this case to add a disastrous 350 feet to the distance Number 313 must travel before she could become airborne, thereby chipping away the remaining 250 feet still left in the bank—and then some.

18 Now the Pilot was in the red. By one hundred feet. Number 313 was bankrupt and prepared to drag down with her a million-dollar fighter and the life of an invaluable combat pilot.

19 Only two hopes of reprieve for this Pilot still lived. First, if it became apparent in the final stage of take-off that he'd never make it, he could jettison his tip tanks and lighten his load by approximately one ton of the extra fuel. Secondly, at a given point down the runway, he would have an opportunity of recognizing that he had not reached a predicted airspeed. Then he could yank the throttles back and abort the take-off in time for a safe stop. But this second safeguard had already been taken out of his hands through an error of omission, committed by someone now far removed from the scene.

20 The runway, originally, had been 7,600 feet long. Recently, 400 feet had been added to the end from which Number 313 took off. But the runway markers—large signs placed at 1,000-foot intervals alongside the runway to enable the pilot to see at a glance during take-off how much runway he still has left—were in their original locations. The fact that they were scheduled to be moved back 400 feet the next day was just twenty-four hours too late.

21 Black smoke pouring from her tail pipe, Number 313 rolled forward, gathering momentum slowly, the thunder of her departure ricocheting off the buildings along the flight line. When the Pilot passed the first 1,000-foot marker, he was really 1,400 feet down the runway. The same misinformation was waiting to mislead him at the 2,000-foot and the 3,000-foot markers, depriving him of his last chance to judge whether or not his take-off was proceeding according to plan.

22 He reached his maximum refusal speed of 106 knots at the 4,000-foot marker. Had his airspeed been appreciably below the briefed speed at this juncture, here is where he could—and undoubtedly would—have refused take-off. But he saw that his airspeed was indicating within two knots of the desired speed. He continued. What he didn't know, because of the hidden extra 400 feet he had covered, was that he should have been going eight knots faster at the critical moment of decision.

23 Now the end of that once endless-looking ribbon of white concrete began to unreel alarmingly fast. It was too late to stop. The Pilot pressed the release button to jettison his tip tanks. Nothing happened. Malfunction in the circuit. Consuming precious seconds, he resorted to hand operation of the manual release. The tanks dropped clear.

24 But Number 313 was still solidly on the runway, still below the minimum take-off speed of her stubby, razor-blade wings as the last foot of the concrete blurred in under the nose. Reacting out of automatic desperation, the Pilot pulled back on the controls. Number 313 staggered a few feet into the air. Instantly he retracted the landing gear, fighting to reduce the drag and gain that two or three knots of airspeed that might still spell the difference. Quivering right at her stalling speed, the heavy fighter squashed back onto the rough, rising terrain beyond the runway, plowing ahead at 140 knots. Seconds later came the explosion.

25   For Number 313, time and distance had run out. And for her Pilot, in that master ledger where no mistakes in the ultimate arithmetic of cause and effect are permitted to occur, the account was now forever closed.

Exercises

CONTENT

True or False? If you think the statement represents what the selection says or implies, mark it "True"; if you do not think so, mark it "False."

1. The pilot was inexperienced.
2. The pilot was unfamiliar with this particular air base.
3. The accident was caused by an accumulation of small human errors.
4. The jet taxied out in slight tail wind.
5. At higher temperatures, a jet engine develops less thrust.
6. An hour's delay in scheduled take-off would have necessitated a new flight plan.
7. When the jet had traveled 6000 feet down the 8000 feet runway the pilot believed he still had 2400 feet of runway ahead of him.
8. The specific gravity of jet fuel is higher at lower temperatures.
9. The pilot was married.
10. A "routine" take-off never really is just routine.

Questions for Discussion

1. List the four "thefts."
2. Explain the paradox of the title.
3. *The Jet That Crashed Before Take-Off* illustrates what Philip Wylie in *Safe and Insane* (page 99) called "the absolute inviolability of [nature's] laws." Explain.

FORM AND STYLE

1. The essay is an analysis bracketed by (or interrupting) a narrative. The narrative tells the story of the take-off crash of a jet airplane; the analysis explains the causes of the crash. Where does the analysis begin and where does it leave off?

2. Lay turns what might have been a dry, technical report into a piece of suspenseful writing. Explain exactly how Paragraph 1 creates suspense. When is the suspense over?

3. Point to other passages where Lay has dramatized his material by means of style. See, for example, the sentence fragment in Paragraph 23.

4. Paragraph 9 contains an analogy. Explain it and the manner in which it organizes the whole middle section of the essay.

5. Comment upon the inexactness of phrasing in this sentence in Paragraph 20: "The fact that they were scheduled to be moved back 400 feet the next day was just twenty-four hours too late."

6. Why does the metaphor at the very end of the essay—"the account was now forever closed"—seem particularly appropriate?

VOCABULARY

Which of the four words or phrases to the right seems to you to be *closest* in meaning to the word in heavy type to the left? Put a check mark after your choice.

shimmering (3)   warm . . . steamy . . . glimmering . . . seeming to tremble . . .

irrevocably (4)   beyond recall . . . fatally . . . stupidly . . . erroneously . . .

stark (4)   cruel . . . strong . . . stern . . . awful . . .

primary (7)   assigned . . . first . . . most important . . . instructive . . .

consistently (7)   considerably . . . by way of consisting of . . . very much . . . steadily . . .

reverse (8)   behind . . . in a backward direction . . . set-back . . . contradiction . . .

petty (9)   mean . . . small . . . pretty . . . avoidable . . .

relay (10)   radio (*verb*) . . . send as warning . . . pass on . . . call attention to . . .

valid (11)   long . . . valuable . . . fatal . . . justifiable . . .

negligible (11)   neglected . . . unimportant . . . unnoticed . . . small . . .

transient (12)   substitute . . . guest . . . visitor . . . one who is passing through . . .

confronted (12)   faced . . . greeted . . . confused . . . surprised

imperceptible (12)   small . . . gradual . . . not apparent to the senses . . . unimportant . . .

pertinent (13)   painful . . . relevant . . . important . . . serious . . .

convivial (14)   congenial . . . living together . . . jovial . . . mutual . . .

inadvertently *(16)*   unintentionally . . . carelessly . . . without telling anybody . . . inexplicably . . .

accuracy *(17)*   skill . . . skill with accounting . . . experience . . .
exactness . . .

conscientiousness *(17)*   responsibility . . . conscience . . . consciousness . . . careful from a sense of moral duty . . .

reprieve *(19)*   safety . . . rescue . . . pardon from death . . . relief . . .

apparent *(19)*   probable . . . clear . . . possible . . . visible . . .

abort *(19)*   stop . . . kill . . . divert . . . delay . . .

THEME SUGGESTIONS

According to the author, no single known jet plane crash has occurred exactly like the one related in *The Jet That Crashed Before Take-
Off*. The account combines details from several real crashes. What difference, if any, does this information make as far as your attitude to the
essay is concerned? Give reasons for your answer.

Jet pilot

Protection against human error in —— (a dangerous job you know of)

Why it happened (analyze and explain the causes of an accident)

31

BERTON ROUECHÉ

Eleven Blue Men

1   At about eight o'clock on Monday morning, September 25, 1944,
a ragged, aimless old man of eighty-two collapsed on the sidewalk on Dey
Street, near the Hudson Terminal. Innumerable people must have
noticed him, but he lay there alone for several minutes, dazed, doubled
up with abdominal cramps, and in an agony of retching. Then a policeman came along. Until the policeman bent over the old man, he may
have supposed that he had just a sick drunk on his hands; wanderers
dropped by drink are common in that part of town in the early morning.
It was not an opinion that he could have held for long. The old man's
nose, lips, ears, and fingers were sky-blue. The policeman went to a telephone and put in an ambulance call to Beekman-Downtown Hospital,
half a dozen blocks away. The old man was carried into the emergency
room there at eight-thirty. By that time, he was unconscious and the blue-

ELEVEN BLUE MEN. From *Eleven Blue Men* by Berton Roueché. Copyright, 1953, by Berton Roueché. This piece first appeared in *The New Yorker*.
Reprinted by permission of Little, Brown & Company.

ness had spread over a large part of his body. The examining physician attributed the old man's morbid color to cyanosis, a condition that usually results from an insufficient supply of oxygen in the blood, and also noted that he was diarrheic and in a severe state of shock. The course of treatment prescribed by the doctor was conventional. It included an instant gastric lavage, heart stimulants, bed rest, and oxygen therapy. Presently, the old man recovered an encouraging, if painful, consciousness and demanded, irascibly and in the name of God, to know what had happened to him. It was a question that, at the moment, nobody could answer with much confidence.

2   For the immediate record, the doctor made a free-hand diagnosis of carbon-monoxide poisoning—from what source, whether an automobile or a gas pipe, it was, of course, pointless even to guess. Then, because an isolated instance of gas poisoning is something of a rarity in a section of the city as crammed with human beings as downtown Manhattan, he and his colleagues in the emergency room braced themselves for at least a couple more victims. Their foresight was promptly and generously rewarded. A second man was rolled in at ten-twenty-five. Forty minutes later, an ambulance drove up with three more men. At eleven-twenty, two others were brought in. An additional two arrived during the next fifteen minutes. Around noon, still another was admitted. All of these nine men were also elderly and dilapidated, all had been in misery for at least an hour, and all were rigid, cyanotic, and in a state of shock. The entire body of one, a bony, seventy-three-year-old consumptive named John Mitchell, was blue. Five of the nine, including Mitchell, had been stricken in the Globe Hotel, a sunless, upstairs flophouse at 190 Park Row, and two in a similar place, called the Star Hotel, at 3 James Street. Another had been found slumped in the doorway of a condemned building on Park Row, not far from City Hall Park, by a policeman. The ninth had keeled over in front of the Eclipse Cafeteria, at 6 Chatham Square. At a quarter to seven that evening, one more aged blue man was brought in. He had been lying, too sick to ask for help, on his cot in a cubicle in the Lion Hotel, another flophouse, at 26 Bowery, since ten o'clock that morning. A clerk had finally looked in and seen him.

3   By the time this last blue man arrived at the hospital, an investigation of the case by the Department of Health, to which all outbreaks of an epidemiological nature must be reported, had been under way for five hours. Its findings thus far had not been illuminating. The investigation was conducted by two men. One was the Health Department's chief epidemiologist, Dr. Morris Greenberg, a small, fragile, reflective man of fifty-seven, who is now acting director of the Bureau of Preventable Diseases; the other was Dr. Ottavio Pellitteri, a field epidemiologist, who, since 1946, has been administrative medical inspector for the Bureau. He is thirty-six years old, pale, and stocky, and has a bristling black mustache. One day, when I was in Dr. Greenberg's office, he and Dr. Pellitteri told me about the case. Their recollection of it is, understandably, vivid. The derelicts were the victims of a type of poisoning so rare that only ten previous outbreaks of it had been recorded in medical literature. Of these, two were in the United States and two in Germany; the others had been reported in France, England, Switzerland, Algeria, Australia, and India. Up to September 25, 1944, the largest number of people stricken in a single outbreak was four. That was in Algeria, in 1926.

4   The Beekman-Downtown Hospital telephoned a report of the occurrence to the Health Department just before noon. As is customary, copies of the report were sent to all the Department's administrative officers. "Mine was on my desk when I got back from lunch," Dr. Greenberg said to me. "It didn't sound like much. Nine persons believed to be suffering from carbon-monoxide poisoning had been admitted during the morning, and all of them said that they had eaten breakfast at the Eclipse Cafeteria, at 6 Chatham Square. Still, it was a job for us. I checked with the clerk who handles assignments and found that Pellitteri had gone out on it. That was all I wanted to know. If it amounted to anything, I knew he'd phone me before making a written report. That's an arrangement we have here. Well, a couple of hours later I got a call from him. My interest perked right up."

5   "I was at the hospital," Dr. Pellitteri told me, "and I'd talked to the staff and most of the men. There were ten of them by then, of course. They were sick as dogs, but only one was in really bad shape."

6   "That was John Mitchell," Dr. Greenberg put in. "He died the next night. I understand his condition was hopeless from the start. The others, including the old boy who came in last, pulled through all right. Excuse me, Ottavio, but I just thought I'd get that out of the way. Go on."

7   Dr. Pellitteri nodded. "I wasn't at all convinced that it was gas poisoning," he continued. "The staff was beginning to doubt it, too. The symptoms weren't quite right. There didn't seem to be any of the headache and general dopiness that you get with gas. What really made me suspicious was this: Only two or three of the men had eaten breakfast in the cafeteria at the same time. They had straggled in all the way from seven o'clock to ten. That meant that the place would have had to be full of gas for at least three hours, which is preposterous. It also indicated that we ought to have had a lot more sick people than we did. Those Chatham Square eating places have a big turnover. Well, to make sure, I checked with Bellevue, Gouverneur, St. Vincent's, and the other downtown hospitals. None of them had seen a trace of cyanosis. Then I talked to the sick men some more. I learned two interesting things. One was that they had all got sick right after eating. Within thirty minutes. The other was that all but one had eaten oatmeal, rolls, and coffee. He ate just oatmeal. When ten men eat the same thing in the same place on the same day and then all come down with the same illness . . . I told Greenberg that my hunch was food poisoning."

8 "I was willing to rule out gas," Dr. Greenberg said. A folder containing data on the case lay on the desk before him. He lifted the cover thoughtfully, then let it drop. "And I agreed that the oatmeal sounded pretty suspicious. That was as far as I was willing to go. Common, ordinary, everyday food poisoning—I gathered that was what Pellitteri had in mind—wasn't a very satisfying answer. For one thing, cyanosis is hardly symptomatic of that. On the other hand, diarrhea and severe vomiting are, almost invariably. But they weren't in the clinical picture, I found, except in two or three of the cases. Moreover, the incubation periods—the time lapse between eating and illness—were extremely short. As you probably know, most food poisoning is caused by eating something that has been contaminated by bacteria. The usual offenders are the staphylococci—they're mostly responsible for boils and skin infections and so on—and the salmonella. The latter are related to the typhoid organism. In a staphylococcus case, the first symptoms rarely develop in under two hours. Often, it's closer to five. The incubation period in the other ranges from twelve to thirty-six hours. But here we were with something that hit in thirty minutes or less. Why, one of the men had got only as far as the sidewalk in front of the cafeteria before he was knocked out. Another fact that Pellitteri had dug up struck me as very significant. All of the men told him that the illness had come on with extraordinary suddenness. One minute they were feeling fine, and the next minute they were practically helpless. That was another point against the ordinary food-poisoning theory. Its onset is never that fast. Well, that suddenness began to look like a lead. It led me to suspect that some drug might be to blame. A quick and sudden reaction is characteristic of a great many drugs. So is the combination of cyanosis and shock."

9 "None of the men were on dope," Dr. Pellitteri said. "I told Greenberg I was sure of that. Their pleasure was booze."

10 "That was O.K.," Dr. Greenberg said. "They could have got a toxic dose of some drug by accident. In the oatmeal, most likely. I couldn't help thinking that the oatmeal was relevant to our problem. At any rate, the drug idea was very persuasive."

11 "So was Greenberg," Dr. Pellitteri remarked with a smile. "Actually, it was the only explanation in sight that seemed to account for everything we knew about the clinical and environmental picture."

12 "All we had to do now was prove it," Dr. Greenberg went on mildly. "I asked Pellitteri to get a blood sample from each of the men before leaving the hospital for a look at the cafeteria. We agreed he would send the specimens to the city toxicologist, Dr. Alexander O. Gettler, for an overnight analysis. I wanted to know if the blood contained methemoglobin. Methemoglobin is a compound that's formed only when any one of several drugs enters the blood. Gettler's report would tell us if we were at least on the right track. That is, it would give us a yes-or-no answer on drugs. If the answer was yes, then we could go on from there to

identify the particular drug. How we would go about that would depend
on what Pellitteri was able to turn up at the cafeteria. In the meantime,
there was nothing for me to do but wait for their reports. I'd theorized
myself hoarse."

13   Dr. Pellitteri, having attended to his bloodletting with reasonable
dispatch, reached the Eclipse Cafeteria at around five o'clock. "It was
about what I'd expected," he told me. "Strictly a horse market, and dirtier
than most. The sort of place where you can get a full meal for fifteen
cents. There was a grind house on one side, a cigar store on the other,
and the 'L' overhead. Incidentally, the Eclipse went out of business a
year or so after I was there, but that had nothing to do with us. It was
just a coincidence. Well, the place looked deserted and the door was
locked. I knocked, and a man came out of the back and let me in. He
was one of our people, a health inspector for the Bureau of Food and
Drugs, named Weinberg. His bureau had stepped into the case as a
matter of routine, because of the reference to a restaurant in the noti-
fication report. I was glad to see him and to have his help. For one thing,
he had put a temporary embargo on everything in the cafeteria. That's
why it was closed up. His main job, though, was to check the place for
violations of the sanitation code. He was finding plenty."

14   "Let me read you a few of Weinberg's findings," Dr. Greenberg
said, extracting a paper from the folder on his desk. "None of them had
any direct bearing on our problem, but I think they'll give you a good
idea of what the Eclipse was like—what too many restaurants are like.
This copy of his report lists fifteen specific violations. Here they are:
'Premises heavily infested with roaches. Fly infestation throughout premises. Floor defective in rear part of dining room. Kitchen walls and ceiling encrusted with grease and soot. Kitchen floor encrusted with dirt.
Refuse under kitchen fixtures. Sterilizing facilities inadequate. Sink defective. Floor and walls at serving tables and coffee urns encrusted with
dirt. Kitchen utensils encrusted with dirt and grease. Storage-cellar walls,
ceiling, and floor encrusted with dirt. Floor and shelves in cellar covered
with refuse and useless material. Cellar ceiling defective. Sewer pipe
leaking. Open sewer line in cellar.' Well . . ." He gave me a squeamish
smile and stuck the paper back in the folder.

15   "I can see it now," Dr. Pellitteri said. "And smell it. Especially the
kitchen, where I spent most of my time. Weinberg had the proprietor
and the cook out there, and I talked to them while he prowled around.
They were very coöperative. Naturally. They were scared to death. They
knew nothing about gas in the place and there was no sign of any, so I
went to work on the food. None of what had been prepared for breakfast
that morning was left. That, of course, would have been too much to
hope for. But I was able to get together some of the kind of stuff that had
gone into the men's breakfast, so that we could make a chemical determination at the Department. What I took was ground coffee, sugar, a mix-

ture of evaporated milk and water that passed for cream, some bakery rolls, a five-pound carton of dry oatmeal, and some salt. The salt had been used in preparing the oatmeal. That morning, like every morning, the cook told me, he had prepared six gallons of oatmeal, enough to serve around a hundred and twenty-five people. To make it, he used five pounds of dry cereal, four gallons of water—regular city water—and a handful of salt. That was his term—a handful. There was an open gallon can of salt standing on the stove. He said the handful he'd put in that morning's oatmeal had come from that. He refilled the can on the stove every morning from a big supply can. He pointed out the big can—it was up on a shelf—and as I was getting it down to take with me, I saw another can, just like it, nearby. I took that one down, too. It was also full of salt, or, rather, something that looked like salt. The proprietor said it wasn't salt. He said it was saltpetre—sodium nitrate—that he used in corning beef and in making pastrami. Well, there isn't any harm in saltpetre; it doesn't even act as an antiaphrodisiac, as a lot of people seem to think. But I wrapped it up with the other loot and took it along, just for fun. The fact is, I guess, everything in that damn place looked like poison."

16 After Dr. Pellitteri had deposited his loot with a Health Department chemist, Andrew J. Pensa, who promised to have a report ready by the following afternoon, he dined hurriedly at a restaurant in which he had confidence and returned to Chatham Square. There he spent the evening making the rounds of the lodging houses in the neighborhood. He had heard at Mr. Pensa's office that an eleventh blue man had been admitted to the hospital, and before going home he wanted to make sure that no other victims had been overlooked. By midnight, having covered all the likely places and having rechecked the downtown hospitals, he was satisfied. He repaired to his office and composed a formal progress report for Dr. Greenberg. Then he went home and to bed.

17 The next morning, Tuesday, Dr. Pellitteri dropped by the Eclipse, which was still closed but whose proprietor and staff he had told to return for questioning. Dr. Pellitteri had another talk with the proprietor and the cook. He also had a few inconclusive words with the rest of the cafeteria's employees—two dishwashers, a busboy, and a counterman. As he was leaving, the cook, who had apparently passed an uneasy night with his conscience, remarked that it was possible that he had absent-mindedly refilled the salt can on the stove from the one that contained saltpetre. "That was interesting," Dr. Pellitteri told me, "even though such a possibility had already occurred to me, and even though I didn't know whether it was important or not. I assured him that he had nothing to worry about. We had been certain all along that nobody had deliberately poisoned the old men." From the Eclipse, Dr. Pellitteri went on to Dr. Greenberg's office, where Dr. Gettler's report was waiting.

18 "Gettler's test for methemoglobin was positive," Dr. Greenberg said. "It had to be a drug now. Well, so far so good. Then we heard from Pensa."

19 "Greenberg almost fell out of his chair when he read Pensa's report," Dr. Pellitteri observed cheerfully.

20 "That's an exaggeration," Dr. Greenberg said. "I'm not easily dumfounded. We're inured to the incredible around here. Why, a few years ago we had a case involving some numskull who stuck a fistful of potassium-thiocyanate crystals, a very nasty poison, in the coils of an office water cooler, just for a practical joke. However, I can't deny that Pensa rather taxed our credulity. What he had found was that the small salt can and the one that was supposed to be full of sodium nitrate both contained sodium *nitrite*. The other food samples, incidentally, were O.K."

21 "That also taxed my credulity," Dr. Pellitteri said.

22 Dr. Greenberg smiled. "There's a great deal of difference between nitrate and nitrite," he continued. "Their only similarity, which is an unfortunate one, is that they both look and taste more or less like ordinary table salt. Sodium nitrite isn't the most powerful poison in the world, but a little of it will do a lot of harm. If you remember, I said before that this case was almost without precedent—only ten outbreaks like it on record. Ten is practically none. In fact, sodium-nitrite poisoning is so unusual that some of the standard texts on toxicology don't even mention it. So Pensa's report was pretty startling. But we accepted it, of course, without question or hesitation. Facts are facts. And we were glad to. It seemed to explain everything very nicely. What I've been saying about sodium-nitrite poisoning doesn't mean that sodium nitrite itself is rare. Actually, it's fairly common. It's used in the manufacture of dyes and as a medical drug. We use it in treating certain heart conditions and for high blood pressure. But it also has another important use, one that made its presence at the Eclipse sound plausible. In recent years, and particularly during the war, sodium nitrite has been used as a substitute for sodium nitrate in preserving meat. The government permits it but stipulates that the finished meat must not contain more than one part of sodium nitrite per five thousand parts of meat. Cooking will safely destroy enough of that small quantity of the drug." Dr. Greenberg shrugged. "Well, Pellitteri had had the cook pick up a handful of salt—the same amount, as nearly as possible, as went into the oatmeal—and then had taken this to his office and found that it weighed approximately a hundred grams. So we didn't have to think twice to realize that the proportion of nitrite in that batch of cereal was considerably higher than one to five thousand. Roughly, it must have been around one to about eighty before cooking destroyed part of the nitrite. It certainly looked as though Gettler, Pensa, and the cafeteria cook between them had given us our answer. I called up Gettler and told him what Pensa had discovered and asked him to run a specific test for nitrites on his blood samples. He had, as a matter of course, held some blood back for later examination. His confirmation came through in a couple of hours. I went home that night feeling pretty good."

23 Dr. Greenberg's serenity was a fugitive one. He awoke on Wednesday morning troubled in mind. A question had occurred to him that he was unable to ignore. "Something like a hundred and twenty-five people ate oatmeal at the Eclipse that morning," he said to me, "but only eleven of them got sick. Why? The undeniable fact that those eleven old men were made sick by the ingestion of a toxic dose of sodium nitrite wasn't enough to rest on. I wanted to know exactly how much sodium nitrite each portion of that cooked oatmeal had contained. With Pensa's help again, I found out. We prepared a batch just like the one the cook had made on Monday. Then Pensa measured out six ounces, the size of the average portion served at the Eclipse, and analyzed it. It contained two and a half grains of sodium nitrite. That explained why the hundred and fourteen other people did not become ill. The toxic dose of sodium nitrite is three grains. But it didn't explain how each of our eleven old men had received an additional half grain. It seemed extremely unlikely that the extra touch of nitrite had been in the oatmeal when it was served. It had to come in later. Then I began to get a glimmer. Some people sprinkle a little salt, instead of sugar, on hot cereal. Suppose, I thought, that the busboy, or whoever had the job of keeping the table salt shakers filled, had made the same mistake that the cook had. It seemed plausible. Pellitteri was out of the office—I've forgotten where—so I got Food and Drugs to step over to the Eclipse, which was still under embargo, and bring back the shakers for Pensa to work on. There were seventeen of them, all good-sized, one for each table. Sixteen contained either pure sodium chloride or just a few inconsequential traces of sodium nitrite mixed in with the real salt, but the other was point thirty-seven per cent nitrite. That one was enough. A spoonful of that salt contained a bit more than half a grain."

24 "I went over to the hospital Thursday morning," Dr. Pellitteri said. "Greenberg wanted me to check the table-salt angle with the men. They could tie the case up neatly for us. I drew a blank. They'd been discharged the night before, and God only knew where they were."

25 "Naturally," Dr. Greenberg said, "it would have been nice to know for a fact that the old boys all sat at a certain table and that all of them put about a spoonful of salt from that particular shaker on their oatmeal, but it wasn't essential. I was morally certain that they had. There just wasn't any other explanation. There was one other question, however. Why did they use so *much* salt? For my own peace of mind, I wanted to know. All of a sudden, I remembered Pellitteri had said they were all heavy drinkers. Well, several recent clinical studies have demonstrated that there is usually a subnormal concentration of sodium chloride in the blood of alcoholics. Either they don't eat enough to get sufficient salt or they lose it more rapidly than other people do, or both. Whatever the reasons are, the conclusion was all I needed. Any animal, you know, whether a mouse or a man, tends to try to obtain a necessary substance that his body lacks. The final question had been answered."

Exercises

CONTENT

True or False? If you think the statement represents what the selection says or implies, mark it "True"; if you do not think so, mark it "False."

1. None of the stricken men died.
2. All of them had had oatmeal for breakfast.
3. Some of the men were first picked up as drunks before the police realized they were sick.
4. Diarrhea and severe vomiting are rarely symptoms of cyanide poisoning.
5. There had been only two previous recorded cases of this type of poisoning.
6. There was never any question of crime.
7. In most cases of food poisoning, symptoms appear well within the first half-hour after ingestion.
8. This case led to the permanent closing of the Eclipse Cafeteria by the New York City Department of Health.
9. The presence of sodium nitrite in the kitchen of the Eclipse Cafeteria was never explained.
10. Sodium chloride is ordinary table salt.

Question for Discussion

In your opinion, which of the following statements comes closest to stating the theme of *Eleven Blue Men?*

1. Thanks to the alertness, skill, and excellent equipment of the New York Department of Health, widespread epidemics are virtually impossible in New York City.
2. Subhygienic public eating places should clean up or close up.
3. The case of the "eleven blue men" provides a good example of the methodical and ingenious medical detective work often performed by public health officials.
4. Often in medicine a first diagnosis has to be changed as later symptoms develop.
5. Heavy drinking makes a person more liable to poisoning from otherwise harmless or relatively harmless drugs.

FORM AND STYLE

1. Think for a moment of *Eleven Blue Men* as a kind of detective story. Who is the criminal? The detective?

2. Define the principle of organization used here.

3. Try to find reasons why certain passages are written as objective summarizing reports, while others are direct quotations.

4. Is there any advantage in having both Dr. Greenberg and Dr. Pellitteri tell about the case? Explain.

5. What is the effect of such words and expressions as "sick as dogs" (Paragraph 5), "their pleasure was booze" (Paragraph 9), "I'd theorized myself hoarse" (Paragraph 12), "in that damn place" (Paragraph 15), "old boys" (Paragraph 24)?

6. What is the significance of the words "in which he had confidence" in the first sentence of Paragraph 16?

7. Explain the sentence fragments in Paragraph 14 and the use of single quotation marks on either side of them.

VOCABULARY

Which of the four words or phrases to the right seems to you to be *closest* in meaning to the word in heavy type to the left? Put a check mark after your choice.

agony (*1*)   pain . . . spasm . . . violent activity . . . horror . . .

attributed (*1*)   gave as to the cause of . . . explained . . . recorded . . . diagnosed for the time being . . .

lavage (*1*)   purgation . . . washing . . . pumping . . . examination . . .

therapy (*1*)   treatment . . . putting in a tent . . . application . . . cure . . .

irascibly (*1*)   in a bewildered manner . . . loudly . . . like a rascal . . . angrily . . .

immediate (2)   in between time . . . temporary . . . right away . . . medical . . .

dilapidated (2)   poor . . . wretched . . . ruined . . . depraved . . .

rigid (2)   unconscious . . . limp . . . stiff . . . cold . . .

fragile (3)   frail . . . thin . . . agile . . . intelligent . . .

derelicts (3)   victims . . . patients . . . delirious persons . . . wrecks

preposterous (7)   absurd . . . hard to believe . . . dangerous . . . unlikely . . .

persuasive (10)   attractive . . . convincing . . . eloquent . . . fruitful . . .

toxicologist (12)   expert on intoxication . . . diagnostician . . . specialist on diseases of the blood . . . expert on poisons . . .

dispatch (13)   care . . . speed . . . send-off . . . distinction . . .

embargo (13)   suspicion . . . prohibition . . . seal . . . closure . . .

sanitation (13)   purity . . . cleanliness . . . health . . . public welfare . . .

extracting *(14)*   producing . . . showing . . . taking out . . . look-
      ing at . . .
squeamish *(14)*   delicate . . . easily nauseated . . . odd-looking . . .
      reluctant . . .
repaired *(16)*   returned . . . fixed . . . retired . . . reported . . .
inured *(20)*   injured . . . insured . . . accustomed . . . prepared . . .
credulity *(20)*   reason . . . strength . . . theory . . . belief . . .
precedent *(22)*   record . . . evidence . . . previous example . . .
      something earlier . . .
stipulates *(22)*   orders . . . makes condition . . . desires . . . allows
serenity *(23)*   unruffledness . . . happiness . . . pride . . . self-flat-
      tery . . .
fugitive *(23)*   short-lived . . . fleeing . . . insubstantial . . . false . . .
ingestion *(23)*   eating . . . swallowing . . . digestion . . . presence
inconsequential *(23)*   quality of not following . . . slight . . . unim-
      portant . . . microscopic . . .

THEME SUGGESTIONS

The use of humor in *Eleven Blue Men*
Public health measures in our town
High taxes are/are not worth it
How I pieced evidence together to solve a problem

32

I. M. LEVITT

Schedule for the Space Age

1   The Soviet earth satellite whose successful launching so startled
the world on October 4 [1957] was thrust to a height of about 560
miles—or roughly one four-hundredth of the distance to the moon. If that
seems to leave a long way to go, the achievement was nevertheless a
momentous first step into an era of space travel in which not only the
moon but far more distant celestial bodies will be within the reach of
man. Already it is possible to predict with fair certainty the probable
timetable of man's conquest of space.

2   The present first phase will continue with the launching of pro-
gressively more complex and longer-lived satellites. The next phase,

SCHEDULE FOR THE SPACE AGE. "Now the Space Age Opens" by I. M.
Levitt, in the *New York Times Magazine,* October 13, 1957. Reprinted by
permission of the *New York Times Magazine* and the author.

which will ultimately take man to the moon and the planets, will begin within a few years—let us say by 1960—with the mastery of the problem of putting a television transmitter in a satellite. Much work remains to be done. Solar mirrors to produce the necessary power must be developed. Telemetering—transmission of data by radio—must be improved. The tape machines now used to record TV programs must be miniaturized to be taken aloft. But the principles of these devices are known now; only technical development work remains to make them applicable to the satellite.

3   The TV picture which we will thus get from on high will be a vast panorama of the earth. Its most important application will probably be in weather forecasting: Meteorologists will have data gathered by looking in toward the earth from outside its atmosphere, instead of the other way around, and their whole science will be revolutionized.

4   By 1964 a rocket plane will go into the sky carrying a full complement of small animals. These will be monkeys, rats, mice and guinea pigs. They will be in capsule chambers and will spend a considerable amount of time in gravity-free space. These animals will be wired for everything. Technicians on the surface will have telemetered to them the heart beat, the blood pressure, the temperature, the respiration rate and every other bit of information needed to disclose the complete behavior of these creatures in space. Not only will there be recordings of the actions of the animals but pictures will be relayed back to the surface showing their reactions to various stimuli induced as part of the experiments.

5   In this fashion we shall gain an insight into the probable behavior of man when he gets into space. But the animals used in this experiment will not return to earth. When the satellite orbit has decayed to the point where atmospheric drag becomes a factor, gravity will accelerate it and bring the ship into the denser atmosphere, where it will burn out like a meteor.

6   Thus the next step must await the solution to the staggering problem of "re-entry." But by 1968 there should be a rocket ship going aloft with a man aboard (it may be a woman, for a woman packs the same amount of skill and brains into a smaller package). The pilot will be wired so that scientists on the earth can keep him (or her) under constant surveillance. Cameras will picture and relay to the earth the behavior of the pilot. Every conceivable device will be employed to obtain a complete picture of the first man in space.

7   Scientists should know then whether further space travel is feasible. While today it appears that there should be no question of this, actually no man has been subject to these conditions for more than forty seconds—the maximum period of gravity-free flight so far experienced by pilots in experimental rocket planes. We must live with this condition for a considerable length of time before we are certain that man can adapt to it.

8 After a few weeks in the sky the pilot will be ready to return to the surface of the earth. Now an inordinately complex electronic computer will take over to bring the rocket plane down. The speed of the rocket plane will be so high and the reaction time of the pilot so slow that only an electronic "brain" will be capable of performing this exacting task.

9 Assuming that the human being comes through this adventure with no mishaps, then the establishment of a huge, spinning, doughnut-shaped space station can begin by 1978. Tremendous three-stage rockets will be launched to enter a region 1,000 miles above the surface of the earth. Into this area will come rocket ship after rocket ship carrying payloads from which to fashion the huge wheel-shaped structure. When complete, the space station will constitute the finest physical laboratory ever conceived by man. Here, above even the thinnest atmosphere, it will orbit the earth indefinitely.

10 Such a space station will become an essential stepping stone to other bodies in the solar system. To escape from the earth's gravity en route to the moon or the planets the "velocity of escape"—seven miles per second—must be reached. This is an enormous speed when we consider that our fastest rockets may attain a speed at the surface of the earth of less than one and one-quarter miles per second.

11 To achieve seven miles per second, inordinate amounts of fuel must be consumed. Thus any method by which this speed can be reduced will enhance the possibility of success. This is precisely why the space station is such a crucial item in any attempt to reach the other celestial bodies. To establish the space station requires a speed of only five miles per second. This saving in speed means that appreciably higher payloads can be taken to the space station. And once the station is available, then a speed of only about two miles per second is necessary to escape from it to voyage farther.

12 However, following completion of the space station about 1980, there will come a hiatus in which our scientific cupboard will be replenished—new developments integrated into our sciences. Perhaps twenty years will elapse from the time man establishes the space station until he is ready to leave for the moon and the planets. This brings us to the year 2000.

13 The key to all travel beyond the moon is the exploitation of the moon itself as a "superbase." The reason for this is readily understood. The moon is a small body, 2,160 miles in diameter. Its mass is $\frac{1}{81}$ that of the earth. The combination of these two factors means that the lunar escape velocity is about one and one-half miles per second. The ease with which we can leave the moon makes it a certainty that it will be the most important base in deep space travel.

14 But a base needs more than just a low velocity of escape. A base means a place where the travelers can take on a full load of fuel. It means a place where the space ship can be provisioned. It means a place where personnel can recuperate from strenuous trips. The moon is all of these.

15 It may come as a surprise to those people who have long considered the moon as a dead, lifeless body to hear it described as the perfect base. The truth is that the moon *is* a cold and lifeless body, but once man gets to its surface he may make it bloom into a habitable planet.

16 By the year 2000 it is certain that man will have tapped tremendous stores of energy. It may take the form of energy from the nucleus of the atom or it may take the form of energy from the sun. Already man can convert sunlight into electrical energy with an efficiency of about 11 per cent. While this particular approach may not be capable of much higher efficiency, in the next forty years it is conceivable that new materials may be discovered to yield higher efficiencies. Given sufficient energy—and at the moment this is a reasonable assumption—then man can remake the moon to his own liking.

17 On the moon are rocks which in many cases are similar to those on the earth. Dr. Harold C. Urey, one of our foremost authorities on the composition of planets, believes that some of the lunar rocks are like the magnesium silicates on earth. These rocks contain water in varying amounts. Some contain none while others contain about 13 per cent, locked in as the water of crystallization. In the case of the latter, 100 tons of rock will yield thirteen tons of water. The only agency necessary to make the rocks give up their water is energy in the form of heat.

18 These rocks can be ground up by machines brought from the earth by way of the space station. Once pulverized, the rock powder can be baked at a temperature of about 1,000 degrees F. In this process the water will be vaporized and collected and man will have acquired one of the basic necessities for survival.

19 Water is but a starting point. When water vapor is subject to the ultra-violet radiation of the sun or other forms of energy it will dissociate into oxygen and hydrogen. Thus another necessity—an atmosphere—immediately becomes available. The oxygen can also be used as the oxidizer in the rocket propellant system, and even the hydrogen can be used as a fuel.

20 The presence of oxygen and water also means that a form of metallurgy can begin on the moon. We must realize that no one has been on the moon to plunder it of its resources, and thus virgin metals may abound on its surface. Once metals are available, then a technology can begin. Machines can be built for many purposes.

21 By the year 2000 our chemical technology should also have advanced to the point where the synthesis of many of our commonplace materials will be possible. On the moon are materials which can be broken down into basic elements. Once the carbon, nitrogen, hydrogen, oxygen and other elements are acquired, then man can synthesize many of the compounds which are in use today or which may come into use in the future. Thus, shortly after man sets foot on the moon, he will be able to build huge plastic-domed villages which will trap and hold an atmosphere and which will permit the growing of plant life. After plant life obtains a foothold on the moon, animals may be brought to our satellite.

22 Perhaps fifty years after man has reached the moon we on the earth may once more look into the sky at our satellite and be astounded at the changes taking place. There may be entire cities built under plastic domes which will glitter in the sunlight. The full moon will be a remarkable sight, with myriad reflections from the tops of the plastic domes and from the artificial lakes which may then abound there.

23 Thus the moon will become the center of another civilization similar to that on earth. The moon will provide every necessity for the further adventures of man.

Exercises

CONTENT

True or False? If you think the statement represents what the selection says or implies, mark it "True"; if you do not think so, mark it "False."

1. Sputnik was the name of the first artificial earth satellite.

2. About 1960 the first man (or woman) will travel into space and return alive.

3. Meteorology is the science that will benefit most directly and immediately from TV-equipped satellites.

4. Women can probably adapt themselves more easily to space travel than men.

5. Until the space pilot has been thoroughly trained, "re-entry" will have to be made by means of electronic "brains."

6. By 1980 a space station will have been built.

7. Less speed per second is required to establish a space station than to reach the moon.

8. The mass of the moon is only about $\frac{1}{28}$ that of the earth.

9. Before the moon can be made habitable, man must find a method by which sunlight can be converted into electrical energy.

10. It will never be possible to eat a completely moon-produced meal that will include milk, meat, and vegetables.

Questions for Discussion

1. Levitt's time schedule for man's conquest of near space involves six phases or periods, including the present. Go through the essay and list them with the dates indicated.

2. Explain the ten-year interval without new space achievements between 1968 and 1978.

3. What do you think is meant by "the further adventures of man" (Paragraph 23)? Does Levitt's conclusion here agree or disagree with Clarke's in *The Earth and Its Neighbors* (p. 81)?

FORM AND STYLE

1. Choose one: the development of the essay is (a) by spatial movement, (b) by chronological movement, (c) by comparison-contrast, (d) from the specific to the general, (e) from the simple to the complex, (f) by a combination of two or more methods.

2. Excluding the first, introductory paragraph, into which two main parts does the essay naturally divide?

3. Which sentence in Paragraph 1 may be said to serve as a topic sentence or statement of theme for the whole essay?

4. Explain the meaning of "thus," the first word in Paragraph 6.

5. Try to explain why Levitt's vision of the moon's future fifty years from now (Paragraph 22) does not seem like just another piece of science fiction fantasy. What qualities of style contribute to our feeling that the prophecy will be realized—that the time table is correct?

VOCABULARY

Which of the four words or phrases to the right seems to you to be *closest* in meaning to the word in heavy type to the left? Put a check mark after your choice.

momentous (1)   momentary . . . very important . . . long awaited . . . promising . . .

ultimately (2)   in the end . . . probably . . . sooner or later . . . in a wonderful manner . . .

miniaturized[1] (2)   perfected . . . strengthened . . . made small . . . radically changed in design . . .

applicable (2)   practical . . . useful . . . capable of being used . . . available . . .

panorama (3)   show . . . very large view . . . study . . . viewpoint . . .

respiration (4)   perspiration . . . pulsation . . . metabolism . . . breathing . . .

induced (4)   caused . . . introduced . . . designed . . . inducted . . .

surveillance (6)   examination . . . observation . . . control . . . protection . . .

[1] Word coined by Levitt; not listed in standard dictionaries.—*Ed.*

feasible (7)   safe . . . desirable . . . justifiable . . . practicable . . .
inordinately (8)   unusually . . . excessively . . . impossibly . . .
    chaotically . . .
exacting (8)   difficult . . . demanding . . . important . . . complex
enhance (11)   reduce . . . advance . . . slow down . . . speed up
crucial (11)   important . . . painful . . . decisive . . . difficult . . .
hiatus (12)   pause . . . gap . . . time of hibernation . . . delay . . .
replenished (12)   refilled . . . completed . . . reorganized . . . im-
    proved . . .
recuperate (14)   rest . . . be re-created . . . relax . . . recover . . .
strenuous (14)   frequent . . . strained . . . strength-consuming . . .
    stern . . .
habitable (15)   habit-forming . . . liveable on . . . delightful . . .
    useful . . .
convert (16)   produce . . . subject to chemical process . . . change
    . . . turn to use . . .
myriad (22)   beautiful . . . ten million . . . innumerable . . . fas-
    cinating . . .
abound (22)   exist . . . be many . . . be made . . . be found . . .

THEME SUGGESTIONS

First man in space/on the moon
I'm getting dizzy, or I liked it better before Sputnik
Why space travel?
A day in Moon City, A.D. 2060

Self and Society

COLE • VAN DOREN • LOVE • ETHRIDGE
SUCKOW • HAMILTON • KOSOBUD

The essays in "Nature and Science" dealt with man's relationship with the physical world: the selections in this section deal with his relationship with other men. Almost inevitably, this involves in some way or another his relationship with himself.

Cole compares dating in the 1920's with dating today and concludes that modern youth are more serious-minded and more conservative in their romantic life than their parents. According to Van Doren, we are not helping other people by doing things to please them rather than ourselves; the secret of success is to know one's own mind and to act on that knowledge. Love's report on the strange and aimless existence of an educated, self-respecting New York vagrant may perhaps be taken to support Van Doren's thesis: Henry Shelby is obviously a man who does *not* know what he wants. Ethridge's review of a book by Robert Penn Warren is a sane analysis of a sane book on racial segregation in the South. Ruth Suckow's short story deals with a different kind of clash between people, but one that is equally sad and more poignant: the distance between generations, the breaking of bonds, the changing of ways and values that are inevitable in a society as fluid as ours. Edith Hamilton goes far beyond Ruth Suckow's recent past, but she, too, deals with contrasts: those between the unsentimental, idea-loving, versatile Athenian citizen in the times of Pericles and Socrates, and our own hurried, practical-minded specialist. Patricia Kosobud looks into a possible future—the product, perhaps, of specialists—and describes a way of life that has had to sacrifice all that makes democracy worth while in order to preserve even a hollow semblance of itself.

209

33

CHARLES W. COLE

American Youth Goes Monogamous

1   It was an autumn Saturday in 1935 when I was eight years out of college that I first realized I belonged to the older generation. But I did not understand that I was witnessing the first stages of a revolution which has dramatically altered the folkways of American youth and created a new and strange chasm between my generation and the next. Across the gulf which divides the adults who reached maturity in the early 1930s and the youngsters growing up today, communication on some subjects is difficult if not impossible.

2   The occasion was a dance at a fraternity house. My wife and I were chaperons. It was the first such dance we had attended since 1927. We noticed that the stag line was very small in comparison to our day, but thought that perhaps it was harder to get stags to come in depression times. One of my students was a tall dark basketball player named Fred. We saw him dancing with a vivacious girl in a bright yellow dress. Twenty minutes later he was still dancing with the same girl. We commented to each other on the fact that he was stuck with the girl and felt sorry for him. Another twenty minutes passed. He was still dancing with the same girl over in a corner by the fireplace. At this point I felt so perturbed about his plight that I went up to one of his fraternity brothers and said:

3   "Fred is stuck with that girl in the yellow dress; can't one of you do something about it?"

4   The young man looked at me wide-eyed and replied, "Oh, no! That's Fred's girl."

5   It was another five years before "going steady" was fully established as the standard and persuasive pattern for the social life of the young. But today it is so completely dominant that the debutante parties in some large cities where, through a kind of stubborn conservatism, stags are still used and the girl brings two or three young men with her are regarded as oddities by the young people.

6   Youth at present is almost completely monogamous in a thoroughly established fashion, and it is aggressively sure that its customs and ways are right.

7   Not long ago, I was talking with three college seniors. They had been questioning me about the social customs of the 'twenties, which to them are as quaint (and as remote) as the 'nineties were to my generation, but appealing because of the good music like "Tea for Two" or "St. Louis Blues" and dances like the Charleston. I had been telling about stag lines and cutting in and getting stuck and the old story of the five-dollar bill held behind the girl's back. One of the seniors asked:

8 "But why did you cut in on a girl?"

9 I replied, "Well, maybe you knew her and she was a good dancer, or fun to talk to or had what we called a 'good line.' Or perhaps you didn't know her and got introduced and cut in. Then if the two of you got on together you asked her for a date."

10 There was a hushed pause. Then another of the seniors questioned me a little timidly. "Do you mean that when another man brought the girl, you felt you could ask her for a date right at the dance?"

11 "Certainly," I answered; "in fact, that was the way you met new girls."

12 A pall of disapproving silence settled over us, as the young men contemplated the immorality, the stark and blatant indecency of their parents' generation. Then one of them with visible tact changed the subject.

13 A boy today who seeks to make friends with a girl somebody else brings to a dance is known as a "bird-dog" and what he does is called "bird-dogging." The origin of the phrase is neither known nor obvious. But the activity is frowned on in the most thoroughgoing fashion. There was the case of Weston Brewer. He was a member of the Alpha Beta Gamma fraternity. At one of the house dances to which he had brought his own girl, he met a girl named Maureen, from Boston, who had been brought by one of the other brothers, Tim Morton. With Weston and Maureen it was love at first sight in the best romantic tradition. Weston went to Boston to see her. He went every weekend. When this fact became known, the matter was brought up at the next chapter meeting and it was proposed that Weston be expelled from the fraternity for bird-dogging a brother's girl. But Weston's friends—though in no way condoning his actions—pointed out that Maureen was not really Tim's girl, since he had only one date with her before the dance. It was concluded, therefore, that, while Weston was guilty of the worst taste, expulsion from the chapter would not be justified.

14 One of the delicate questions in going steady is when the relationship may be said to have been established. Here, there is some difference of opinion. But in general three dates in fairly rapid succession are not enough and six dates are plenty. So the fourth or the fifth date may be considered crucial. I once saw a girl from the Middle West in tears. She had had three dates with a boy and had got on well with him. But she felt she did not like him enough to go with him on a steady basis and therefore was compelled to refuse the fourth date. "Like" is now, by the way, a word of art. In "Bill likes Sue," it implies the first stages of what, if all goes well, may result in love.

15 Going steady is a rather stylized relationship. (The phrase "going steady" is used in high schools though not much in college circles. But the institution is as strong in the latter as the former.) When it is fully established, it means that the boy will not go out with any other girl or the girl with any other boy. It means further that each can count on the other for any date, dance, or other social event. There are certain exceptions—concessions as it were to the weakness of the flesh. Let us say that Jack comes from Missoula, Montana, and is attending an Eastern college. In Missoula, he is going steady with Mary. But to be denied female companionship for months at a time is more than he can be expected to endure. It is not, then, wholly improper for Jack, under these conditions, to go out with Nancy from Vassar while he is in the East. Ideally Jack should tell Nancy about Mary and Mary about Nancy. And Nancy (or perhaps Mary) should be aware that she is secondary, the under-steady so to speak.

16 But it would be even better and Jack would be more admired by his fellows—granted that Mary is really his girl—if he lived a completely celibate and monastic life while at college. This would be regarded as a great sacrifice, but it would bring him respect and sympathy.

17 This sympathy might even take concrete form. There was the case of Donald, a junior in the Gamma Beta Alpha house. He was a scholarship boy with means so limited that he could not go home to Beaver Falls, Minnesota, for Christmas vacation. At home he had a girl named Grace, whom he dearly liked and to whom he was completely faithful. The time came for the spring house dance and all the chapter members were urged to bring dates. Don sadly refused and thought mournfully of Grace. The brothers were so deeply impressed by his constancy that they raised a pool to buy Grace an airplane ticket East and to pay all her expenses. The big scene took place before the dance when his friends said to Don, "We've got a blind date for you," led him protesting to the library, threw open the doors, and there was Grace beaming over a corsage of orchids. This romantic denouement made the weekend a happy and thrilling one for the whole chapter.

18 Going steady is a progressive not a static relationship. At the start, it means merely a monogamous social arrangement, but it is likely to move on to a point where the couple gets "pinned." (The typical symbol is the fraternity pin, but if the college has no fraternities, a Phi Bete key, a club emblem, or military insignia may be used.) Overtly "pinning" merely means that the girl can and does wear the boy's fraternity pin. Inwardly it means more than that, though there are various degrees. Merely "pinned" implies that the boy and girl plan to go steady in the future, like each other a good deal, and expect the relationship to develop further. To be seriously pinned means "engaged to be engaged" or perhaps even "engaged" preparatory to getting a ring, securing parental approval, and clearing up other details.

19 Since pinning is in many ways the equivalent of the betrothal of earlier times, it is frequently quite ceremonious. Friends of the pinned couple may give a little party, at which the girl appears with the pin on for the first time, and toasts may be drunk in champagne. There was the case of a returning alumnus of elder vintage who started to go into the music room in his fraternity house, but was stopped with the admonition, "Don't go in there, Joe is pinning his girl." The alumnus completely misunderstood the situation until the young couple emerged wreathed in smiles, the girl with the pin on her bosom, to receive congratulations.

20 The relationship of going steady, even of a pinned couple, may be ended with somewhat more ease than an engagement can be broken. It may be terminated by either party or by mutual agreement. If either the boy or the girl ends it firmly, he or she is said to have "axed" the other.

21 The duration of the "steady" arrangement is most variable. It may last from a few days to many years. There are instances where a couple started going steady in junior high school, continued through high school and college, and got married after eight or more years of going together. A boy or girl on the other hand may have several "steadies" in the course of a single year. But it is considered frivolous and light-minded to change too often. So monogamous (pro tem) is the younger generation that after losing a steady, it is thought proper to wait a decent interval before seeking another.

22 The philanderer of the 'twenties who dated a different girl every night and went out with dozens in the course of a year has disappeared. So has the prom trotter of earlier times. A clever girl today might conceivably have a male friend in four or five different colleges, but she would not be much admired if she had two at the same college. If she collected an array of fraternity pins from several boys—I knew of girls in the 'twenties who had as many as seven—she would be condemned by her acquaintances.

23 The dances have perhaps changed most visibly of all the social institutions. While the system of going steady has become more formalized, dances have tended to become more informal. (Why dress up for someone you see so often and know so well?) They have tended to become shorter. (When you dance with only one partner, two hours or so is enough.) There is a good deal of sitting around and listening to music or entertainment instead of dancing. In fact, an effort is made to secure bands worth listening to rather than those whose music is especially suitable for dancing. The dances are a little heavy and somber because the excitement and shifting around of cutting in has disappeared and because neither the boys nor the girls feel under any special obligation to be gay or entertaining. The big dance of the prom type is fading slowly away.

Since a couple is going to dance together anyhow they may as well do it in an informal fashion to phonograph records, or at a night spot, without going to the trouble and expense of attending a big formal affair.

24   The revolution in the courtship and dating procedures of our youth has had profound effects on our society and even on our economy.

25   The average age of marriage has dropped very rapidly. A college girl of the 1920s *said*, at least, that she was looking forward to a career. Most of them did not expect to get married until two or three years after graduation. The college girl today declares quite frankly that she wants to get married and she frequently does so while still in college. A girl who gets as far as junior year in college without having acquired a man is thought to be in grave danger of becoming an old maid. A manless senior is considered to be more or less on the shelf.

26   Matrimony at an early age is facilitated by the disappearance of the idea that a man should be able to support a wife before he gets married. The GI Bill of Rights with its higher allowances for married veterans seems to have destroyed the older notions, and to have made the idea of married undergraduate students acceptable. Nowadays, one or both sets of parents are expected to "help." If the parents cannot be of assistance it is perfectly normal for the girl to take a job and help to support her husband through medical school or law school.

27   And then there is the birth rate. Thirty years ago a young couple usually planned to have two children and usually did. Today the ideal seems to be four or five children. The effect of this shift in attitude on the birth rate has been spectacular. Among college graduates of both sexes the classes ten years out already have substantially as many children as the classes twenty-five years out. It is known also of course that all by itself an earlier average age of marriage will raise the birth rate.

28   Why young people want more children is by no means clear. Partly the new attitude may arise from the fact that there is no servant problem. Since there are no servants, there is no question of waiting till it is possible to afford a maid to look after the baby. Housekeeping has, moreover, been much simplified by washing machines, frozen foods, diaper services, and a score of other developments. Baby-sitting has become a national and fairly well organized institution. Partly the trend to large families may arise from the fact that many of the young people marrying today were only children or had a single sibling. They seem to envy the children who come from large families and had a more varied and exciting family circle. Partly, too, young people seem to be seeking in their own families the security that is outwardly denied by the unsettled state of the world.

29   In the 'twenties and early 'thirties, when the social pattern was one of multiple or polygamous dating—on the part of both boys and girls— young people did not think nearly so much about marriage as they do today. Thirty years ago a boy and a girl could have dates over a long period without considering that they might some day get married. They dated each other for the fun of it, because they enjoyed each other's company, because they liked the same things, or merely because in the competitive social life of their time it was a good thing to have dates—the more, the better. Today young people often play with the idea of marriage as early as the second or third date, and they certainly think about it by the fifth or sixth. By the time they have been going steady for a while they are quite apt to be discussing the number and names of their future children. The fact that the steady may well be a future spouse gives a different color to the social life of the youth. It makes it more serious, less frivolous. The boys and girls spend a lot of time discussing their relationship and whether it is solidly founded on bases of long-run compatibility.

30   The oddest thing about the revolution in the social life of youth in the last twenty years is that it constitutes the triumph of rural nineteenth-century American mores in the urban and suburban society of the mid-twentieth century. Anybody over seventy who was brought up in a country village or town finds the social customs of young people today strangely familiar. In the 1880s or 1890s it was normal to have boys and girls pair off in a more or less stable fashion, and such pairing often ended eventually in marriage. The very phrase "going steady" has the ring of rural America under President Cleveland.

31   Why have our young people reverted so sharply to the ways of an earlier era and a simpler society? There seems to be no clear-cut answer. The change has often been ascribed to the second world war, when the sudden shortage of men made each girl eager to hold on to any available male. But it was well under way before 1939. The new folkways may be related to the Great Depression when a boy putting out money for a girl on dances, movies, or the like wanted to be sure of some return on his investment. It is also true that the fiercely competitive social life of the 'twenties with the stag lines and the cutting in and the multiple dates meant that a popular girl had a very good time indeed. But the majority of girls were not popular. They dreaded being wall flowers. They were the ones with whom boys sometimes got stuck. It may be that the less popular majority of girls slowly created the present democratic system, under which any girl with a steady is just as well off as any other girl with a steady. Since each boy wants a steady too and since the numbers of boys and girls are about equal everybody seems better off at present, though it is possible that some polygamous male instincts are thwarted. On the other hand, girls would insist that the new system was created by the boys who are aggressive, possessive, and jealous of all rivals.

32   The new ways may also be related to the search for security. The boy or girl who has a steady is secure. Each partner knows that the other can be counted on for the coming high-school dance or the next football game. In a day when the population moves from home to home with such freedom and when so many homes are broken by divorce or otherwise, this kind of security is very precious to young people. Perhaps, too, the general decline of competition under the welfare state has led to less competitive social customs. Just as the retail stores have tried to shelter themselves from all price competition behind the so-called Fair Trade laws, so our young people have divided into noncompeting twosomes.

33 Whatever the origin of the present pre-marital monogamy of youth, it is one of the most important phenomena of recent times. Already it is responsible for the new birth rate that has exploded the predictions that our population would become stable in numbers in the 1970s. It looks as if the United States would grow in population rapidly and indefinitely. Already it has produced the tidal wave of babies that will overwhelm the high schools in 1961 and the colleges in 1964. Already it has created a situation where parents and children find it hard to communicate on social matters. The mother who says to a daughter, "Why do you always have dates with Jimmy? Aren't there other nice boys?" seems to the daughter to be lacking in elementary understanding of the facts of social life.

34 It is too early to determine what the new system will do for the stability of marriage. On *a priori* grounds the oldsters would predict that a boy who had dated only one girl or at the most half-a-dozen would be less likely to find a permanently compatible mate than one who had gone out with fifty or a hundred. It would seem even that there might be anti-eugenic consequences, since the intelligent girl would have less chance of finding an intelligent boy to marry.

35 But it is also possible that a marriage relationship based on an elaborate system of pre-marital companionship progressing through recognized stages (dating, going steady, getting pinned, becoming engaged) may be built in a solid and enduring fashion. It is conceivable too that the fiercely monogamous pre-marital folkways may carry over into married life and erect strong buttresses to the institutions of marriage and the family.

Exercises

CONTENT

True or False? If you think the statement represents what the selection says or implies, mark it "True"; if you do not think so, mark it "False."

1. Modern youth has higher morals than youth of the 1920's.

2. At dances in the 'twenties, boys often made dates with their friends' dates.

3. A boy who did the same thing today would be considered behaving in bad taste.

4. Dances are less formal now than they used to be because they are shorter.

5. Early marriages tend to lower the birth rate.

6. The "polygamous" dating pattern of the 'twenties favored the pretty girl.

7. It is never right for a man to let his wife support him.

8. The custom of "going steady" was common in rural America in the years around the first World War.

9. "Going steady" is a system created by jealous boys.

10. Its effects on marriage stability and happiness are probably going to be harmful.

Questions for Discussion

1. In a single phrase, state the *subject matter* of Cole's essay.

2. In a single phrase state its *theme*. In trying to do so, you may find it helpful first to pick the noun from the following list that seems to you best to suggest Cole's attitude to the social custom he describes: (a) regret, (b) amusement, (c) bewilderment, (d) interest, (e) fear.

3. Explain ". . . the old story of the five-dollar bill held behind the girl's back" (Paragraph 7) and "bird-dogging" (Paragraph 13).

4. What do Weston and Maureen (Paragraph 13) have in common with Donald and Grace (Paragraph 17)? Explain how your answer is relevant to a value judgment of the monogamous dating pattern.

FORM AND STYLE

1. Why are the paragraphs on the whole longer in the later parts of the essay than in the earlier ones?

2. What is the transition between Paragraphs 13 and 14?

3. *American Youth Goes Monogamous* falls into five main parts. The first is an anecdote that dramatically illustrates the difference between the boy-girl relationship in college in the author's youth and the same relationship today. The second is the main part of the essay. It describes, with frequent use of examples, the institution of "going steady" and modern youth's attitude to it. The fifth evaluates the "going steady," suggesting its possible bad and good effects on marriage. What do the third and fourth parts deal with? Indicate where the divisions between the five parts occur.

4. Explain the sarcasm, "It is not, then, wholly improper for Jack, under these conditions, to go out with Nancy from Vassar while he is in the East" (Paragraph 15).

5. What is an "under-steady" (Paragraph 15)? What word does it remind you of? Is the similarity in sound significant? If so, explain how. What is this kind of play on words called?

VOCABULARY

Which of the four words or phrases to the right seems to you to be *closest* in meaning to the word in heavy type to the left? Put a check mark after your choice.

chasm (*1*)   gap . . . difference . . . dividing line . . . obstacle . . .

vivacious (*2*)   plain . . . tall . . . lively . . . beautiful . . .

perturbed (*2*)   sorry . . . upset . . . shaken . . . indignant . . .

monogamous (*6*)   moral . . . idealistic . . . single . . . having only one spouse . . .

aggressively (*6*)   more and more . . . smugly . . . in a fighting manner . . . absolutely . . .

quaint (*7*)   silly . . . incomprehensible . . . odd . . . questionable

timidly (*10*)   in an embarrassed manner . . . in a shocked manner . . . hesitatingly . . . fearfully . . .

blatant (*12*)   horrible . . . obvious . . . blameworthy . . . revolting . . .

condoning (*13*)   overlooking . . . pardoning . . . praising . . . reprimanding . . .

expulsion (*13*)   act of expelling . . . blackballing . . . condemnation . . . exclusion . . .

compelled (*14*)   forced . . . tempted . . . supposed . . . advised . . .

stylized (*15*)   stylish . . . conventional . . . indefinite . . . new . . .

concessions (*15*)   gifts . . . confessions . . . victories . . . yieldings

endure (*15*)   experience . . . last . . . enjoy . . . suffer . . .

celibate (*16*)   without fun . . . unmarried . . . virtuous . . . devoted . . .

constancy (*17*)   depth of feeling . . . love . . . romance . . . faithfulness . . .

denouement (*17*)   stripping . . . triumph . . . outcome . . . reunion

static (*18*)   unchanging . . . reactionary . . . steady . . . finished . . .

vintage (*19*)   habits . . . generation . . . outlook . . . age . . .

pro tem (*21*)   apparently . . . by themselves . . . for the time being . . . believe it or not . . .

philanderer (*22*)   one who collects philanders . . . playboy . . . seducer . . . an indiscriminate person . . .

array (*22*)   series . . . bunch . . . shelf . . . lot . . .

facilitated (*26*)   encouraged . . . prevented . . . made a fact . . . made easier . . .

compatibility (*29*)   attraction . . . like-mindedness . . . sympathy . . . harmony . . .

mores (*30*)   laws . . . customs . . . excesses . . . morals . . .

reverted (*31*)   changed . . . turned back . . . worshiped . . . preferred . . .

ascribed (*31*)   attributed . . . written as for . . . described . . . made responsible for . . .

thwarted (*31*)   sublimated . . . frustrated . . . checked . . . turned away . . .

eugenic (*34*)   wholesome . . . hygienic . . . having to do with the production of sound offspring . . . intellectual . . .

buttresses (35)   foundations . . . aids . . . fortifications . . . supports . . .

THEME SUGGESTIONS

Advantages and disadvantages in going steady
Stop picking on us!
A critical comment on Cole's essay
Morals of modern youth
Mother/father and I discuss dating customs

34

MARK VAN DOREN

Know What You Want

1   My brother Carl, the biographer of Benjamin Franklin, was famous for his generosity. Asked for anything, he was likely to give it. And nothing was more valuable than his advice, which he gave freely when asked. He was not one of those men who pull long faces and wonder whether you oughtn't to decide things for yourself. If you wanted his help, and said so, he never doubted that you did; nor did he foolishly assume that you were bound to take it; the final decision would of course be yours, but meanwhile he was happy to throw what light he could upon your problem.

2   I owe him more than I can say, and not merely in this one department of advice. Here, though, he was better than generous to me; he was prodigal, he gave me every thought he had. Books to read, people to meet, trips to take, restaurants to try—he included me in his world, so that I lived doubly while he lived. He was nine years my senior, and when we were boys in Illinois he did not hesitate to counsel me sometimes as if I were his son. If I didn't know enough to ask, he told me.

3   But as I grew up, and later when I followed him to New York, this changed. Nothing, I think, interested him more than what I did or did not do, but he was never in my way. He took it for granted now that I knew enough to ask; and when I did, which was often enough, he held back nothing. I was never dependent upon him unless I chose to be. It was always my choice. And the wonderful thing—wonderful, I mean,

about him, not me—was that when I made it I felt stronger rather than weaker because I did. My problem immediately became his own; it excited him, it aroused his imagination; so that as we talked I could believe the alternatives to be his as well as mine, and the pleasure too of doing whatever thing would eventually be done, even though in the nature of the case I was to do that thing alone. There was the time, for example, when I begged him to tell me what I should write about for my doctor's dissertation at Columbia. He suggested a criticism of John Dryden's poetry; and within a few minutes was racing through the subject with such contagious zest that I caught fire and contributed a few ideas myself—to his work, as it were, though in the end it was entirely mine.

4   The one great comprehensive piece of advice Carl gave me, however, came later than that, and I am sorry to say I do not precisely remember the occasion that called it forth—perhaps it was a teaching position I had doubts about, or a job of editing I was afraid I should not stop other work to do. But no matter, it was what he said that counted. I have never forgotten it, nor do I expect to while I live. It has made all the difference to me. And I gladly pass it on.

5   "The real question is," said Carl, "do you *want* to do it?" "Why," I said, "that's what I can't decide." He laughed. "It seems to me you have decided." "What?" "That you don't want to do it." "How can you tell?" "Why, by your doubt. In my own case this would be decisive." "But doubts are not decisions." "Yes, they are. I have made it a rule never to do anything I didn't want to do—immediately, that is, or else without much thought one way or the other. The longer I hesitate the better I know my answer must be negative." "But you do hesitate. You've even come to me and asked me what I thought you ought to decide."

6   He laughed again. "Well, then, I was weak. I didn't know the strength of my own inclinations—or disinclinations. Believe me, *they* are clear. And the thing to do is to be as clear yourself. Of course things get in the way—duty, obligation, the desire not to disappoint or offend, the wish always to be liked. But in the end, my boy, do only what you want to do. And do nothing you *don't* want to do. Now in this case you surely don't expect me to tell you what your inclination is—or your disinclination. You are the only one in the world that knows. I think I understand you pretty well, but here is private ground. I'm keeping off."

7   Now in one sense this was not advice at all. But in the best sense it was the best; and I needed it the most. Not, of course, that it was easy to take. For it threw me back upon the question of who and what I was, and whether I had knowledge of this person. How far should I trust my doubts and my desires? How confident could I afford to be that even if I knew my feelings I should let them master me? Who was I to announce that I would never do anything I didn't want to do? It sounded arrogant. It sounded ruthless.

8   And the queer thing was, Carl qualified in neither of those roles.

He was singularly unselfish; everyone said so, and I knew it for a fact. He was generous to a fault; he praised people to their faces and behind their backs; he gave incredible amounts of time and strength to helping others through hard places; he rejoiced in their successes; he was humane to the last ounce. Also, as I told him in our dialogue, he didn't find it easy to follow his own rule. He could be tortured by doubts as to what he should do next, and by misgivings over what he had done last. His large nature was at the same time extremely sensitive; which was why so many loved him, and why there were those who could take advantage of his kindness. I knew these things then, so what should I conclude?

9   What I concluded at that dramatic moment was less important for me than what I have concluded since. Without reservation, I now think Carl was right. His ideal—difficult for him, to be sure, but all the more an ideal because of that—still makes the clearest sense. Nothing else perhaps makes any sense at all.

10   Shall we consult the wishes of others? But what others? And if we could pick the right ones—whatever that means—how could we know that we would please them in the end? We would certainly fail in this if what we did was done unwillingly, unnaturally for us, and therefore against the grain. What they want is that *we* should want the same thing they do. When they invite us to their house they hope that it will give us happiness to come; and we hope they mean the invitation. Unwilling hosts and unwilling guests do not exactly mix; everybody has a poor time. My wife tells me I lean over backward with respect to this; she says I urge people to come only if they want to; she thinks I sound as if I weren't too eager to see them myself. Possibly so, but I defend the principle. There is only one guide through the labyrinth of choice: our own desire, if we know what that is. Sometimes, I grant, it is difficult to know. But I agree with Carl that ignorance is a serious matter. It causes others and ourselves no end of trouble.

11   The principle was stated recently by a man who I might have supposed was too young to understand it. But he had had, evidently, the necessary experience. He is a producer of plays, and I happened to ask him whether the interest he was expressing in a certain play had its origin in the sympathy and affection I knew he felt for the author.

12   "Are you being kind?" I asked. He looked at me in astonishment—I even thought, with pity. "Good Lord, no! I learned long ago that anything like that simply complicates everybody's life." He meant that false hope can produce more misery than no hope at all, that lack of frankness—about important things at any rate—has finally to be paid for by the innocent as well as by the guilty.

13   I remember being asked ten years ago whether I would consider accepting the presidency of a college whose aims I admired. The chairman of the trustees called me on the phone and put it to me in terms that were none too easy to ignore: I was the person they wanted, and I could

do the college good. If I hesitated for as long as one minute it was because Carl's voice was for that minute farther away than the chairman's.
But I heard it in time, and said what I really felt: this was not my kind
of work, I would be unhappy with it, I wouldn't do it well, and therefore
I would do the college harm.

14 "Let me come and see you anyway," he said. "But it wouldn't
change my mind." "Then it will simply be a visit." "All right. You know
I'd like that. But remember what I said. I'll never accept."

15 He did come—it was a day's train trip to my house in Connecticut
where I was spending the winter—and when he left the next morning he
assured me that he liked train trips because they gave him time to read.
The presidency had been scarcely mentioned, and I still don't know if he
was disappointed with respect to it. I do know, however, that his disappointment in me as president, supposing I had been weak enough to
argue down my instinct, would have been enormous and woeful; beginning and ending with me, everybody concerned would have had his life
complicated for nothing.

16 Ruthless? No, I am convinced it is the finest form of scruple. I have
not been describing a curmudgeon. The curmudgeon wants nothing,
whereas the normal thing is to have many desires—and the ideal thing is
to know which ones of them are strongest. The curmudgeon, presumably,
wants neither work nor a wife, and does without them. The normal thing
is to want a wife, and the ideal thing of course is to take (if you can) the
one you want the most. What if you consulted her parents and her
friends? What if you married her only because you promised to, and
meanwhile had changed your mind? This has been done, but neither
party could have benefited by the act. The truly ruthless thing is to do
what you do because you believe you ought to, and for no gentler reason.
That is invoking monsters you have no human right to invoke. It is being,
in the crudest possible sense, impersonal. It will not merely complicate
life, it will ruin it.

17 Why is it that we are flattered when an animal likes us—when,
for instance, we are in somebody's house and the cat, after staring at us
from across the room, comes over and jumps up on our lap? The mistress
of the cat can say nothing better at that moment than: "Look! He doesn't
do it to everybody." We may pretend otherwise, but we are deeply
pleased; and surely the reason is that we know cats—particularly cats—
to be devoid of the sense of duty. They do what they want to do, and
cannot be forced to do anything else. So in this case the motive is pure.
Which is to say, it is purely selfish. Which is to say, it is capable of giving
pleasure unmixed with any other thing. The same is true of small children
—those who are too small to have compromised with complication, the
adult vice that will beset them later.

18 As a vice it has its uses in society, and sometimes its beauty too.
But it is a vice. Which is why I have learned, when someone comes to

me and asks for counsel, that the most helpful thing to do is to let him talk until he has told himself what his own choice is. He probably knew before he came, but doubted that others would approve. Now, though, in an atmosphere free of disapproval, he convinces himself that at last he knows what he wants. He is lucky in the knowledge, and so will those be with whom he is to be concerned.

Exercises

CONTENT

True or False? If you think the statement represents what the selection says or implies, mark it "True"; if you do not think so, mark it "False."

1. Carl Van Doren wrote a book about Thomas Jefferson.
2. The Van Doren brothers spent their boyhood in Indiana.
3. When in doubt, don't do it.
4. Carl Van Doren never gave advice.
5. If a friend asks you for advice on an important decision and you feel like giving it to him, you should give it.
6. You cannot make up your mind whether to go to a show or do your homework. You'd much rather go to the show. Therefore, you ought to go to the show.
7. Mark Van Doren is a college president.
8. He likes cats.
9. He never seeks advice.
10. If, in important matters, you do what you don't want to do in order to please others, you will, in the long run, fail both them and yourself.

Questions for Discussion

1. Could *Know What You Want* be used as a justification of selfishness?
2. Does Van Doren's advice apply to people without moral principles?
3. Does the essay say that you should never do anything simply from a sense of duty?
4. What exactly is the author in doubt about at the end of Paragraph 8?
5. Which two paragraphs first and most clearly state the theme of the essay?
6. In which sense was "this" "not advice at all" (first sentence in Paragraph 7)? In what sense *was* it advice?
7. Paragraph 8 contains a list of what? How would it affect the essay if the list were missing?

FORM AND STYLE

1. What has the first sentence in the essay to do with its theme? In fact, how can the first three paragraphs be said to be relevant to the theme? Your answer here should relate to your answer to question 7 above.

2. What purpose in the argument is served by Paragraphs 11 and 12 and 13-15?

3. Paragraphs 7, 8, 10, 16, and 17 include several questions. Does their presence in any way affect your attitude toward the author? Explain your answer.

VOCABULARY

Which of the four words or phrases to the right seems to you to be *closest* in meaning to the word in heavy type to the left? Put a check mark after your choice.

prodigal (2)   kindhearted . . . understanding . . . lavish . . . wasteful . . .

alternatives (3)   problems . . . subjects . . . choices . . . alterations

contagious (3)   inspiring . . . catching . . . extraordinary . . . encouraging . . .

comprehensive (4)   important . . . understanding . . . decisive . . . inclusive . . .

decisive (5)   deciding . . . final . . . suggestive . . . definite . . .

arrogant (7)   stupid . . . selfish . . . presumptuous . . . snobbish . . .

humane (8)   sympathetic . . . human . . . unselfish . . . kind . . .

sensitive (8)   sensible . . . sensual . . . fine . . . quick and discriminating in feeling . . .

consult (10)   seek advice from . . . comfort . . . try to please . . . submit to . . .

labyrinth (10)   problem . . . maze . . . labor . . . difficulty . . .

ruthless (16)   egotistical . . . cruel . . . unruthed . . . haughty . . .

scruple (16)   principle . . . consideration . . . moral . . . doubt . . .

curmudgeon (16)   idiot . . . beast . . . crank . . . an apathetic person . . .

devoid of (17)   without . . . unbothered by . . . ignorant of . . . in possession of the opposite of . . .

compromised with (17)   given in to . . . come to terms with . . . become aware of . . . played with . . .

THEME SUGGESTIONS

Tell about a personal experience which seems to you to illustrate or to refute Van Doren's rule (advice you wish you had/had not given/

taken). Explain on what grounds Van Doren thinks it unwise to act according to the advice of others against one's own wishes and wants.
  Pleasure vs. duty
  An answer to Van Doren

35

EDMUND G. LOVE

Subways Are for Sleeping

1 On March 4, 1953, at approximately 11:30 P.M., Henry Shelby walked into the New York City hotel where he had maintained an apartment for five months. Upon asking for his key at the desk, he was informed by the clerk that he had been locked out until such time as his bill was settled. The bill amounted to about one hundred and thirteen dollars. At the moment, Shelby had about fourteen dollars, no job, and no friends upon whom he felt free to call for help. Without any argument, he turned and walked back out the door.

2 In the time that has passed since that night, he has returned to the hotel only once, and then merely to see if he had any mail. He has not attempted to retrieve any of his belongings held by the management. With the exception of approximately three and one-half months, in the summer of 1953, he has been one of the thousands of men in various stages of vagrancy who wander the streets of New York City at all hours of the day and night.

3 Henry Shelby, today, is forty-one years old, but looks at least five years younger. He is five feet, eleven and one-half inches tall, weighs 162 pounds. His hair is black but thinning, and his eyes are a deep blue. He has no disfigurements, and his bearing is good. The key to his personality lies in his eyes which express the depth of his feeling, or a quiet humor, depending upon his mood. When he is deep in thought, or troubled, he is apt to trace patterns on the floor, or in the dirt, with the toe of his shoe. At other times he moves briskly, and with some of the grace and sureness of an athlete.

4 He is a graduate of the University of Michigan with a master's degree in economics. He also holds a life teacher's certificate in the state of Michigan and was, at one time, a teacher in the public schools of Lansing. His master's degree studies were concentrated in the field of accounting procedure, and for four years after World War II, he was an

accountant with the Post Office Department in Washington. His associates there consider him an excellent man in this field, and at least two of them say that he could probably qualify as a certified public accountant. In addition to these qualifications, he is experienced and capable in the field of public relations, where his approach has been described as "fresh" and "honest."

5 The city of New York has long been noted for the number and variety of its vagrants. Estimates as to the number of homeless and penniless men and women run from a conservative 10,000 to somewhere around half a million. Vagrants in other parts of the United States are a migratory lot, usually moving with the weather, but the New York variety stay put, occupying park benches, flop houses, gutters, and doorways in all seasons. There are many who possess qualifications as rich as Henry Shelby's. There are many who are literally human derelicts living out their days in a drunken stupor, waiting for an obscure death in the river or a ward at Bellevue. In between there are as many gradations as there are strata in normal society. Almost the only things all vagrants have in common are a hard luck story and an air of bewilderment. Not all of them have lost hope.

6 Henry Shelby is not a hopeless man, but he is certainly bewildered. He himself describes his present life as treading water, waiting to see how things come out. "In the meantime," he says, "I'm getting along all right. I'm perfectly happy."

7 In his months as a vagrant he has become an expert at management and has learned to put first things first. In his case this means food, cleanliness, and shelter, in that order. He prides himself on the fact that he has never panhandled, never visited a soup kitchen, or taken a night's lodging in one of the various hostels maintained by charitable agencies in the city. He has accepted handouts, but he can recall only one instance where anyone ever stepped up to him and gave him money: One night in the middle of winter he noticed advertisements for the première of a motion picture at a Broadway theater. He arrived early and took up a prominent position against the ropes under the marquee. As he stood there, watching the celebrities arrive in their limousines, a man came over to him and placed an unfolded ten dollar bill in his hand.

8 Shelby has never been completely penniless except for one very brief period when he left New York. He has set fifteen cents, which represents subway fare, as the absolute minimum below which he will not allow his finances to sink. He has no maximum, but rarely possesses more than thirty dollars, which represents about one week's salary at present minimum levels. He acquires his money in a variety of ways. He is able to pick up a day's work here and there, carrying sandwich boards, working as a roustabout on the waterfront, washing dishes in cheap restaurants, shoveling snow for the city.

9 When he gets money, he nurses it carefully. He can tell, one minute

after he gets it, exactly how long it will last, because he knows what he's going to eat, how many cigarettes he is going to smoke, and the amount it will cost him for lodging, or incidentals. There are no extras in his life.

10　Virtually all of Shelby's cash goes for food and cigarettes. His breakfasts, invariably, consist of a glass of fruit or vegetable juice; his lunches, of a sandwich, usually a frankfurter, and a glass of milk. His one substantial meal is supper, and into it he piles all the dietary necessities he has missed since he last ate such a meal. His plate is apt to be loaded with green vegetables, cooked vegetables, and meat. He will haggle back and forth with the counterman in order to get these items, usually trading off potatoes and dessert for them. He never looks at the contents of a meal until he looks at the prices and he always chooses the cheapest meal on the menu, unless it contains sea food, which he detests. He knows where all the best food bargains in town are to be found. A bargain means quantity, but once or twice a week he will seek out a place which serves something of which he is especially fond.

11　Between meals he drinks coffee, usually two cups during the morning and three cups during the afternoon and evening. When he is especially broke he cuts out regular meals and subsists entirely on coffee, loading all the sugar and cream he can into his cup. He explains that these are free calories, and that calories, no matter what form they take, will keep him going until he is able to eat regularly again.

12　Shelby says that the truest statement he has ever heard is that no one will ever starve to death in the United States, and his technique for getting food when he is low on money is a simple one. He walks the streets until he finds a restaurant with a sign in the window that reads "dishwasher wanted," or "counterman wanted." He goes in and works long enough to pay for a meal and earn a little extra money. Usually he completes whatever constitutes a full day's work, but if the restaurant is a pleasant place, if he is treated well and the food is good, he may stay a week, or even longer. He is a good worker, and is well liked by his bosses and fellow employees. Many of the latter are men like himself.

13　He has learned a lot of odd jobs around kitchens and has filled in as a chef at two cafeterias, and as a short-order cook at a counter restaurant. At one place where he worked for five weeks, the manager recommended him for the managership of another unit in the chain which had fallen vacant. In this particular restaurant Shelby can always be sure of a job of some kind when he is broke; the manager will put him to work washing windows if there is nothing else available. The same condition holds true at five or six other places in town, but Shelby never uses them unless he is really desperate. He refers to them humorously as his social security.

14　Shelby usually allots no more than fifteen cents a day for shelter. Occasionally he pays more than this, but only when he has gotten by for two or three days without spending anything extra. Shelter means a place to sleep to Shelby, nothing else. His great preference, month in and month out, is for the Sixth and Eighth Avenue subways. He very rarely sleeps on the IRT or BMT. The IRT, with its ramshackle, noisy cars and its seating arrangement, is uncomfortable. The BMT has suitable accommodations, but, as Shelby describes it, "an undesirable clientele."

15 Shelby usually boards the Eighth Avenue subway at Pennsylvania Station between midnight and one in the morning and takes the first express that comes along. At that hour there is usually a seat, especially in the front car, and he immediately settles down and drops off to sleep. He has developed the happy faculty of being able to drop off, or awaken, almost at will. He sleeps lightly, not because he is afraid of being robbed —he never has enough money to worry about that—but because he is very cautious about oversleeping. The vagrant who is still sleeping soundly when the train reaches the end of the line is more than likely to be picked up and lodged in jail by the transportation police.

16 Upon reaching the end of the line, Shelby walks up the stairs from the train platform to the next level. The turnstiles are at this level, and rest rooms have been placed inside the turnstiles. He retires to one of these rest rooms, finds a booth, fastens the door, and smokes a leisurely cigarette. It is supposedly a misdemeanor to carry lighted tobacco within the turnstile area, but Shelby says he discovered quite early in his career that even the police use the privacy of the rest rooms to have a quiet cigarette. Of course, he takes no chances. If there is a policeman anywhere on the turnstile level he will forgo his smoke.

17 After his cigarette, he goes back to the train platform and boards the next train going in the opposite direction from the one he has just come. He quickly settles into a seat and goes to sleep again. He remains asleep until he reaches the other end of the line, then, as before, has his smoke and reboards a train. This time his nap is much shorter because he debarks at the Jay Street-Borough Hall station in Brooklyn and transfers to the Sixth Avenue subway. On this he makes a full round trip, going all the way out to Queens, back to the Brooklyn end of the line, and then back to Jay Street. There he reboards the Eighth Avenue, which he rides back to Penn Station.

18 The whole trip consumes from four and a half to five and a half hours, during the course of which he has probably netted four hours of sleep. Over the months he has learned many of the habits and assignments of the transportation police, and he tries to keep himself from being too familiar a figure. For this reason he does not depend entirely upon the subway and does not dare ride it oftener than every other night.

19 On his off nights, in good weather, he sometimes uses the two great parks, Central and Prospect. By varying his hours of repose, carefully selecting secluded spots, and transferring his resting places often, he can spend one night a week in either one or the other of them. Also, in warm weather, there are fire escapes. Because he knows the city as well

as he does, Shelby has been able to locate several covered, and therefore secluded, ones. Most of them are attached to theaters or warehouses
and offer ideal accommodations. For some reason, the police never seem
to bother vagrants who occupy these emergency exits. And on three or
four occasions during the summer Shelby manages to get out to one of
the beaches near the city. He can sleep unmolested there, especially on
a hot night. There are always legitimate sleepers, as he calls them, who
are trying to escape the heat.

20   Naturally, in the fall, winter, and early spring, Shelby has to find
other places. The benches in the waiting rooms at Grand Central, Penn
Station, and the Port Authority Bus Terminal are his favorites outside of
the subway. As in every other place, however, there are strict rules of
conduct which must be observed. Shelby learned early that the station
police in each of the three establishments have set habits. They make two
routine checks during the course of a night. At Grand Central, for example, these checks come at one-thirty and five-thirty. Between the
checks there are both policemen and plain-clothes men on duty in the
waiting room throughout the night, and they wander up and down, carefully checking trouble spots. Ordinarily, however, these roving guardians
will not disturb people who are stretched out on the benches asleep. Between the checks, therefore, it is possible to get almost four hours of uninterrupted sleep in a prone position. Conditions at Penn Station are
about the same, and at the bus terminal the checks are farther apart, but
the lights are brighter and the crowds larger, giving less room to stretch
out.

21   Shelby keeps, as part of his equipment for sleeping in one of the
three terminals, three tickets: to Poughkeepsie, New York; Princeton,
New Jersey; and Elizabeth, New Jersey, one for each of the three lines.
Inspection of timetables has revealed that there are no busses or trains
leaving New York for these points between one and six in the morning. In
emergencies, should the station police question him too closely, Shelby
flashes the appropriate ticket and claims that he missed the last train and
is waiting for the first one in the morning. This has always worked, but
on one occasion a station policeman escorted him to a six-thirty train and
made certain he got on it. Shelby got off at 125th Street and walked back
to Grand Central.

22   Shelby regards sleeping in hotel lobbies as an unsatisfactory experience, yet he feels bound to try it every now and then. No lobby can
be occupied during the night, and daytime occupancy is limited to about
two hours at most. While house officers will not ordinarily run a respect-
ably dressed man out into the street, they will shake him awake every
hour or so. In order to get four hours of sleep, Shelby estimates that he
has to visit eight hotels during a day. He always apologizes profusely for
having dozed off and never visits the same hotel oftener than every third
month.

23   Shelby says that it is always advisable to carry something when sleeping in a lobby. House officers are apt to respect a man's privacy if he has an umbrella or brief case lying in his lap. When Shelby plans to use a hotel lobby, he will wander up and down the subway trains the day before until he finds what he is looking for. Subways are full of things that are suitable for hotel lobbies. He always turns in whatever he has found to the Board of Transportation's Lost and Found Department after he has used it, and he is always careful to check back later to find out whether there has been any reward. He collected twelve and a half dollars this way last year.

24   Shelby thinks that all-night theaters are the most overrated sleeping places for men like himself. He has used them, and still does occasionally, but compared to the subway, they are inordinately expensive and their seats, though much softer, are much less suited to sleeping. They tip back too much, and the head is apt to snap backwards instead of forward. This always awakens Shelby. Furthermore, one cannot very well lean one's head on one's arm when elbow resting room has to be fought for with one's neighbor. The pictures are noisy in unexpected places, and the sounds that are thrown out from the screen are loud and unorthodox. On top of this, Shelby has found that no matter what picture is being shown, he cannot keep from watching it to see how it comes out. Thus, instead of getting some sleep, he gets entertained.

25   Most people do their personal grooming in the privacy of their own homes. Because Henry Shelby is homeless, he cannot. But for two reasons he places more importance on his personal appearance than he does on having a place to sleep. First, he is naturally a neat and tidy man to whom uncleanliness is distasteful. Second, good grooming is a safety factor in his existence. The police will always pick up an unkempt man and will generally walk right by a tidy man. A shower is not only a comfort, but a good investment.

26   From each five dollar bill he gets, Shelby sets aside enough money to provide himself with a bath. If he goes six days without one, he will stop eating until he can pay for one. Most of Shelby's baths are taken in the public rooms of Grand Central Station and cost sixty-five cents. Shaving is also a problem. At Shelby's age, he cannot go for more than twenty-four hours without acquiring a heavily shaded face. After that his beard is apt to become a heavy stubble. Nevertheless, he tries to stretch the time between shaves to at least thirty-six hours for economic reasons: it costs twenty-five cents to use one of the booths at Grand Central set aside for this purpose. Like most New York City vagrants, Shelby always carries a safety razor in his pocket and will take any opportunity he can to get in a quick, free shave and a chance to brush his teeth. He uses ordinary soap for shaving cream.

27   Clothing is another important item of appearance. With the exception of his outer garments, Shelby owns two of everything: two white shirts, two suits of underwear, two pairs of socks, and two neckties. One set is always on his back and the other is usually in storage at some laundry in the Grand Central area. Whenever he takes his bath, Shelby drops by the laundry first and picks up his clean linen. After his shower he carefully wraps the soiled clothes in a bundle and leaves them in another laundry to be washed.

28 His outer garments are kept as neat as possible. Once or twice a week he drops in at one of the small tailor shops around town and sits in his shirt tails while his coat and trousers are being pressed. Unfortunately, he has never found a place where he can sit in a booth while the clothes are being cleaned. When his garments are quite dirty, and he gets enough money ahead, he picks up his clean laundry and retires to a cheap but good hotel. There he engages a room, paying for it in advance. Once the door is closed on the bellhop, he strips and calls valet service. For the next twenty-four hours, while the cleaners are at work on his coat and trousers, he spends his time in bed, or under the shower. He has slept for twenty-two hours on these occasions, and taken as many as fifteen showers. He never gets too much sleep or too many showers.

29 The whole twenty-four hour period in the hotel, including cleaning, costs him about seven dollars. Shelby considers this gross extravagance, since his weekly average expenditure is about eight dollars, but for some time he never seemed to accumulate enough money to buy a second suit. Besides, he always comes out of his stay with a tremendous sense of pleasure and well being.

30 One of the astounding things about Shelby's existence is that he has become a recluse, just as surely as though he lived on a desert island. For three or four days at a time he will speak to no one, nor will anyone speak to him. He is not solitary by nature, but his way of life and his desire to continue it without molestation impose this penalty upon him. While he might like to engage the policeman in the Grand Central waiting room in conversation, he realizes that if he did, he might be recognized easily the next time he visited there, and all subsequent visits would gradually peg him as a homeless person, making him liable to arrest and harassment.

31 This solitude has brought him one great problem which he senses but finds difficult to describe: the problem of passage of time. Shelby is waiting for something. He himself does not know what it is. When it comes he will either go back into the world from which he came, or sink out of sight in the morass of alcoholism or despair that has engulfed other vagrants. While he is waiting, he is plagued by a restlessness that keeps him on the move for seventeen or eighteen hours a day. He is likely to say that he moves about as much as he does because policemen will not stop a man who looks as though he is coming from some place or going to some place. What he does not say, because he does not realize it, is that he is working to keep his time occupied.

32 Shelby's search for entertainment has led him into every nook and cranny of the city and brought him knowledge which he might not otherwise have gained. One idiosyncrasy that he has discovered but cannot account for is the attitude of station policemen toward book readers. After seven-thirty in the evening, in order to read a book in Grand Central or Penn Station, a person either has to wear horn-rimmed glasses, or look exceptionally prosperous. Anyone else is apt to come under surveillance. On the other hand, newspaper readers never seem to attract attention and even the seediest vagrant can sit in Grand Central all night without being molested if he continues to read a paper. Shelby therefore spends one or two hours a night going over the daily papers. He regularly reads all seven final editions of New York journals, which he picks out of trash baskets.

33 Shelby is extraordinarily fond of museums and galleries and has become something of an art expert. Vagrants are rarely molested in New York museums and galleries. Shelby is apt to smile and say this is because the guards can never distinguish between a legitimate bum and an artistic one. They never disturb a person like him because they never know when they are trying to eject an artist who is holding a one-man show on the third floor.

34 Shelby began frequenting the big marble-coated buildings many months ago in search of shelter and warmth. He followed the guides around on their tours, often three or four times a day. In order to seem part of the group making the tour he would ask questions. And by this time he knows enough to stump most of the guides. He has developed a genuine love for the subject, knows where every show in town is being held and what it contains, and is thinking of trying to do a little painting himself. But when he goes to the shows, he is also still on the lookout for some obscure nook or cranny where he can stretch out and sleep for an hour or two. Even a corner behind a Grecian column where a man can sleep upright without interruption is valuable.

35 Another of Shelby's pastimes is to take the ferry ride from the Battery to Staten Island and back. He calls this the poor man's ocean voyage. Unfortunately, the round trip costs ten cents, which puts it in the luxury class. More often, he boards one of the numerous Central Railroad of New Jersey ferries and makes three or four round trips to the Jersey shore. If he gets on during the rush-hour periods he is not noticed and there is no expense.

36 Pursuing this pastime Shelby has picked up a surprising amount of information on navigation, and he is rapidly becoming an authority on the New York tidal flow. He seems to get a great deal of enjoyment out of criticizing the pilots of the ferries if they do not bring their vessels squarely into the slips, and almost the first thing he reads in the New York papers is the shipping news. Two or three times a week he journeys to the waterfront to watch the arrival or departure of one of the big liners.

On other occasions he will go down to the Jersey ferry slips and board the little vessel that he estimates will come closest to the big ships as they move up the river or put out to sea.

37 The city offers other free sources of diversion too. Shelby always follows a fire engine; has a nose for street fights; and, if he stumbles upon an accident, never leaves the scene until the last policeman has closed his notebook. He stops to listen to every sidewalk preacher he comes across and likes to sing the hymns just for the pleasure of singing something. He knows every major construction project in town, but rarely watches such routine phases of the work as excavation or riveting. He looks the site over and then shows up at the exact moment some critical problem is about to be solved.

38 He is a steady visitor at the various courts around town, and is what he describes as a sucker for band music. For this reason he believes he is happier in New York than he would be in any other city in the world. New York is the only place where there is a parade of some kind every day in the year. On some days there are two or three. Last Armistice Day, Shelby visited five parades and took part in one.

39 The peculiar advantages of the microfilm room of the New York Public Library, which he came upon almost by accident, are probably Shelby's unique discovery. He had been advised by another vagrant that the library was a good place to keep warm on a cold day, and that it offered an opportunity for an hour or two of sleep. Several days later he made his first call there, provided with what he considered a plausible excuse for visiting the institution. He went to the main desk and asked for a copy of the *New York Times* for November 10, 1936. He was referred to the microfilm room, where the attendant produced a roll of film instead of the paper. He was then escorted to one of several viewing machines which were placed helter-skelter in a sort of alcove off to one side of a large room. Shelby put the film in the machine and looked at the image. Within half an hour, as he turned the crank, he dozed off. He was not disturbed and eventually woke up about five hours later.

40 He says, now, that at the time this seemed too good to be true, so a week later he went back again to see if it was an accident. He arrived about nine-fifteen in the morning and slept until almost four-thirty in the afternoon, again without being disturbed.

41 He since has become cognizant of several things. Most men in his condition who visit the Public Library go to the reading rooms. Either they have never heard of the microfilm room, or they underestimate its possibilities. Consequently, the attendants there have never met a real vagrant face to face. They assume that anyone who has heard of microfilm and wishes to use it is in search of learning. They check the film out to the applicant and never follow up. Moreover, the accommodations are very comfortable. The room is warm, and the upright film-display stands give a man an excellent place to rest his head.

42 For some time, Shelby put the microfilm room at the top of his list as a place of shelter, then suddenly he realized that it was a far more valuable place for pure entertainment. He never goes there to sleep now, but he often goes in early in the morning and spends the entire day reading. He has read all the old issues of the *New York Times* that are available on film, all his favorite comic strips from the date of their inception to the present, and every column Damon Runyon ever wrote.

43 A by-product of his many hours in the microfilm room is a system for playing the races which he developed by virtue of having been able to study every racing chart published in New York over the past twenty years. He has put this system to a test twice. At one time he worked quite steadily for almost a month and, with twenty-five dollars in his pocket, visited Aqueduct Race Track where he won eighty-seven dollars and forty cents, after expenses. Prudently, he took the money and bought himself a new suit of clothes, leaving the original twenty-five dollars untouched. A few days later he took the twenty-five and went to Belmont Park, where he lost it all. He hasn't visited the track since, but he remains an avid racing fan and plays the horses regularly in the microfilm room. Nowadays, however, he saves all the races until cold weather sets in and plays during the winter months. He never looks at the racing results beforehand. "I might just as well be honest about it," he says.

44 Shelby's favorite of all forms of recreation is walking. He usually walks the streets of Manhattan for four to ten hours a day, covering anywhere from five to twenty-five miles. He has walked the full length of every up and down avenue in the city and crossed the island on every crosstown street. He is a walking encyclopedia on plaques and knows every traffic bottleneck and short cut in town. He loves to window-shop and knows when most of the stores change their displays. At some time every day he manages to pass the window of the Christian Science Reading Room on Park Avenue and solemnly reads the Bible passage marked there.

45 At one time he estimated that he had about exhausted the possibilities of exploration in Manhattan and decided to concentrate on Brooklyn. He crossed the Brooklyn Bridge on foot one day, and on two other occasions took the subway. At the end of the third trip he gave the project up. "Walking in Brooklyn is like walking in Lansing, Michigan. I have the feeling I've seen everything before," he says. "Manhattan isn't like that."

46 At present, Henry Shelby seems content to take things as they come. "I don't know how long I'll live this life," he said not long ago, as he traced a design in the dirt with his foot. "I don't have much trouble. I've never gotten drunk and lain in a doorway all day. My name's never been on a police blotter for vagrancy. I haven't had to beg. Maybe if things were like they were twenty years ago, when everybody was a bum, I might change. Maybe something will happen that will force me to change, one way or another. Yes, I guess that's about it, but it hasn't happened yet, and things seem so easy and natural this way, the way they are now, that it's just as though it was supposed to be that way. I'm just not going to look at the future. All I can tell anybody, now, is that I intend to be up at a little delicatessen I know on Broadway. They serve a hell of a good boiled beef dinner up there for sixty-eight cents." He looked up at one of the big street clocks. "Which reminds me. If I'm going to get there by six o'clock, I'd better get going. Takes me almost an hour to walk it." His listener asked him why he didn't take the subway.

47   "Subways are for sleeping," Shelby said, smiled, and walked off.

Exercises

CONTENT

True or False? If you think the statement represents what the selection says or implies, mark it "True"; if you do not think so, mark it "False."

1. Cigarettes are not "extras" for Shelby.
2. Shelby has been arrested several times for vagrancy.
3. Though expensive, Shelby's occasional stays in hotels are of psychological value to him.
4. Shelby is a certified public accountant.
5. To avoid having to shave so often, Shelby at one time grew a beard.
6. New York vagrants are lonely people.
7. Reading a book is a better way than reading a newspaper to avoid questioning by the station police in New York railway stations.
8. Shelby is a victim of economic recession.
9. Lack of regular eating and sleeping habits is gradually ruining Shelby's health.
10. Shelby is deeply troubled by the fact that his life is turning out to be a failure.

Questions for Discussion

1. By what set of values is Shelby a failure? By what set of values may he be considered *not* a failure?
2. What is Love's attitude to Shelby? What attitude do you think he wants us to have? What attitude do you have?
3. Aside from its worth as a piece of good prose, what educational value can there be in reading about the purposeless and socially irresponsible existence of a mixed-up New York bum?
4. What are "legitimate sleepers" (Paragraph 19)?

FORM AND STYLE

1. The first six paragraphs identify and describe Shelby for us. The

rest of the essay describes the kind of life he leads. The organization of Paragraphs 7-29 is given in Paragraph 7. Exactly where?

2. Paragraphs 7-29, however, do not follow the outline set up in Paragraph 7: they depart from it with the beginning of Paragraph 14. Explain.

3. What is the significance of, " 'I don't know how long I'll live this life,' he said not long ago, as he traced a design in the dirt with his foot" (second sentence, Paragraph 46)? What earlier passage gives the sentence here its significance?

4. Comment upon the quality of the humor in, "The BMT has suitable accommodations, but, as Shelby describes it, 'an undesirable clientele'" (last sentence, Paragraph 14). How does Shelby's phrase help to characterize him?

5. At the end of Paragraph 46 Shelby hurries off in order to be at the little Broadway delicatessen by six o'clock. Isn't there a suggestion here that Shelby, for all his freedom from the obligations of job and family life, is still, like the rest of us, a slave of clock-measured time? Doesn't he sound a bit like a rushed businessman, anxious to make an important appointment? If you sense the similarity, do you find it funny or not, considering Shelby's circumstances? Discuss the meaning of the essay along the lines suggested by these questions. Do you feel that your attitude to Shelby is part of the meaning? Were your feelings about Shelby influenced by the style and by the choice of specific narrative detail as in Paragraph 46?

VOCABULARY

Which of the four words or phrases to the right seems to you to be *closest* in meaning to the word in heavy type to the left? Put a check mark after your choice.

retrieve (2)   pawn out . . . go through . . . get back . . . ask for . . .

briskly (3)   with authority . . . energetically . . . proudly . . . well

migratory (5)   nomadic . . . sorry . . . variable . . . dependent on the weather . . .

incidentals (9)   extras . . . unforeseen purchases . . . accidents . . . minor expenses . . .

dietary (10)   health (*adj.*) . . . food (*adj.*) . . . caloric (*adj.*) . . . daily . . .

detests (10)   loves . . . loathes . . . gets sick from . . . is indifferent to . . .

subsists (11)   eats just enough . . . substitutes . . . exists . . undergoes hardship . . .

allots (14)   allows . . . uses . . . spends . . . sets aside . . .

ramshackle (14)   dirty . . . rickety . . . smelly . . .old-fashioned . . .

cautious about (15)   afraid of . . . careful about . . . sensitive about . . . particular about . . .

repose (19)   rest . . . sleep . . . retreat . . . lying down . . .

secluded (*19*)   ideal . . . attractive . . . warm . . . protected . . .
prone (*20*)   face down . . . sitting . . . relaxed . . . lying . . .
profusely (*22*)   abundantly . . . humbly . . . with embarrassment . . .
    politely . . .
unkempt (*25*)   shabby . . . ungroomed . . . dirty . . . stubble-faced
tremendous (*29*)   uplifting . . . very great . . . wonderful . . . valu-
    able . . .
astounding (*30*)   bad . . . very surprising . . . secondary . . . strange-
    sounding . . .
recluse (*30*)   outcast . . . hermit . . . lonesome person . . . forgotten
molestation (*30*)   interference . . . harm . . . punishment . . . criti-
    cism . . .
liable (*30*)   subject . . . open . . . probable . . . easily victimized . . .
harassment (*30*)   punishment . . . state of being fined . . . disgrace
    . . . annoyance . . .
morass (*31*)   swamp . . . depth . . . immorality . . . quicksand . . .
diversion (*37*)   distraction . . . amusement . . . cultural activity . . .
    fun . . .
avid (*43*)   well-informed . . . eager . . . thorough . . . habitual . . .
plaques (*44*)   plazas . . . old, culturally interesting houses . . . monu-
    ments . . . inscribed metal plates . . .

THEME SUGGESTIONS

Write a character sketch of Henry Shelby, using as many specific details as you can in making a valid, consistent, and interesting portrait

What is Shelby waiting for? (Theorize, invent a background that does
not contradict the facts of the essay, use him as a symbol of some kind.
The topic is meant to challenge your imagination and thoughtfulness into
explaining an evidently complex man)

The art of being respectable without property
A night among the vagrants
Van Doren on Shelby

36

MARK ETHRIDGE, JR.

Turmoil in the South

1   Since the Supreme Court's decision twenty-seven months ago un-
told millions of words have been written about segregation in the South.

TURMOIL IN THE SOUTH. From *The Saturday Review*, September 1, 1956.
Reprinted by permission of *The Saturday Review* and the author.

Major magazines have acted as clearing houses of opinion. A plague of Northern journalists tours the South like Methodist circuit riders, pouring out copy by the column for home consumption.

2   Yet despite this torrent of words a major part of the picture has been largely overlooked. The facts of segregation and desegregation have been covered, but few if any writers have sought to explain to the rest of the nation the whys of this mid-century Southern turmoil. The depth of Southern convictions, the rationalizations and irrationalizations, the blind and bitter hatreds, and the profound helplessness of people caught in a web not of their own choosing and not entirely of their own making have been ignored in the attempt to categorize the South in terms of black and white.

3   It is just these whys that Robert Penn Warren examines in his short but sensitive and uncluttered book "Segregation." He has set down in interviews with Southerners of all colors and conceptions the first really comprehensive portrait of the racially torn South of 1956.

4   Warren is well qualified to write on this subject. He is a native Kentuckian and a raised Tennesseean. He went to school at Vanderbilt, taught at Southwestern, Vanderbilt, and Louisiana State. He has lived in the North long enough to view the South objectively but, as he has demonstrated in earlier books, the South has lived in him long enough for him to view it compassionately.

5   The book's title is a misnomer. The subject is really about prejudice, which knows no time and no locale. The conflict of the moment, as Warren points out in a unique interview with himself at the end of the book, is only a manifestation of the age-old failure of people to achieve perfect justice. The rigors of the South are typical of the reaction when society sets out to correct a long-standing flaw.

6   Warren puts it this way:

> We have to deal with the problem our historical moment proposes, the burden of our time. We all live with a thousand unsolved problems of justice all the time. We don't even recognize a lot of them. We have to deal only with those which the moment proposes to us. Anyway, we can't legislate for posterity. All we can do for posterity is to try to plug along in a way to make them think we—the old folks—did the best we could for justice, as we could understand it.

7   This book is not an apology for the South. Warren does not attempt to excuse Southern prejudice or Southern failures. But he does try to explain it through the words of people in the South. He has talked to a Southern Negro woman whose husband was killed by white men, to college students, to leaders of the NAACP and the Citizens' Council, to lawyers, plantation owners, preachers, and to the inevitable taxi drivers all interviewers talk to. He heard and reports their explanations for why integration is easier to say than to accomplish. "Pridefulness, money, level of intelligence, race, God's will, filth and disease, power, hate, contempt, legality" are words he quotes. And there's another one, which he calls piety and Hamilton Basso, in "The View from Pompey's Head," called Southern shintoism. This one is ancestor worship or respect for tradition, however you want to put it.

8 But this book is also more than an explanation of the whys. It is an insight into people themselves caught in a storm they can neither conquer nor fully comprehend. Warren shows the conflict among Southern people themselves is not just a division of man against man, but of man against himself. The inner conflict is one of respect for law fighting against tradition, of human decency against inborn prejudice, or long-view economics against personal profits by exploitation. In some areas of the South and in some people resolution came easy. Those who favored integration from the first resolved it quickly. So did Jimmy Byrnes and the South Carolina legislature. To those in the middle resolution comes harder, and the conflict is extremely personal. "I feel it's all happening inside of me, every bit of it," a girl from Mississippi told Warren.

9 Or, as a junk dealer put it:

Somebody ought to tell 'em not to blame no state, not even Alabam' or Mississippi, for what the bad folks do. Like stuff in New York or Chicago. Folks in Mississippi got good hearts as any place. They always been nice and good-hearted to me, for I go up to a man affable. The folks down here is just in trouble and can't claw out. Don't blame 'em, got good hearts but can't claw out of their trouble. It is hard to claw out from under the past and the past way.

10 It is indeed hard to claw out, and Warren does not pretend to know exactly how or when it will happen. It is a moral problem, but it must be solved concretely. It will take mutual education and mutual respect.

11 But Warren does offer hope. If the South, he says, can now face up to itself and its situation it may achieve moral identity. "Then in a country where moral identity is hard to come by, the South, because it has had to deal concretely with a moral problem, may offer some leadership." And because segregation is not really much different from Yankee Phariseeism, from smugness without justification, we as a nation need all the leadership we can get.

Exercises

CONTENT

True or False? If you think the statement represents what the selection says or implies, mark it "True"; if you do not think so, mark it "False."

1. The South has only itself to blame for the race problem.

2. Almost no book before Warren's has tried to explain the reasons for racial conflict in the South today.

3. Robert Penn Warren is Chief Justice of the Supreme Court of the United States.

4. Warren was born and raised in the deep South.

5. His book is pro-segregation.

6. The reviewer likes the book.

7. The title of Warren's book is *Turmoil in the South.*

8. Warren and Ethridge agree that the Southern race problem is due entirely to economic causes.

9. To avoid extreme opinions Warren did not interview Negroes who had suffered from race prejudice, nor whites who had joined white Citizens' Councils to uphold segregation.

10. Warren's thesis is that with a little good will on both sides, the race problem in the South can be solved within a few years.

Questions for Discussion

1. The Supreme Court's decision referred to in the first sentence of Paragraph 1 was handed down on May 17, 1954. What was it?

2. What is the N.A.A.C.P.?

3. A book review has two main functions: (a) to tell the reader what the book is about and—at least in the case of a book on a controversial topic like this—what the author says about his topic, and (b) to give the reviewer's opinion whether the book is good, indifferent, or bad. By these standards, is *Turmoil in the South* a good book review? Support your answer by reference to the review.

4. Choose one: Warren's book is (a) a series of interviews with Southerners, (b) a short history of segregation in the South, (c) an analysis of the causes of racial turmoil in the South, (d) a set of directives for how racial integration can be achieved, (e) a passionate defense of the traditional Southern way of life, including segregation.

5. Justify calling sentences 3 and 4 in Paragraph 8 the most important passage in the whole review.

FORM AND STYLE

1. What is the importance of Paragraph 4 to the review as a whole?

2. Does or does not the second sentence of Paragraph 5 explain the first? Explain your answer.

3. Point out the paragraphs in the review that do *not* deal directly with Warren's book. Justify their inclusion. (Compare your answer to question 1, above, concerning Paragraph 4.)

4. Explain the pun at the end of Paragraph 2.

5. Justify the "bad" English in Paragraph 9.

6. What is meant by "inevitable taxi drivers" (Paragraph 7)?

7. What shade of meaning would Ethridge have lost if near the end of Paragraph 11 he had written "Northern sense of moral superiority" instead of "Yankee Phariseeism"?

VOCABULARY

Which of the four words or phrases to the right seems to you to be *closest* in meaning to the word in heavy type to the left? Put a check mark after your choice.

turmoil (2)   rebellion . . . civil war . . . revolution . . . confusion

categorize (2)   criticize . . . classify . . . explain . . . oversimplify

uncluttered (3)   non-partisan . . . calm . . . well-organized . . . unhurried . . .

compassionately (4)   understandingly . . . sympathetically . . . wisely . . . with emotion . . .

locale (5)   place . . . limitation . . . room . . . space . . .

unique (5)   final . . . interesting . . . excellent . . . being the only one . . .

manifestation (5)   demonstration . . . result . . . repetition . . . declaration . . .

rigors (5)   sufferings . . . acts of violence . . . prejudices . . . cruelties . . .

flaw (5)   defect . . . injustice . . . failure . . . disease . . .

comprehend (8)   understand . . . be aware of . . . forgive . . . yield to . . .

exploitation (8)   confiscation . . . unfair use . . . trade prejudice . . . suppression . . .

affable (9)   courteous . . . fabulous . . . often . . . honest . . .

concretely (10)   legally . . . forcefully . . . in practice . . . by means of things . . .

identity (11)   splendor . . . sameness . . . individuality . . . meaning . . .

smugness (11)   pride . . . prejudice . . . complacency . . . coziness

THEME SUGGESTIONS

Write a review of a nonfiction book or long article
School integration in practice (describe a situation you know)
The case for segregation
The case against segregation
A prejudice conquered

Four Generations

1   "Move just a little closer together—the little girl more toward the center—that's good. Now I think we'll get it."

2   The photographer dived once more under the black cloth.

3   "Stand back, Ma," a husky voice said. "You'll be in the picture."

4   Aunt Em stepped hastily back with a panicky look. Mercy, she didn't want to show! She hadn't had time to get her dress changed yet, had come right out of the kitchen where she was baking pies to see the photograph taken. She was in her old dark blue kitchen dress and had her hair just wadded up until she could get time to comb it. It didn't give her much time for dressing up, having all this crowd to cook for.

5   The boys, and Uncle Chris, standing away back on the edges, grinned appreciatively. Fred whispered to Clarence, "Laugh if Ma'd got in it." The way she had jumped back, and her unconsciousness of the ends sticking up from her little wad of hair delighted the boys. When they looked at each other, a little remembering glint came into their eyes.

6   There was quite a crowd of onlookers. Aunt Em. Uncle Chris in his good trousers, and his shirt sleeves, his sunburned face dark brown above the white collar that Aunt Em had made him put on because of Charlie's. Uncle Gus and Aunt Sophie Spfierschlage had come over to dinner, and stood back against the white house wall, Aunt Sophie mountainous in her checked gingham. The boys, of course, and Bernie Schuldt who was working for Chris; and another fellow who had come to look at some hogs and who was standing there, conscious of his old overalls and torn straw hat, mumbling, "Well, didn't know I was gona find anything like this goin' on." . . . Charlie's wife, Ella, had been given a chair where she could have a good view of the proceedings. She tried to smile and wave her handkerchief when little Phyllis looked around at her. Then she put the handkerchief to her eyes, lifting up her glasses with their narrow light shell rims, still smiling a little painfully. She had to think from how far Katherine had come.

7   Aunt Em and Aunt Sophie were whispering, "Ain't it a shame Edna couldn't get over! They coulda took one of Chris and her and Marine and Merle, with Grandpa, too. . . . That little one looks awful cute, don't she? . . . Well, what takes him so long? Grandpa won't sit there much longer. I should think they coulda had it taken by this time a'ready."

FOUR GENERATIONS. From *Iowa Interiors* by Ruth Suckow. Copyright, 1926, by Rinehart & Company, Inc. Copyright renewed 1954 by Ruth Suckow Nuhn. Reprinted by permission of Rinehart & Company, Inc., New York, Publishers.

8 They all watched the group on the lawn. They had decided that the snowball bushes would "make a nice background." The blossoms were gone, but the leaves were dark green, and thick. What a day for taking a picture! It would be so much better out here than in the house. Katherine had made them take it right after dinner, so that little Phyllis would not be late for her nap—nothing must ever interfere with that child's nap. It was the brightest, hottest time of day. The tall orange summer lilies seemed to open and shimmer in the heat. Things were so green—the country lawn with its thick grass, the heavy foliage of the maple trees against the blue summery sky of July. The thin varnished supports of the camera stand glittered yellow and sticky. The black cloth of the lens looked thick, dense, hot. The photographer's shirt was dazzling white in the sun, and when he drew his head out from under the cloth his round face shone pink. His coat made a black splotch tossed on the grass.

9 "The little girl more toward the center."

10 All three of the others tried anxiously to make little Phyllis more conspicuous. "Here, we've got to have you showing—my, my!—whether the rest of us do or not," Charlie said jovially. Grandpa's small aged frail hand moved a little as if he were going to draw the child in front of him—but, with a kind of delicacy, did not quite touch her little arm.

11 They had to wait while a little fleecy cloud crossed the sun, putting a brief, strange, cool shadow over the vivid lawn. In that moment the on-lookers were aware of the waiting group. Four generations! Great-grand-father, grandfather, mother, daughter. It was all the more impressive when they thought of Katherine and Phyllis having come from so many miles away. The snowball bushes were densely green behind them—almost dusky in the heat. Grandpa's chair had been placed out there—a homemade chair of willow branches. To think that these four belonged together!

12 Grandpa, sitting in the chair, might have belonged to another world. Small, bent like a little old troll, foreign with his black cambric skull cap, his blue far-apart peasant eyes with their still gaze, his thin silvery beard. His hands, gnarled from years of farm work in a new coun-try, clasped the homemade knotted stick that he held between his knees. His feet, in old felt slippers with little tufted wool flowers, were set flat on the ground. He wore the checked shirt of an old farmer. . . . It hardly seemed that Charlie was his son. Plump and soft, dressed in the easy gar-ments, of good quality and yet a trifle careless, of Middle Western small-town prosperity. His shaven face, paler now than it used to be and show-ing his age in the folds that had come about his chin; his glasses with shell rims and gold bows; the few strands of grayish hair brushed across his pale, luminous skull. A small-town banker. Now he looked both impressed and shamefaced at having the photograph taken. . . . And then Kath-erine, taking after no one knew whom. Slender, a little haggard and worn, still young, her pale, delicate face and the cords in her long, soft throat, her little collar bones, her dark, intelligent weak eyes behind her thick black-rimmed glasses. Katherine had always been like that. Refined, "finicky," studious, thoughtful. Her hand, slender and a trifle sallow, lay on Phyllis's shoulder.

13 Phyllis. . . . Her little yellow frock made her vivid as a canary bird against the dark green of the foliage. Yellow—the relatives did not know whether they liked that, bright yellow. Still, she did look sweet. They hadn't thought Katherine's girl would be so pretty. Of course the care that Katherine took of her—everything had to revolve around that child. There was something faintly exotic about her liquid brown eyes with their jet-black lashes, the shining straight gold-brown hair, the thick bangs that lay, parted a little and damp with the heat, on the pure white of her forehead. Her little precise "Eastern accent." . . . Grandpa looked wonderingly at the bare arms, round and soft and tiny, white and moist in the heat. Fragile blue veins made a flowerlike tracery of indescribable purity on the white skin. Soft, tender, exquisite . . . ach, what a little girl was here, like a princess!

14 The cloud passed. Katherine's white and Phyllis's yellow shone out again from the green. The others stood back watching, a heavy stolid country group against the white wall of the farmhouse that showed bright against the farther green of the grove. Beyond lay the orchard and the rank green spreading cornfields where little silvery clouds of gnats went shimmering over the moist richness of the leaves.

15 "Watch—he's taking it now!"

16 In the breathless silence they could hear the long whirr and rush of a car on the brown country road beyond the grove.

17 Well, the picture was taken. Everyone was glad to be released from the strain.

18 Grandpa's chair had been placed nearer the house, under some maple trees. Charlie stayed out there with him a while. It was his duty, he felt, to talk to the old man a while when he was here at the farm. He didn't get over very often—well, it was a hundred miles from Rock River, and the roads weren't very good up here in Sac township. His car stood out at the edge of the grove in the shade. The new closed car that he had lately bought, a "coach," opulent, shining, with its glass and upholstery and old-blue drapes, there against the background of the evergreen grove with its fallen branches and pieces of discarded farm machinery half visible in the deepest shade.

19 It wasn't really very hard to get away from Rock River and the bank. He and Ella took plenty of trips. He ought to come to see his father more than he did. But he seemed to have nothing to say to Grandpa. The old man had scarcely been off the place for years.

20 "Well, Pa, you keep pretty well, do you?"

21 "Ja, pretty goot . . . ja, for so old as I am—"

22 "Oh, now, you mustn't think of yourself as so old."

23 Charlie yawned, recrossed his legs. He lighted a cigar.

24 "Chris's corn doing pretty well this season?"

25 "Ach, dot I know nuttings about. Dey don't tell me nuttings."

26 "Well, you've had your day at farming, Pa."

27 "Ja . . . ja, ja . . ."

28 He fumbled in the pocket of his coat, drew out an ancient black pipe.

29 Charlie said cheerfully, "Have some tobacco?" He held out a can.

30 The old man peered into it, sniffed. "Ach, dot stuff? No, no, dot is shust like shavings. I smoke de real old tobacco."

31 "Like it strong, hey?"

32 They both puffed away.

33 Grandpa sat in the old willow chair. His blue eyes had a look half wistful, half resentful. Charlie was his oldest child. He would have liked to talk with Charlie. He was always wishing that Charlie would come, always planning how he would tell him things—about how the old ways were going and how the farmers did now, how none of them told him things—but when Charlie came, then that car was always standing there ready to take him right back home again, and there seemed nothing to be said. He always remembered Charlie as the young man, the little boy who used to work beside him in the field—and then when Charlie came, he was this stranger. Charlie was a town man now. He owned a bank! He had forgotten all about the country, and the old German ways. To think of Charlie, their son, being a rich banker, smoking cigars, riding around in a fine carriage with glass windows. . . .

34 "Dot's a fine wagon you got dere."

35 Charlie laughed. "That's a coach, Pa."

36 "So? Coach, is dot what you call it? Like de old kings, like de emperors, de kaisers, rode around in. Ja, you can live in dot. Got windows and doors, curtains—is dere a table too, stove—no? Ja, dot's a little house on wheels."

37 He pursed out his lips comically. But ach, such a carriage! He could remember when he was glad enough to get to town in a lumber wagon. Grandma and the children used to sit in the back on the grain sacks. His old hands felt of the smooth knots of his stick. He went back, back, into reverie. . . . He muttered just above his breath, "Ach, ja, ja, ja . . . dot was all so long ago . . ."

38 Charlie was silent, too. He looked at the car, half drew out his watch, put it back. . . . Katherine crossed the lawn. His eyes followed her. Bluish-gray, a little faded behind his modern glasses—there was resentment, bewilderment, wistfulness in them at the same time, and loneliness. He was thinking of how he used to bring Kittie out here to the farm when she was a little girl, when Chris used to drive to Germantown and get them with a team and two-seated buggy. They had come oftener than

now when they had the car. . . . "Papa, *really* did you live out here—on this farm?" He had been both proud and a little jealous because she wasn't sunburned and wiry, like Chris's children. A little slim, long-legged, soft-skinned, dark-eyed girl. "Finicky" about what she ate and what she did—he guessed he and Ella had encouraged her in that. Well, he hadn't had much when he was a child, and he'd wanted his little girl to have the things he'd missed. He'd wanted her to have more than his brothers' and sisters' children. He was Charlie, the one who lived in town, the successful one. Music lessons, drawing lessons, college . . . and here she had grown away from her father and mother. Chris's children lived close around him, but it sometimes seemed to him that he and Ella had lost Kittie. Living away off there in the East. And when she came home, although she was carefully kind and dutiful and affectionate, there was something aloof. He thought jealously, maybe it would have been better if they hadn't given her all those things, had kept her right at home with them. . . . It hadn't been as much pleasure as he had anticipated having his little grandchild there. There was her "schedule" that Kittie was so pernickety about. He'd been proud to have people in Rock River see her beauty and perfection, but he hadn't been able to take her around and show her off as he'd hoped.

39 All day he had been seeing a little slim fastidious girl in a white dress and white hair ribbons and black patent leather slippers, clinging to his hand with little soft fingers when he took her out to see the cows and the pigs. . . . "Well, Kittie, do you wish we lived out here instead of in town?" She shook her head, and her small under lip curled just a little. . . .

40 He saw Chris and Gus off near the house. They could talk about how crops were coming, and he could tell them, with a banker's authority, about business conditions. He stirred uneasily, got up, yawned, stretched up his arms, said with a little touch of shame:

41 "Well, Pa, guess I'll go over and talk to Chris a while. I'll see you again before we leave."

42 "Ja—" The old man did not try to keep him. He watched Charlie's plump figure cross the grass. Ja, he had more to say to the young ones.

43 Aunt Em was through baking. She had gone into the bedroom to "get cleaned up." She had brought out chairs to the front porch. "Sit out here. Here's a chair, Ella—here, Katherine. Ach, Sophie, take a better chair than that." "Naw, this un'll do for me, Em."

44 "The womenfolks"—Katherine shuddered away from that phrase. She had always, ever since she was a little girl, despised sitting about this way with "the womenfolks." Planted squat in their chairs, rocking, yawning, telling over and over about births and deaths and funerals and sicknesses. There was a kind of feminine grossness about it that offended what had always been called her "finickiness."

45 Her mother enjoyed it. She was different from Aunt Em and Aunt Sophie, lived in a different way—a small plump elderly woman with waved grayish-silvery hair and a flowered voile dress with little fussy laces, feminine strapped slippers. But still there was something that she liked about sitting here in the drowsy heat and going over and over things with the other women. Sometimes, to Katherine's suffering disgust, she would add items about the birth of Katherine herself—"Well, I thought sure Kittie was going to be a boy. She kicked so hard—" "Oh, *Mother*, spare us!" Aunt Em would give a fat, comfortable laugh—"Don't look so rambunctious now, does she? Kittie, ain't you ever gona get a little flesh on your bones? You study too hard. She oughta get out and ride the horses like Edna does."

46 Aunt Sophie Spfierschlage—that was the way she sat rocking, her feet flat on the floor, her stomach comfortably billowing, beads of sweat on her heavy chin and lips and around the roots of her stiff, dull hair. Well, thank goodness she was only Aunt Em's sister, she wasn't really related to the Kleins. Aunt Em was bad enough.

47 They used to laugh over her fastidious disgust, when she sat here, a delicate, critical little girl who didn't want to get on one of the horses or jump from rafters into the hay. "Kittie thinks that's terrible. Well, Kittie, that's the way things happen." "Ach, she won't be so squeamish when she grows up and has three or four of her own." Now she sat beside them, delicate, still too thin to Aunt Em's amazement. "Ain't you got them ribs covered up yet? What's the matter? Don't that man of yours give you enough to eat?"—her soft skin pale and her eyes dark from the heat, dressed with a kind of fastidious precision, an ultra-refinement. A fragile bar pin holding the soft white silk of her blouse, her fine dark hair drooping about her face. "Well, you ain't changed much since you got married!" Aunt Em had said. They expected to admit her now to their free-masonry, to have *her* add interesting items about the birth of Phyllis.

48 Phyllis—her little darling! As if the exquisite miracle of Phyllis could have anything in common with these things! Katherine suffered just as she had always suffered from even small vulgarities. But she sat courteous and ladylike now, a slight dutiful smile on her lips.

49 "Where does she get them brown eyes? They ain't the color of yours are they? Turn around and let's have a look at you—no, I thought yours was kinda darker."

50 Aunt Em had come out now, had squatted down into another chair. "I guess her papa's got the brown eyes."

51 "Yes, I think she looks a little like Willis."

52 Ella said almost resentfully, "Well, I don't know whether she takes after Willis's folks or not, but I can't see that she looks one bit like Kittie or any of us."

53 "Well," Aunt Em said, "but look at Kittie. She don't look like you or Charlie neither. But I guess she's yours just the same, ain't she, Ella?

. . . Say, you remember that Will Fuchs? Ja, his girl's got one they say
don't belong to who it ought to. Her and that young Bender from over
south—"

54   Katherine did not listen. How long before they could leave? She
had thought it right to bring Phyllis over here where her great-grand-
father lived, as her father had wished. But it seemed worse to her than
ever. She knew that Aunt Em wouldn't let them go without something
more to eat, another of her great heavy meals with pie and cake and
coffee. Her mother had always said, as if in extenuation of her visible enjoyment of the visit and the food, "Well, Aunt Em means well. Why don't
you try and talk with her? She wants to talk with you." But Aunt Em and
the Spfierschlages and the whole place seemed utterly alien and horrible
to Katherine. For a moment, while they had been taking the photograph
out on the lawn, she had felt touched with a sense of beauty. But she had
never belonged here. She felt at home in Willis's quiet old frame house
in New England, with his precise, elderly New England parents—"refinement," "culture," Willis's father reading "the classics," taking the *Atlantic
Monthly* ever since their marriage. She had always felt that those were
the kind of people she ought to have had, the kind of home. Of course
she loved Father and Mother and was loyal to them. They depended upon
her as their only child.

55   This porch! It seemed to express the whole of her visits to the farm.
It was old-fashioned now—a long narrow porch with a fancy railing, the
posts trimmed with red. Her ancestral home! It was utterly alien to her.

56   They were talking to her again.

57   "Where's the girl—in taking her nap yet?"

58   "Yes, she's sleeping."

59   "Ach, you hadn't ought to make her sleep all the time when she's
off visiting. I baked a little piece of pie crust for her. I thought I'd give it
to her while it was nice and warm."

60   "Oh, better not try to give her pie crust," Ella said warningly.

61   "Ach, that ain't gona hurt her—nice homemade pie. Mine always
et that."

62   "Ja, mine did too."

63   Katherine's lips closed firmly. She couldn't hurry and hurt Father
and Mother—but oh, to get Phyllis home! Father—he was always trying
to give the child something she shouldn't have, he wanted to spoil her as
he had tried to spoil Katherine herself. . . . She shut her lips tight to
steel herself against the pitifulness of the sudden vision of Father—getting
so much older these last few years—looking like a child bereft of his toy
when she had firmly taken away the things with which he had come trot-
ting happily home for his grandchild. He had gradually drawn farther
and farther away. Once he had hurt her by saying significantly, when
Phyllis had wanted a pink blotter in the bank—"You'll have to ask your
mother. Maybe there's something in it to hurt you. *Grandpa* don't know."

He had wanted to take Phyllis to a little cheap circus that had come to town, to show her off and exhibit her. Mother was more sympathetic, even a little proud of retailing to the other "ladies" how careful Katherine was in bringing up the child, what a "nice family" Willis had. But even she was plaintive and didn't understand. Both she and Father thought that Katherine and Willis were "carrying it too far" when they decided to have Willis teach the child until they could find the proper school for her.

64 She heard a little sleepy startled voice from within the house— "Moth-uh!"

65 "Uh—huh! There's somebody!" Aunt Em exclaimed delightedly.

66 Katherine hurried into the darkened bedroom where Phyllis lay on Aunt Em's best bedspread. The shades were down, but there was the feeling of the hot sunlight back of them. Phyllis's bare arms and legs were white and dewy. Her damp golden-brown bangs were pushed aside. Katherine knelt adoring. She began to whisper.

67 "Is Mother's darling awake? . . . Shall we go home soon—see Father? Sleep in her own little room?" . . . Her throat tightened with a homesick vision of the little room with the white bed and the yellow curtains.

68 They had left Grandpa alone again. Charlie and the other men were standing out beside the car, bending down and examining it, feeling of the tires, trying the handles of the doors.

69 Grandpa had left his chair in the yard and gone to the old wooden rocker that stood just inside the door of his room. His room was part of the old house, the one that he and Grandma had had here on the farm. It opened out upon the back yard, with a little worn, narrow plank out from the door. It looked out upon the mound of the old cyclone cellar, with its wooden door, where now Aunt Em kept her vegetables in sacks on the damp, cool floor, with moist earthen jars of plum and apple butter on the shelf against the cobwebbed wall. The little triangular chicken houses were scattered about in the back yard, and beyond them was the orchard where now small apples were only a little lighter than the vivid summer green of the heavy foliage and where little dark, shiny bubbles of aromatic sap had oozed out from the rough, crusty bark.

70 The shadows in the orchard were drawing out long toward the east, and the aisles of sunlight, too, looked longer. The groups of people moved about more. Everything had the freshened look of late afternoon. Grandpa rocked a little. He puffed on his pipe, took it out and held it between his fingers. It left his lower lip moistened and shining above the fringe of silvery beard. His blue eyes kept looking toward the orchard, in a still, fathomless gaze. His lips moved at times.

71 "Ach, ja, ja, ja . . ." A kind of mild, sighing groan. It had pleased him that they had wanted the photograph taken, with the little great-grandchild. But that was over now. They had left him alone. And again, with a movement of his head, "Ja, dot was all so long ago."

72 Beyond the orchard, beyond the dark green cornfields that lay behind it, beyond the river and the town, beyond all the wide western country, and the ocean . . . what were his fixed blue eyes, intent and inward and sad, visioning now?

73 The rocker was framed in the doorway of his room. Even the odor of the room was foreign. His bed with a patchwork quilt, a little dresser, a chest of drawers. The ancient wall paper had been torn off and the walls calcimined a sky-blue. Against the inner one hung his big silver watch, slowly ticking. . . . His eyes blue, and his hair under the little black cap, his beard, were silvery. . . . A German text with gaudy flowers hung on a woolen cord above the bed. "*Der Herr is mein Hirte.*"

74 He started. "Nun—who is dot?"

75 He did not know that little Phyllis had been watching him. Standing outside the door, in her bright canary yellow, her beautiful liquid brown eyes solemnly studying him. She was half afraid. She had never seen anything so old as "Great-grandfather." The late afternoon sunlight shimmered in the fine texture of his thin silvery beard. It brought out little frostings and marks and netted lines on his old face in which the eyes were so blue. One hand lay upon his knee. She stared wonderingly at the knots that the knuckles made, the brownish spots, the thick veins, the queer, stretched, shiny look of the skin between the bones. She looked at his black pipe, his funny little cap, his slippers with the tufted flowers. . . .

76 "Ach, so? You t'ink Grandpa is a funny old man den? You want to look at him? So?"

77 He spoke softly. A kind of pleased smiling look came upon his face. He stretched out his hand slowly and cautiously, as if it were a butterfly poised just outside his door. A sudden longing to get this small pretty thing nearer, an ingenuous delight, possessed him now that he was alone with her. He spoke as one speaks to a bird toward which one is carefully edging nearer, afraid that a sudden motion will startle its bright eyes and make it take wing.

78 "Is dis a little yellow bird? Can it sing a little song?"

79 A faint smile dawned on the serious parted lips. He nodded at her. She seemed to have come a little closer. He, too, looked in wonderment, as he had done before, at the shining hair, the fragile blue veins on the white temples, the moist pearly white of the little neck, marveling at her as he would have marveled at some beautiful strange bird that might have alighted a moment on his door step. . . .

80 "Can't sing a little song? No? Den Grandpa will have to sing one to you."

81 He had been thinking of songs as he sat here, they had been murmuring somewhere in his mind. Old, old songs that he had known long ago in the old country. . . . His little visitor stood quite still as his faint, quavering voice sounded with a kind of dim sweetness in the sunshine. . . .

82   *"Du, du, liegst mir im Herzen,*
            Du, du, liegst mir im Sinn,
            Du, du, machst mir viel Schmerzen,
            Weisst nicht wie gut ich dir bin—
            Ja, ja, ja, ja, weisst nicht wie gut ich dir bin."

83   The gaze of her brown shining eyes never wavered, and a soft glow of fascinated interest grew in them as the sad wailing simplicity of the old tune quavered on the summer air. For a moment she was quite near, they understood each other.

84   "You like dot? Like Grandpa's song?"

85   She nodded. A tiny pleased smile curved her fresh lips. . . . Then suddenly, with a little delicate scared movement, as if after all she had discovered that the place was strange, she flitted away to her mother.

Exercises

CONTENT

True or False? If you think the statement represents what the selection says or implies, mark it "True"; if you do not think so, mark it "False."

1. The family has gathered to celebrate Grandpa's 90th birthday.
2. We never learn the name of the family.
3. Katherine lives in New England.
4. Her husband is a professor at Harvard.
5. Aunt Em has a sister whose name is Sophie.
6. Katherine has a cousin whose name is Fred.
7. Katherine has not seen her parents for some years.
8. Phyllis' grandfather took her to a cheap little circus.
9. When visiting the farm, Charlie spends most of his time talking to his father.
10. Though this has not been stated in so many words, Katherine is not really Charlie's daughter.

Questions for Discussion

1. Draw a chart showing the family relationship among Grandpa, Charlie, Ella, Uncle Chris, Aunt Em, Katherine, and Phyllis.
2. Name the four characters who represent the "four generations."
3. Is there a "villain" in the story? If so, who is it?
4. As the title says, this is a story about four generations of one family. But what does it say *about* the four generations? What is the theme of the story?
5. How many different kinds of contrast can you find in the story?

FORM AND STYLE

1. Paragraph 12 begins and Paragraph 13 ends with Grandpa. What does the story deal with in between? What determines the organization of the two paragraphs and what is the significance of their circular form?

2. After the introductory section, dealing with the taking of the picture (Paragraphs 1-16), the story focuses in turn on the four main characters. What is the sequence in which the characters are being spotlighted?

3. Why would "described" have been a less accurate word than "spotlighted" in question 2?

4. Through whose eyes do we "see" the story in Paragraph 18? In Paragraph 33? How is the change in viewpoint accomplished?

5. On the basis of the story alone, how would you define "finicky" and "finickiness"?

6. This is a translation of the German song Grandpa sings in Paragraph 82:

> You, you are in my heart,
> You, you are on my mind,
> You, you bring me great sorrow,
> Do not know how I love you—
> Yes, yes, yes, yes, you do not know how I love you.

What is the significance of the song? Of course, it shows how Grandpa tries to make friends with little Phyllis and how his mind goes back to his youth in Germany. But does it not suggest something even more important to the story as a whole? Can it not almost be said to state its theme? Explain.

7. Comment upon the use of the word "flitted" in Paragraph 85. Why not "skipped," or "fled," or simply "ran"?

8. What difference to the story would the omission of the last sentence in Paragraph 85 have made?

VOCABULARY

Which of the four words or phrases to the right seems to you to be *closest* in meaning to the word in heavy type to the left? Put a check mark after your choice.

conspicuous (*10*)   centered . . . evident . . . important . . . appearing to one's advantage . . .

jovially (*10*)   sentimentally . . . suddenly . . . good-naturedly . . . anxiously . . .

troll (*12*)   root . . . dwarf . . . wizard . . . stump of tree . . .

haggard (*12*)   wasted . . . wild . . . glum . . . old-looking . . .

sallow (*12*)   bony . . . freckled . . . thin . . . pale yellow . . .

exotic (*13*)   exciting . . . strange . . . foreign . . . mysterious . . .

tracery (*13*)   design . . . marks . . . branchwork . . . tint . . .

stolid (*14*)   impassive . . . dull . . . solid . . . substantial . . .

opulent *(18)*   flashy . . . large . . . rich . . . brand new . . .
wistful *(33)*   thoughtful . . . pleased . . . yearning . . . mischievous
reverie *(37)*   memory . . . longing . . . daydreaming . . . ecstasy . . .
aloof *(38)*   distant . . . superior . . . critical . . . wrong . . .
anticipated *(38)*   hoped . . . expected . . . said beforehand . . .
     guessed . . .
fastidious *(39)*   too delicate . . . beautiful . . . sickly . . . whining
squat *(44)*   firmly . . . square . . . forever . . . short and thick . . .
grossness *(44)*   silliness . . . vulgarity . . . largeness . . . ugliness
rambunctious *(45)*   strong . . . unruly . . . full of fight . . . lively
extenuation *(54)*   excuse . . . defense . . . explanation . . . praise
alien *(54)*   mean . . . foreign . . . ridiculous . . . repulsive . . .
bereft of *(63)*   robbed of . . . without . . . looking for . . . grieving
     for . . .
retailing *(63)*   sell in detail . . . boasting . . . informing . . . tell in
     detail . . .
plaintive *(63)*   complaining . . . sorrowful . . . blind . . . unsympa-
     thetic . . .
fathomless *(70)*   meaningless . . . without seeing . . . unmeasurable
     . . . shallow . . .
texture *(75)*   sheen . . . mixture . . . manner of composition . . .
     covering . . .
ingenuous *(77)*   ingenious . . . sudden . . . frank . . . overwhelm-
     ing . . .

THEME SUGGESTIONS

Customs in my grandparents' home
Old and young: distance, conflict, or understanding?
Changing environment
Revisiting my childhood

38

EDITH HAMILTON

The Greek Way

1   It is clear that in Greece the values were different from our own today. Indeed we are not able really to bring into one consistent whole their outlook upon life; from our point of view it seems to involve a self-

THE GREEK WAY. From *The Greek Way* by Edith Hamilton. By permission of W. W. Norton & Company, Inc. Copyright, 1930, 1942, by W. W. Norton & Company, Inc.

contradiction. People so devoted to poetry as to make it a matter of practical importance must have been, we feel, deficient in the sense for what is practically important, dreamers, not alive to life's hard facts. Nothing could be farther from the truth. The Greeks were pre-eminently realists. The temper of mind that made them carve their statues and paint their pictures from the living human beings around them, that kept their poetry within the sober limits of the possible, made them hard-headed men in the world of everyday affairs. They were not tempted to evade facts. It is we ourselves who are the sentimentalists. We, to whom poetry, all art, is only a superficial decoration of life, make a refuge from a world that is too hard for us to face by sentimentalizing it. The Greeks looked straight at it. They were completely unsentimental. It was a Roman who said it was sweet to die for one's country. The Greeks never said it was sweet to die for anything. They had no vital lies.

2   The great funeral oration of Pericles,[1] delivered over those fallen in the war, stands out as unlike all other commemoration speeches ever spoken. There is not a trace of exaltation in it, not a word of heroic declamation. It is a piece of clear thinking and straight talking. The orator tells his audience to pray that they may never have to die in battle as these did. He does not suggest or imply to the mourning parents before him that they are to be accounted happy because their sons died for Athens. He knows they are not and it does not occur to him to say anything but the truth. His words to them are:

3   Some of you are of an age at which they may hope to have other children, and they ought to bear their sorrow better. To those of you who have passed their prime, I say: Congratulate yourselves that you have been happy during the greater part of your days; remember that your life of sorrow will not last long, and take comfort in the glory of those who are gone.

4   Cold comfort, we say. Yes, but people so stricken cannot be comforted, and Pericles knew his audience. They had faced the facts as well as he had. To read the quiet, grave, matter-of-fact words is to be reminded by the force of opposites of all the speeches everywhere over the tombs of the Unknown Soldier.

5   Completely in line with this spirit is the often quoted epitaph on the Lacedemonians who fell at Thermopylæ.[2] Every one of them fell, as they knew beforehand they would. They fought their battle to the death with no hope to help them and by so dying they saved Greece, but all the great poet who wrote their epitaph found it fitting to say for them was:

6   O passer by, tell the Lacedemonians that we lie here in obedience to their laws.

7   We rebel; something more than that, we feel, is due such heroism.

[1] Athenian statesman, about 500-429 B.C.—*Ed.*
[2] In 480 B.C., during the Persian invasion of Greece. The Lacedemonians were Spartans.—*Ed.*

But the Greeks did not. Facts were facts and deeds spoke for themselves. They did not need ornament.

8 Often we are repelled by words that seem to us wanting in common human sympathy. When Œdipus[3] appears for the last time before his exile and speaks his misery, all that his friends say is:

9 These things were even as thou sayest.

10 And to his wish that he had died in infancy they answer:

11 I also would have had it thus.

12 The attitude seems hard but it is always to be borne in mind that the Greeks did not only face facts, they had not even a desire to escape from them. When Iphigenia says that Orestes must die but Pylades[4] may go free, he refuses to take his life on such terms, but he refuses like a Greek and not a modern. It is not love of his friend alone that constrains him but also fear of what people would say, and he knows it and speaks it straight: "Men will whisper how I left my friend to die. Nay—I love you and I dread men's scorn." That is honest but we cannot any more be honest like that. It shocks us. The combination that resulted in the Athenian is baffling to us, lovers of beauty who held poetry and music and art to be of first importance—in their schools the two principal subjects the boys learned were music and mathematics—and at the same time, lovers of fact, who held fast to reality. Pindar prays: "With God's help may I still love what is beautiful and strive for what is attainable." "What I aspire to be and am not, comforts me,"[5] would never have appealed to a Greek.

13 The society these men made up, whose sense of values is so strange to us, can be in some sort reconstructed, an idea of what their ways and their manner of life was like is to be had, even though the historical records, as usual, say nothing about the things we most want to know. Stories like those given above were not told of the Greeks because one man or two, a Pericles, a Socrates, had such notions. The golden deeds of a nation, however mythical, throw a clear light upon its standards and ideals. They are the revelation that cannot be mistaken of the people's conscience, of what they think men should be like. Their stories and their plays tell more about them than all their histories. To understand the Mid-Victorians one must go not to the history writers but to Dickens and Anthony Trollope.[6] For the Athenians of the great age we turn not to

---

[3] King of Thebes, the hero of *King Œdipus*, a tragedy by Sophocles. Œdipus was destined to kill his father and marry his mother, and when he discovered that the prophecy had been fulfilled, he blinded himself and left Thebes forever.—*Ed.*

[4] Iphigenia, Orestes, and Pylades are characters in *Iphigenia in Tauris* by Euripides. Iphigenia was a priestess who was required to sacrifice her brother Orestes but succeeded in escaping from Tauris together with him and his friend Pylades.—*Ed.*

[5] Robert Browning, in "Rabbi Ben Ezra" (1864)—*Ed.*

[6] 19th century English novelists.—*Ed.*

Thucydides, the historian, interested in Athens rather than her citizens, but to two writers unlike in every respect but one, their power to understand and depict the men they lived with: to Aristophanes, who made fun of them and scolded them and abused them and held them up for themselves to see in every play he wrote, and to Plato, who, for all that his business lay with lofty speculations on the nature of the ideal, was a student and lover of human nature too, and has left us in the personages of his dialogues characters so admirably drawn, they still live in his pages.

14 Many of the men met there are known to us from other writers. Some of the most famous persons of the day take part in the discussions. Whether all of them were real people or not there is no means of knowing, but there can be no doubt that they all are true to life, and that they seemed to Plato's hearers perfectly natural men, such as any upper-class Athenian was used to. Nothing else is credible. To suppose that Plato's idealism extended to his dramatis personæ, and that he put his doctrines in the mouths of personages who would appear unreal and absurd to his pupils, is to insult their intelligence and his. It is true that he does not give a cross-section of Athens, any more than Trollope does of England. A few people "not in society" make their appearance—a man who earns his living by giving recitations from Homer; a soothsayer, to Plato on the same social level as a clergyman to Sir Roger de Coverley[7]—but the people he really knows are the gentlemen of Athens and he knows them as Trollope knows his parsons and his M. P.'s.[8]

15 This society he introduces us to is eminently civilized, of men delighting to use their minds, loving beauty and elegance, as Pericles says in the funeral oration, keenly alive to all the amenities of life, and, above all, ever ready for a talk on no matter how abstract and abstruse a subject: "When we entered the house"—the speaker is Socrates—"we found Protagoras walking in the cloister; a train of listeners accompanied him; he, like Orpheus,[9] attracting them by his voice and they following. Then, as Homer says, 'I lifted up my eyes and saw' Hippias the Elean sitting in the opposite cloister and many seated on benches around him. They were putting to him questions on physics and astronomy and he was discoursing of them. Also Prodicus the Cean was there, still in bed—the day, be it noted, was just dawning—and beside him on the couches near, a number of young men. His fine deep voice re-echoed through the room." Socrates begs Protagoras to talk to them of his teaching and when the great man agrees: "As I suspected that he would like a little display and glorification in the presence of Prodicus and Hippias, I said: 'But why should we not summon the rest to hear?' 'Suppose,' said Callias, the host, 'we hold a council in which you may sit and discuss?' This was agreed

----

[7] A character in the *Spectator* essays written by Joseph Addison and Richard Steele in the early 18th century.—*Ed.*

[8] Members of [the British] Parliament.—*Ed.*

[9] Legendary Greek poet and musician.—*Ed.*

upon and great delight was felt at the prospect of hearing wise men talk."
And so they all settle down happily to argue about the identity of virtue
and knowledge and whether virtue can be taught.

16 It is, one perceives, a leisured society. Socrates speaks to the young
Theatetus of "The ease which free men can always command. They can
have their talk out in peace, wandering at will from one subject to
another, their only aim to attain the truth." But the direct witness is
hardly needed; an atmosphere of perfect leisure is the setting of all the
dialogues and to immerse oneself in them is to be carried into a world
where no one is ever hurried and where there is always time and to spare:
"I went down yesterday to the Piræus with Glaucon," so the *Republic*
begins, "to offer up my prayers to the goddess and also to see how they
would celebrate the festival. When we had finished and were turned
toward the city, Polemarchus appeared and several others who had been
at the procession. 'You are on your way to the city?' he said. 'But do you
see how many we are? And are you stronger than all these? If not, you
will have to stay.' 'But,' said I, 'may there not be an alternative? May we
not persuade you to let us go?' 'Can you, if we refuse to listen? And you
may be sure we shall. Stay and see the torch race on horseback this evening. And there will be a gathering of young men and we will have a
good talk.' "

17 After some such fashion nearly every dialogue begins. The most
charmingly leisured of them is, perhaps, the *Phædrus*. "Where are you
bound?" Socrates asks Phædrus, to which the young man answers that he
is going for a walk outside the wall to refresh himself after a morning
spent in talk with a great rhetorician: "You shall hear about it if you can
spare time to accompany me." Well, Socrates says, he so longs to hear it
that he would go all the way to Megara and back rather than miss it.
With this, Phædrus begins to be doubtful if he can do justice to the great
man: "Believe me, Socrates, I did not learn his very words—O no. Still,
I have a general notion of what he said and can give you a summary."
"Yes, dear lad," replies Socrates, "but you must first of all show what you
have under your cloak—for that roll I suspect is the actual discourse, and
much as I love you, I am not going to have you exercise your memory at
my expense." Phædrus gives in—he will read the whole essay; but where
shall they sit? O yes, under "that tallest plane tree, where there is shade
and gentle breezes and grass on which to sit or lie." "Yes," Socrates answers, "a fair resting place, full of summer sounds and scents, the stream
deliciously cool to the feet, and the grass like a pillow gently sloping to
the head. I shall lie down and do you choose the position you can best
read in. Begin." A number of hours are spent under that plane tree, discussing "the nature of the soul—though her true form be ever a theme of
large and more than mortal discourse"; and "beauty shining in company
with celestial forms"; and "the soul of the lover that follows the beloved
in modesty and holy fear"; and "the heavenly blessings of friendship";

and "all the great arts, which require high speculation about the truths of nature"; and men who "are worthy of a proud name befitting their serious pursuit of life. Wise, I may not call them, for that is a great name which belongs to God alone—lovers of wisdom is their fitting title." That is the way two gentlemen would while away a summer morning in the Athens of Plato.

18 It is a society marked also by an exquisite urbanity, of men gently bred, easy, suave, polished. The most famous dinner-party that was ever given was held at the house of Agathon the elegant, who declared to his guests as they took their places that he never gave orders to his servants on such occasions: "I say to them, Imagine that you are our hosts and I and the company your guests; treat us well and we shall commend you." Into this atmosphere of ease and the informality past masters in the social art permit themselves, an acquaintance is introduced by mistake who had not been invited, a mishap with awkward possibilities for people less skilled in the amenities than our banqueters. Instantly he is made to feel at home, greeted in the most charming fashion: "'Oh, welcome, Aristodemus,' said Agathon, 'You are just in time to sup with us. If you come on any other matter put it off and make one of us. I was looking for you yesterday to invite you if I could have found you.'"

19 Socrates is late. It appears that he has fallen into a meditation under a portico on the way. When he enters, "Agathon begged that he would take the place next to him 'that I may touch you and have the benefit of that wise thought which came into your mind in the portico.' 'How I wish,' said Socrates, taking his place as he was desired, 'that wisdom could be infused by touch. If that were so how greatly should I value the privilege of reclining at your side, for you would fill me with a stream of wisdom plenteous and fair, whereas my own is of a very questionable sort.'" An argument is started and Agathon gives way: "I cannot refute you, Socrates." "Ah no," is the answer. "Say rather, dear Agathon, that you cannot refute the truth, for Socrates is easily refuted." It is social intercourse at its perfection, to be accounted for only by a process of long training. Good breeding of that stamp was never evolved in one generation nor two, and yet these men were the grandsons of those that fought at Marathon and Salamis.[10] Heroic daring and the imponderables of high civilization were the inheritance they were born to.

20 Through the dialogues moves the figure of Socrates, a unique philosopher, unlike all philosophers that ever were outside of Greece. They are, these others, very generally strange and taciturn beings, or so we conceive them, aloof, remote, absorbed in abstruse speculations, only partly human. The completest embodiment of our idea of a philosopher is Kant, the little stoop-shouldered, absent-minded man, who moved only between his house and the university, and by whom all the housewives in Königsberg set their clocks when they saw him pass on his way to the

10 Scenes of Greek victories in the Persian Wars, 490 and 480 B.C.—*Ed.*

lecture-room of a morning. Such was not Socrates. He could not be, being a Greek. A great many different things were expected of him and he had to be able to meet a great many different situations. We ourselves belong to an age of specialists, the result, really, of our belonging to an age that loves comfort. It is obvious that one man doing only one thing can work faster, and the reasonable conclusion in a world that wants a great many things is to arrange to have him do it. Twenty men making each a minute bit of a shoe, turn out far more than twenty times the number of shoes that the cobbler working alone did, and in consequence no one must go barefoot. We have our reward in an ever-increasing multiplication of the things every one needs but we pay our price in the limit set to the possibilities of development for each individual worker.

21 In Greece it was just the other way about. The things they needed were by comparison few, but every man had to act in a number of different capacities. An Athenian citizen in his time played many parts. Æschylus was not only a writer of plays; he was an entire theatrical staff, actor, scenic artist, costumer, designer, mechanician, producer. He was also a soldier who fought in the ranks, and had probably held a civic office; most Athenians did. No doubt if we knew more about his life we should find that he had still other avocations. His brother-dramatist, Sophocles, was a general and a diplomat and a priest as well; a practical man of the theatre too, who made at least one important innovation. There was no artist class in Greece, withdrawn from active life, no literary class, no learned class. The soldiers and their sailors and their politicians and their men of affairs wrote their poetry and carved their statues and thought out their philosophy. "To sum up"—the speaker is Pericles—"I say that Athens is the school of Greece and that the individual Athenian in his own person seems to have the power of adapting himself to the most varied forms of action with the utmost versatility and grace"—that last word a touch so peculiarly Greek.

Exercises

CONTENT

True or False? If you think the statement represents what the selection says or implies, mark it "True"; if you do not think so, mark it "False."

1. The Greeks were realists.
2. The Greeks thought it was sweet to die for one's country.
3. We are less sentimental than the Greeks.
4. We find it difficult to understand how anyone can *both* love beauty *and* face facts.
5. Greek history is our best source of information about the Greeks.
6. Nobody worked very hard in Athens.

7. We live in an age of specialization; the Greeks did not.
8. Kant lived in Königsberg.
9. Æschylus, Sophocles, and Socrates were Athenian playwrights
10. Everybody ought to become more like the Greeks.

Questions for Discussion

1. Is *The Greek Way* exposition or argument? Explain your answer.

2. In your opinion, which of the following statements comes closest to stating the theme of the essay: (a) The Greeks were more realistic than we are; (b) Greek values were different from our values; (c) the Greeks were wiser than we are because they had more leisure; (d) study of Greek civilization should be encouraged.

3. What is meant by "vital lies" (last sentence of Paragraph 1)? Discuss the implications of the statement.

4. In your own words, state the point of the contrast between "With God's help may I still love what is beautiful and strive for what is attainable," and "What I aspire to be and am not, comforts me" (Paragraph 12). Discuss the relevance of idealism (belief in the importance of striving for ideals) to the issue raised by the contrast in meaning between the two quotations.

FORM AND STYLE

1. The first twelve paragraphs include several quotations. What ties them together?

2. Paragraphs 13 and 14 serve as justification for the emphasis on Plato's writings in Paragraphs 15-19. Explain.

3. Explain Socrates' function as a means of transition in the beginning of Paragraph 20.

4. Arrange the following items in the order that most closely reflects the outline of the essay: leisure, nonsentimentality, versatility, intellectualism, gracefulness.

VOCABULARY

Which of the four words or phrases to the right seems to you to be *closest* in meaning to the word in heavy type to the left? Put a check mark after your choice.

deficient (1)   weak . . . wanting . . . abnormal . . . negligent . . .
pre-eminently (1)   nothing else but . . . to a superior degree . . . first
  of all . . . emphatically . . .
evade (1)   cover up . . . make pretty . . . escape . . . overlook . . .
refuge (1)   antidote . . . excuse . . . one who flees . . . shelter . . .
oration (2)   speech . . . occasion . . . ceremony . . . hymn . . .

commemoration (2)   memorizing . . . funeral . . . memorial . . . commendation . . .

exaltation (2)   phoniness . . . sentimentality . . . glory . . . high and intense feeling . . .

declamation (2)   speech-making . . . gesture . . . declaration . . . inspiration . . .

repelled (8)   driven back . . . awed . . . surprised . . . disgusted . . .

exile (8)   banishment . . . death . . . execution . . . exit . . .

constrains (12)   inspires . . . makes . . . moves . . . binds . . .

attainable (12)   good . . . heroic . . . reachable . . . lovable . . .

aspire (12)   hope . . . struggle . . . aim . . . intend . . .

mythical (13)   mystical . . . strange . . . untrue . . . impossible . . .

revelation (13)   truth . . . disclosure . . . essence . . . analysis . . .

depict (13)   portray . . . discuss . . . despise . . . be interested in . . .

lofty (13)   profound . . . high . . . abstract . . . theological . . .

personages (13)   pages of a diary . . . personifications . . . persons . . . famous men . . .

dramatis personae (14)   dramatists . . . subjects . . . persons who like drama . . . characters in a drama . . .

amenities (15)   friendly acts . . . pleasant activities . . . luxuries . . . virtues . . .

abstruse (15)   farfetched . . . abstract . . . trivial . . . difficult . . .

immerse (16)   interest . . . project . . . plunge . . . lose . . .

urbanity (18)   delicacy . . . good manners . . . city life . . . courtesy

suave (18)   arrogant . . . polished . . . polite . . . persuasive . . .

infused (19)   learned . . . injected . . . given . . . acquired . . .

plenteous (19)   virtuous . . . plentiful . . . gracious . . . plain . . .

refute (19)   confuse . . . prove wrong . . . disprove . . . argue against . . .

imponderables (19)   improbabilities . . . mysteries . . . what cannot be thought about . . . what cannot be weighed . . .

taciturn (20)   silent . . . unfriendly . . . unattractive . . . incapable of being well known . . .

avocations (21)   enterprises . . . pastimes . . . vocations . . . duties

versatility (21)   elegance . . . many-sidedness . . . speed . . . skill

THEME SUGGESTIONS

Summarize *The Greek Way*. Do not interpret or evaluate. Simply state in your own words what the essay says. Your summary will, of course, be much shorter than the essay. The assignment will test your ability to discriminate between the essentials and the nonessentials in a long essay, between main points (which you should include in your summary) and the elaboration and illustration of the main points (which usually you will have to exclude).

A comparison between the ideal Greek and the ideal man of our culture

The usefulness of art

Hypocrisy in public life

Thoughts on death

The age of the specialist

39

PATRICIA ALVIS KOSOBUD

Interim

A Short Story Set in the Future

1 In the afternoons I take the children to play in the city's one remaining strip of park, which lies between the Memorial Cannon and the district anti-missile base. What a marvelous history lesson it provides for them—the quaint old First World War weapon and the latest in intricate design for defense. We've made tremendous progress in the fifty short years that lie between them. Of course, the children prefer the old cannon, on which they climb or play at old-fashioned war games, to the new one, which is fenced off from them and well guarded.

2 I always make it a point to leave by 4:30, no matter how the children protest, because John has to go to Civil Defense at seven o'clock so he only sees them for two hours each day. On the street we walk along, many of the shops have been converted for family living. The plate-glass windows have either been replaced with boards or draped and painted in gay colors. The food and supply outlets are in some of the larger stores, and we pick up our Freedom Ration on the way home.

3 We live in the old Kominski School building. They were going to tear it down when the board of education was dissolved, but our local citizens' committee protested and was able to salvage it. We were awfully pleased when we were accepted as tenants. We have a whole classroom just for the five of us, and since it had been condemned we don't have to pay any rent, just taxes and what we have to spend for upkeep.

4 At first everybody chipped in and bought coal for the furnace, but when it broke down two years ago the tenants' committee voted not to fix it. Coal rationing was about to start and we felt that the ration wouldn't be adequate for the furnace anyway. John has rigged up an ingenious fireplace for us. He got some bricks from an apartment house

INTERIM: A SHORT STORY SET IN THE FUTURE. From *The Reporter*, April 18, 1957. Reprinted by permission of *The Reporter*.

that collapsed not far away and bought some old stovepipe to make an outlet in the window. It hardly smokes at all, and the coal ration is enough for at least a little fire on the coldest winter days. We wear coats all winter in the house and the children have had very few colds. All in all, our arrangement is much better than the one small room in an old apartment where we used to live.

5   The children think it's very funny when we tell them that one family used to take a whole apartment. When I stop to think, it *is* strange. When John and I were first married ten years ago, we had a three-room place and we talked of needing more space when we had children. Of course, no one could then have foreseen how successful our industrial leaders would be at bringing people from unproductive farms and small towns into the big cities where they are needed.

6   When they did begin coming, in droves, just at the time C.D. ordered the curtailment of all nondefense building, everybody thought it wouldn't work, but then the zoning laws were relaxed. People quickly began to move in with others who were compatible, and for a time there were actually vacant apartments to the west of us.

7   I was rather sorry when the schools closed because I didn't feel at all equal to the job of educating the children at home, but on the whole it has turned out pretty well. We tell them all we can about what is happening, and of course they listen to the TV for hours, especially in winter when they have to stay bundled up in bed to keep warm. There is quite a wide range of programs geared to the various age groups throughout the day, so that all the children can know at least something about history, geography, science, and the arts. My children, who have never been to school (Mike was not quite five when the schools closed), find nothing unusual in the situation. The older children missed the classroom at first, but they adjusted quickly, as children do, and for the teenagers, of course, the Civil Defense Cadets began soon afterward.

8   Some of the women in our block have been discussing the possibility of starting some sort of pre-cadet group for the children between six and twelve. We think it would be a good thing for them to get more experience in group projects. They could do much the same sort of thing they do now, but in small organized groups. Certainly the scavenging trips could be improved by a little organization. As it is now, they just wander about aimlessly the whole morning, picking up whatever they find. Very often the younger ones like Mike and Joe will find a bit of cardboard or wood for window repair and fuel supplement, only to have the bigger boys take it away from them. There are always fights, and neither John nor I want them to grow up believing that the strong rule the weak.

9   John and I have tried our best to instill in them the democratic principles that are our heritage, but we and many parents like us feel that it is becoming more difficult in these times to make our words have

any meaning. John tells me that I should be careful not to say anything that might sound like prejudice, and I must say it disturbs me that we must live in such close contact with people who have no thought in life but their own well-being. Many of these people only came to the city because of the money to be made in the factories. They have no concept of the real meaning of our great defense preparations. And as far as I can tell, they have more impact on our children than we have on theirs. Certainly we have always taught them fair play and the peaceful solution of differences.

10 Last Sunday we went to see the new shelter that's just been finished at the University. We're assigned to it so we thought it was particularly important for the children to see it. They were very excited, even little Laura, and ran from room to room. They were especially fascinated by the hospital section. It is admirably equipped and will even handle maternity cases, they tell me. I found myself wondering if our fourth child would be born there. A lot can happen in seven months. Mike was born at Lying-In just before C.D. took it over. Joe and Laura were "do-it-yourself projects," as we call them.

11 You have to see a shelter to appreciate it. They have everything imaginable to make life easy and comfortable, a veritable monument to American technology. There are sleeping cubicles for individual families, with bunks on the walls and foam-rubber mattresses. I could have carried them away, thinking of our lumpy beds at home. There are bathrooms, beautifully tiled, with ample fixtures for the corridor of families each serves. And then there are spacious recreation rooms, with books and records and games. The children's facilities are separate and furnished to fit the tastes of different age groups, much better planned than any of the public or private schoolrooms I taught in before Mike was born. There is a modern kitchen with facilities to cook for the whole shelter and a delightfully pleasant dining room. The laundry room is equipped with automatic washers and dryers. Here again I felt pangs of longing. We didn't see the storerooms but were told that there are enough frozen foods there to take care of the entire population for a month. All the utilities are powered by an atomic generator and there are tanks of water more than adequate for a month's needs.

12 One misses windows at first, but the whole building is so cheerfully lighted and so well air-conditioned that after the first few moments I forgot that windows had ever existed.

13 We came aboveground well pleased, and John said he didn't begrudge one bit the evenings he spends working for C.D. When we got home we felt dissatisfied with our surroundings and indulged our selfish feelings for a while.

14 At bedtime, Mike and Joe, still exhilarated by what they had seen, kept chattering long after little Laura had gone to sleep and even after lights-out at nine.

15 "Are we really going to live there some day?" Joe asked.

16 "Some day," said John with a smile.

17 "When?"

18 "Oh, I suppose when the attack comes," I said.

19 "Yippee!" shouted Mike. "I hope they hurry up."

20 "It probably won't be long," John assured them. "Now you'd better get to sleep. Come on, into bed, both of you!"

21 John and I sat on the edge of our bed long after they had gone to sleep. Through the window, a gentle spring breeze brought fresh cool air to the room. The moon shone brightly on the abandoned play yard outside, casting lights and shadows in the broken concrete.

22 "I'm glad we went," John said. "It helps to bring meaning to what we tell them."

Exercises

CONTENT

True or False? If you think the statement represents what the selection says or implies, mark it "True"; if you do not think so, mark it "False."

1. The setting of the story is a completely socialistic state.
2. The narrator does not believe in democracy.
3. The narrator has four children and is expecting a fifth.
4. The family owns a car.
5. There are no lights allowed in the "apartment" after 9:00.
6. C.D. means "Citizens for Defense."
7. The narrator used to be a schoolteacher.
8. Her husband's name is Joe.
9. She was born before 1960.
10. Everybody in the story fears the Russians.

Questions for Discussion

1. Explain the title of the story.
2. How would you answer the charge that the story in presenting Civil Defense as a potential threat to present values and ways of life itself is dangerous, subversive, unpatriotic?
3. What *is* the "meaning of our great defense preparations" (Paragraph 9), as the father and mother see it?

FORM AND STYLE

1. What does the author gain by using a fictitious "I" as narrator? How does the character of the narrator contribute to the meaning of the story?
2. The story is full of irony in the sense that we frequently see a sig-

nificance in the narrator's remarks that she is unaware of herself. Explain the irony of, "We've made tremendous progress in the fifty short years that lie between them" (Paragraph 1), ". . . and neither John nor I want them to grow up believing that the strong rule the weak" (Paragraph 8), "Certainly we have always taught them fair play and the peaceful solution of differences" (Paragraph 9), "Yippee!" (Paragraph 14).

3. The story is also full of *symbols*—that is, facts and objects that suggest without stating meanings other than their literal one. In answering the questions that follow, keep in mind that there are no "correct" answers, that most authors and critics agree that symbols are effective exactly because they are not definite statements the truth of which can be proved or disproved, but because they *are* suggestive only, elusively haunting and teasing the mind, engaging your imagination and feeling, enriching the meaning of their context. What symbolic meaning do you find in the following:

(a) ". . . the city's one remaining strip of park, which lies between the Memorial Cannon and the district anti-missile base" (Paragraph 1)?

(b) The narrator's unborn baby (Paragraph 10)?

(c) The air-raid shelter considered as "a veritable monument to American technology" (Paragraph 11)?

(d) The lack of windows in the shelter (Paragraph 12)?

(e) "The moon shone brightly on the abandoned play yard outside . . ." (Paragraph 15)?

4. The narrator reveals more about herself and her condition by what she does *not* say than by what she says. Explain.

VOCABULARY

Which of the four words or phrases to the right seems to you to be *closest* in meaning to the word in heavy type to the left? Put a check mark after your choice.

intricate (*1*)   complicated . . . effective . . . advanced . . . systematic . . .

converted (*2*)   rented out . . . changed . . . redecorated . . . cheapened . . .

salvage (*3*)   rescue . . . use . . . make fit for savages . . . fix . . .

adequate (*4*)   available . . . usable . . . inexpensive enough . . . sufficient . . .

ingenious (*4*)   wonderful . . . beautiful . . . clever . . . passable . . .

curtailment (*6*)   reduction . . . end . . . prohibition . . . cancellation . . .

compatible (*6*)   feeling the same . . . helpful . . . having a home . . . willing . . .

geared to (7)   adapted for . . . planned for . . . popular with . . . addressed to . . .

scavenging (8)   revengeful . . . educational . . . garbage picking . . . door-to-door collecting . . .

heritage (9)   privilege . . . inheritance . . . duty . . . belief . . .

veritable (*11*)   impressive . . . actual . . . splendid . . . long-lasting

spacious (*11*)   pleasant . . . well-spaced . . . roomy . . . as in a space ship . . .

exhilarated (*14*)   excited . . . made happy . . . interested . . . upset

THEME SUGGESTIONS

The day it happened
Disarmament—or else
CD in my home town
An answer to *Interim*
The use of irony in *Interim*

Language and Learning

JAMESON • KNIGHT • HAYAKAWA • HUFF

SELDIN • BRACKEN • CHUTE • THURBER • KRUTCH

These essays all deal with learning through language. What college teaches is, ultimately, not facts and techniques, but *ideas,* and ideas can be communicated only through words.

In the first essay Robert Jameson discusses hows and whys of going to college. A series of essays dealing with the ways of words follows. Knight presents an amusing story of linguistic simplemindedness in his dialogue with a none-too-bright plumber. Hayakawa calls our attention to the frightening implications of the fact that what we call things largely determines our attitudes to them. The next three essays deal with the misuse of words in one way or another, showing how language can be used as an obstacle in the way to truth. Huff gives examples of intentional or unintentional fraud in the use of statistics to "prove" whatever the writer wants to prove; Seldin writes about the unscrupulous manipulation of children's minds by TV and radio commercials; and Peg Bracken parodies the prefabricated "realism" in a certain kind of popular fiction that pretends to be honest.

The last three essays are about the pursuit of truth. Marchette Chute describes the difficulties even a conscientious researcher has in preserving objectivity when his desires try to slant the facts away from the truth. Her research has been biographical, but what she says applies to other fields of study as well. In subject matter and attitude her essay is similar to Huff's on the irresponsible and subjective use of statistics. Thurber tells a story of a possibly foolish moth who sought truth and who, in a sense, found it. And Krutch reminds us that truth, despite a general human tendency to believe otherwise, has a way of keeping soberly and undramatically in the middle.

40

ROBERT U. JAMESON

How to Stay in College

1   At least 2,500,000 young Americans are in college this fall. Of these, about 1,000,000 are freshmen. These figures are impressive; they seem to indicate that the ideal of a college-educated democracy is on the way to realization. Yet the unhappy fact is that more than a third of the men and women who enter college fail to graduate. Why?

2   To find the answer to this question, I have talked to deans and instructors in several colleges and to a large number of young men and women who have just finished their freshman year in colleges all across the United States. Some facts are clear.

3   Of those who drop out of college, some leave for financial reasons, and this is often tragic because these people in many cases do well in college before they have to leave. Some leave because of poor health. A few are drafted. Many leave for "personal" reasons—marriage, family mixups or just the realization that college is not the place for them.

4   But the principal concern of the colleges is the disappearance of students who should graduate, but who simply fail instead. Therefore the real question is this: Why do students fail in college?

5   Although they may state it differently, all college deans from coast to coast agree on one point: The major problem of the college freshman is that of adjusting to a new kind of life, in which he is expected to behave like an adult. The Assistant Dean of Freshmen at Yale, Harold B. Whiteman, Jr., calls this "the acquiring of self-discipline." Dr. J. W. Graham, Assistant Dean at Carnegie Tech, calls the same process "learning to think." Diogenes, among others, said simply "Know thyself." In one way or another, what happens in the first year or two of college depends largely upon this one thing: Is the college student ready to grow up, to understand what college is?

6   What is college? By the end of this article, I believe that the question will be answered fairly. To begin with, here are some general statements about what college is. Robert B. Cox, Dean of Men at Duke University, says that his fervent wish is to be able some day to prove to an entering class that the freshman year is not Grade 13 in high school. Father Edward Dwyer, of Villanova College, says this: "I wish that it were possible for us to demonstrate that college is a place for adults, not an advanced school for children." And a young man who has just finished his first year at Princeton says this: "The most important problems

How to Stay in College. From *The Saturday Evening Post*, October 2, 1954. Reprinted by permission of the author.

facing a freshman are those of adjustment to a unique society, one totally different from high school."

7   Can college be defined?

8   In the first place, college is a place in which a person can learn how to learn. In school, boys and girls are taught something about how to pass courses in order to get a school diploma. Often enough they get the diploma at a certain age even with a record of failure. In college, on the other hand, these boys and girls are asked to learn to think, to meet complex intellectual problems and to handle these problems on their own. Intellectual independence, the first requisite of college, is often a distinct shock to a freshman.

9   An example of one college's method will perhaps make the point clearer. At The Carnegie Institute of Technology, English composition courses are quite unlike high-school courses. Students may be given several opposing points of view about a single topic and told to reach a logical, unbiased conclusion in a composition about this topic. The unwary freshman is thus faced with the necessity of using logic, of discarding personal prejudices and of writing carefully in order to prove to his instructor that he is capable of thinking through a problem. This "case-study" method is used in more than one freshman course in college.

10   Another course will present a student with the necessity of doing a large volume of reading and drawing conclusions from the reading. Or an instructor may say something like this: "What happened in England during the first week of July, 1751?" The freshman who asks how to find out such things will probably be rewarded with an icy stare and a map showing where the college library is—no more.

11   How do freshmen react to situations like these? Unfortunately, many will react badly because the spoon feeding of the high school, the parents eager to help with homework, the teacher who leads classes by the nose are all missing. Now the human brain, perhaps the least-used "muscle" in the human body, has to start working on its own.

12   A student who has finished a year at Washington and Lee says this: "I have just begun to realize, at the end of a rough year, what college has to offer. I hope that next year I will do a better job." "In college," says a girl at Michigan, "you get nowhere until you grow up."

13   But no college dean or adviser can possibly walk up to a floundering freshman and say, "You will do all right as soon as you grow up." Instead, all colleges provide elaborate programs to introduce the college to the freshmen, to warn the young people about what is ahead.

14   When the 1,000,000 new freshmen arrive for Freshman Week at any of the nearly 2,000 colleges in the land, they are put through a complicated and sometimes bewildering mill. They meet their roommates. They meet their advisers. They take placement tests and aptitude tests and reading tests and physical examinations. They meet the president. They are invited to buy the school paper, pennants, beer mugs, rugs, laundry service and everything else under the sun. They attend a football rally and chapel and a dance or two and a picnic and a number of meetings for indoctrination in the methods of study.

15 They are breezed through a very pleasant week—dizzying, perhaps, but new and different. They don't even have time to get homesick. That comes about two weeks later. Now, during this week, deans and advisers say many things which freshmen may, to their sorrow, ignore:

Start studying at once.

Get to know the library immediately.

Set up a schedule for yourself—revise it later, if necessary—to include both social and academic activities.

Join one or two extracurricular activities, but not every one in sight.

Get enough sleep.

Don't forget chapel.

Don't cut classes.

You're on your own; make the most of your independence. But if you get into trouble, see your adviser right away.

16 Then classes begin, and the realities of college are suddenly all too evident. The first theme is written; the first history test is taken; the first physics experiment is done. And the first blast comes from a teacher, who, unlike lovable old Mr. Chips at home in the high school, is apparently half devil and half dragon.

17 An angry English instructor throws a theme on the desk in front of the dean of admissions and says acidly, "Would you be good enough to tell me why this man, who is obviously an idiot, has been admitted to this college?"

18 A freshman hands in a paper two days late and wonders why he gets an E. Another is stymied by the fact that his edition of *King Lear* has no footnotes to explain the text. "How am I supposed to be able to understand this stuff?"

19 A freshman's reaction to failure is a clear indication of whether he is a child or an adult. The adult simply works harder. The child may get surly. . . . He may look for excuses to explain his failure—headaches, a loud-mouthed roommate, the radio across the hall. . . . One common reaction is to blame the instructor. But no college adviser has much time for such an attitude. "I always tell characters like that," says a dean of a Southern college, "that I don't care what he thinks of the teacher. I tell him the library is right across the street. He can learn a lot there."

20 Or failure may bring a defeatist attitude, particularly to a student who has always done well in school. Colleges are on the watch for the defeatist, because they want to salvage at least something which the student has to offer, and they want also to keep him on an even keel emotionally. Deans, advisers, the college health service, coaches and others go into action. The student who fails to react to the collective wisdom of a group like this eventually will probably be dropped.

21 Many failures in college happen because freshmen think that college is a place in which to learn a trade or business. Having received high-school credit for typing, shorthand, automobile driving, band, and what not, they are chagrined to learn that college is not like that. Dean Whiteman, of Yale, says that students often complain about courses such as economics on the ground that these courses do not tell anyone how to run a business; they just teach theories. In much the same way, every college of engineering has on its hands a number of freshmen who are misfits at the start because they are not working with their hands, but are exposed to English, history and psychology. A college course in electricity is not for the embryo television-repair man, who should go to trade school, not college.

22 Those who have this mistaken idea often drop out of the technical schools, where mortality is high anyway. In liberal-arts colleges, students more often than not can adjust themselves to the idea of a liberal education. But the adjustment is painful and often takes two or three years.

23 Colleges aim not to produce what Dr. J. W. Graham, of Carnegie Tech, calls the "complete technician," but instead a man whose education makes him able to fit a problem into its historical frame. Or, as a professor of chemistry in a small liberal-arts college puts it, "In three or four years all one can learn is that there are unsolved problems for research."

24 There are two real reasons for college education, and the two are actually the same stated differently: preparation for one of the professions, and acquisition of an idea of culture. Together, these two things mean the beginning of the development of the adult mind. Woodrow Wilson once said, "The object of a university is intellect."

25 Part of a circular given to each entering freshman at Columbia in 1953 reads as follows: "A liberal-arts education is one that aids the youth to grow into a mature, well-rounded individual who knows how to think objectively, to make the best use of his talents and to understand his responsibilities in a democratic society."

26 A liberal-arts education means, of course, a general education in which the humanities (literature, language, fine arts), the social sciences (history, economics, political science) and the natural sciences (chemistry, biology, physics) are about equally balanced.

27 During the war, emphasis in colleges lay in the turning out of people with the specific skills which a complicated war economy required. But today, all over the United States, the trend is returning to the kind of education described as the liberal arts. Even professional schools are now asking for students who have a broad academic background. For example, the Harvard Medical School does not require its candidates to have majored in science any more: some science, of course, but not just science. About a quarter of the curriculum at Carnegie Tech is made up of humanities courses. Massachusetts Institute of Technology has working arrangements with a number of small liberal-arts colleges under which students take "general-education" courses for two or three years and then transfer to M.I.T. for engineering.

28 Understanding the aims of the liberal-arts program in the American college is probably the hardest and also the most important job for the freshman today. Some freshmen—indeed, some graduate students—will never understand why general education is valuable. They may finish their course, but they will have wasted a lot of time and money. Some freshmen will drop out of college because, not understanding, they will simply fail their courses for lack of direction. Fortunately many freshmen will get the point and will come out of college with at least the beginning of a conception of what learning is.

29 If the freshman will take advantage of his adviser's experience, of his teachers' knowledge and of the wealth of his college library, and if he will study on his own, most of his minor adjustment problems will disappear. He will stop thinking of the college degree as a high-class work permit, a ticket of admission to this or that job. He will know that hard, analytical study is required in college. He will realize that liberal education means a good balance between academic, athletic and social life. And he will quite surely, out of his broad background, find a special interest to develop into a college major, even if it turns out to be an "impractical" field like Chinese, Indic philology or archaeology.

30 And the man or woman who finds out what education means has grown up. Surely the proof of the broad education which Americans can get if they want it is a deep understanding of how good that education can be.

Exercises

CONTENT

True or False? If you think the statement represents what the selection says or implies, mark it "True"; if you do not think so, mark it "False."

1. More than one-third of the entering freshmen fail to graduate.
2. The main reason why male students leave college before graduation is that they are being drafted into military service.
3. Some high schools graduate all their students, regardless of their academic record.
4. Most college teachers expect too much of the freshmen.
5. There are almost 5,000 colleges and universities in the United States.
6. In a democracy like ours, every young man or woman who wants a college education is entitled to one.
7. It is unwise to major in an impractical field like archaeology.
8. Our institutions of higher learning do not provide sufficient training for specific occupations.

9. More and more professional schools refuse to accept students with a liberal arts degree.

10. Biology is a social science.

Questions for Discussion

1. Which statement from among the following comes closest, in your opinion, to stating the theme of the essay:
   (a) American higher education must learn to adjust itself to an age of science.
   (b) A student's success in college is almost entirely up to himself.
   (c) In order to stay in college, a student should plan all his courses with a definite career in mind.
   (d) "A liberal-arts education is one that aids the youth to grow into a mature, well-rounded individual who knows how to think objectively, to make the best use of his talents and to understand his responsibilities in a democratic society."
   (e) Colleges teach principles and attitudes, not facts and techniques.

2. To whom is *How to Stay in College* primarily addressed: students? parents? teachers? college administrators? two or more or all of these? the general public? Explain your answer.

3. How do you interpret Jameson's definition of college as "a place in which a person can learn how to learn"?

4. How do you feel about the freshman who failed to make much sense out of Shakespeare's *King Lear* and asked how he was "supposed to be able to understand this stuff" (Paragraph 18)? Do you feel he has a legitimate complaint? Discuss.

FORM AND STYLE

1. The main body of the essay is an answer to which question, asked specifically where?

2. Point out the words in the beginning of Paragraphs 2, 4, 10, 11, 13, 15, 16, 17, and 22 that connect their respective paragraphs with what has gone before.

3. Paragraphs 16-20 deal with failures due to student immaturity. What is the logical relationship between these paragraphs and Paragraph 21?

4. What single term could serve as title for Paragraphs 23-30?

5. Go through the essay and find passages where Jameson tries to dramatize and make concrete what he is discussing.

VOCABULARY

Which of the four words or phrases to the right seems to you to be *closest* in meaning to the word in heavy type to the left? Put a check mark after your choice.

principal *(4)*   principle . . . head of a high school . . . main . . . as a matter of principle . . .

requisite *(8)*   hurdle . . . something required before something else can be had . . . demand . . . ideal . . .

distinct *(8)*   severe . . . definite . . . distinguished . . . discouraging . . .

unbiased *(9)*   sound . . . unfounded . . . not base . . . unprejudiced

unwary *(9)*   careless . . . unprepared . . . fresh . . . innocent . . .

discarding *(9)*   disregarding . . . discerning . . . not making use of . . . throwing off . . .

floundering *(13)*   immature . . . having difficulties . . . badly prepared . . . in a muddle . . .

acidly *(17)*   bitingly . . . coldly . . . irritably . . . sarcastically . . .

stymied *(18)*   blocked . . . confused . . .overwhelmed . . . made indignant . . .

surly *(19)*   sullen . . . angry . . . childish . . . spoiled . . .

defeatist *(20)*   admitting defeat too easily . . . defiant . . . resentful . . . unaccomplishing . . .

chagrined *(21)*   upset . . . disappointed . . . saddened . . . surprised . . .

conception *(28)*   idea . . . knowledge . . . appreciation . . . illumination . . .

philology *(29)*   logic . . . ancient history . . . philosophy . . . study of language and literature . . .

THEME SUGGESTIONS

Why go to college?
A college freshman's evaluation of his high school education
Liberal arts vs. vocational training
My study habits
A helpful flunk

41

RIXFORD KNIGHT

Street Elbow

1   It seemed to me that while the plumber was right there in the house was naturally a good time to find out why a street elbow was

STREET ELBOW. From *The Atlantic Monthly*, May, 1955. Reprinted by permission of the author.

called a street elbow, so I went down cellar and said, "Good morning. How is everything going this morning?" And then I said, "Say—by the way, why is a street elbow called a *street* elbow? I can see why it is an elbow all right. But where does the *street* part come from?"

2   The plumber explained. He said, "I'll tell you. You see a street elbow has one male and one female end. On a regular elbow both ends are female. Here; let me show you."

3   I said, "Yes, I understand about that; but what I mean is: why does its having one male and one female end make a *street* elbow of it? Streets don't have one male and one female end that I know of. So why a *street* elbow?"

4   The plumber said, "Wait now. Just let me show you. Look at this here. See? On this end the threads are on the outside. That's because it is the male end. And on this end the threads are on the inside. That's the female end. Now you take a regular elbow—like this here—the threads are on the inside on both ends. That makes it a regular elbow instead of a street elbow. *You* can see how it is."

5   I told the plumber I could see what the difference was between a street elbow and a regular elbow. "Only what I can't understand is why they show the difference by calling one a *street* elbow. Why not call it a mixed elbow? Or a hermaphrodite elbow? Or something that would mean something? *Street* doesn't mean anything, so far as I know; that is, not in this connection."

6   The plumber said, "But it does mean something. Like I've just been telling you: it means a street elbow has one male and one female end. If it had two female ends it would be just a regular elbow."

7   "Listen," I said. "Take a piece of pipe, now. If you say 'This is a brass pipe,' that means something different from what it does if you say 'This is galvanized pipe.' Anybody would know what you meant. But when you say 'This is a *street* elbow,' that doesn't mean anything except to somebody who already knows what a street elbow is."

8   "I can't help that," said the plumber. "There's a lot of things people don't know about the plumbing business. But any plumber knows what a street elbow is. You ask any plumber, I don't care who he is, and he will tell you a street elbow has got one male and one female end. That's what makes it a *street* elbow."

9   I said, "Yes, sure. It is *called* a street elbow. But it could be called a whattentot elbow and it would still have one male and one female end; so why pick on *street* to call it?"

10   The plumber said, "Well, I've been in the plumbing business for thirty-five years now and a street elbow has always been called a street elbow for as long as I can remember. And my father was in the plumbing business for longer than that and *he* always called it a street elbow, and I guess he ought to know if anybody would."

11   "Of course he would," I told the plumber. "All I'm saying is, how

did they come to be called *street* elbows in the first place? Why did your father or whoever it was pick out *street* as the name to call them?"

12 "Jeez, I wouldn't know about that," said the plumber. "I suppose they had to call them something or nobody would know what anybody else was talking about. Why do you call a pipe a pipe or a house a house or a kitchen a kitchen? You just do, that's all."

13 "But calling a pipe a pipe or a house a house is altogether different from calling a street elbow a street elbow. The word for house may have come from the ancient Aryans or something and we call it that because they did. There is a reason for it. But I can't see any reason at all for calling this thing a *street* elbow."

14 "Maybe the ancient Aryans called them street elbows," said the plumber.

15 "But for cripe sake, the ancient Aryans didn't have street elbows. They didn't have pipes and I doubt if they even had streets; and even if they did, why would they call a piece of curved pipe a *street* elbow unless they called one end of a street the male end and the other end female? Maybe they did. That's what I am trying to find out. Why did somebody start calling this thing a *street* elbow?"

16 "You mean, why did they call it a *street* elbow?" said the plumber.

17 "That's it! Why did they call this thing a *street* elbow? Did maybe a man named Street invent it or something?"

18 The plumber said, "Well, I couldn't say as to that. I never knew of a man named Street in the plumbing business; though of course they might have been, sometime. I don't claim to know everything. Maybe if you were to look in some of those books or something."

19 I said, "I have already looked in the encyclopedia. All it says is that a street elbow has one male and one female end."

20 "That's right. The book is right about that," said the plumber.

21 "But what has that got to do with its being called a *street* elbow? Why call it of all things a *street* elbow?"

22 The plumber thought that one over. He said, "Y'know, I've been wondering about that myself. Why," he wanted to know, "do they call it a *street* elbow?"

Exercises

CONTENT

True or False? If you think the statement represents what the selection says or implies, mark it "True"; if you do not think so, mark it "False."

1. The author did not know that the plumber's father had invented street elbows.

2. A street elbow is any L-shaped piece of pipe.

3. For a long time, the plumber thinks the author is trying to find out what a street elbow is.

4. The ancient Aryans had no word for street.

5. The whole discussion is silly because it can never be settled.

Questions for Discussion

1. Why doesn't the author wonder about the use of the word "elbow?"

2. Explain why "hermaphrodite elbow" would indeed be a more fitting term for this particular kind of pipe than "street elbow."

3. The essay raises a problem about language. The problem is not what the plumber at one point (Paragraph 12) thinks it is: why we call anything what we call it—why a house is a "house" and a kitchen a "kitchen." (This, incidentally, is a problem that can be answered, up to a point, by historians of language.) What *is* the problem?

4. Choose one: The joke of the essay is that (a) the question asked remains unanswered at the end, (b) the plumber is so slow in understanding exactly what the author is asking, (c) he claims at the end to have asked himself the same question, (d) both (b) and (c) are true.

FORM AND STYLE

1. How are the paragraphs divided?

2. Comment upon the use of "they" in "though of course they might have been" (Paragraph 18), and of "For cripe sake" (Paragraph 15). Can you justify these usages?

3. Point out specifically how the author suggests a difference in cultural background between the plumber and himself.

4. Discuss the opinion that the plumber's statement in Paragraph 18, "I don't claim to know everything," is the funniest in the whole essay.

5. The little identifying tags for the speeches are nearly all of the same kind: "the plumber said," "said the plumber," "I said," and so on. Is this a stylistic defect that creates monotony, or can it be said that by making them all the same or nearly the same, Knight succeeds in drawing the reader's attention away from the speech tags to what really matters in the essay: what the author and the plumber are saying? Discuss.

VOCABULARY

Try to explain why it is not surprising that—with the exception of one or two technical terms—there are no "difficult" words needing definition in this essay.

THEME SUGGESTIONS

Define the two attitudes toward language represented by the plumber and the author.

Write an essay illustrating one or more examples of what *Street El-bow* deals with: the use of a familiar word (like "street" here) in an un-expected, but not necessarily unexplainable, context. For example: "match *book*," "typewriter *key*," "car *hood*," or any others you can think of.

42

S. I. HAYAKAWA

Classification

1   The figure below shows eight objects, let us say animals, four large and four small, a different four with round heads and another four with square heads, and still another four with curly tails and another four with straight tails. These animals, let us say, are scampering about your village, but since at first they are of no importance to you, you ignore them. You do not even give them a name.

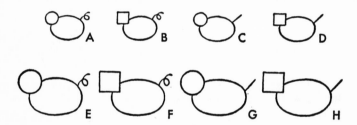

2   One day, however, you discover that the little ones eat up your grain, while the big ones do not. A differentiation sets itself up, and abstracting the common characteristics of A, B, C, and D, you decide to call these *gogo;* E, F, G, and H you decide to call *gigi.* You chase away the *gogo,* but leave the *gigi* alone. Your neighbor, however, has had a different experience; he finds that those with square heads bite, while those with round heads do not. Abstracting the common characteristics of B, D, F, and H, he calls them *daba,* and A, C, E, and G he calls *dobo.* Still another neighbor discovers, on the other hand, that those with curly tails kill snakes, while those with straight tails do not. He differentiates them, abstracting still another set of common characteristics: A, B, E, and F are *busa,* while C, D, G, and H are *busana.*

3   Now imagine that the three of you are together when E runs by.

You say, "There goes the *gigi*"; your first neighbor says, "There goes the *dobo*"; your other neighbor says, "There goes the *busa*." Here immediately a great controversy arises. What is it really, a *gigi*, a *dobo*, or a *busa*? What is its *right name*? You are quarreling violently when along comes a fourth person from another village who calls it a *muglock*, an edible animal, as opposed to *uglock*, an inedible animal—which doesn't help matters a bit.

4   Of course, the question, "What is it *really*? What is its *right name*?" is a nonsense question. By a nonsense question is meant one that is not capable of being answered. Things can have "right names" only if there is a necessary connection between symbols and things symbolized, and . . . there is not. That is to say, in the light of your interest in protecting your grain, it may be necessary for you to distinguish the animal E as a *gigi*; your neighbor, who doesn't like to be bitten, finds it practical to distinguish it as a *dobo*; your other neighbor, who likes to see snakes killed, distinguishes it as a *busa*. What we call things and where we draw the line between one class of things and another depend upon the interests we have and the purposes of the classification. For example, animals are classified in one way by the meat industry, in a different way by the leather industry, in another different way by the fur industry, and in a still different way by the biologist. None of these classifications is any more final than any of the others; each of them is useful for its purpose.

5   This holds, of course, regarding everything we perceive. A table "is" a table to us, because we can understand its relationship to our conduct and interests; we eat at it, work on it, lay things on it. But to a person living in a culture where no tables are used, it may be a very big stool, a small platform, or a meaningless structure. If our culture and upbringing were different, that is to say, our world would not even look the same to us.

6   Many of us, for example, cannot distinguish between pickerel, pike, salmon, smelts, perch, crappies, halibut, and mackerel; we say that they are "just fish, and I don't like fish." To a seafood connoisseur, however, these distinctions are real, since they mean the difference to him between one kind of good meal, a very different kind of good meal, or a poor meal. To a zoologist, even finer distinctions become of great importance, since he has other and more general ends in view. When we hear the statement, then, "This fish is a specimen of the pompano, *Trachinotus carolinus*," we accept this as being "true," even if we don't care, not because that is its "right name," but because that is how it is *classified* in the most complete and most general system of classification which people most deeply interested in fish have evolved.

7   When we name something, then, we are classifying. *The individual object or event we are naming, of course, has no name and belongs to no class until we put it in one.* To illustrate again, suppose that we were to give the *extensional* meaning of the word "Korean." We would have to

point to all "Koreans" living at a particular moment and say, "The word 'Korean' denotes at the present moment these persons: A_1, A_2, A_3 . . . A_n." Now, let us say, a child, whom we shall designate as Z, is born among these "Koreans." *The extensional meaning of the word "Korean," determined prior to the existence of Z, does not include Z.* Z is a new individual belonging to no classification, since all classifications were made without taking Z into account. Why, then, is Z also a "Korean"? *Because we say so.* And, saying so—fixing the classification—we have determined to a considerable extent future attitudes toward Z. For example, Z will always have certain rights in Korea; he will always be regarded in other nations as an "alien" and will be subject to laws applicable to "aliens."

8   In matters of "race" and "nationality," the way in which classifications work is especially apparent. For example, the present writer is by "race" a "Japanese," by "nationality" a "Canadian," but, his friends say, "essentially" an "American," since he thinks, talks, behaves, and dresses much like other Americans. Because he is "Japanese," he is excluded by law from becoming a citizen of the United States[1]; because he is "Canadian," he has certain rights in all parts of the British Commonwealth; because he is "American," he gets along with his friends and teaches in an American institution of higher learning without any noticeable special difficulties. Are these classifications "real"? Of course they are, and *the effect that each of them has upon what he may and may not do constitutes their "reality."*

9   There was, again, the story some years ago of the immigrant baby whose parents were "Czechs" and eligible to enter the United States by quota. The child, however, because it was born on what happened to be a "British" ship, was a "British subject." The quota for Britishers was full for that year, with the result that the new-born infant was regarded by immigration authorities as "not admissible to the United States." How they straightened out this matter, the writer does not know. The reader can multiply instances of this kind at will. When, to take another example, is a person a "Negro"? By the definition accepted in the United States, any person with even a small amount of "Negro blood"—that is, whose parents or ancestors were classified as "Negroes"—is a "Negro." *It would be exactly as justifiable to say that any person with even a small amount of "white blood" is "white."* Why do they say one rather than the other? Because the former system of classification *suits the convenience of those making the classification.*

10   There are few complexities about classifications at the level of dogs and cats, knives and forks, cigarettes and candy, but when it comes to classifications at high levels of abstraction, for example, those describing conduct, social institutions, philosophical and moral problems, serious difficulties occur. When one person kills another, is it an act of murder, an act of temporary insanity, an act of homicide, an accident, or an act of

[1] Since 1952 "race" is no bar to U.S. citizenship.

heroism? As soon as the process of classification is completed, our attitudes and our conduct are to a considerable degree determined. We hang
the murderer, we lock up the insane man, we free the victim of circumstances, we pin a medal on the hero.

Exercises

CONTENT

True or False? If you think the statement represents what the selection says or implies, mark it "True"; if you do not think so, mark it
"False."

1. A "nonsense" question is a question that cannot be answered.
2. There is no "right" name for anything.
3. The square-headed animals ought to be called "daba."
4. Hayakawa does not like fish.
5. What you call things influences your attitude toward them.
6. It makes no difference whether you refer to a certain child as
"brat," "darling," or "the Hathaways' little girl who'll be six in August,"
since the child stays the same whatever you call her.
7. Hayakawa resents the fact that his race prevents him from becoming an American citizen.
8. The point of the story told in Paragraph 9 is that the baby obviously was Czech and that the immigration authorities should have realized this.
9. "Murder is murder, whatever you choose to call it."
10. Since there is no necessary connection between things and the
names of things, we are free to call anything anything we like to call it.

Questions for Discussion

1. Hayakawa uses two terms that need to be understood before his
essay can be fully understood. By *abstracting* (Paragraph 2 and later)
Hayakawa means the mental process by which we ignore the individual
peculiarities of anything for the sake of grouping (or classifying) it with
other individuals of the same kind. For example, I may refer to a man as
"Herman Bucklebelt," or as "a machine-shop foreman," or as "a father," or
as "an American," or as "a human being," or as "a mammalian." With each
new term I apply to Mr. Bucklebelt I give him a new classification, and
each new classification puts him in a larger group than the preceding one
did. I keep ignoring more and more of the characteristics that make
Bucklebelt a unique individual. Instead I pick out, or *abstract*, those
characteristics he has in common with others and classify him by means
of these characteristics. Since the characteristics become increasingly general, I end up losing sight of Bucklebelt in the vast inclusiveness of the

zoological term "mammalian": he has become one with whales and mice and elephants.

The second term Hayakawa uses that may cause difficulty is *extensional meaning* (Paragraph 7). The extensional meaning of a word is the physical object, or collection of physical objects, the word refers to. The extensional meaning of the word "cat," for instance, is not a dictionary definition but the actual animal, the physical creature you can pick up and give milk to and be scratched by. The opposite of the *extensional* meaning is the *intensional* meaning, or the ideas and feelings the word suggests to your mind.

Now answer the following questions:

(a) Arrange the following terms in the order of increased abstraction, i.e., from the individual to the general: food, apple, fruit, economic asset, McIntosh, farm product.

(b) What is the extensional meaning of "S. I. Hayakawa"?

2. According to Hayakawa, is the following a sensible statement: "It's vicious nonsense for the Communists to say that their system of government is democratic"? Discuss.

3. Would you accept this as a fair statement of Hayakawa's main point in this essay? "Since there is no necessary connection between the object and its name, anything can be classified (or named) in any number of ways. This is not to say that classification is meaningless and unimportant. In fact, using language is mainly a matter of giving things names, or classifying them, and how we think and feel about things and act toward them is to a large extent determined by the way we classify them." Discuss.

4. In terms of Hayakawa's ideas here, how would you describe the problem that puzzled the author of *Street Elbow?*

5. Does or does not Hayakawa in Paragraph 10 say that a war hero is no better and no worse than a murderer? Discuss.

FORM AND STYLE

1. Define the function of the first three paragraphs in the overall organization of the essay.

2. What do Paragraphs 8 and 9 have in common? How do they differ from Paragraphs 1-3? How are they similar to Paragraphs 1-3?

3. Complete the analogy: Paragraphs 5 and 6 are to Paragraph 4 as Paragraphs 8 and 9 are to Paragraph —. Explain your answer and define the relationships.

VOCABULARY

Which of the four words or phrases to the right seems to you to be *closest* in meaning to the word in heavy type to the left? Put a check mark after your choice.

scampering (*1*)   scurrying . . . rooting . . . nesting . . . plundering

differentiation (*2*)   definition . . . difference . . . distinction . . . disagreement . . .

inedible (*3*)   untrainable . . . unfriendly . . . indigestible . . . uneatable . . .

connoisseur (*6*)   lover . . . expert in matters of taste . . . dealer . . . cook . . .

denotes (*7*)   means . . . implies . . . suggests . . . makes a note of

designate (*7*)   draw . . . mark . . . call . . . define . . .

prior to (*7*)   in preference to . . . earlier than . . . without reference to . . . more important than . . .

alien (*7*)   suspect . . . oriental . . . noncitizen . . . somebody different . . .

constitutes (*8*)   affects . . . determines . . . makes up . . . corresponds to . . .

THEME SUGGESTIONS

The prejudice of language

Write an essay, as personal or impersonal as you want to make it, on the manner in which we tend to express our attitudes by our choice of words, and how—conversely—our attitudes are determined by the words we hear and see applied. A man may be "a great statesman" to you and "a dirty politician" to me, and the girl a doctor may call "thin" is "slim" to her fiancé and "nothing but skin and bones" to her frustrated rival. These remarks are suggestive only: you are free to use Hayakawa's essay in any way you wish in a theme on the relationship between language and attitudes.

Moral implications in *Classification*

43

DARRELL HUFF

The Semiattached Figure

1   If you can't prove what you want to prove, demonstrate something else and pretend that they are the same thing. In the daze that follows the collision of statistics with the human mind, hardly anybody will notice the difference. The semiattached figure is a device guaranteed to stand you in good stead. It always has.

2 You can't prove that your nostrum cures colds, but you can publish (in large type) a sworn laboratory report that half an ounce of the stuff killed 31,108 germs in a test tube in eleven seconds. While you are about it, make sure that the laboratory is reputable or has an impressive name. Reproduce the report in full. Photograph a doctor-type model in white clothes and put his picture alongside.

3 But don't mention the several gimmicks in your story. It is not up to you—is it?—to point out that an antiseptic that works well in a test tube may not perform in the human throat, especially after it has been diluted according to instructions to keep it from burning throat tissue. Don't confuse the issue by telling what kind of germ you killed. Who knows what germ causes colds, particularly since it probably isn't a germ at all?

4 In fact, there is no known connection between assorted germs in a test tube and the whatever-it-is that produces colds, but people aren't going to reason that sharply, especially while sniffling.

5 Maybe that one is too obvious, and people are beginning to catch on, although it would not appear so from the advertising pages. Anyway, here is a trickier version.

6 Let us say that during a period in which race prejudice is growing you are employed to "prove" otherwise. It is not a difficult assignment. Set up a poll or, better yet, have the polling done for you by an organization of good reputation. Ask that usual cross section of the population if they think Negroes have as good a chance as white people to get jobs. Repeat your polling at intervals so that you will have a trend to report.

7 Princeton's Office of Public Opinion Research tested this question once. What turned up is interesting evidence that things, especially in opinion polls, are not always what they seem. Each person who was asked the question about jobs was also asked some questions designed to discover if he was strongly prejudiced against Negroes. It turned out that people most strongly prejudiced were most likely to answer Yes to the question about job opportunities. (It worked out that about two-thirds of those who were sympathetic toward Negroes did not think the Negro had as good a chance at a job as a white person did, and about two-thirds of those showing prejudice said that Negroes were getting as good breaks as whites.) It was pretty evident that from this poll you would learn very little about employment conditions for Negroes, although you might learn some interesting things about a man's racial attitudes.

8 You can see, then, that if prejudice is mounting during your polling period you will get an increasing number of answers to the effect that Negroes have as good a chance at jobs as whites. So you announce your results: Your poll shows that Negroes are getting a fairer shake all the time.

9 You have achieved something remarkable by careful use of a semi-attached figure. The worse things get, the better your poll makes them look.

10 Or take this one: "27 per cent of a large sample of eminent physicians smoke Throaties—more than any other brand." The figure itself may be phony, of course, in any of several ways, but that really doesn't make any difference. The only answer to a figure so irrelevant is "So what?" With all proper respect toward the medical profession, do doctors know any more about tobacco brands than you do? Do they have any inside information that permits them to choose the least harmful among cigarettes? Of course they don't, and your doctor would be the first to say so. Yet that "27 per cent" somehow manages to sound as if it meant something.

11 Now slip back one per cent and consider the case of the juice extractor. It was widely advertised as a device that "extracts 26 per cent more juice" as "proved by laboratory test" and "vouched for by Good Housekeeping Institute."

12 That sounds right good. If you can buy a juicer that is twenty-six per cent more effective, why buy any other kind? Well now, without going into the fact that "laboratory tests" (especially "independent laboratory tests") have proved some of the darndest things, just what does that figure mean? Twenty-six per cent more than what? When it was finally pinned down it was found to mean only that this juicer got out that much more juice than an old-fashioned hand reamer could. It had absolutely nothing to do with the data you would want before purchasing; this juicer might be the poorest on the market. Besides being suspiciously precise, that twenty-six per cent figure is totally irrelevant.

13 Advertisers aren't the only people who will fool you with numbers if you let them. An article on driving safety, published by *This Week* magazine undoubtedly with your best interests at heart, told you what might happen to you if you went "hurtling down the highway at 70 miles an hour, careening from side to side." You would have, the article said, four times as good a chance of staying alive if the time were seven in the morning than if it were seven at night. The evidence: "Four times more fatalities occur on the highways at 7 P.M. than at 7 A.M." Now that is approximately true, but the conclusion doesn't follow. More people are killed in the evening than in the morning simply because more people are on the highways then to be killed. You, a single driver, may be in greater danger in the evening, but there is nothing in the figures to prove it either way.

14 By the same kind of nonsense that the article writer used you can show that clear weather is more dangerous than foggy weather. More accidents occur in clear weather, because there is more clear weather than foggy weather. All the same, fog may be much more dangerous to drive in.

15 You can use accident statistics to scare yourself to death in connection with any kind of transportation . . . if you fail to note how poorly attached the figures are.

16 More people were killed by airplanes last year than in 1910. Therefore modern planes are more dangerous? Nonsense. There are hundreds of times more people flying now, that's all.

Exercises

CONTENT

True or False? If you think the statement represents what the selection says or implies, mark it "True"; if you do not think so, mark it "False."

1. Any germ-killing drug cures a cold.
2. All advertising is fraudulent.
3. Doctors pictured in ads are never real doctors.
4. One of the ways in which advertising can mislead is by the loose use of comparatives: "more," "better," "finer," etc.
5. Negroes find it easier to get jobs, and *better* jobs, all the time.
6. An ad can be truthful and still be meaningless.
7. The following ad uses the "semiattached figure": "A total of three hundred hi-fi sets were sold in America in 1948. In 1958 the Full-o'-Noise Company, Inc., *alone* sold more than three thousand sets! We're clearly way ahead of our competitors!"
8. "In 1902 my grandfather made $6000 a year as a bank president. Last year I made more than $7000 as a gas station attendant. If this doesn't prove that a guy is better off in almost any kind of job today than he would have been fifty-sixty years ago, I don't know what it proves."
9. Public opinion polls are rigged.
10. Much advertising counts on the fact that the public is impressed by exact figures.

Questions for Discussion

1. What, exactly, is a "semiattached figure"?
2. Do you accept the statement that "more people are killed in the evening than in the morning simply because more people are on the highway then to be killed"? What does the author overlook? Does the fact that his logic is weak here ruin his argument in Paragraphs 13-16?
3. Can you explain the psychology behind the fact that people who were prejudiced against Negroes also were likely to believe that Negroes were not being discriminated against on the labor market (Paragraph 7)? (There is no one correct answer to this question; it just provokes some interesting speculation.)

FORM AND STYLE

1. In form, *The Semiattached Figure* consists of a general statement

followed by a series of specific examples. How many? Identify them. Divide them into two groups and distinguish the groups.

2. What metaphor is suggested by "the collision of statistics with the human mind" (Paragraph 1)?

3. What is sarcastic about Paragraph 3?

4. Paragraph 5 and the first sentence in Paragraph 11 serve as transitions. Explain how.

5. Point out specific examples of colloquial usage in the essay. What relationship between author and reader does the style suggest? Does it seem relevant to the theme of the essay? Explain.

VOCABULARY

Which of the four words or phrases to the right seems to you to be *closest* in meaning to the word in heavy type to the left? Put a check mark after your choice.

daze *(1)*   fog . . . shock . . . confusion . . . darkness . . .

nostrum *(2)*   product . . . quack medicine . . . invention . . . prescription . . .

reputable *(2)*   famous . . . esteemed . . . supposedly competent . . . impressive . . .

diluted *(3)*   processed . . . made safe . . . changed . . . thinned . . .

assorted *(4)*   sorted out . . . certain . . . diseased . . . varied . . .

eminent *(10)*   famous . . . prominent . . . excellent . . . outstanding

irrelevant *(10)*   small . . . having nothing to do with the issue in question . . . indefinite . . . without support . . .

vouched for *(11)*   guaranteed . . . tested . . . attested to . . . sponsored . . .

reamer *(12)*   juicer . . . sharp tool for making holes . . . curved knife . . . squeezer . . .

approximately *(13)*   more or less . . . by estimate . . . nearly . . . exactly . . .

THEME SUGGESTION

Analyze an ad or commercial using the "semiattached figure."

44

JOSEPH J. SELDIN

Selling the Kiddies

1   Several years ago, when television was in its infancy, an advertisement appeared in a trade publication pointing out to alert manufacturers the remarkable ability of television to indoctrinate pre-school children with commercial brand names. The ad, quoted in E. S. Turner's "The Shocking History of Advertising," described the following family scene:

2   Speaking of surveys, we tried an experiment the other evening. . . . To a curly-headed four-year-old being tucked under the covers we posed this question: Susie, which product brushes teeth whiter? "Colgate's, of course, Gramp." We couldn't resist another. Which product washes clothes cleaner? Without a moment's hesitation: "Tide." We tried once more. Which coffee gives the best value? When she replied, "A and P, and now good-night, Gramp," we hurried out of the child's room with other questions beating at our brain.

3   Where else on earth is brand consciousness fixed so firmly in the minds of four-year-old tots? How many pre-school Americans are pre-sold on how many different products? What is it worth to a manufacturer who can close in on this juvenile audience and continue to sell it under controlled conditions, year after year, right up to its attainment of adulthood and full-fledged buyer status? It CAN be done. Interested?

4   This ad appeared around 1950 when there were 5,000,000 television sets in the United States. Since then, the number of sets has spiraled to 32,000,000, entering two out of every three households in the nation. This rapid growth has afforded advertisers of soaps, cigarettes, detergents, cereals, beers, etc., the chance to "plant their feet on the nation's hearth," as one trade observer put it. It also has enabled them to "close in" on the 18,000,000 children under five years of age and the 16,000,000 in the five-to-nine group—successfully capturing many of these young listeners with their commercials. How successfully is shown in the research findings by the Youth Research Institute that "youngsters eagerly repeat television and radio commercials which strike their fancy. Even five-year-olds sing beer commercials over and over again with gusto." Assurance is offered advertisers by the Youth Research Institute that "millions of youngsters" in homes throughout the nation are singing the merits of advertised products "with the same vigor displayed by the most enthusiastic announcers." An additional bright spot is that a catchy commercial is repeatedly sung during the day by youngsters at no extra cost to the advertiser. "They are also much more difficult to turn off," the report adds.

5   Nor do the children limit their activities on behalf of the advertiser

SELLING THE KIDDIES. From *The Nation*, October 8, 1955. Reprinted by permission of *The Nation*.

to the singing of commercials. As every parent knows, they exert a major influence on family spending. One survey reveals that they urge their parents to buy a specified brand of breakfast cereal 71 per cent of the time, pressure for the purchase of 44 per cent of the packaged desserts, 35 per cent of the milk-fortifiers, and 32 per cent of the toothpastes.

6   The trick in turning children into the extended selling arm of the advertiser is easily accomplished by using child-appeal premiums. These premiums are generally fabricated of inexpensive plastics, metal, or paper products, and their cost is ordinarily more than covered by the charge to the consumer. Often there is room in the consumer charge for a profit for the distributor and retailers handling the premium for the advertiser. But the essence of the premium's purpose is not to return an immediate profit, but rather to excite the children and create in them an overwhelming yen for possession of the premium. This simple technique of using the premium as bait for the children, and children as bait for their parents, effectively mangles the parents' usual marketing considerations of need, price, quality, and budget.

7   For example, General Electric offered a sixty-piece circus, a magic-ray gun, and a space helmet as premiums for children who brought their parents into dealers' stores to witness demonstrations of new GE refrigerator models. Sylvania offered a complete Space Ranger kit, replete with space helmet, distintegrator, flying saucer, and space telephone, to children who brought their parents into dealers' stores to see the new line of television sets. Nash blandished a toy service station that pulled countless thousands of youngsters into showrooms where their parents' buying-potential was courted. Quaker Oats sent workmen into the Yukon to transplant five tons of dirt to Anchorage, Alaska, where a prospector's pouch containing a bit of the dirt was mailed to any child in return for 25 cents and a Quaker Oats boxtop. General Mills offered youngsters Lone Ranger masks in millions of Wheaties boxes and Lone Ranger comic books in millions of Cheerio boxes. Sunkist Growers offered four giant circus masks for 25 cents and a wrapper from a three-can package; Standard Brands gave away Howdy Doody coloring cards with Royal pudding boxes; Armour and Company used baseball buttons to promote the consumption of its frankfurters, and Colgate pushed up its soap sales with a "name Lassie's puppies" contest, the prizes including a year's supply of Fab for "mother." These were only a few of the many scores of juvenile premium offers.

8   Manipulation of children's minds in the fields of religion or politics would touch off a parental storm of protest and a rash of congressional investigations. But in the world of commerce children are fair game and legitimate prey.

Exercises

CONTENT

True or False? If you think the statement represents what the selection says or implies, mark it "True"; if you do not think so, mark it "False."

1. In 1950 there were about five million TV sets in the United States.
2. In 1955 there were about thirty-four million children below nine years in the United States.
3. Singing commercials are bad for children.
4. The longer a parent has to listen to a child singing a commercial it has picked up on radio or TV, the more infuriated he or she is likely to be with the product.
5. Surveys reveal that in most American families the children have little or no influence on family spending.

Questions for Discussion

1. Which paragraph contains the essence of the author's thesis?
2. The discussion of the influence of advertising on children deals with two forms of advertising. Which two?
3. Is *Selling the Kiddies* pure exposition or argument? Explain your answer.

FORM AND STYLE

1. Where do you first become aware of Seldin's attitude to the phenomenon he describes? Is his attitude ever openly stated? If so, where?
2. Outline the essay.
3. What difference to the meaning does it make whether you consider "the kiddies" of the title the direct or the indirect object?

VOCABULARY

Which of the four words or phrases to the right seems to you to be *closest* in meaning to the word in heavy type to the left? Put a check mark after your choice.

infancy (*1*)   beginning . . . clothing proper for babies . . . growing pains . . . babyhood . . .
alert (*1*)   eager . . . enterprising . . . forewarned . . . watchful . . .
indoctrinate with (*1*)   inject into . . . corrupt with . . . teach . . . suggest to . . .

attainment (3) goal . . . fulfillment . . . maturity . . . reaching . . .
afforded (4) had the money for . . . given . . . tempted with . . .
 delighted with . . .
gusto (4) spirit . . . pleasure . . . taste . . . bad consequence . . .
exert (5) practice . . . want . . . have . . . expect . . .
yen (6) liking . . . desire . . . fad . . . rapture . . .
mangles (6) spoils . . . overrides . . . upsets . . . goes against . . .
replete (7) complete . . . disgustingly full . . . splendid . . . filled
rash (8) eruption . . . lot . . . rush . . . hasty action . . .

THEME SUGGESTIONS

An advertiser replies to Seldin
What is a "good" commercial? Does it exist?
Around the universe for a boxtop and 25 cents
"Next time you go shopping, be sure to tell Mom to buy . . . ," or
Commercials vs. parental authority
Why I sold/smashed/gave away my TV set

45

PEG BRACKEN

The New Mallarkey

1 There are more tricks to the glossy fiction trade than the casual reader probably thinks. One of the writer's big problems, as he creates his beautiful, brave, lovable characters, is making them beautiful enough and brave enough, and still keeping them lovable.

2 The fact is, times have changed. Today's sophisticated reader will no longer buy yesterday's heroine, who walked in virtue, her eyes blue as the sky over Naples, with cheeks that shamed the rose. He is equally unconvinced by yesterday's hero, that big handsome broad-shouldered curly-haired package of incorruptibility.

3 A thing called Reader Identification has set in. The reader knows, deep down, that *he* is not as beautiful and lovable as that, and furthermore he doubts whether anyone is.

4 Thus, the twin horns of the writer's dilemma are distressingly

THE NEW MALLARKEY. From *The Atlantic Monthly*, July, 1955. Copyright, 1955, by the Atlantic Monthly Company. Reprinted by permission of *The Atlantic Monthly* and the author.

clear. The writer must, to put it bluntly, lay off the mallarkey. But he knows, too, that his feminine readers will refuse just as flatly to identify themselves with a thick-waisted heroine or one who has a front tooth out; nor will his masculine readers stay long with a potbellied hero.

5 It is encouraging to be able to report that writers have solved the problem—not with the faint praise which damns, but with the faint damn which praises. For example: "Brad looked at Pam. She was too thin, her cheekbones too high, her eyes too wide apart. . . ."

6 Now, there is Reader Identification with a hey-nonnie. Every woman wants to be too thin. And love those high cheekbones, those wide-set eyes! But here she finds them brusquely dismissed as faults.

7 Well, the reader has faults too. She knows how it is. And while she privately imagines the heroine to be about as beautiful as any girl can be, she derives a certain feminine comfort from hearing that not everyone thinks so. The reader immediately joins the heroine's team. She becomes her Secret Pal.

8 It is not easy, this matter of presenting virtues as faults; the writer must remember at all times that Pam's legs may be too long, but not so her nose. Her eyes may be too large, but never, under any circumstances, her knuckles. "Pam's too-generous mobile mouth" is always acceptable to the reader, but "Pam's big flapping mouth" would be rejected instantly. No, it isn't easy. And the writer encounters the same problem when he describes the house or room Pam lives in. Yet, here again, the same approach will ease the way to Reader Identification:—

9 "It wasn't a smart room. Obviously no interior decorator had had a hand in assembling this casual collection of odd pieces; no decorator would have condoned the faded chintzes and the clutter of books. Even the kindly firelight burnishing the rocker and the copper kettle couldn't quite hide the shabbiness of the rug. Yet Brad liked the room, felt at home there. . . ."

10 Note the shrewd use of the "yet" instead of a "therefore." Observe its magical effect in making the reader feel superior to the writer, as well as at home in the room, "Why, that's my kind of place!" the reader thinks. "What does this silly writer want, a store window? My stuff doesn't match either. And as for books, well, I always say a room isn't a room without books. . . ." So the reader is more than ever ready to share Pam's problems and eventual joys.

11 An aspiring glossy fiction writer should know that his heroes will respond just as nicely to the faint damn as will his heroines and his settings. When a man reads that "Brad's face was casually put together, the nose jutting, the lines deep—a face marked by the hard living of forty-one years," he feels better about his own face, which was designed a bit haphazardly too. Also, the suggestion of manly dissipation enables him to write off his own extra rounds at the nineteenth hole. At the same time, he senses that none of these things is going to handicap Brad in the slight-

est. Brad is obviously a nice combination of valor and virility. He will go far, and the reader will follow him all the way.

12 It is true that there are pitfalls with heroes, as with heroines, and the alert writer will keep them in mind. For instance, a tight-lipped hero who grins an occasional crooked grin will be readily accepted by the reader, even though these traits, in real life, are usually an indication of bad bridgework. But the reader will quickly shy away from Brad should he have foot trouble. Foot trouble, for some reason, belongs to men named Harold Buebke, not Brad Reynolds; and heroes are never named Harold Buebke.

13 It is all a matter of knowing how and what to insult without insulting. It is for this reason that the writer so often seems preoccupied with the hero's hair. Brad can have hair like old rope, and often does. Or he can have mussed-up hair, although a better adjective is "unruly," or he can even have hair that's growing thin on top—no matter, it will lower him no whit in the reader's estimation; moreover, it will provide a comfortable bond of Reader Identification.

14 No discussion of the praise-while-damning method would be complete without mention of the flashback to adolescence—a technique which has been often and profitably used by writers who know their business. One of its many merits is that it permits the heroine to be an absolute dilly from the first moment she appears.

15 "Brad looked at Pam Harrison, slim, poised, perfect. There had been a little Pam Harrison once, years ago, before the war had torn and twisted so many things. . . . Pam Harrison, the little kid next door.

16 " 'Pam, are you the same girl that—' Brad stopped, feeling like a fool. This girl, this copper-haired beauty with the exquisite legs, the warm ivory skin, the marvelous laughing mouth—she could never have been that skinny brat with the freckles, that kid with the braces on her teeth.

17 " 'You mean, was I the kid you used to chase home from school with snowballs?' Pam wrinkled her nose, charmingly. 'Yes. Wasn't I *awful?*'

18 "Brad grinned.

19 " 'I was pretty awful myself,' he said ruefully. 'Remember how. . . .' "

20 Now, this isn't quite as easy as it looks. It's quite all right for the child Pam to be remembered with braces on her teeth, a skinny freckled gamin. But the reader will never make contact with Pam if she used to be dough-faced and over-weight. Once in a long time a writer will fatten up a young heroine and get away with it, but the trick lies in the use of the word "pudgy," which has a rollicking cherubic quality that's rather fun.

21 However, once these problems have been met and mastered, the writer finds himself in a nice position, and can get on with his story; he has given his principals a reasonably repulsive adolescence, and the reader shouldn't quibble over their distinct charms as adults. After all, fair's fair.

22 This takes care of all the description the writer has to worry about, with one exception. If it is ever necessary to describe someone asleep in bed—and it is surprising how often this *is* necessary—there is only one way to do it: "Lying there asleep in the rumpled bedclothes, he looked defenseless."

23 A querulous critic might object, unless he is Lucky Luciano lying there asleep with his gat under his pillow and his finger on the trigger, how in the world else can he look? But that is mere carping, and it need not be considered here.

Exercises

CONTENT

True or False? If you think the statement represents what the selection says or implies, mark it "True"; if you do not think so, mark it "False."

1. Heroes and heroines of popular romantic fiction used to be unbelievably brave and handsome, lovable and beautiful.
2. Modern readers reject such characters as false and sentimental.
3. "Reader identification" means that the reader is able to see some similarity between himself and the hero (or heroine).
4. The "new mallarkey" consists in the writer's finding fault with his chief characters for something the reader sees in himself and therefore finds attractive.
5. A "new mallarkey" heroine may have eyes set too wide apart—
6. —but she cannot be wide-hipped.
7. And a "new mallarkey" hero may be pot-bellied—
8. —but he cannot be losing his hair.
9. Lucky Luciano is a man of lovable faults.
10. The writer of "new mallarkey" praises with a faint damn.

Questions for Discussion

1. Miss Bracken makes fun of the "new mallarkey." Is she, therefore, in favor of the "old mallarkey"? Or of no "mallarkey" whatever? How can she be defended against the criticism that she wants her heroes and heroines all perfect and hence unrealistic? Discuss.
2. Why may the heroine's legs be too long but not her nose, the hero craggy-faced but not flat-footed?
3. In Paragraph 5 there is an *allusion,* or reference, to a poem by the 18th century English poet Alexander Pope, who describes a jealous and hypocritical critic as one who would

> Damn with faint praise, assent with civil leer,
> And without sneering, teach the rest to sneer. . . .

In good writers, allusions are not simply a means by which they show off their reading. Allusions can contribute to the meaning by reminding the reader of the original context and thus enrich the present context. Here in Paragraph 5, once we think of the line from Pope that Miss Bracken first refers to and then reverses, we also think of the insincerity, the falseness of feeling, of the man about whom Pope's line originally was written. Is an allusion to insincerity and falseness of feeling relevant here? Explain.

4. What is meant by "his own extra rounds at the nineteenth hole" (Paragraph 11), and by "these traits, in real life, are usually an indication of bad bridgework" (Paragraph 12)?

FORM AND STYLE

1. Would it have made any difference to the organization of the essay if in Paragraph 1 the author had written "brave, beautiful, lovable" instead of "beautiful, brave, lovable"? Explain.

2. Sarcasm may be defined as expressing a negative attitude (hate, contempt, disgust, ridicule, etc.) to something by a positive statement about it: the motorist saying "that's all I needed," when he has a flat tire; the angry mother telling the child to "go ahead, why don't you break all the dishes?" The speaker in such cases says exactly the opposite of what he really means, and sarcasm may therefore be considered a form of irony, since irony results from disagreement between what has been stated and what is implied. Explain the sarcasm in Paragraphs 5 and 23.

3. Comment upon the use of slang and colloquialism in the essay. Can it be justified? If so, how?

4. Try to imagine the essay without the examples of the "new mallarkey." Obviously, not much is left. What rule for writing of this sort has been suggested?

5. Assuming that the quotations are all intended to ridicule a particular kind of popular, romantic fiction by parody, what, exactly, is wrong with Paragraph 15—why is it an example of bad literature?

VOCABULARY

Which of the four words or phrases to the right seems to you to be *closest* in meaning to the word in heavy type to the left? Put a check mark after your choice.

sophisticated (2) bored . . . worldly . . . intellectual . . . cynical
dilemma (4) a rare Asiatic animal with horns . . . difficulty . . .
danger . . . a choice between disagreeable alternatives . . .

with a hey-nonnie (6)   too much . . . emphatically . . . nonsensically . . . with a bang . . .

mobile (8)   large . . . lively . . . movable . . . loose . . .

encounters (8)   faces . . . solves . . . avoids . . . opposes . . .

condoned (9)   condemned . . . liked . . . designed . . . approved

burnishing (9)   scorching . . . burning . . . making shiny . . . illuminating . . .

aspiring (11)   ambitious . . . hopeful . . . skillful . . . young . . .

haphazardly (11)   ruggedly . . . dangerously . . . not handsomely . . . in a careless manner . . .

dissipation (11)   feeling . . . crime . . . vice . . . sportsmanship . . .

virility (11)   masculinity . . . good looks . . . nice personality . . . strength . . .

pitfalls (12)   difficulties . . . traps . . . techniques . . . tricks . . .

cherubic (20)   cheerful . . . mischievous . . . like a puppy . . . like a baby angel . . .

carping (23)   silliness . . . irrelevance . . . fault-finding . . . hair-splitting . . .

THEME SUGGESTIONS

What is wrong with the slicks
Good and bad escape literature
I *like* Pam and Brad!
A parody

46

MARCHETTE CHUTE

Getting at the Truth

1   This is a rather presumptuous title for a biographer to use, since truth is a very large word. In the sense that it means the reality about a human being it is probably impossible for a biographer to achieve. In the sense that it means a reasonable presentation of all the available facts it is more nearly possible, but even this limited goal is harder to reach than it appears to be. A biographer needs to be both humble and cautious when he remembers the nature of the material he is working with, for a historical fact is rather like the flamingo that Alice in Wonderland tried to use as a croquet mallet. As soon as she got its neck nicely straightened out

GETTING AT THE TRUTH. From *The Saturday Review*, September 19, 1953. Reprinted by permission of *The Saturday Review* and the author.

and was ready to hit the ball, it would turn and look at her with a puzzled expression, and any biographer knows that what is called "a fact" has a way of doing the same.

2   Here is a small example. When I was writing my forthcoming biography, "Ben Jonson of Westminster," I wanted to give a paragraph or two to Sir Philip Sidney, who had a great influence on Jonson. No one thinks of Sidney without thinking of chivalry, and to underline the point I intended to use a story that Sir Fulke Greville told of him. Sidney died of gangrene, from a musket shot that shattered his thigh, and Greville says that Sidney failed to put on his leg armor while preparing for battle because the marshal of the camp was not wearing leg armor and Sidney was unwilling to do anything that would give him a special advantage.

3   The story is so characteristic both of Sidney himself and of the misplaced high-mindedness of late Renaissance chivalry that I wanted to use it, and since Sir Fulke Greville was one of Sidney's closest friends the information seemed to be reliable enough. But it is always well to check each piece of information as thoroughly as possible and so I consulted another account of Sidney written by a contemporary, this time a doctor who knew the family fairly well. The doctor, Thomas Moffet, mentioned the episode but he said that Sidney left off his leg armor because he was in a hurry.

4   The information was beginning to twist in my hand and could no longer be trusted. So I consulted still another contemporary who had mentioned the episode, to see which of the two he agreed with. This was Sir John Smythe, a military expert who brought out his book a few years after Sidney's death. Sir John was an old-fashioned conservative who advocated the use of heavy armor even on horseback, and he deplored the current craze for leaving off leg protection, "the imitating of which . . . cost that noble and worthy gentleman Sir Philip Sidney his life."

5   So here I was with three entirely different reasons why Sidney left off his leg armor, all advanced by careful writers who were contemporaries of his. The flamingo had a legitimate reason for looking around with a puzzled expression.

6   The only thing to do in a case like this is to examine the point of view of the three men who are supplying the conflicting evidence. Sir Fulke Greville was trying to prove a thesis: that his beloved friend had an extremely chivalric nature. Sir John Smythe also was trying to prove a thesis: that the advocates of light arming followed a theory that could lead to disaster. Only the doctor, Thomas Moffet, was not trying to prove a thesis. He was not using his own explanation to reinforce some point he wanted to make. He did not want anything except to set down on paper what he believed to be the facts; and since we do not have Sidney's own explanation of why he did not put on leg armor, the chances are that Dr. Moffet is the safest man to trust.

7   For Moffet was without desire. Nothing can so quickly blur and

distort the facts as desire—the wish to use the facts for some purpose of your own—and nothing can so surely destroy the truth. As soon as the witness wants to prove something he is no longer impartial and his evidence is no longer to be trusted.

8   The only safe way to study contemporary testimony is to bear constantly in mind this possibility of prejudice and to put almost as much attention on the writer himself as on what he has written. For instance, Sir Anthony Weldon's description of the Court of King James is lively enough and often used as source material; but a note from the publisher admits that the pamphlet was issued as a warning to anyone who wished to "side with this bloody house" of Stuart. The publisher, at any rate, did not consider Weldon an impartial witness. At about the same time Arthur Wilson published his history of Great Britain, which contained an irresistibly vivid account of the agonized death of the Countess of Somerset. Wilson sounds reasonably impartial; but his patron was the Earl of Essex, who had good reason to hate that particular countess, and there is evidence that he invented the whole scene to gratify his patron.

9   Sometimes a writer will contradict what he has already written, and in that case the only thing to do is to investigate what has changed his point of view. For instance, in 1608 Captain John Smith issued a description of his capture by Powhatan, and he made it clear that the Indian chief had treated him with unwavering courtesy and hospitality. In 1624 the story was repeated in Smith's "General History of Virginia," but the writer's circumstances had changed. Smith needed money, "having a prince's mind imprisoned in a poor man's purse," and he wanted the book to be profitable. Powhatan's daughter, the princess Pocahontas, had recently been in the news, for her visit to England had aroused a great deal of interest among the sort of people that Smith hoped would buy his book. So Smith supplied a new version of the story, in which the once-hospitable Powhatan would have permitted the hero's brains to be dashed out if Pocahontas had not saved his life. It was the second story that achieved fame, and of course it may have been true. But it is impossible to trust it because the desire of the writer is so obviously involved; as Smith said in his prospectus, he needed money and hoped that the book would give "satisfaction."

10   It might seem that there was an easy way for a biographer to avoid the use of this kind of prejudiced testimony. All he has to do is to construct his biography from evidence that cannot be tampered with—from parish records, legal documents, bills, accounts, court records, and so on. Out of these solid gray blocks of impersonal evidence it should surely be possible to construct a road that will lead straight to the truth and that will never bend itself to the misleading curve of personal desire.

11   This might be so if the only problem involved were the reliability of the material. But there is another kind of desire that is much more subtle, much more pervasive, and much more dangerous than the occasional distortions of fact that contemporary writers may have permitted themselves to make; and this kind of desire can destroy the truth of a biography even if every individual fact in it is as solid and as uncompromising as rock. Even if the road is built of the best and most reliable materials it can still curve away from the truth because of this other desire that threatens it: the desire of the biographer himself.

12 A biographer is not a court record or a legal document. He is a human being, writing about another human being, and his own temperament, his own point of view, and his own frame of reference are unconsciously imposed upon the man he is writing about. Even if the biographer is free from Captain Smith's temptation—the need for making money—and wants to write nothing but the literal truth, he is still handicapped by the fact that there is no such thing as a completely objective human being.

13 An illustration of what can happen if the point of view is sufficiently strong is the curious conclusion that the nineteenth-century biographers reached about William Shakespeare. Shakespeare joined a company of London actors in 1594, was listed as an actor in 1598 and 1603, and was still listed as one of the "men actors" in the company in 1609. Shortly before he joined this company Shakespeare dedicated two narrative poems to the Earl of Southampton, and several years after Shakespeare died his collected plays were dedicated to the Earl of Pembroke. This was his only relationship with either of the two noblemen, and there is nothing to connect him with them during the fifteen years in which he belonged to the same acting company and during which he wrote nearly all his plays.

14 But here the desire of the biographers entered in. They had been reared in the strict code of nineteenth-century gentility and they accepted two ideas without question. One was that there are few things more important than an English lord; the other was that there are few things less important than a mere actor. They already knew the undeniable fact that Shakespeare was one of the greatest men who ever lived; and while they could not go quite so far as to claim him as an actual member of the nobility, it was clear to them that he must have been the treasured friend of both the Earl of Southampton and the Earl of Pembroke and that he must have written his plays either while basking in their exalted company or while he was roaming the green countryside by the waters of the river Avon. (It is another basic conviction of the English gentleman that there is nothing so inspiring as nature.) The notion that Shakespeare had spent all these years as the working member of a company of London actors was so abhorrent that it was never seriously considered. It could not be so; therefore it was not.

15 These biographers did their work well. When New South Wales built its beautiful memorial library to Shakespeare, it was the coat of arms of the Earl of Southampton that alternated with that of royalty in digni-

fied splendor over the bookshelves. Shakespeare had been re-created in the image of desire, and desire will always ignore whatever is not relevant to its purpose. Because the English gentlemen did not like Shakespeare's background it was explained away as though it had never existed, and Shakespeare ceased to be an actor because so lowly a trade was not suited to so great a man.

16 All this is not to say that a biography should be lacking in a point of view. If it does not have a point of view it will be nothing more than a kind of expanded article for an encyclopedia—a string of facts arranged in chronological order with no claim to being a real biography at all. A biography must have a frame of reference. But it should be a point of view and a frame of reference implicit in the material itself and not imposed upon it.

17 It might seem that the ideal biographical system, if it could be achieved, would be to go through the years of research without feeling any kind of emotion. The biographer would be a kind of fact-finding machine and then suddenly, after his years of research, a kind of total vision would fall upon him and he would transcribe it in his best and most persuasive English for a waiting public. But research is fortunately not done by machinery, nor are visions likely to descend in that helpful manner. They are the product not only of many facts but also of much thinking, and it is only when the biographer begins to get emotional in his thinking that he ought to beware.

18 It is easy enough to make good resolutions in advance, but a biographer cannot altogether control his sense of excitement when the climax of his years of research draws near and he begins to see the pieces fall into place. Almost without his volition, A, B, and D fit together and start to form a pattern, and it is almost impossible for the biographer not to start searching for C. Something turns up that looks remarkably like C, and with a little trimming of the edges and the ignoring of one very slight discrepancy it will fill the place allotted for C magnificently.

19 It is at this point that the biographer ought to take a deep breath and sit on his hands until he has had time to calm down. He has no real, fundamental reason to believe that his discovery is C, except for the fact that he wants it to be. He is like a man looking for a missing piece in a difficult jigsaw puzzle, who has found one so nearly the right shape that he cannot resist the desire to jam it into place.

20 If the biographer had refused to be tempted by his supposed discovery of C and had gone on with his research, he might have found not only the connecting, illuminating fact he needed but much more besides. He is not going to look for it now. Desire has blocked the way. And by so much his biography will fall short of what might have been the truth.

21 It would not be accurate to say that a biographer should be wholly lacking in desire. Curiosity is a form of desire. So is the final wish to get the material down on paper in a form that will be fair to the reader's in-

terest and worthy of the subject. But a subconscious desire to push the facts around is one of the most dangerous things a biographer can encounter, and all the more dangerous because it is so difficult to know when he is encountering it.

22 The reason Alice had so much trouble with her flamingo is that the average flamingo does not wish to be used as a croquet mallet. It has other purposes in view. The same thing is true of a fact, which can be just as self-willed as a flamingo and has its own kind of stubborn integrity. To try to force a series of facts into a previously desired arrangement is a form of misuse to which no self-respecting fact will willingly submit itself. The best and only way to treat it is to leave it alone and be willing to follow where it leads, rather than to press your own wishes upon it.

23 To put the whole thing into a single sentence: you will never succeed in getting at the truth if you think you know, ahead of time, what the truth ought to be.

Exercises

CONTENT

True or False? If you think the statement represents what the selection says or implies, mark it "True"; if you do not think so, mark it "False."

1. *Alice in Wonderland* is a biography.
2. Sir Philip Sidney died from a wound in the foot.
3. Dr. Moffet's account of Sidney's death has been proved to be the only true one.
4. Captain John Smith lived in the early 17th century.
5. Princess Pocahontas did not save his life.
6. Shakespeare had no connection with the nobility.
7. A biographer should have a viewpoint.
8. There is no such thing as a completely objective human being.
9. Shakespeare was born in the town of Avon.
10. A biographer should never want to prove anything.

Questions for Discussion

1. What do Ben Jonson, Sir Philip Sidney, Sir Fulke Greville, King James I, Captain John Smith, and William Shakespeare have in common, beyond the fact that they are all mentioned in this essay?
2. Name the three different reasons, given in the contemporary accounts of Sir Philip Sidney's death, for his having left off his armor.
3. Why did the 19th century biographers try so hard to associate Shakespeare with the nobility?

4. Choose a single sentence from the essay that seems to you to sum up its main idea, and explain its particular position in the essay.

FORM AND STYLE

1. The main body of the essay falls into two parts. Name them. Where does the division between them occur? How is the transition worked out?

2. What structural function in the essay do the following three passages have in common: Paragraphs 2-7, Paragraph 8, Paragraph 9? Can you find a passage from the second part of the essay that serves a similar function?

3. The metaphor implied in "the information was beginning to twist in my hand . . ." (beginning of Paragraph 4) refers to something mentioned earlier in the essay? What?

4. Comment upon the tone and meaning of the last sentence in Paragraph 18: "Something turns up that looks remarkably like C, and with a little trimming of the edges and the ignoring of one very slight discrepancy it will fill the place allotted for C magnificently." Make clear how a correct reading of the sentence depends upon the reader's understanding of the author's tone or attitude.

5. What purpose or purposes (you should be able to think of at least two) are served by the allusions to *Alice in Wonderland?*

6. Find an example of parallel phrasing in Paragraph 11.

7. Explain the metaphor at the end of Paragraph 11. If the biography is like a road and the facts in the biography are like materials used for building the road, what in the writing of the biography is like the curve of the road, and what in the building of the road is like "the desire of the biographer himself"? Comment upon the effectiveness of the metaphor.

VOCABULARY

Which of the four words or phrases to the right seems to you to be *closest* in meaning to the word in heavy type to the left? Put a check mark after your choice.

presumptuous (*1*)   very sumptuous . . . irrelevant . . . arrogant . . . big . . .

chivalry (2)   horsemanship . . . adventure . . . ideal knighthood . . . bravery . . .

reliable (3)   trustworthy . . . fair . . . accurate . . . factual . . .

advocated (4)   opposed . . . called out . . . argued for . . . was pleased with . . .

deplored (4)   regretted . . . welcomed . . . argued against . . . raged against . . .

distort (7)　　obscure . . . twist . . . disturb . . . destroy . . .

impartial (7)　　open-minded . . . trustworthy . . . imparting . . . objective . . .

testimony (8)　　witnesses . . . tests . . . documents . . . evidence . . .

agonized (8)　　horrible . . . fighting . . . famous . . . painful . . .

unwavering (9)　　unusual . . . unchanging . . . strong . . . wonderful

prospectus (9)　　vision . . . preface . . . advertisement . . . advance information . . .

tampered with (10)　　destroyed . . . secretly altered . . . looked at by anybody . . . corrupted . . .

pervasive (11)　　forceful . . . persuasive . . . spreading throughout . . . difficult to discover . . .

imposed upon (12)　　forced upon . . . placed as a burden upon . . . presented falsely to . . . modified according to . . .

reared (14)　　raised . . . conditioned . . . accustomed . . . prepared

gentility (14)　　quality of being well born . . . stuffiness . . . snobbery . . . gentleness . . .

basking (14)　　wallowing . . . lying in warmth . . . romping . . . taking delight . . .

exalted (14)　　fine . . . high . . . exciting . . . aristocratic . . .

abhorrent (14)　　impossible-seeming . . . dreadful . . . repulsive . . . strange . . .

alternated (15)　　was exchanged . . . showed splendidly . . . took turns . . . hung high . . .

expanded (16)　　long . . . boring . . . regular . . . enlarged . . .

implicit (16)　　really . . . directly . . . made necessary . . . involved in the nature of . . .

transcribe (17)　　translate . . . write . . . copy . . . express . . .

persuasive (17)　　glittering . . . causing agreement . . . penetrating . . . eloquent . . .

volition (18)　　will . . . intention . . . realization . . . knowledge . . .

discrepancy (18)　　something superfluous . . . irrelevance . . . disagreement . . . doubt . . .

integrity (22)　　identity . . . independence . . . moral soundness and strength . . . intractability . . .

THEME SUGGESTIONS

Fact vs. desire, or the disappointing truth

Discuss *Getting at the Truth.* What does it say, how effectively does it say it, how relevant is it to your own college work?

Establishing the truth (report on a research project or scientific experiment you have successfully completed—for instance, in some other college course.)

47

JAMES THURBER

The Moth and the Star

1   A young and impressionable moth once set his heart on a certain star. He told his mother about this and she counseled him to set his heart on a bridge lamp instead. "Stars aren't the thing to hang around," she said; "lamps are the thing to hang around." "You get somewhere that way," said the moth's father. "You don't get anywhere chasing stars." But the moth would not heed the words of either parent. Every evening at dusk when the star came out he would start flying toward it and every morning at dawn he would crawl back home worn out with his vain endeavor. One day his father said to him, "You haven't burned a wing in months, boy, and it looks to me as if you were never going to. All your brothers have been badly burned flying around street lamps and all your sisters have been terribly singed flying around house lamps. Come on, now, get out of here and get yourself scorched! A big strapping moth like you without a mark on him!"

2   The moth left his father's house, but he would not fly around street lamps and he would not fly around house lamps. He went right on trying to reach the star, which was four and one-third light years, or twenty-five trillion miles away. The moth thought it was just caught in the top branches of an elm. He never did reach the star, but he went right on trying, night after night, and when he was a very, very old moth he began to think that he really had reached the star and went around saying so. This gave him a deep and lasting pleasure, and he lived to a great old age. His parents and his brothers and his sisters had all been burned to death when they were quite young.

3   *Moral: Who flies afar from the sphere of our sorrow is here today and here tomorrow.*

Exercises

CONTENT

True or False? If you think the statement represents what the selection says or implies, mark it "True"; if you do not think so, mark it "False."

1. The moth was disobedient.
2. The moth was small for his age.

THE MOTH AND THE STAR. From *The New Yorker*, February 18, 1939. Permission the author, © 1939, The New Yorker Magazine, Inc.

3. The moth died young but happy.
4. It is normal for moths to be burned to death.
5. The moth's parents were conformists.

Question for Discussion

In your opinion, which of the following statements best expresses the meaning of the story?
(a) If you insist on being different, you'll end up being lonely.
(b) There is survival value in idealism.
(c) It is one of the ironies of life that the escapist is sometimes better off than people who face their responsibilities.
(d) It doesn't pay off to be like everybody else.
(e) There is no hidden meaning; it's just a little story about a moth.

FORM AND STYLE

1. *The Moth and the Star* is an example of *allegory*, or—more specifically—of *beast fable*. An allegory is a narrative in which characters and events have symbolic significance in addition to their literal, surface, meaning. The story of the shepherd's boy who cried "Wolf!" so often in fun that when the wolf really did come the villagers did not believe him is an allegory, the boy signifying (representing, "standing for") people who lie so often that when disaster really comes their truth is taken for another lie. A beast fable is an allegory that uses animals and animal behavior to symbolize human affairs.

Allegory (including beast fable) can also be looked upon as a form of analogy: the relationship between shepherd's boy, wolf, and villagers is analogous to that between liar or false alarmist, real danger, and other people, with the cry of "Wolf!" when the wolf is really there being analogous to the truth that is taken for a lie because it has been a lie so often in the past.

Work out the analogy—that is, explain the allegory—in *The Moth and the Star* by giving the symbolic, human significance of the moth, the star, the bridge lamp, the parents, singeing, and burning.

2. Why would it seem "wrong" if the sentence in Paragraph 1 had read: "All your brothers have been badly burned flying around house lamps and all your sisters have been terribly singed flying around street lamps"? Explain your answer. And explain what both the original sentence and the new version of it mean in case you do *not* find the latter inferior to the former.

3. List examples of contrast—between "characters," objects, attitudes, ideas—in the story.

4. Why, in your opinion, did Thurber put his "moral" in rhyme?

VOCABULARY

Which of the four words or phrases to the right seems to you to be *closest* in meaning to the word in heavy type to the left? Put a check mark after your choice.

impressionable *(1)*   idealistic . . . susceptible . . . easily awed . . . not easily impressed . . .

endeavor *(1)*   labor . . . struggle . . . plan . . . attempt . . .

strapping *(1)*   strong . . . huge . . . in good health . . . capable of taking care of himself . . .

THEME SUGGESTIONS

The character of the moth
A question of values
In defense of conformity, or What about responsibility?, or The price of idealism
Self-delusion

48

JOSEPH WOOD KRUTCH

The Golden Mean

1   Reading the other day a certain Victorian book by a moralizing author, I was suddenly struck by a difference between the Victorian point of view and ours which just possibly may be quite as important as the much discussed change in sex morality. This writer was fearfully concerned with the "spoiled child," and it occurred to me that not only the Victorian but all ages from the first Christian down to the beginning of our own were constantly expressing the fear that not only children but young ladies, the laboring classes, the middle classes, and in fact nearly everybody except the writer himself was being "spoiled." Today we have recovered from that obsession, but we seem to have fallen victim to another. Although we are no longer afraid that children or anybody else may be "spoiled," we have become just as fearful that they may be "underprivileged."

2   In both cases the remote consequences of the ever-present threat

THE GOLDEN MEAN. From "If You Don't Mind My Saying So," in *The American Scholar*, Spring, 1957. Reprinted by permission of *The American Scholar*.

are assumed to be even worse than the immediate ones. The spoiled child would end on the gallows; the underprivileged one is now headed for a whole gallery of neuroses and almost sure to turn out "antisocial." Our concern is certainly the more amiable, but I am not sure that it is any less extravagant. People survived a lot of abuse in former times, and not getting everything you want is not always as fatal to normality as we assume today. The old-fashioned parent who believed in the necessity of "breaking the child's will" was certainly wrong, but so perhaps is the modern who supposes that he is heading his offspring for the psychoanalyst's couch if he forbids him to saw the leg off the dining-room table. Yet if you argue the question, the general opinion seems to be that there is no course in between; and if you agree that "breaking the will" is bad, then you are supposed to have to admit that the "permissive system" must be right.

3   An article I once wrote at the request of the general editor of one of the popular "home magazines" was vetoed by the editor of its mother-and-child department because I said that although parents should know the great truth that "children should be loved," it was more important for the children themselves to realize its corollary: "Children should be lovable." Thriftily I managed to use this notion elsewhere, but the mother-and-child editor said it would lead readers to conclude that the magazine was advising parents to beat their babies. The golden mean may seem to represent an easy sort of compromise. I remember that the first time it was expounded to me I was not at all impressed. But Aristotle must have made so much of it because he realized that there is nothing to which the human being takes less readily.

4   From experience I have learned that you can't criticize anything without having it supposed that you favor some opposite extreme. If you say, for example, that automobiles should not be built to run ninety miles an hour, you are asked scornfully if you want to go back to the horse and buggy, as though nothing between ninety miles an hour and eight were possible—as, indeed, seems to be the case where human beings are involved. This line of argument used to be used chiefly against "liberals" and "progressives" when they were in the minority. If one of them opposed the twelve-hour day it was assumed that he was advocating a life of almost uninterrupted leisure for labor. Nowadays it is more often used, as the woman editor used it, against every middle-of-the-road proposal. If you confess the suspicion that a certain specific demand of some single union is unreasonable, then you are accused of wanting to hand the manacled workingman over to exploiters, just as you have already been accused of maintaining that the automobile should be abolished and children beaten daily. This is no doubt the reason why it sometimes seems that progress is a delusion, that change is never anything except a switch from one excess to another, and that we never get rid of an evil except by exchanging it for its opposite.

Exercises

CONTENT

True or False? If you think the statement represents what the selection says or implies, mark it "True"; if you do not think so, mark it "False."

1. We fear "spoiling" our children just as much as parents in the Victorian age did.
2. Krutch believes in spanking.
3. Krutch is against extremes.
4. Krutch believes in the principle of "if you aren't *for* me, you're against me."
5. Aristotle first introduced the idea of "the golden mean."
6. It is called "the *golden* mean" because it stands for a valuable principle.
7. The essay is neither pro- nor anti-labor.
8. Krutch used to edit a "home" magazine.
9. There is no such thing as progress.
10. Human beings find it difficult to follow the middle of the road.

Questions for Discussion

1. In your own words, state the theme of the essay.
2. The essay deals with something which in logic is known as "the black-and-white fallacy." (A fallacy is a false idea or a piece of illogical reasoning.) Explain the term on the basis of the examples Krutch gives here.
3. With Krutch's essay in mind, discuss the reasonableness or unreasonableness of the following attitudes:

   (a) "What do you want, white meat or dark?" "Just give me a piece of dark, please." "What's wrong with the white, may I ask?"
   (b) "Since you don't believe the prosecution's only witness, I assume you consider the defendant innocent?"
   (c) "You think it's too hot in here! Want us to freeze to death or something?"
   (d) "So you don't like high school football, eh? Guess you want kids to grow up to be weaklings."
   4. What single sentence best sums up the whole essay?

FORM AND STYLE

1. At which point in the essay is its main idea first introduced?
2. Discuss the relevance of the portions of the essay that precede this point.
3. Write an outline of Paragraph 4.

VOCABULARY

Which of the four words or phrases to the right seems to you to be *closest* in meaning to the word in heavy type to the left? Put a check mark after your choice.

Victorian (*1*)   victorious . . . of the time of Queen Victoria of England . . . morally uplifting . . . successful . . .

moralizing (*1*)   moral . . . strait-laced . . . preaching morality . . . argumentative . . .

obsession (*1*)   fear . . . danger . . . obstruction . . . fixed idea . . .

gallery (*2*)   string . . . collection . . . long and narrow room . . . exhibition . . .

amiable (*2*)   kindly . . . admirable . . . plausible . . . leading to friendship . . .

extravagant (*2*)   silly . . . wrong . . . unusual . . . excessive . . .

abuse (*2*)   neglect . . . frustration . . . suffering . . . mistreatment

corollary (*3*)   opposite . . . other side of the coin . . . cause . . . something that follows logically . . .

expounded (*3*)   told . . . explained . . . pounded into . . . revealed

manacled (*4*)   oppressed . . . poor . . . long-suffering . . . shackled

delusion (*4*)   hallucination . . . deceptive belief . . . mockery . . . absurdity . . .

THEME SUGGESTIONS

When I was a victim of the black-and-white fallacy

The dangers of the middle of the road

Everything is simple in the Westerns, or If he's not a good guy he must be a bad guy

On seeing faults and virtues on both sides

The golden mean as an educational ideal